BUREAU FOR PARANORMAL RESEARCH AND DEFENSE

B.P.R.D. HELL ON EARTH: THE DEVIL'S ENGINE & THE LONG DEATH

created by MIKE MIGNOLA

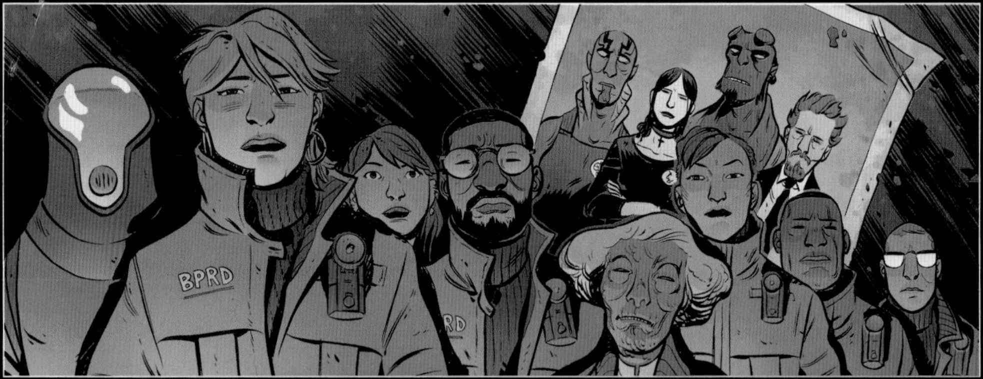
BPRD

Since Liz Sherman destroyed the frog army and the Black Flame in Agartha, the Bureau for Paranormal Research and Defense has seen their charter expanded to oversee international threats, leading to collaborations with Russia's occult bureau. With Liz missing and Abe Sapien on the verge of death, the burden lies upon Kate Corrigan, Johann, and the more conventional agents of the B.P.R.D.

MIKE MIGNOLA'S

B.P.R.D.™ HELL ON EARTH

THE DEVIL'S ENGINE & THE LONG DEATH

story by **MIKE MIGNOLA** and **JOHN ARCUDI**

art for *The Devil's Engine* by **TYLER CROOK**

art for *The Long Death* by **JAMES HARREN**

colors by **DAVE STEWART**

letters by **CLEM ROBINS**

cover art by **MIKE MIGNOLA** with **DAVE STEWART**

chapter break art by **DUNCAN FEGREDO**

editor **SCOTT ALLIE**

assistant editor **DANIEL CHABON**   collection designer **AMY ARENDTS**

publisher **MIKE RICHARDSON**

DARK HORSE BOOKS®

Special thanks to Jason Hvam

Mike Richardson PRESIDENT AND PUBLISHER · Neil Hankerson EXECUTIVE VICE PRESIDENT
Tom Weddle CHIEF FINANCIAL OFFICER · Randy Stradley VICE PRESIDENT OF PUBLISHING
Michael Martens VICE PRESIDENT OF BOOK TRADE SALES · Anita Nelson VICE PRESIDENT OF
BUSINESS AFFAIRS · Matt Parkinson VICE PRESIDENT OF MARKETING · David Scroggy VICE
PRESIDENT OF PRODUCT DEVELOPMENT · Dale LaFountain VICE PRESIDENT OF INFORMATION
TECHNOLOGY · Darlene Vogel SENIOR DIRECTOR OF PRINT, DESIGN, AND PRODUCTION
Ken Lizzi GENERAL COUNSEL · Davey Estrada EDITORIAL DIRECTOR · Scott Allie SENIOR
MANAGING EDITOR · Chris Warner SENIOR BOOKS EDITOR · Diana Schutz EXECUTIVE EDITOR
Cary Grazzini DIRECTOR OF PRINT AND DEVELOPMENT · Lia Ribacchi ART DIRECTOR · Cara
Niece DIRECTOR OF SCHEDULING · Tim Wiesch DIRECTOR OF INTERNATIONAL LICENSING

DarkHorse.com   Hellboy.com

This book collects the comic-book series *B.P.R.D. Hell on Earth: The Devil's Engine* #1–#3 and *B.P.R.D.
Hell on Earth: The Long Death* #1–#3, originally published by Dark Horse Comics.

Published by Dark Horse Books
A division of Dark Horse Comics, Inc.
10956 SE Main Street
Milwaukie, OR 97222

First edition: December 2012
ISBN 978-1-59582-981-8

10 9 8 7 6 5 4 3 2 1
Printed by Midas Printing International, Ltd., Huizhou, China.

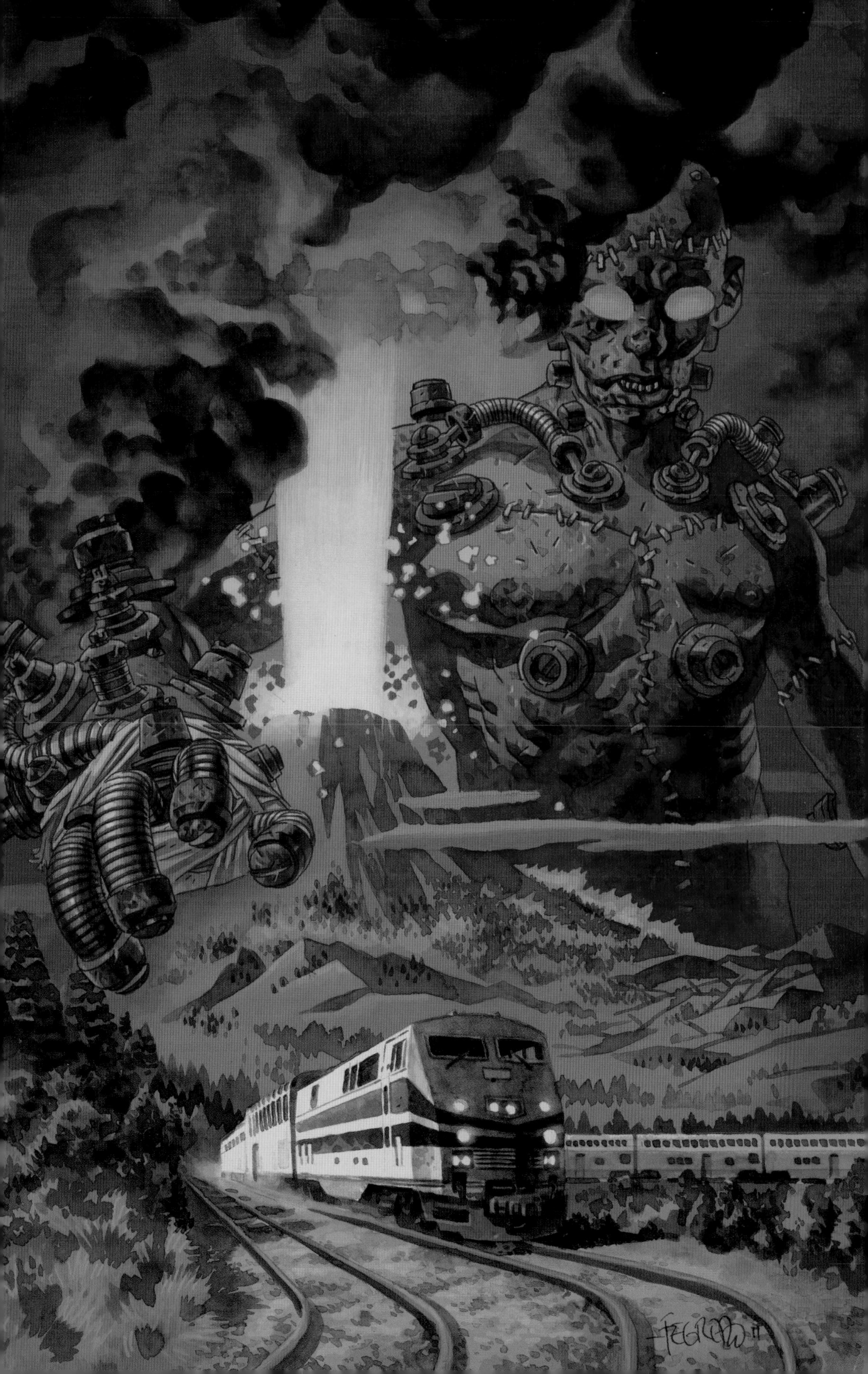

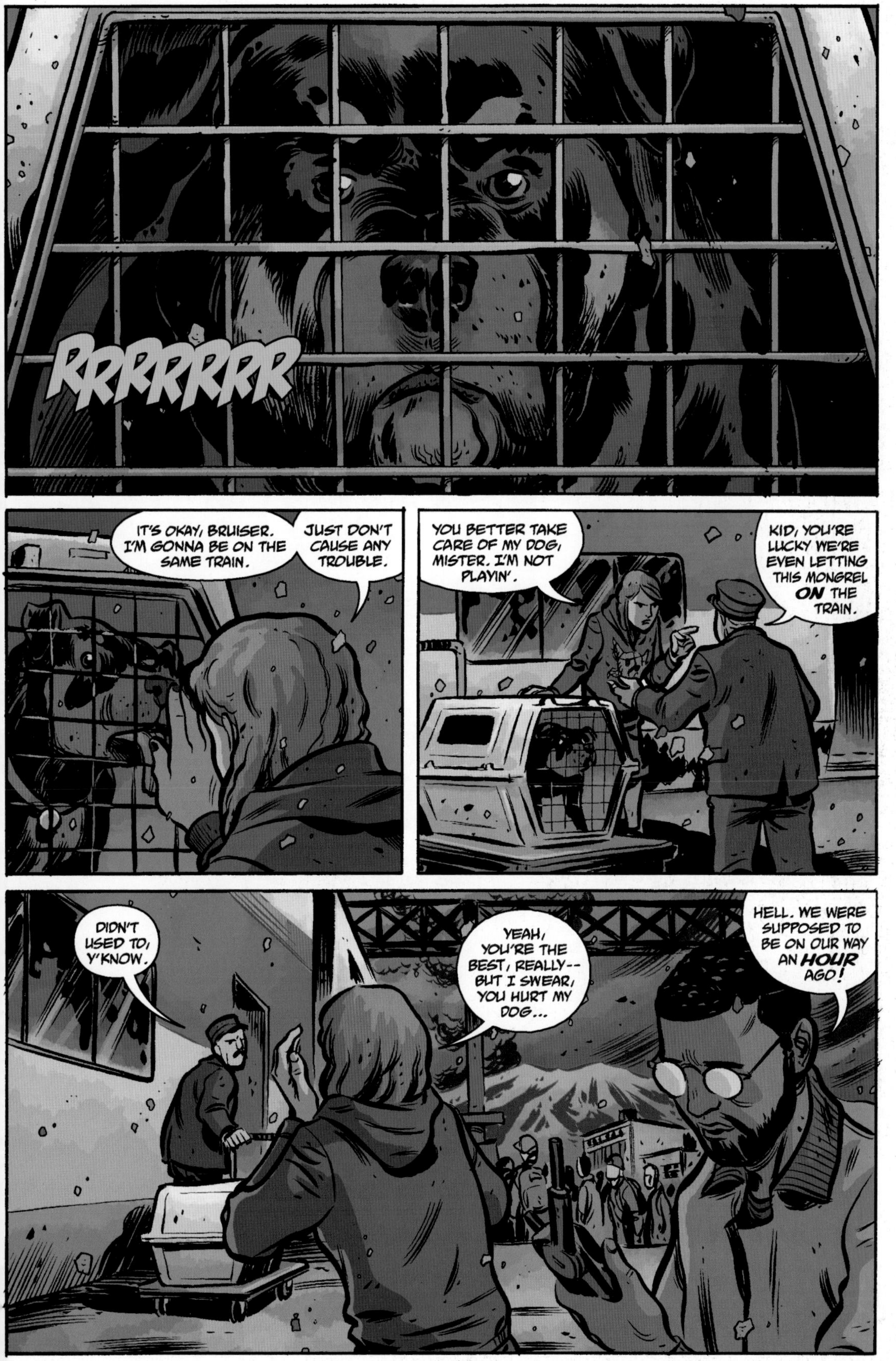
RRRRRRR
IT'S OKAY, BRUISER. I'M GONNA BE ON THE SAME TRAIN.
JUST DON'T CAUSE ANY TROUBLE.
YOU BETTER TAKE CARE OF MY DOG, MISTER. I'M NOT PLAYIN'.
KID, YOU'RE LUCKY WE'RE EVEN LETTING THIS MONGREL ON THE TRAIN.
DIDN'T USED TO, Y'KNOW.
YEAH, YOU'RE THE BEST, REALLY-- BUT I SWEAR, YOU HURT MY DOG...
HELL. WE WERE SUPPOSED TO BE ON OUR WAY AN HOUR AGO!

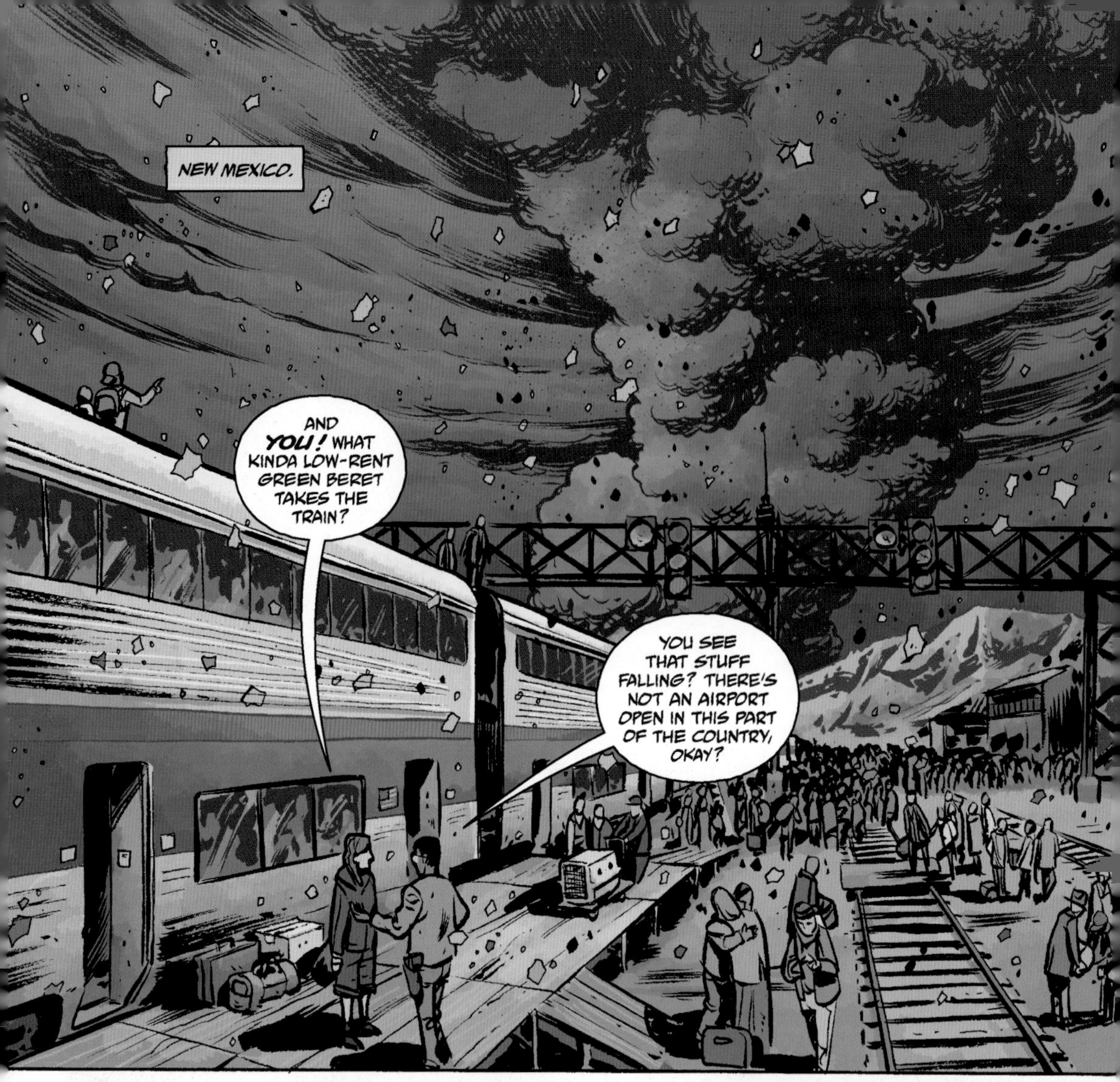
NEW MEXICO.
AND YOU! WHAT KINDA LOW-RENT GREEN BERET TAKES THE TRAIN?
YOU SEE THAT STUFF FALLING? THERE'S NOT AN AIRPORT OPEN IN THIS PART OF THE COUNTRY, OKAY?

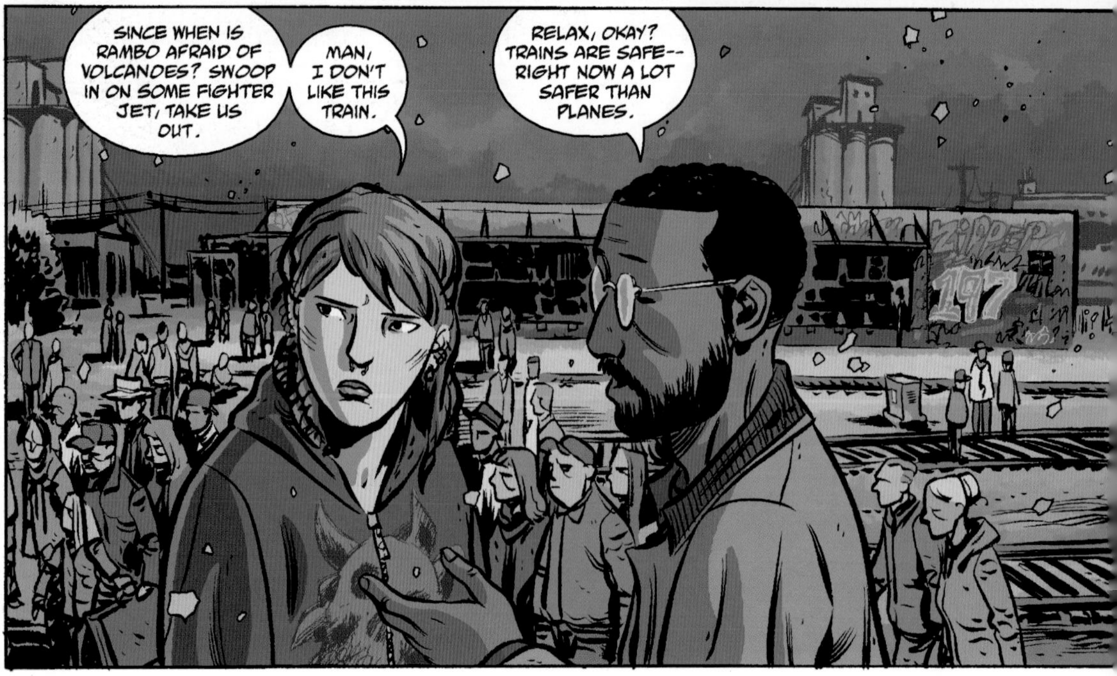
SINCE WHEN IS RAMBO AFRAID OF VOLCANOES? SWOOP IN ON SOME FIGHTER JET, TAKE US OUT.
MAN, I DON'T LIKE THIS TRAIN.
RELAX, OKAY? TRAINS ARE SAFE--RIGHT NOW A LOT SAFER THAN PLANES.

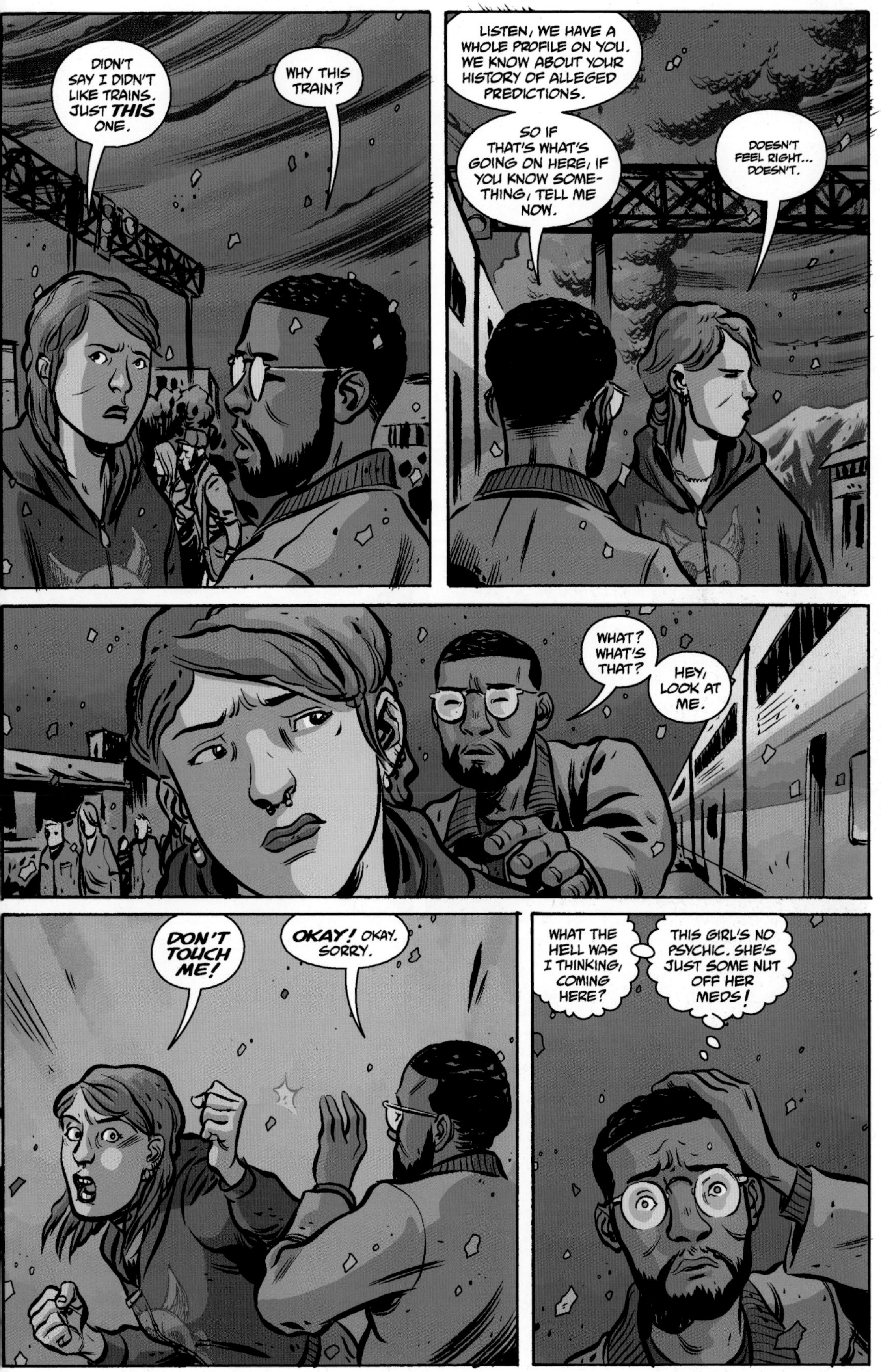
DIDN'T SAY I DIDN'T LIKE TRAINS. JUST THIS ONE.
WHY THIS TRAIN?
LISTEN, WE HAVE A WHOLE PROFILE ON YOU. WE KNOW ABOUT YOUR HISTORY OF ALLEGED PREDICTIONS.
SO IF THAT'S WHAT'S GOING ON HERE, IF YOU KNOW SOME-THING, TELL ME NOW.
DOESN'T FEEL RIGHT... DOESN'T.
WHAT? WHAT'S THAT?
HEY, LOOK AT ME.
DON'T TOUCH ME!
OKAY! OKAY. SORRY.
WHAT THE HELL WAS I THINKING, COMING HERE?
THIS GIRL'S NO PSYCHIC. SHE'S JUST SOME NUT OFF HER MEDS!

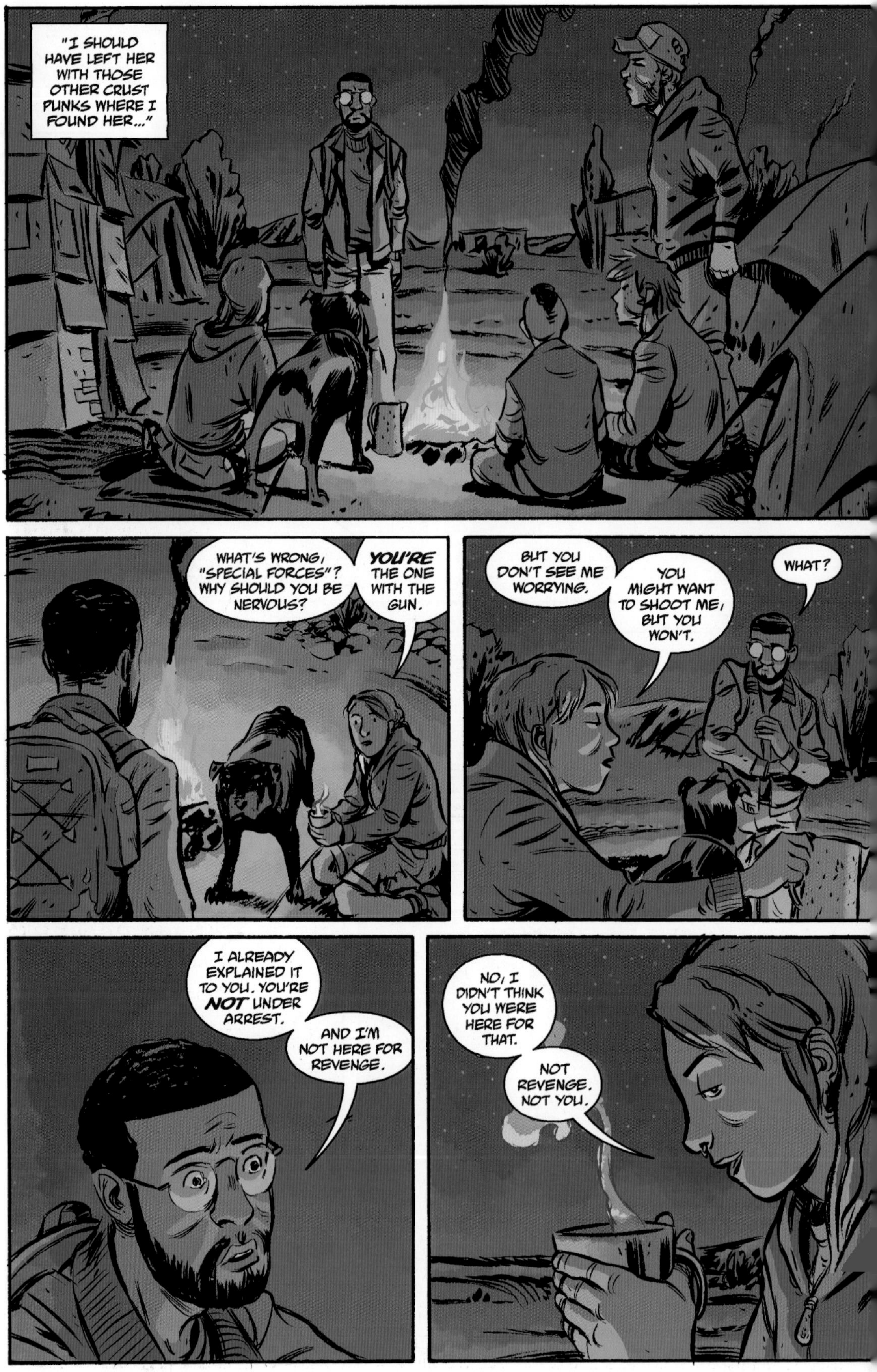
"I SHOULD HAVE LEFT HER WITH THOSE OTHER CRUST PUNKS WHERE I FOUND HER..."
WHAT'S WRONG, "SPECIAL FORCES"? WHY SHOULD YOU BE NERVOUS?
YOU'RE THE ONE WITH THE GUN.
BUT YOU DON'T SEE ME WORRYING.
YOU MIGHT WANT TO SHOOT ME, BUT YOU WON'T.
WHAT?
I ALREADY EXPLAINED IT TO YOU. YOU'RE ***NOT*** UNDER ARREST.
AND I'M NOT HERE FOR REVENGE.
NO, I DIDN'T THINK YOU WERE HERE FOR THAT.
NOT REVENGE. NOT YOU.

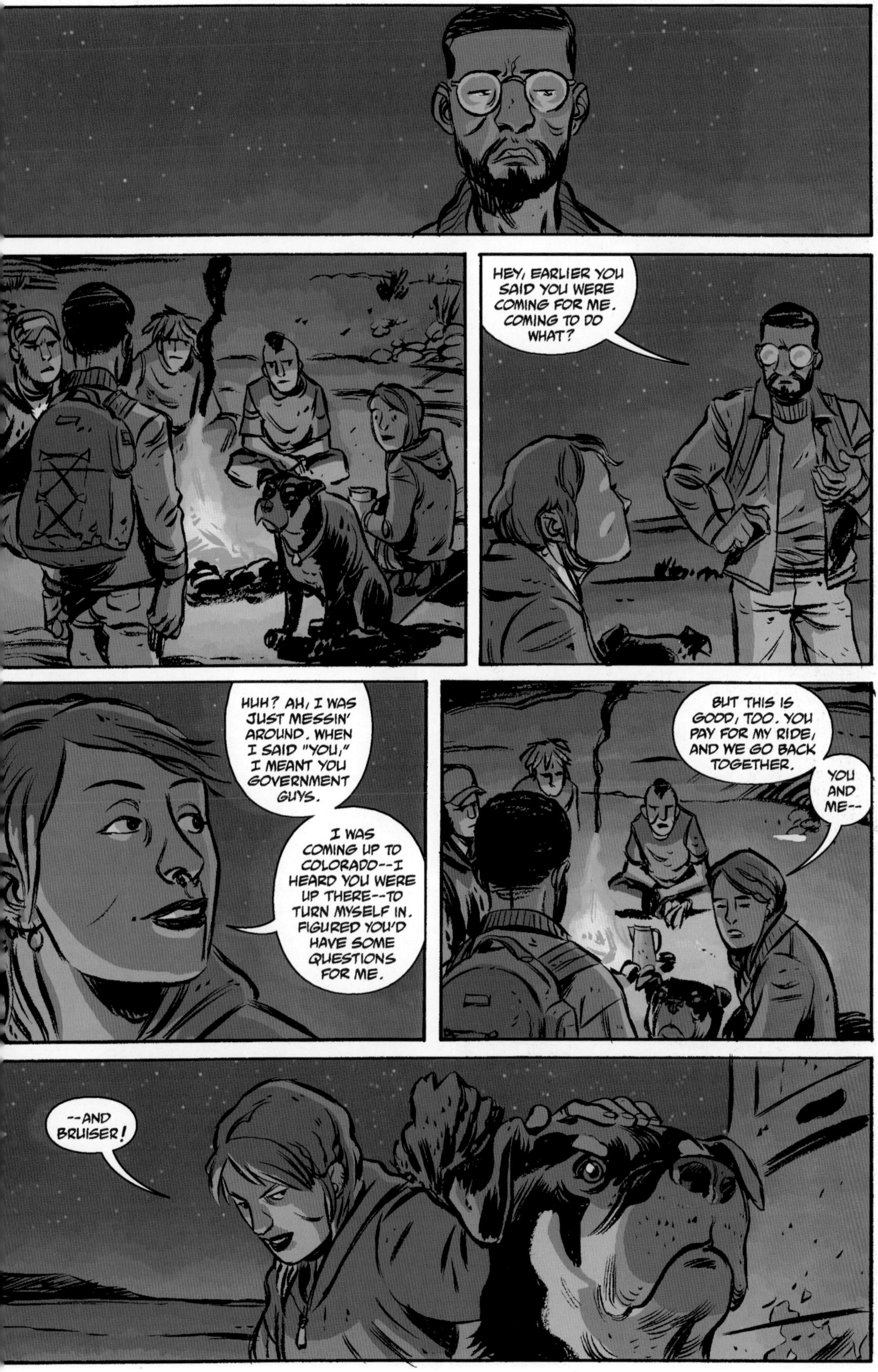
HEY, EARLIER YOU SAID YOU WERE COMING FOR ME. COMING TO DO WHAT?
HUH? AH, I WAS JUST MESSIN' AROUND. WHEN I SAID "YOU," I MEANT YOU GOVERNMENT GUYS.
I WAS COMING UP TO COLORADO--I HEARD YOU WERE UP THERE--TO TURN MYSELF IN. FIGURED YOU'D HAVE SOME QUESTIONS FOR ME.
BUT THIS IS GOOD, TOO. YOU PAY FOR MY RIDE, AND WE GO BACK TOGETHER.
YOU AND ME--
--AND BRUISER!

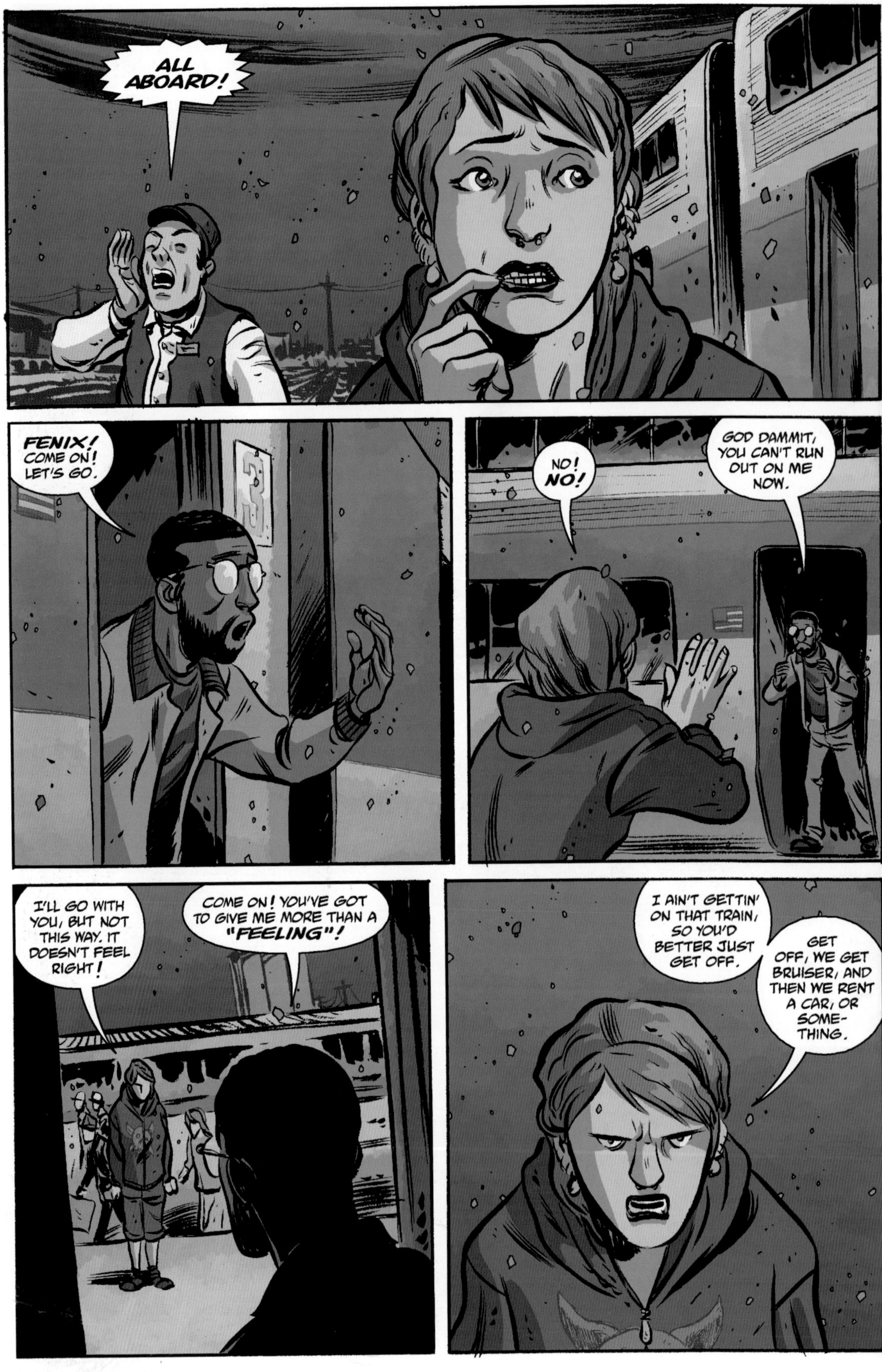
ALL ABOARD!
FENIX! COME ON! LET'S GO.
NO! NO!
GOD DAMMIT, YOU CAN'T RUN OUT ON ME NOW.
I'LL GO WITH YOU, BUT NOT THIS WAY. IT DOESN'T FEEL RIGHT!
COME ON! YOU'VE GOT TO GIVE ME MORE THAN A "FEELING"!
I AIN'T GETTIN' ON THAT TRAIN, SO YOU'D BETTER JUST GET OFF.
GET OFF, WE GET BRUISER, AND THEN WE RENT A CAR, OR SOME-THING.

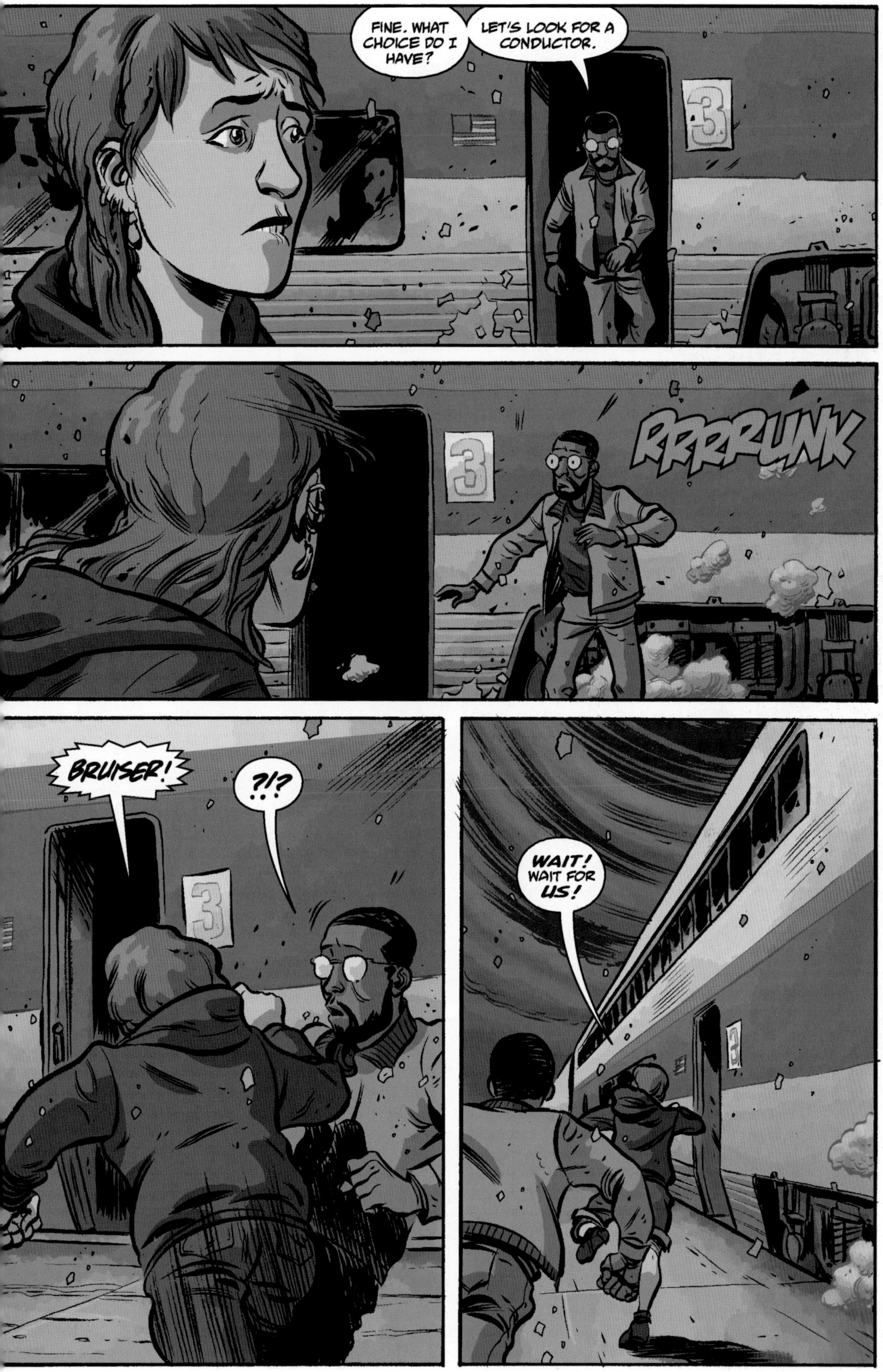
FINE. WHAT CHOICE DO I HAVE?
LET'S LOOK FOR A CONDUCTOR.
RRRRUNK
BRUISER!
?!?
WAIT! WAIT FOR US!

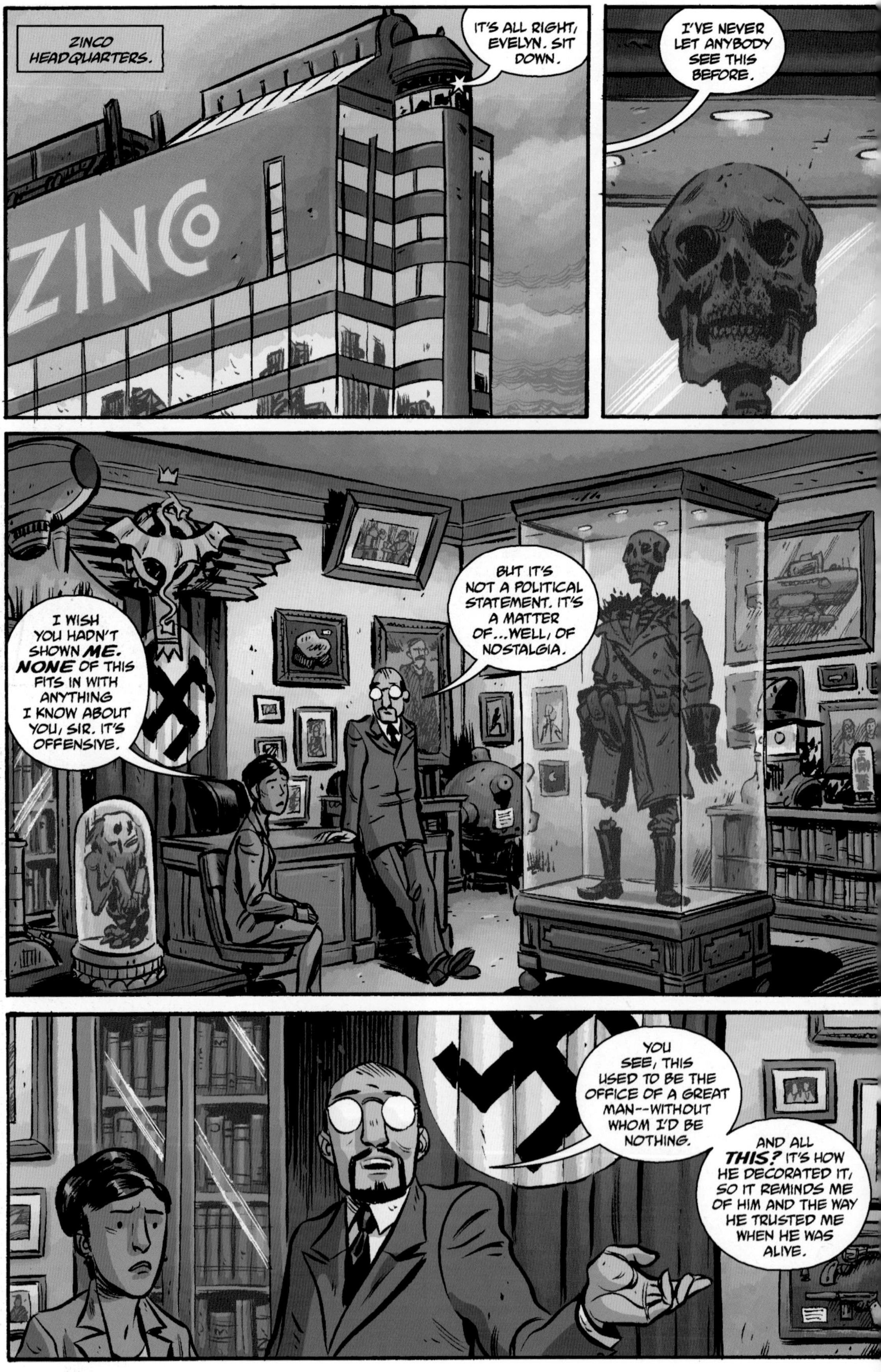
ZINCO HEADQUARTERS.
IT'S ALL RIGHT, EVELYN. SIT DOWN.
ZINCO
I'VE NEVER LET ANYBODY SEE THIS BEFORE.
I WISH YOU HADN'T SHOWN ME. NONE OF THIS FITS IN WITH ANYTHING I KNOW ABOUT YOU, SIR. IT'S OFFENSIVE.
BUT IT'S NOT A POLITICAL STATEMENT. IT'S A MATTER OF...WELL, OF NOSTALGIA.
YOU SEE, THIS USED TO BE THE OFFICE OF A GREAT MAN--WITHOUT WHOM I'D BE NOTHING.
AND ALL THIS? IT'S HOW HE DECORATED IT, SO IT REMINDS ME OF HIM AND THE WAY HE TRUSTED ME WHEN HE WAS ALIVE.

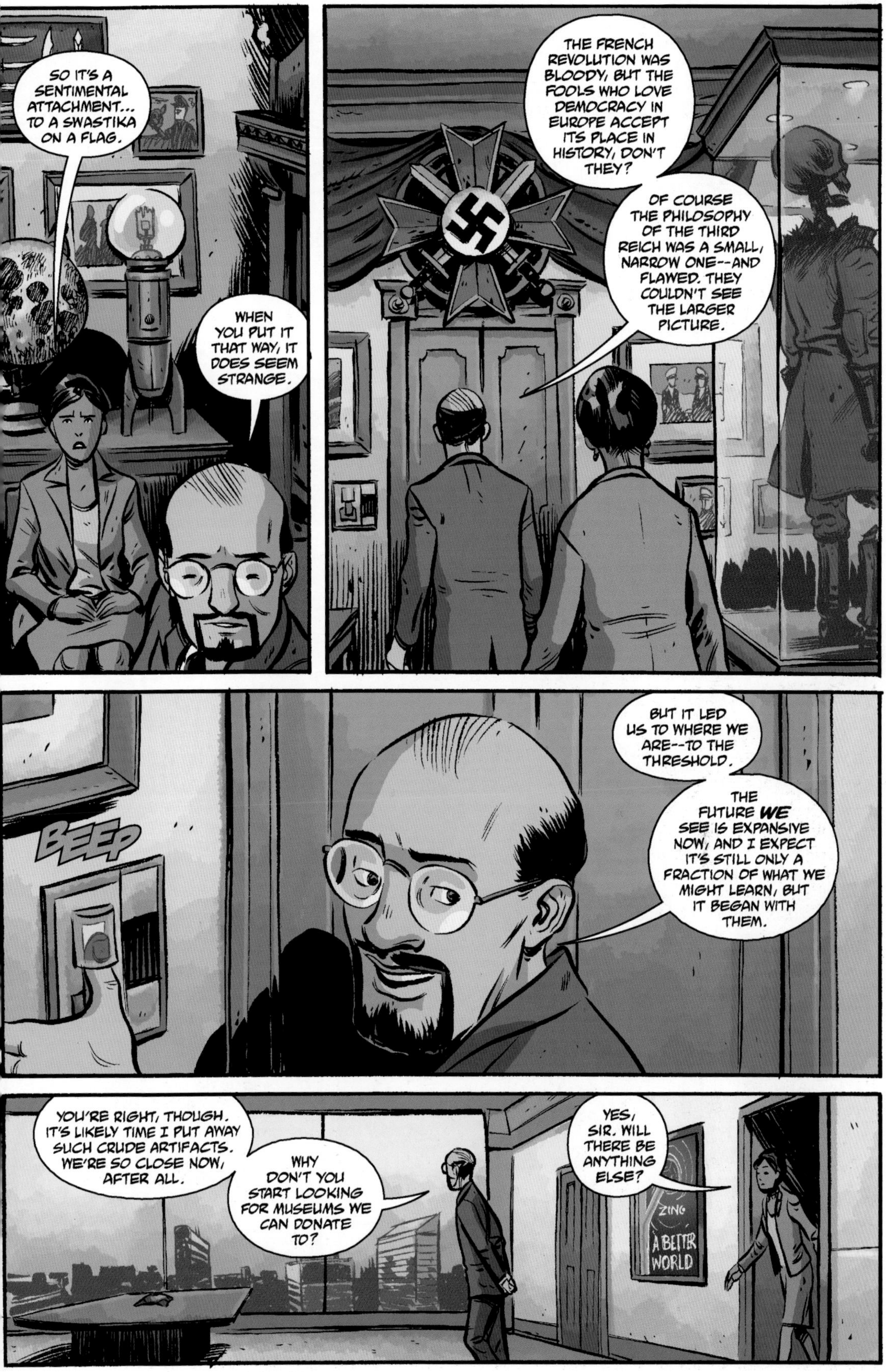

SO IT'S A SENTIMENTAL ATTACHMENT... TO A SWASTIKA ON A FLAG.
WHEN YOU PUT IT THAT WAY, IT DOES SEEM STRANGE.
THE FRENCH REVOLUTION WAS BLOODY, BUT THE FOOLS WHO LOVE DEMOCRACY IN EUROPE ACCEPT ITS PLACE IN HISTORY, DON'T THEY?
OF COURSE THE PHILOSOPHY OF THE THIRD REICH WAS A SMALL, NARROW ONE--AND FLAWED. THEY COULDN'T SEE THE LARGER PICTURE.
BEEP
BUT IT LED US TO WHERE WE ARE--TO THE THRESHOLD.
THE FUTURE *WE* SEE IS EXPANSIVE NOW, AND I EXPECT IT'S STILL ONLY A FRACTION OF WHAT WE MIGHT LEARN, BUT IT BEGAN WITH THEM.
YOU'RE RIGHT, THOUGH. IT'S LIKELY TIME I PUT AWAY SUCH CRUDE ARTIFACTS. WE'RE SO CLOSE NOW, AFTER ALL.
WHY DON'T YOU START LOOKING FOR MUSEUMS WE CAN DONATE TO?
YES, SIR. WILL THERE BE ANYTHING ELSE?
ZING
A BETTER WORLD

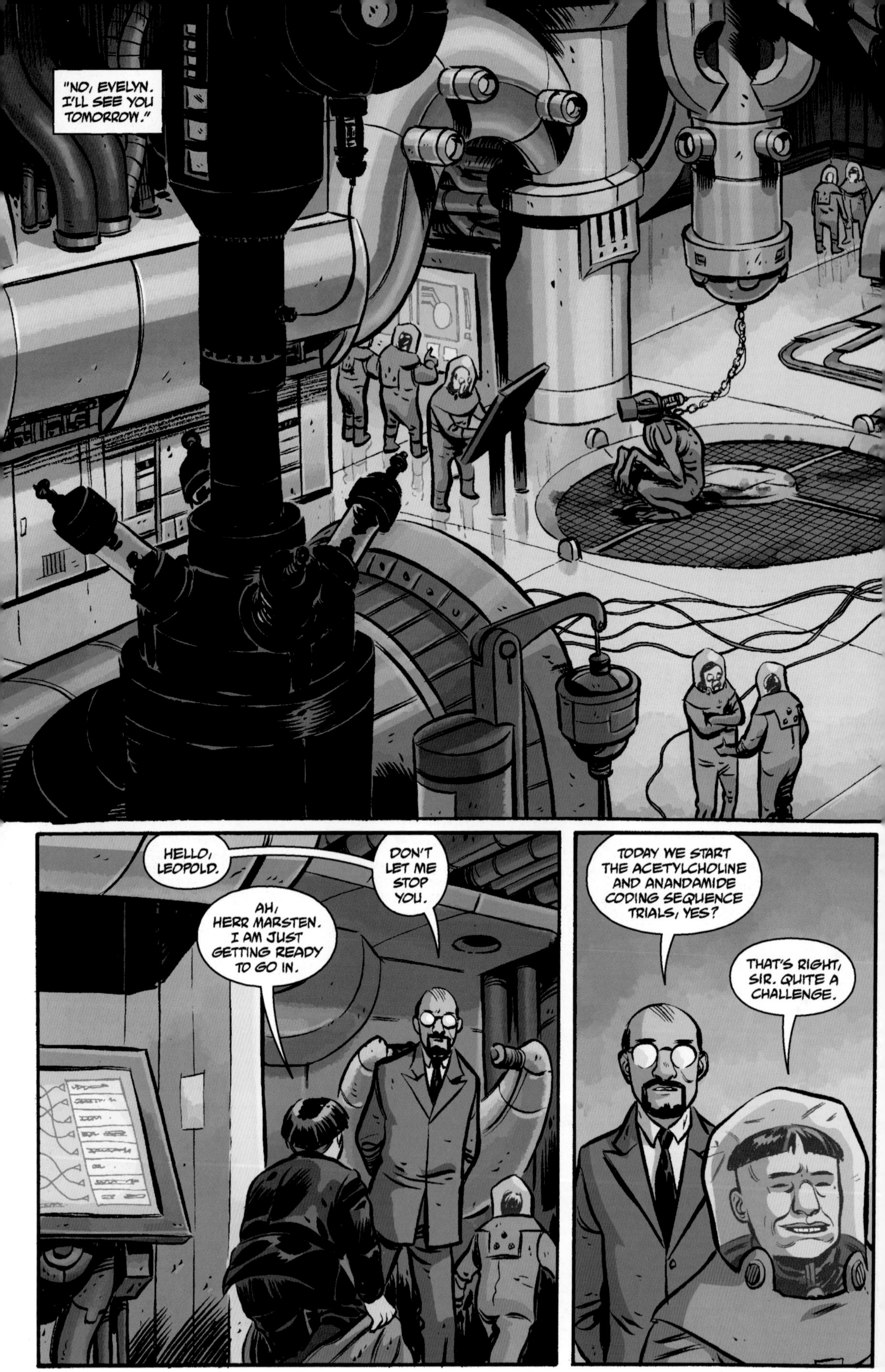
"NO, EVELYN. I'LL SEE YOU TOMORROW."
HELLO, LEOPOLD.
DON'T LET ME STOP YOU.
AH, HERR MARSTEN. I AM JUST GETTING READY TO GO IN.
TODAY WE START THE ACETYLCHOLINE AND ANANDAMIDE CODING SEQUENCE TRIALS, YES?
THAT'S RIGHT, SIR. QUITE A CHALLENGE.

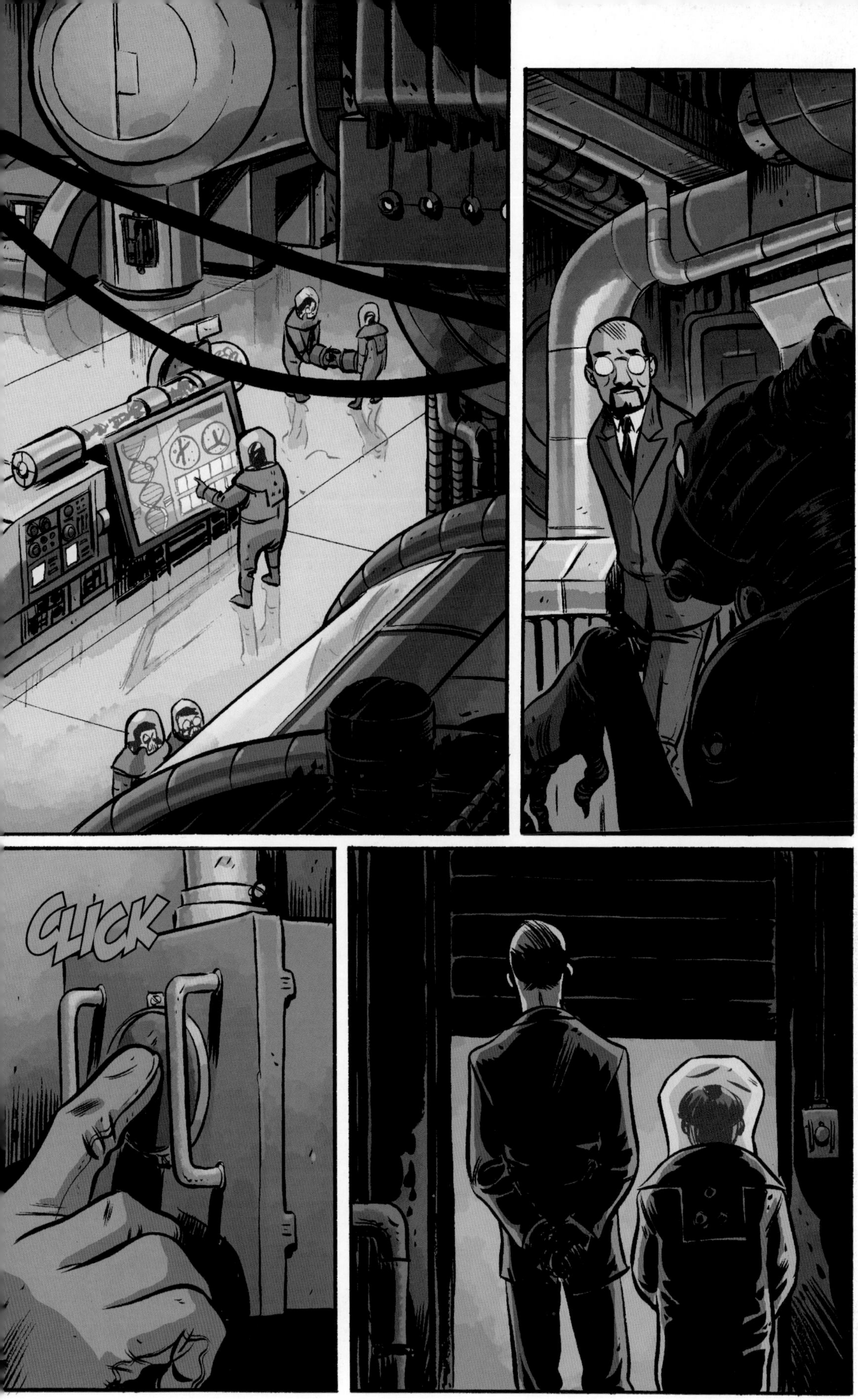
CLICK

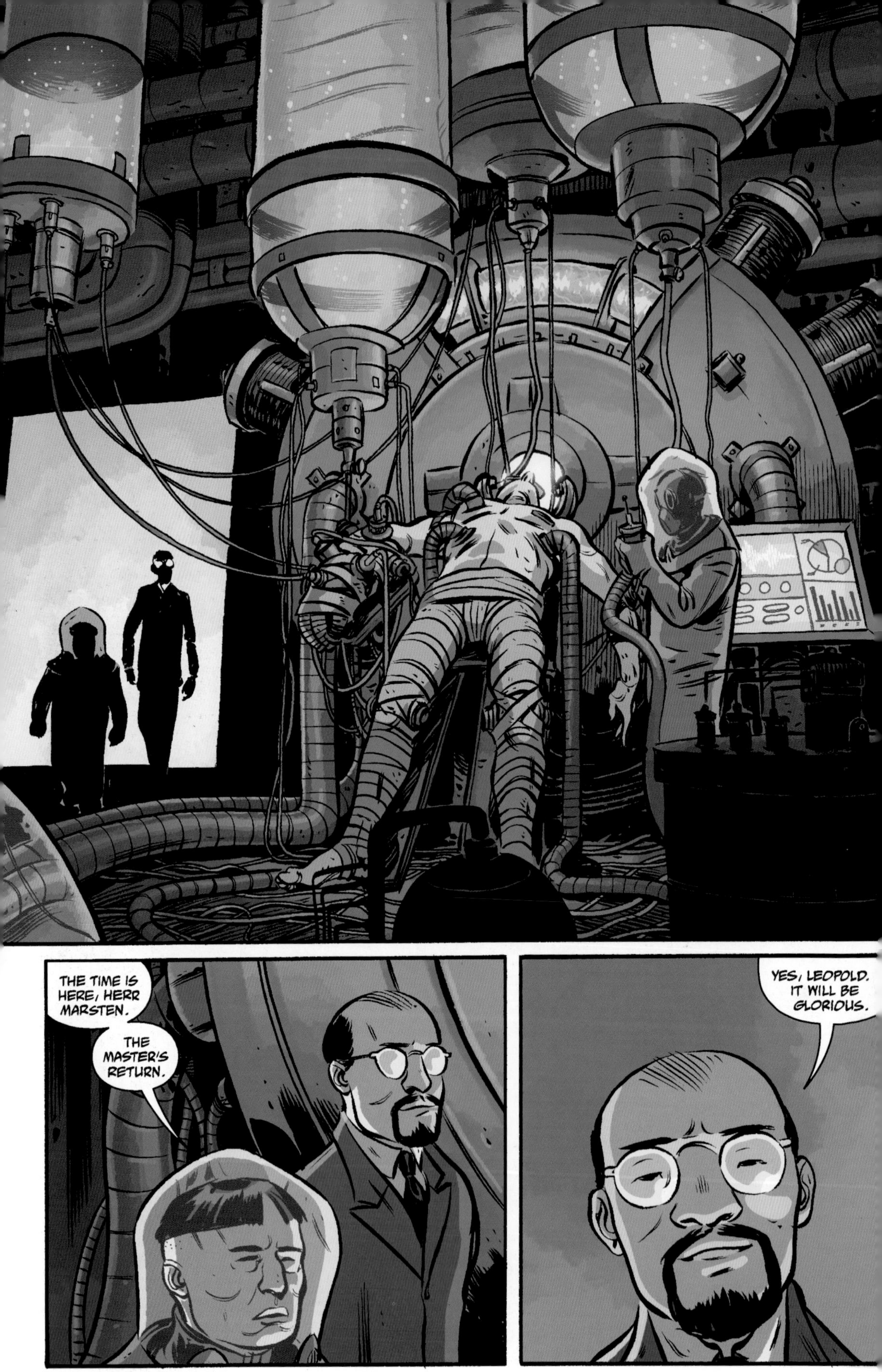
THE TIME IS HERE, HERR MARSTEN.
THE MASTER'S RETURN.
YES, LEOPOLD. IT WILL BE GLORIOUS.

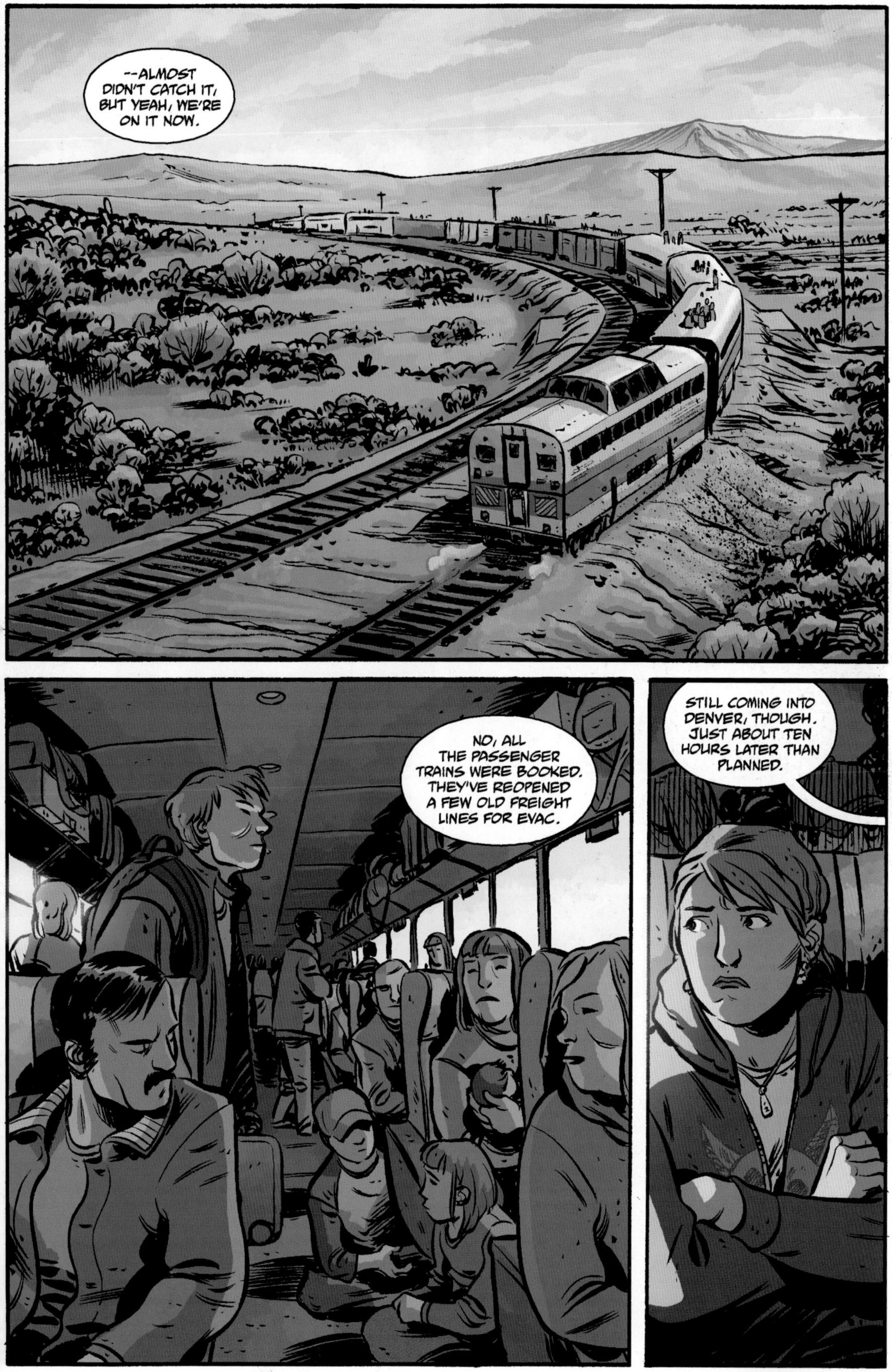
--ALMOST DIDN'T CATCH IT, BUT YEAH, WE'RE ON IT NOW.
NO, ALL THE PASSENGER TRAINS WERE BOOKED. THEY'VE REOPENED A FEW OLD FREIGHT LINES FOR EVAC.
STILL COMING INTO DENVER, THOUGH. JUST ABOUT TEN HOURS LATER THAN PLANNED.

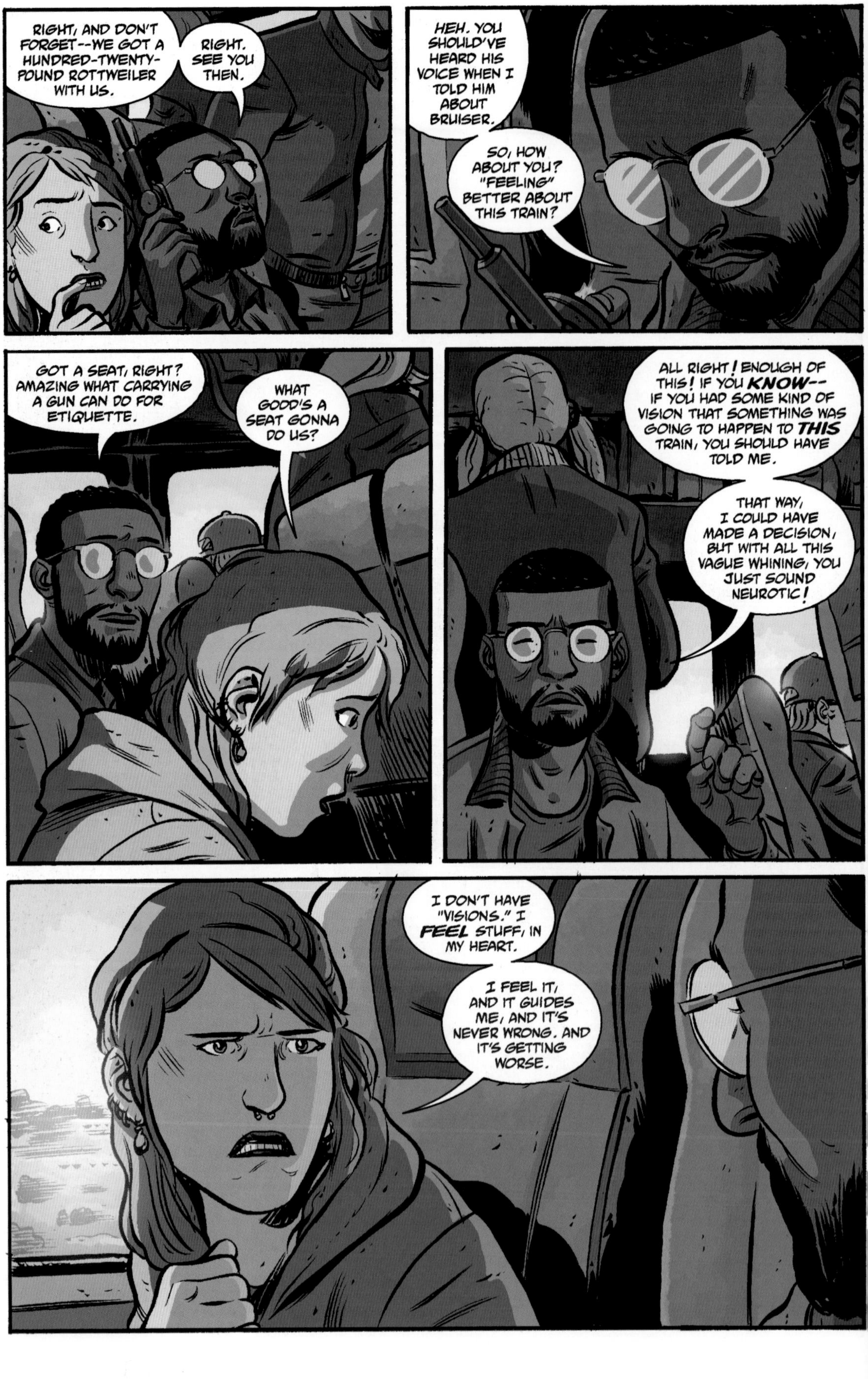
RIGHT, AND DON'T FORGET--WE GOT A HUNDRED-TWENTY-POUND ROTTWEILER WITH US.
RIGHT. SEE YOU THEN.
HEH. YOU SHOULD'VE HEARD HIS VOICE WHEN I TOLD HIM ABOUT BRUISER.
SO, HOW ABOUT YOU? "FEELING" BETTER ABOUT THIS TRAIN?
GOT A SEAT, RIGHT? AMAZING WHAT CARRYING A GUN CAN DO FOR ETIQUETTE.
WHAT GOOD'S A SEAT GONNA DO US?
ALL RIGHT! ENOUGH OF THIS! IF YOU KNOW-- IF YOU HAD SOME KIND OF VISION THAT SOMETHING WAS GOING TO HAPPEN TO THIS TRAIN, YOU SHOULD HAVE TOLD ME.
THAT WAY, I COULD HAVE MADE A DECISION, BUT WITH ALL THIS VAGUE WHINING, YOU JUST SOUND NEUROTIC!
I DON'T HAVE "VISIONS." I FEEL STUFF, IN MY HEART.
I FEEL IT, AND IT GUIDES ME, AND IT'S NEVER WRONG. AND IT'S GETTING WORSE.

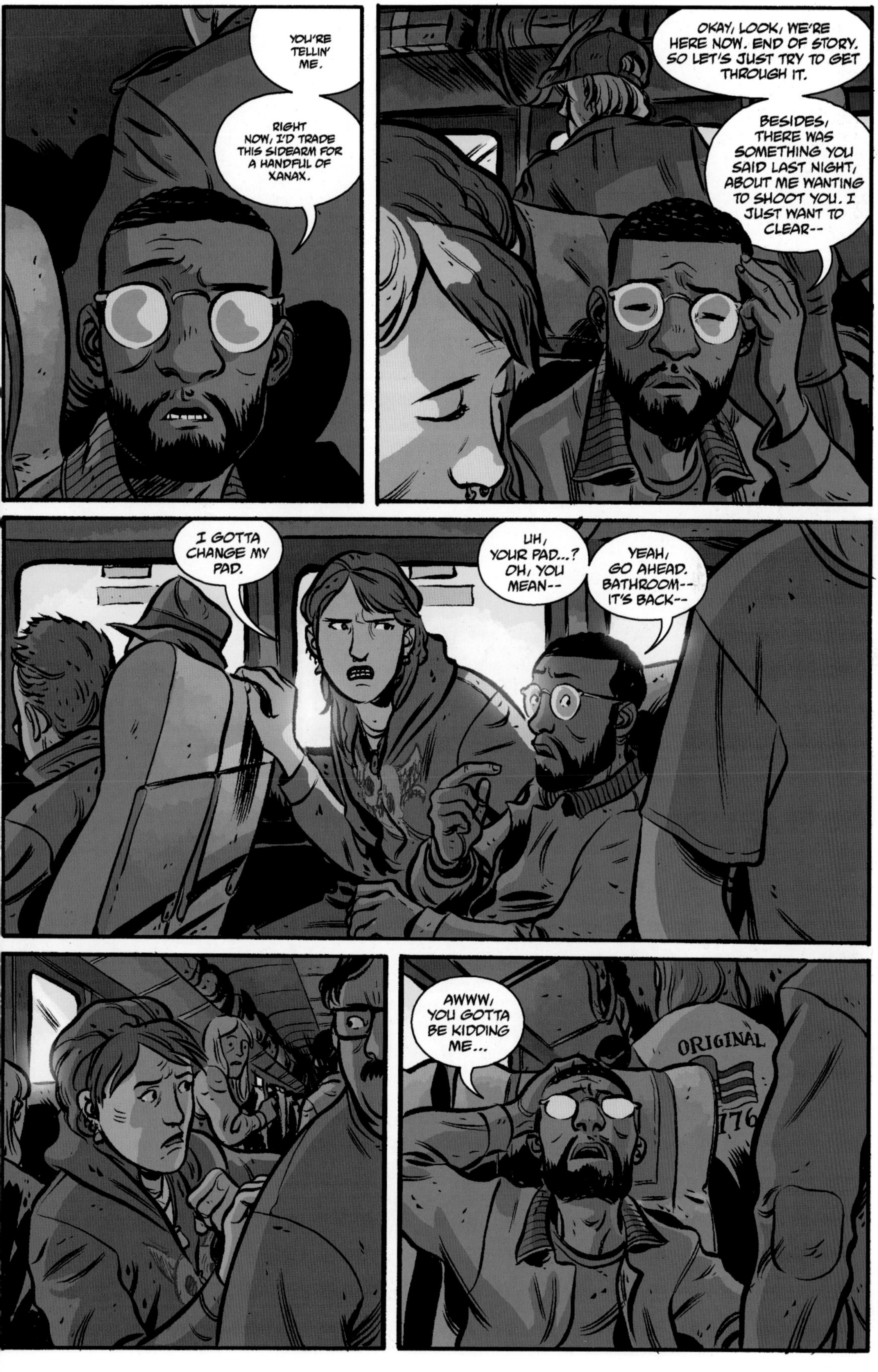
YOU'RE TELLIN' ME.
RIGHT NOW, I'D TRADE THIS SIDEARM FOR A HANDFUL OF XANAX.
OKAY, LOOK, WE'RE HERE NOW. END OF STORY. SO LET'S JUST TRY TO GET THROUGH IT.
BESIDES, THERE WAS SOMETHING YOU SAID LAST NIGHT, ABOUT ME WANTING TO SHOOT YOU. I JUST WANT TO CLEAR--
I GOTTA CHANGE MY PAD.
UH, YOUR PAD...? OH, YOU MEAN--
YEAH, GO AHEAD. BATHROOM-- IT'S BACK--
AWWW, YOU GOTTA BE KIDDING ME...
ORIGINAL

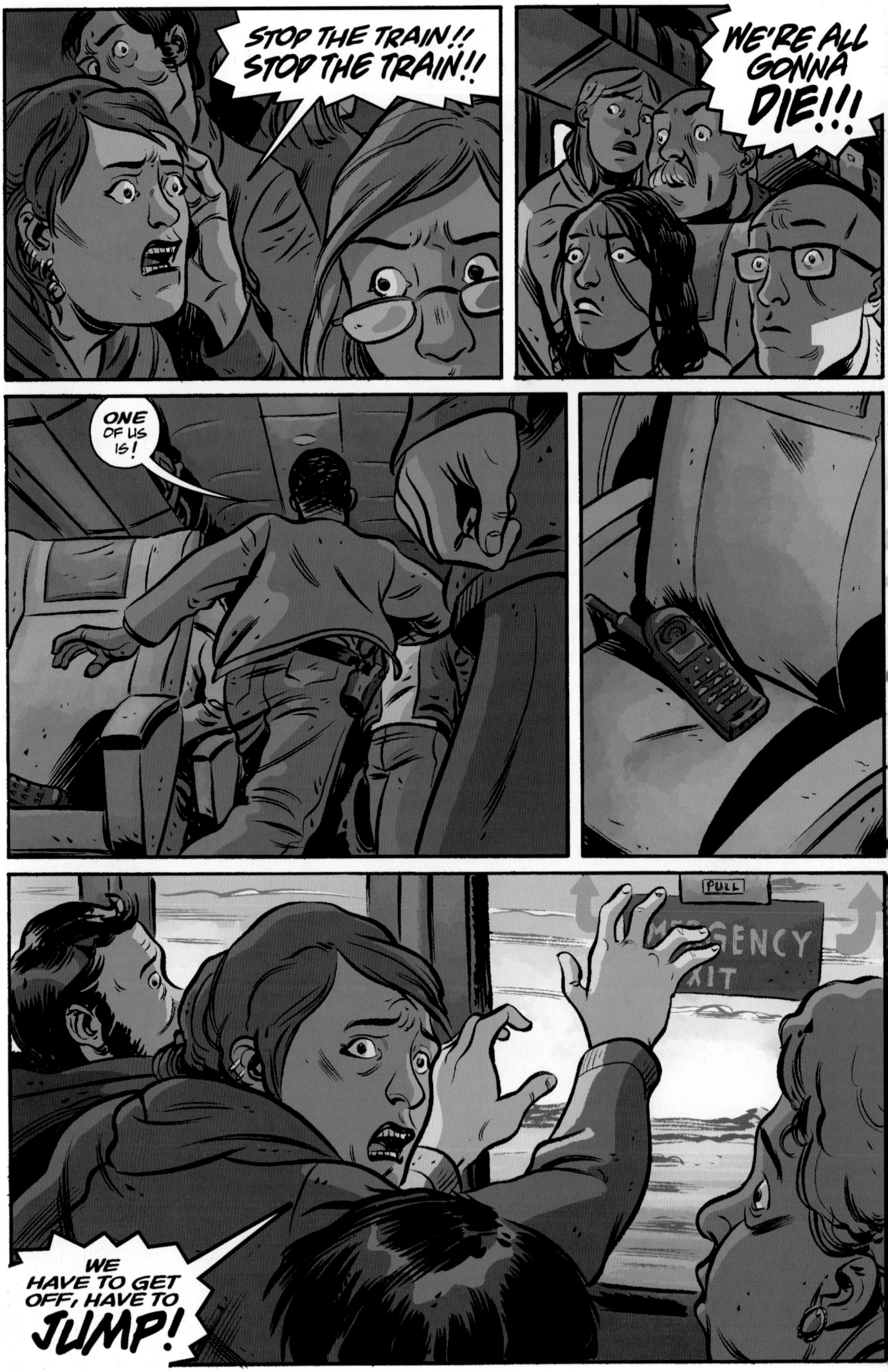
STOP THE TRAIN!!
STOP THE TRAIN!!
WE'RE ALL GONNA DIE!!!
ONE OF US IS!
PULL
WE HAVE TO GET OFF, HAVE TO JUMP!

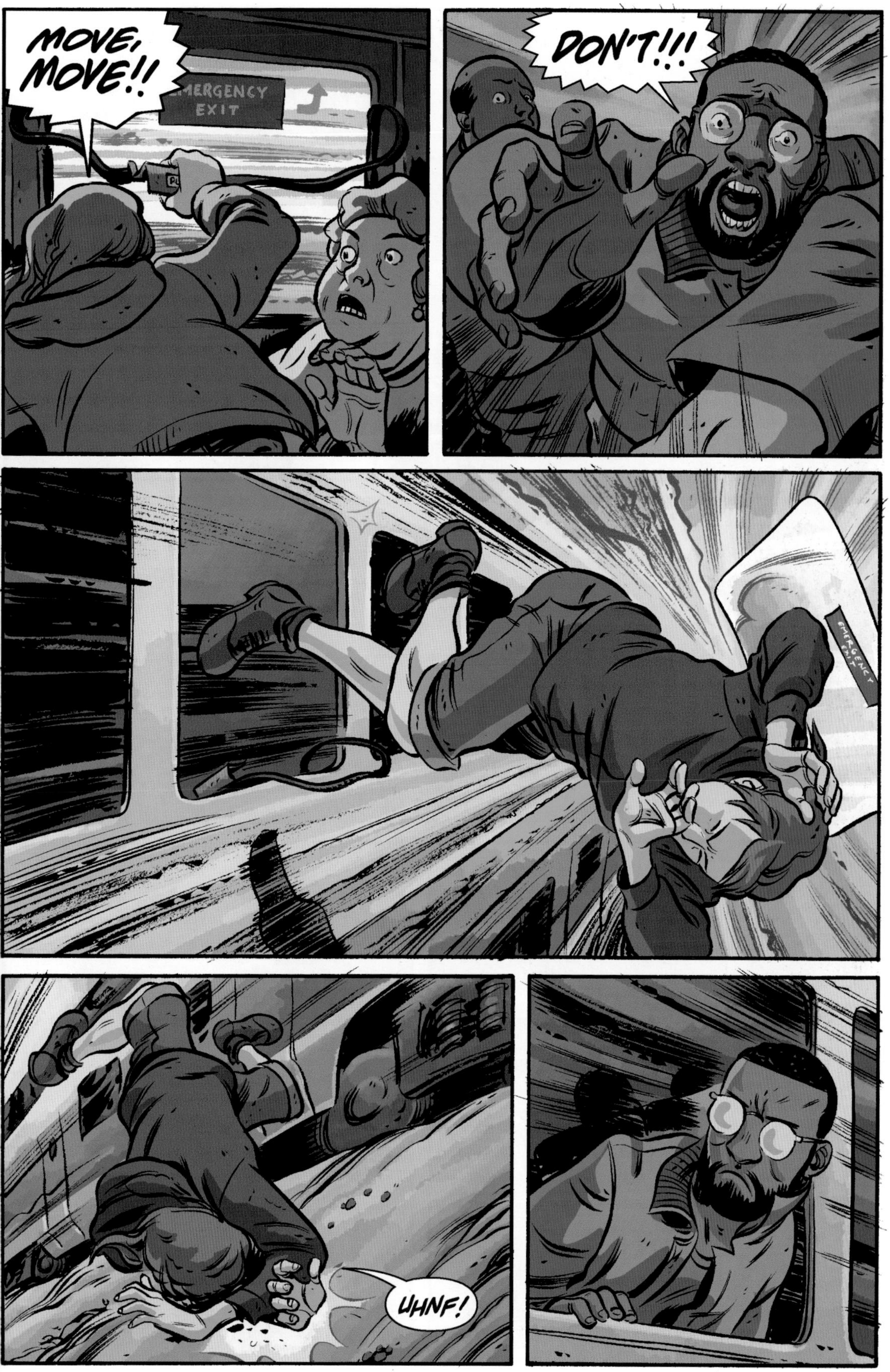
MOVE, MOVE!!
EMERGENCY EXIT
DON'T!!!
EMERGENCY EXIT
UHNF!

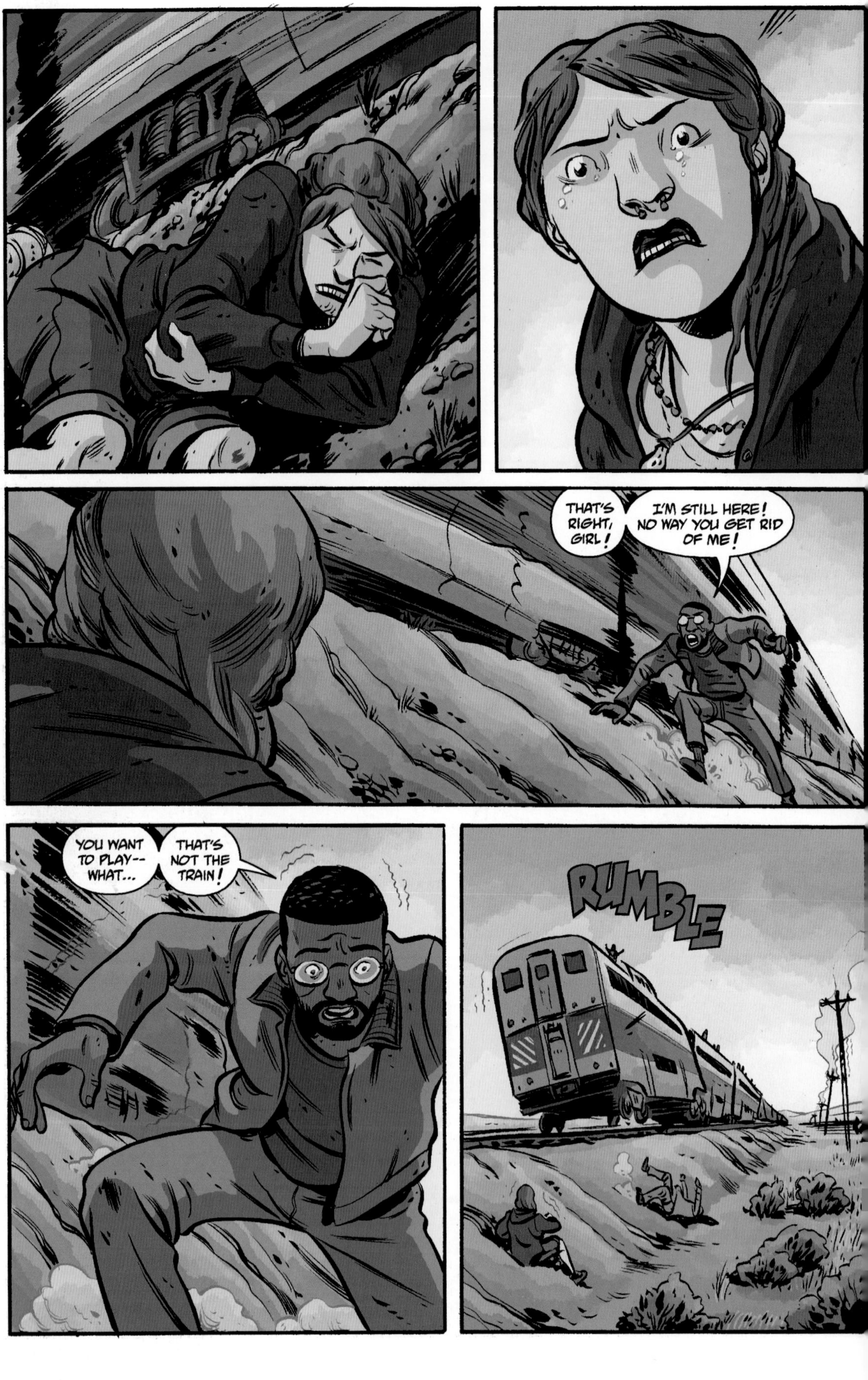
THAT'S RIGHT, GIRL!
I'M STILL HERE! NO WAY YOU GET RID OF ME!
YOU WANT TO PLAY-- WHAT...
THAT'S NOT THE TRAIN!
RUMBLE

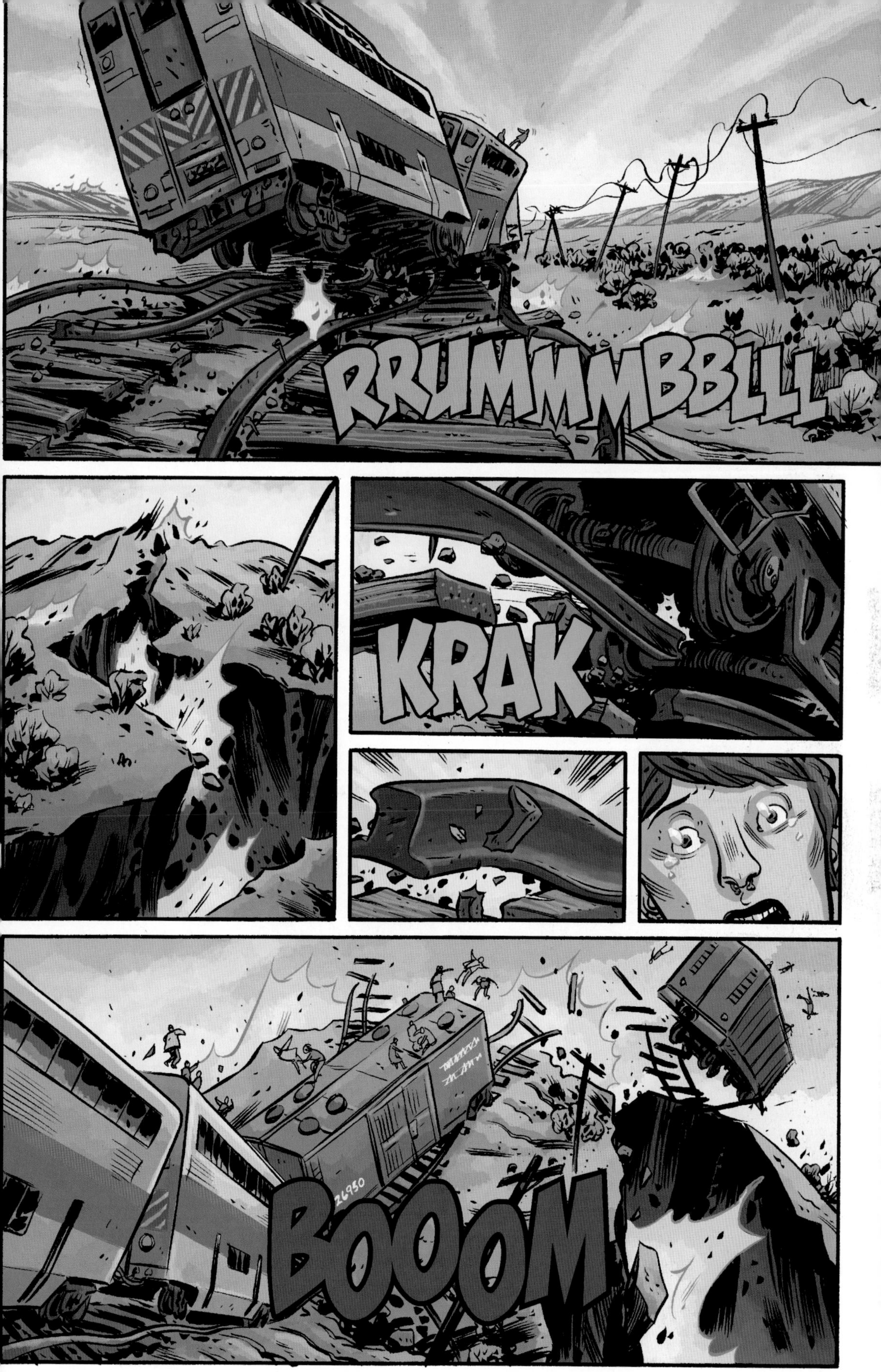
RRUMMMBBLLL
KRAK
BOOOM

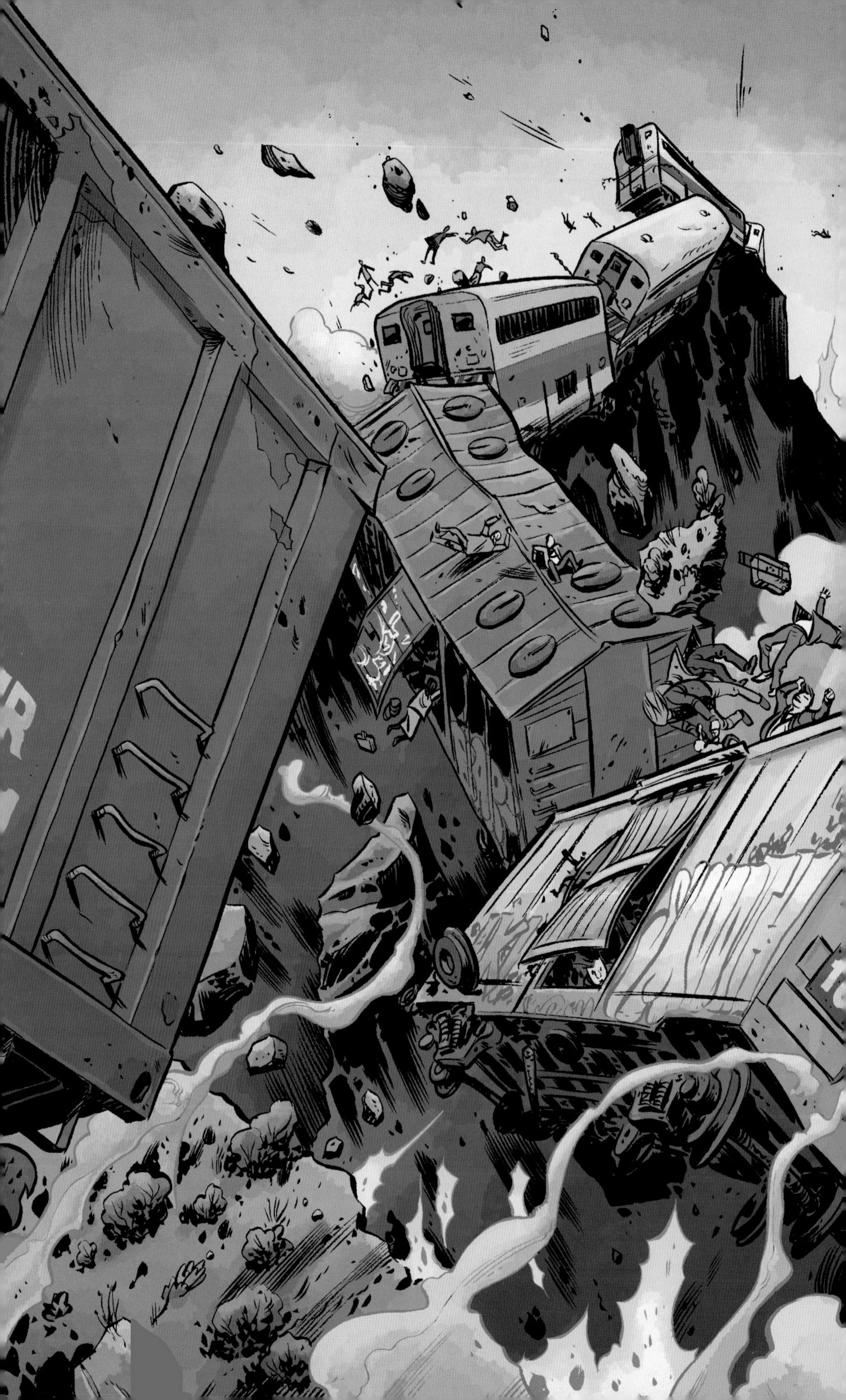

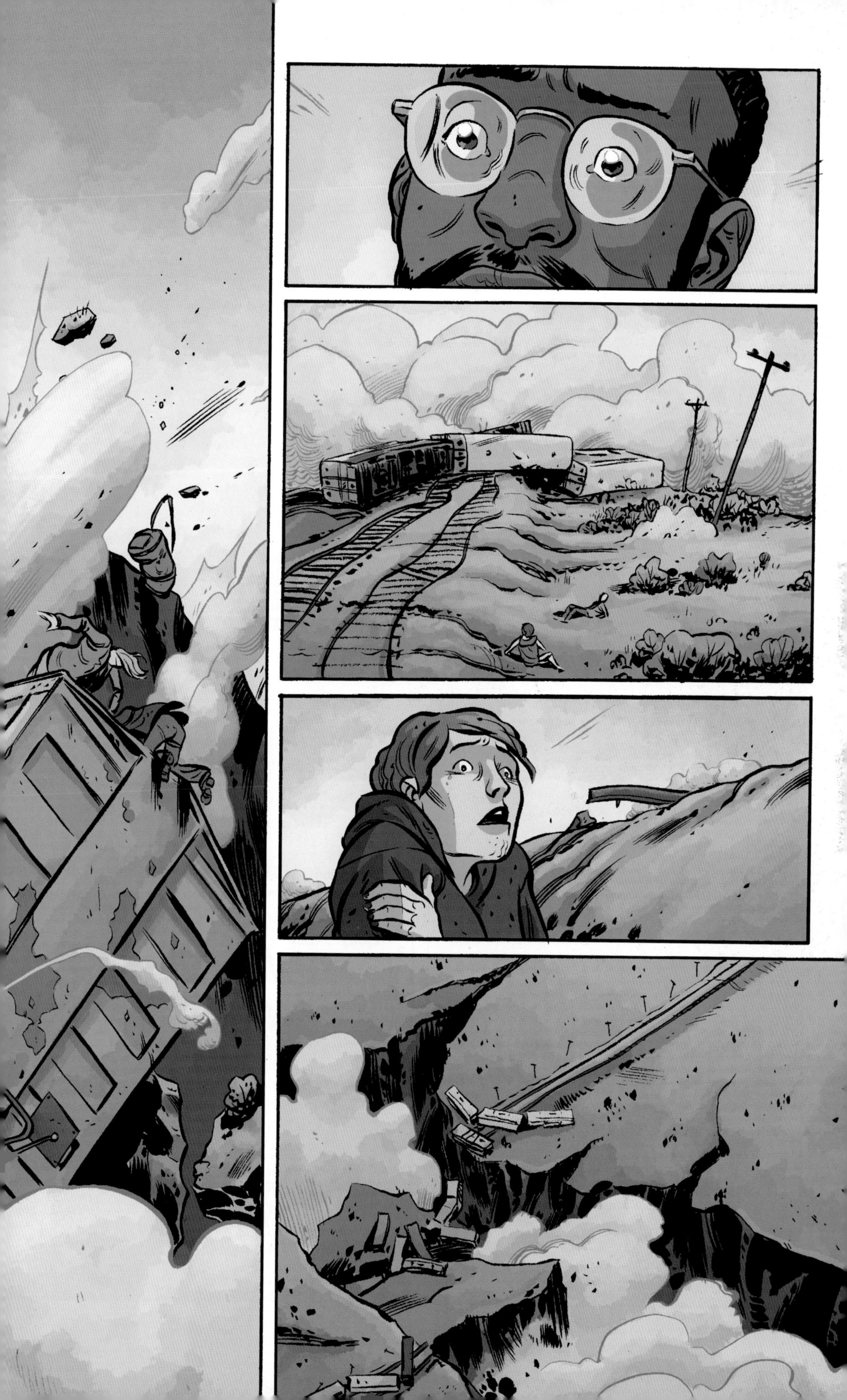

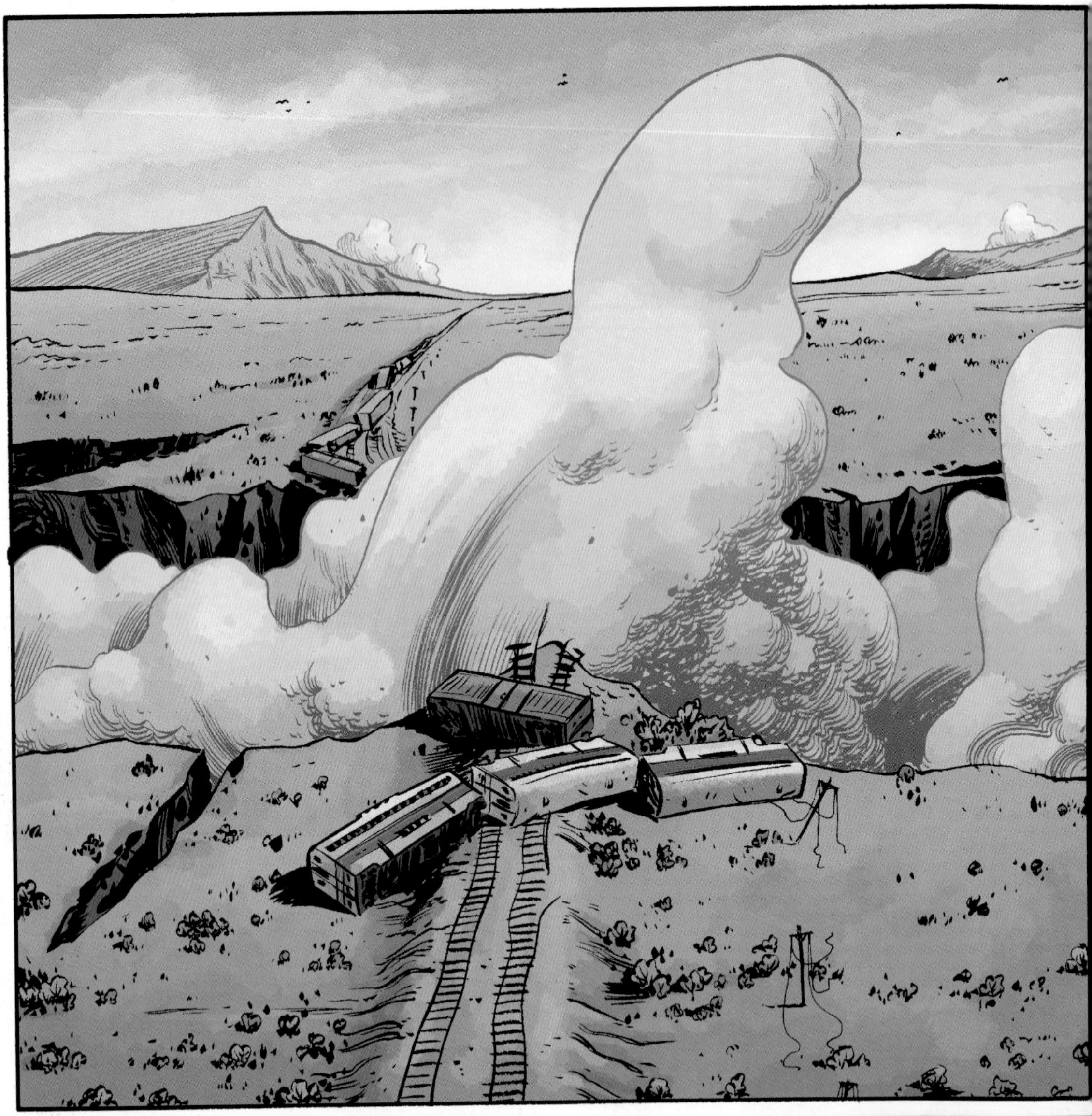

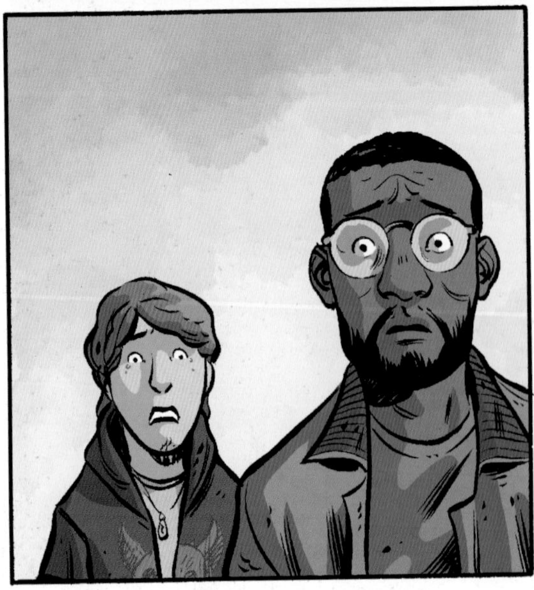

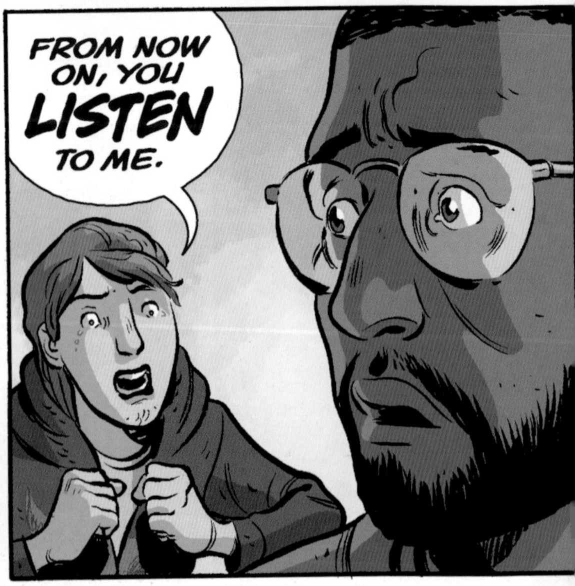
FROM NOW ON, YOU LISTEN TO ME.

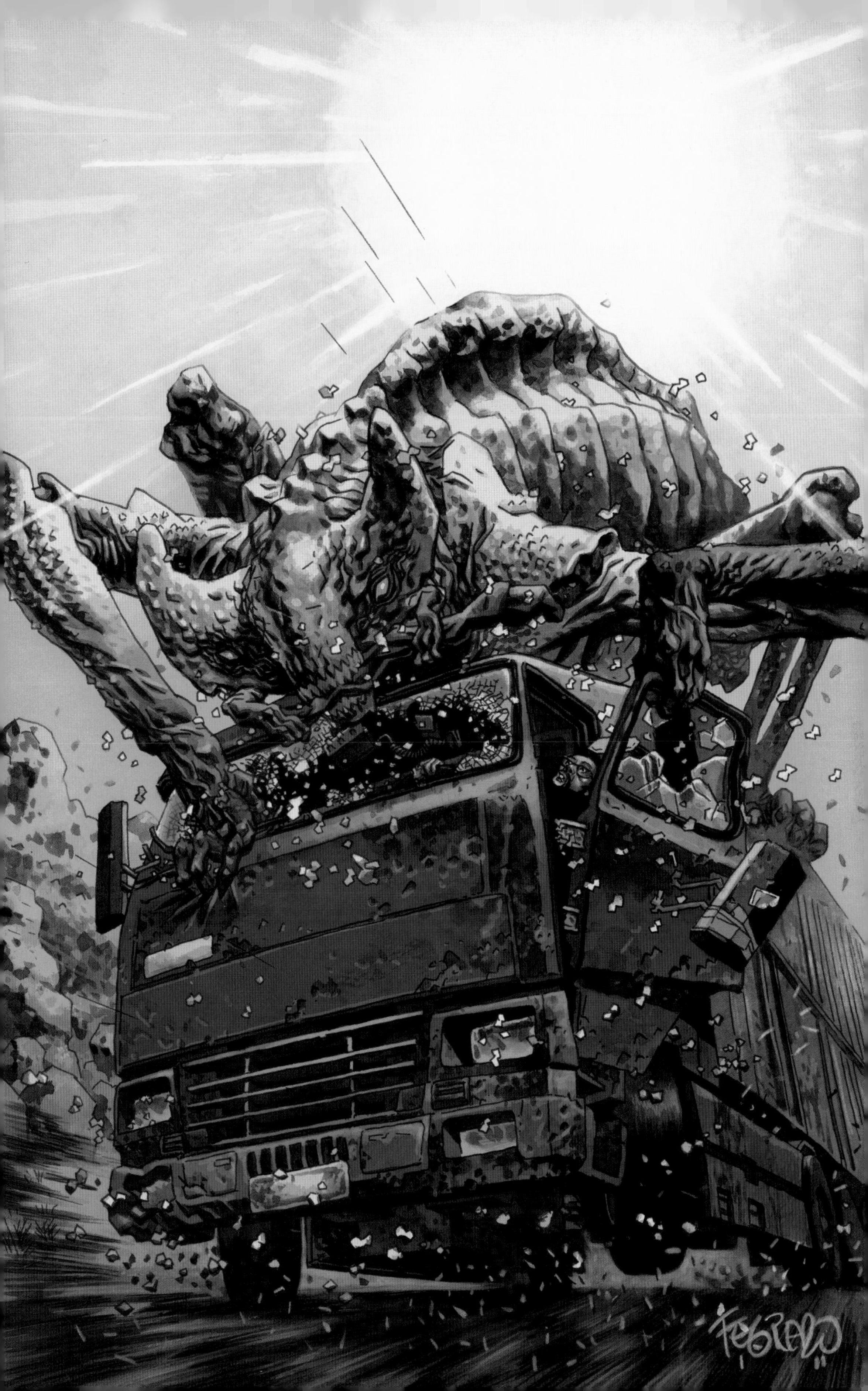
FEGREDO

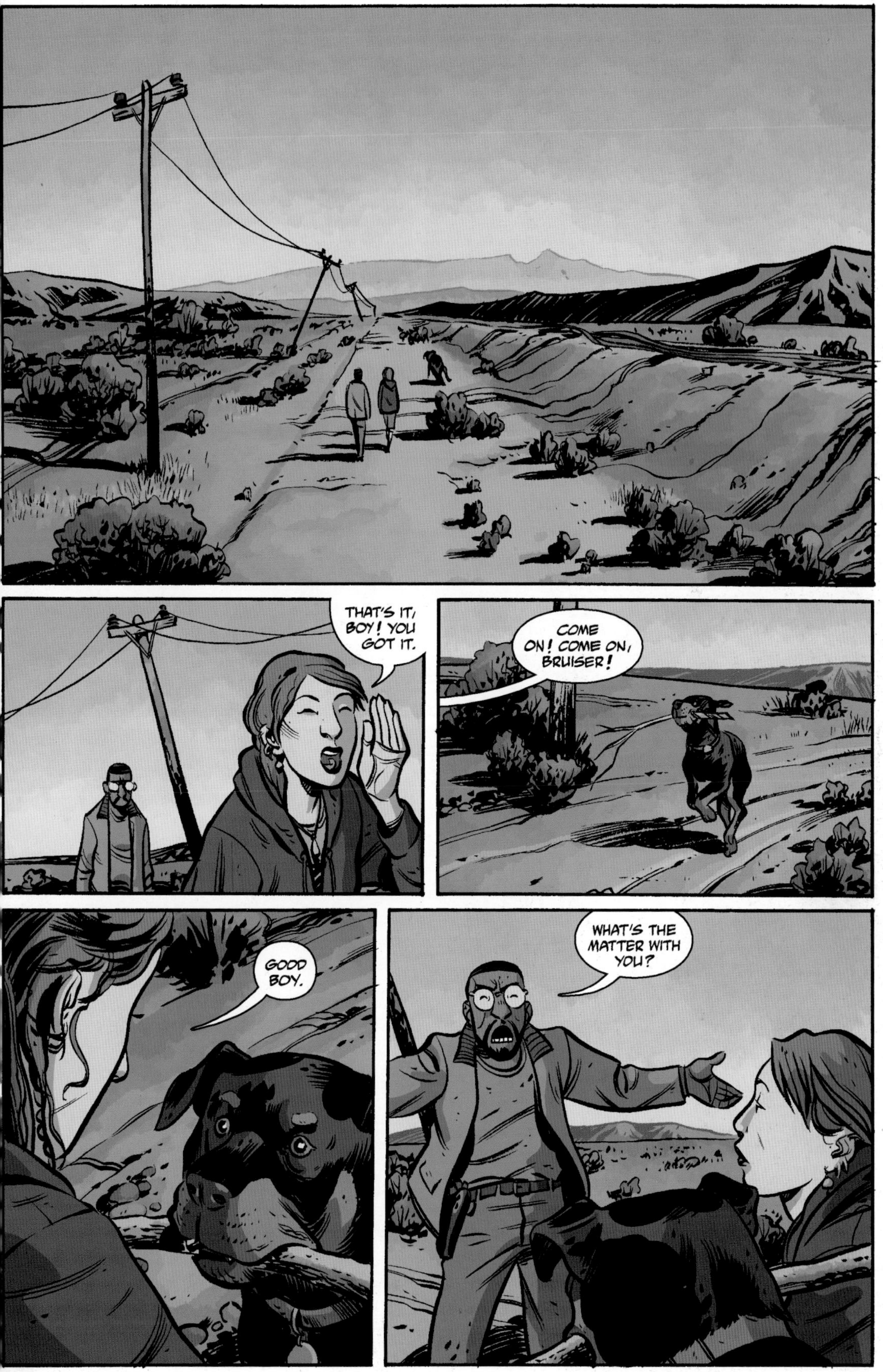
THAT'S IT, BOY! YOU GOT IT.
COME ON! COME ON, BRUISER!
GOOD BOY.
WHAT'S THE MATTER WITH YOU?

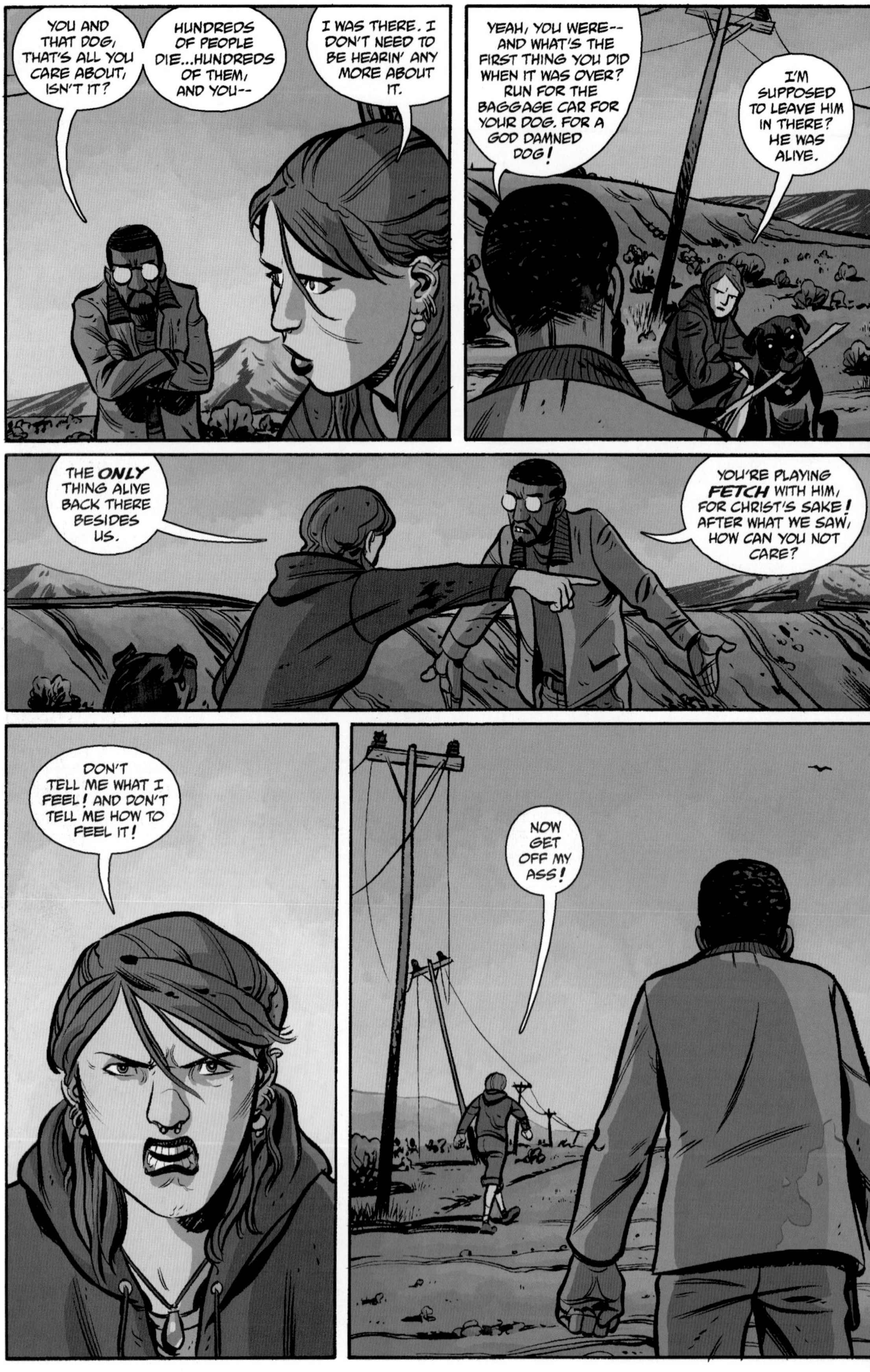
YOU AND THAT DOG, THAT'S ALL YOU CARE ABOUT, ISN'T IT?
HUNDREDS OF PEOPLE DIE...HUNDREDS OF THEM, AND YOU--
I WAS THERE. I DON'T NEED TO BE HEARIN' ANY MORE ABOUT IT.
YEAH, YOU WERE-- AND WHAT'S THE FIRST THING YOU DID WHEN IT WAS OVER? RUN FOR THE BAGGAGE CAR FOR YOUR DOG. FOR A GOD DAMNED DOG!
I'M SUPPOSED TO LEAVE HIM IN THERE? HE WAS ALIVE.
THE ONLY THING ALIVE BACK THERE BESIDES US.
YOU'RE PLAYING FETCH WITH HIM, FOR CHRIST'S SAKE! AFTER WHAT WE SAW, HOW CAN YOU NOT CARE?
DON'T TELL ME WHAT I FEEL! AND DON'T TELL ME HOW TO FEEL IT!
NOW GET OFF MY ASS!

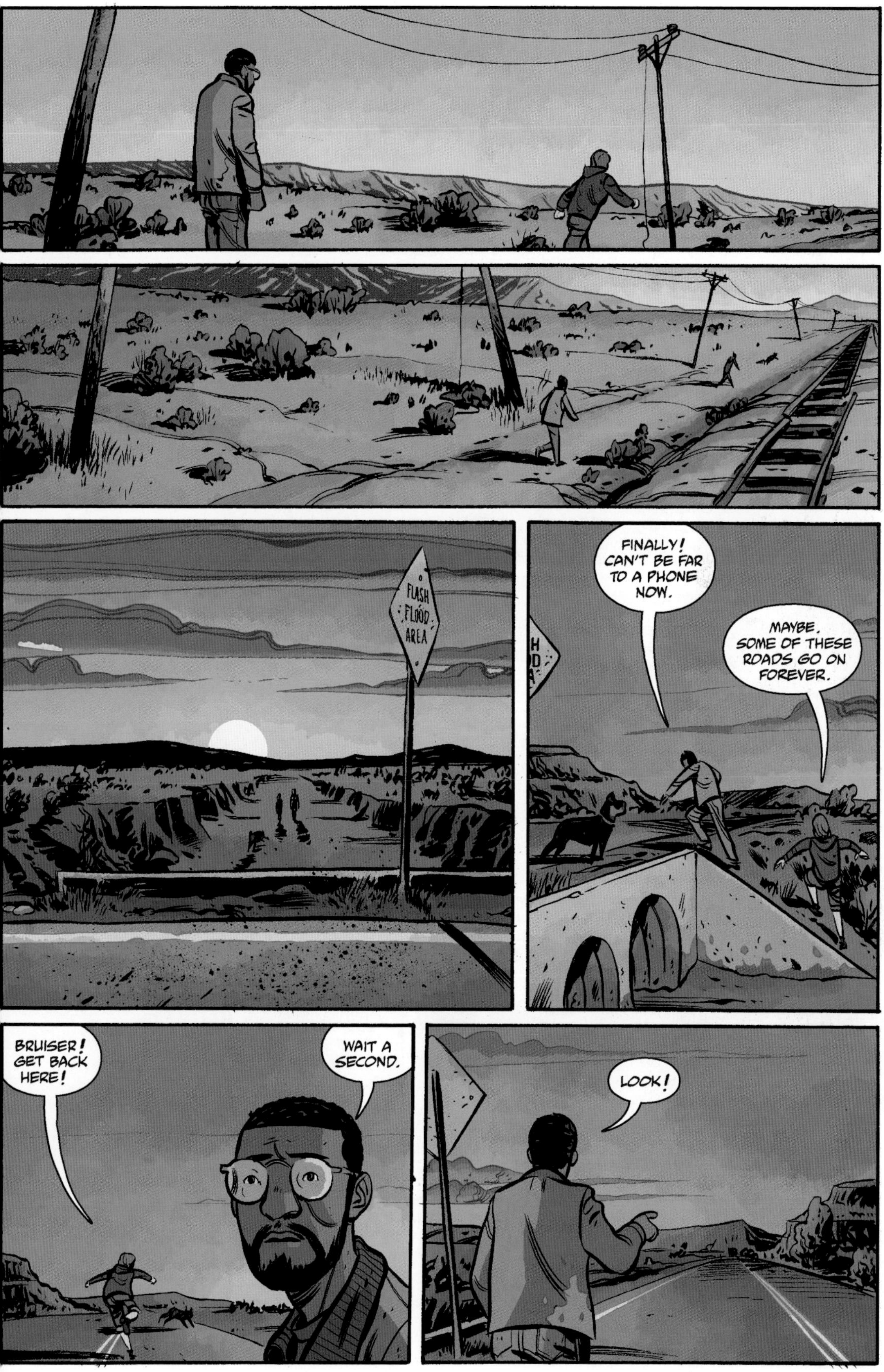
FLASH FLOOD AREA
FINALLY! CAN'T BE FAR TO A PHONE NOW.
MAYBE. SOME OF THESE ROADS GO ON FOREVER.
BRUISER! GET BACK HERE!
WAIT A SECOND.
LOOK!

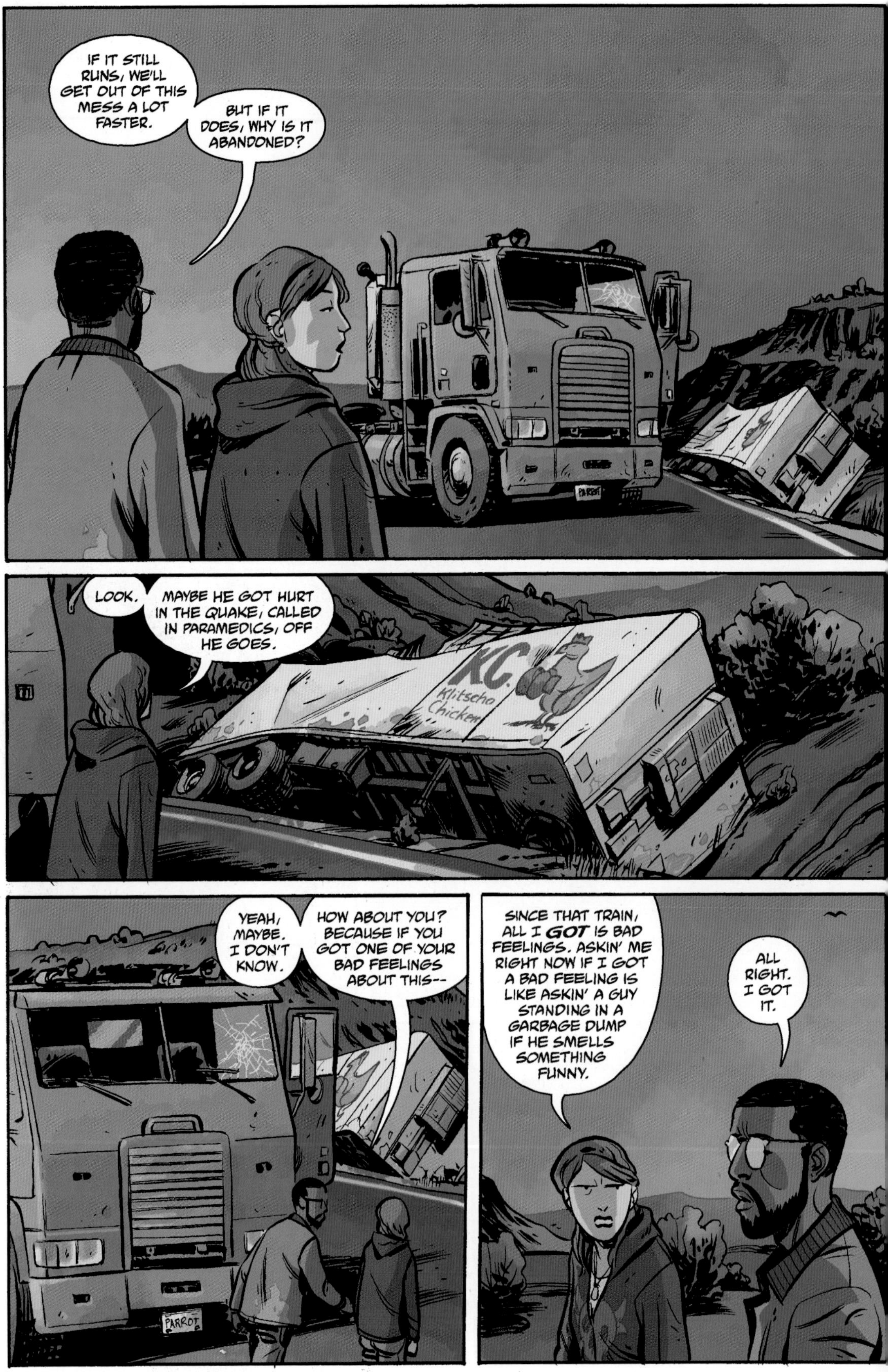
IF IT STILL RUNS, WE'LL GET OUT OF THIS MESS A LOT FASTER.
BUT IF IT DOES, WHY IS IT ABANDONED?
PARROT
LOOK.
MAYBE HE GOT HURT IN THE QUAKE, CALLED IN PARAMEDICS, OFF HE GOES.
K.C. Klitscho Chicken
YEAH, MAYBE. I DON'T KNOW.
HOW ABOUT YOU? BECAUSE IF YOU GOT ONE OF YOUR BAD FEELINGS ABOUT THIS--
PARROT
SINCE THAT TRAIN, ALL I GOT IS BAD FEELINGS. ASKIN' ME RIGHT NOW IF I GOT A BAD FEELING IS LIKE ASKIN' A GUY STANDING IN A GARBAGE DUMP IF HE SMELLS SOMETHING FUNNY.
ALL RIGHT. I GOT IT.

DRIVER'S-SIDE DOOR'S OPEN. LEFT IN A HURRY.

YOU KNOW...SOMETHING *DOES* SMELL FUNNY.

JESUS!

I'M GONNA BE SICK. I'M GONNA PUKE.

BUFFETT

SSSSSSSSSSSS

K.C. itscho icken

NO. NO, I DON'T THINK YOU'LL HAVE THE TIME.

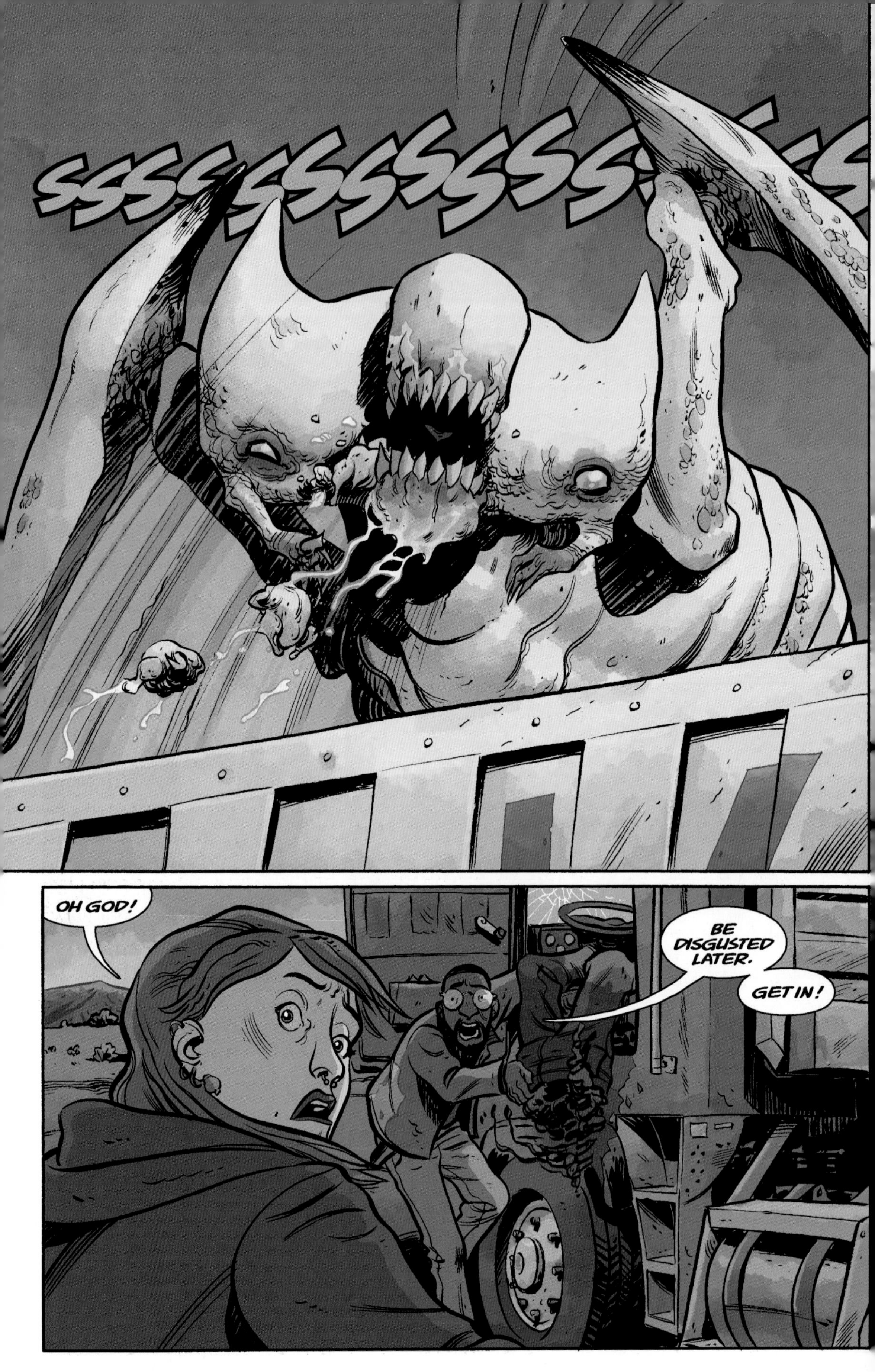
SSSSSSSSSSSSSSS
OH GOD!
BE DISGUSTED LATER.
GET IN!

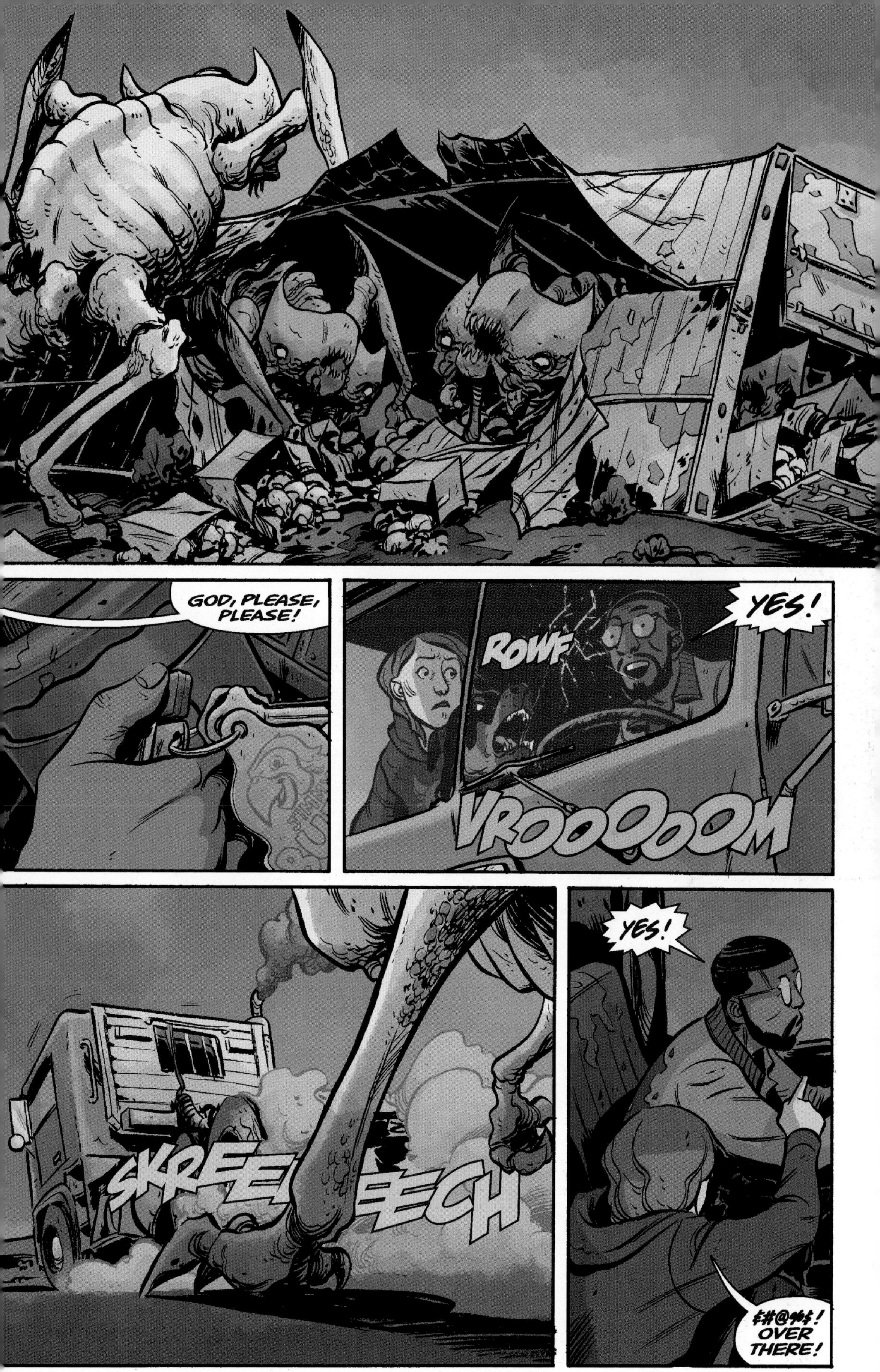
GOD, PLEASE, PLEASE!
YES!
ROWF
VROOOOOOM
SKREEEEEECH
YES!
₤#@%$! OVER THERE!

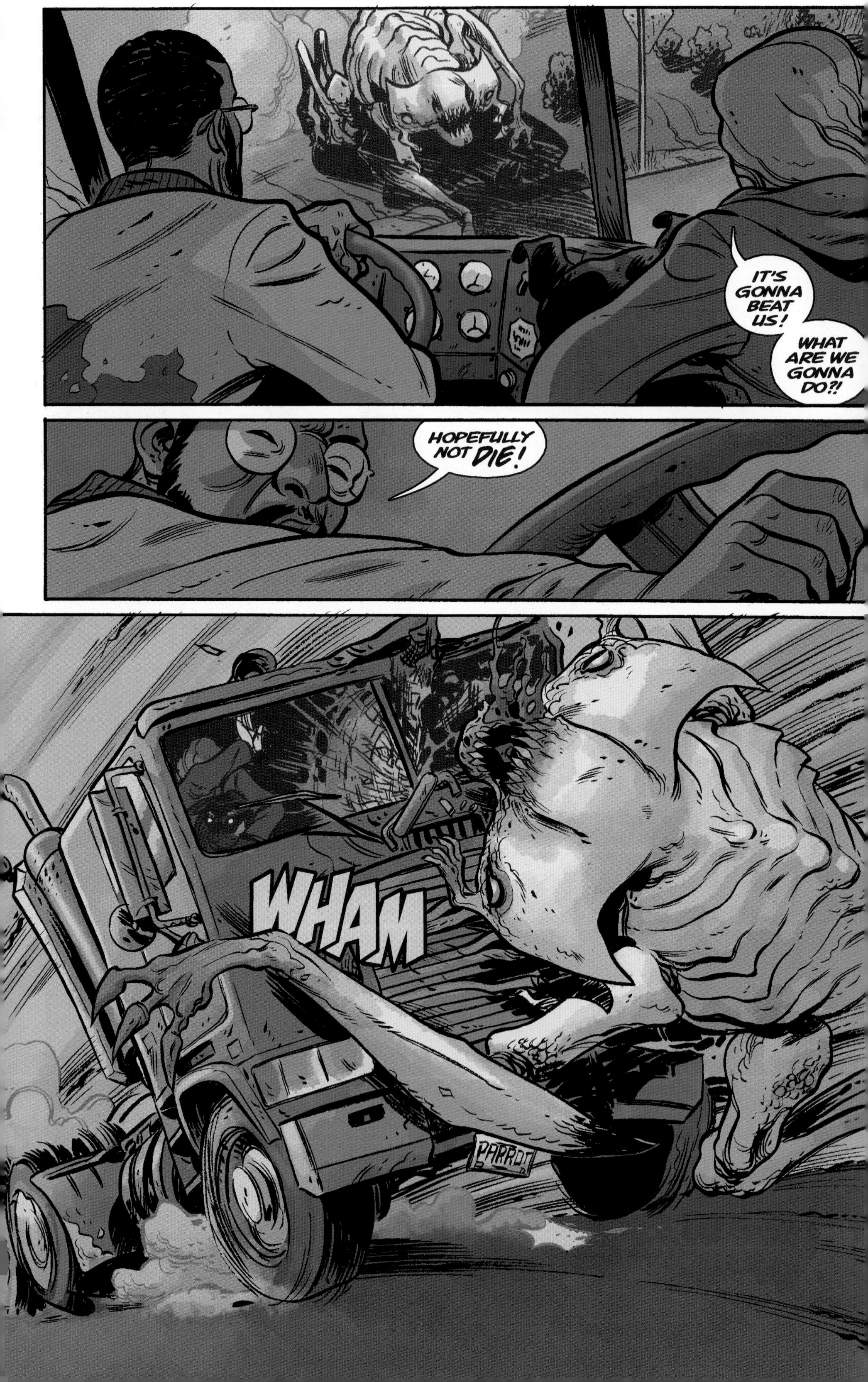
IT'S GONNA BEAT US!
WHAT ARE WE GONNA DO?!
HOPEFULLY NOT DIE!
WHAM
PARROT

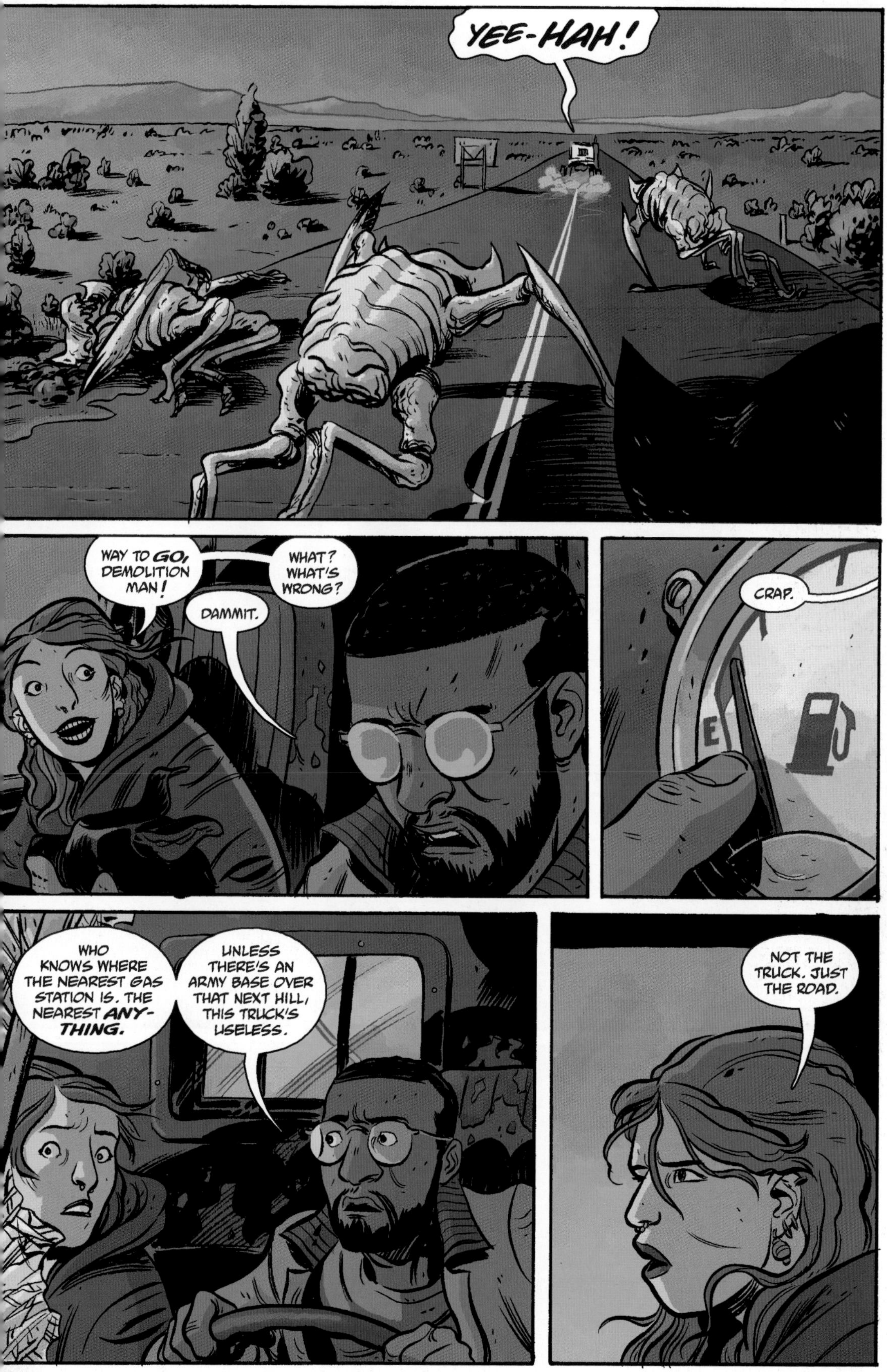
YEE-HAH!
WAY TO GO, DEMOLITION MAN!
WHAT? WHAT'S WRONG?
DAMMIT.
CRAP.
WHO KNOWS WHERE THE NEAREST GAS STATION IS. THE NEAREST ANY-THING.
UNLESS THERE'S AN ARMY BASE OVER THAT NEXT HILL, THIS TRUCK'S USELESS.
NOT THE TRUCK. JUST THE ROAD.

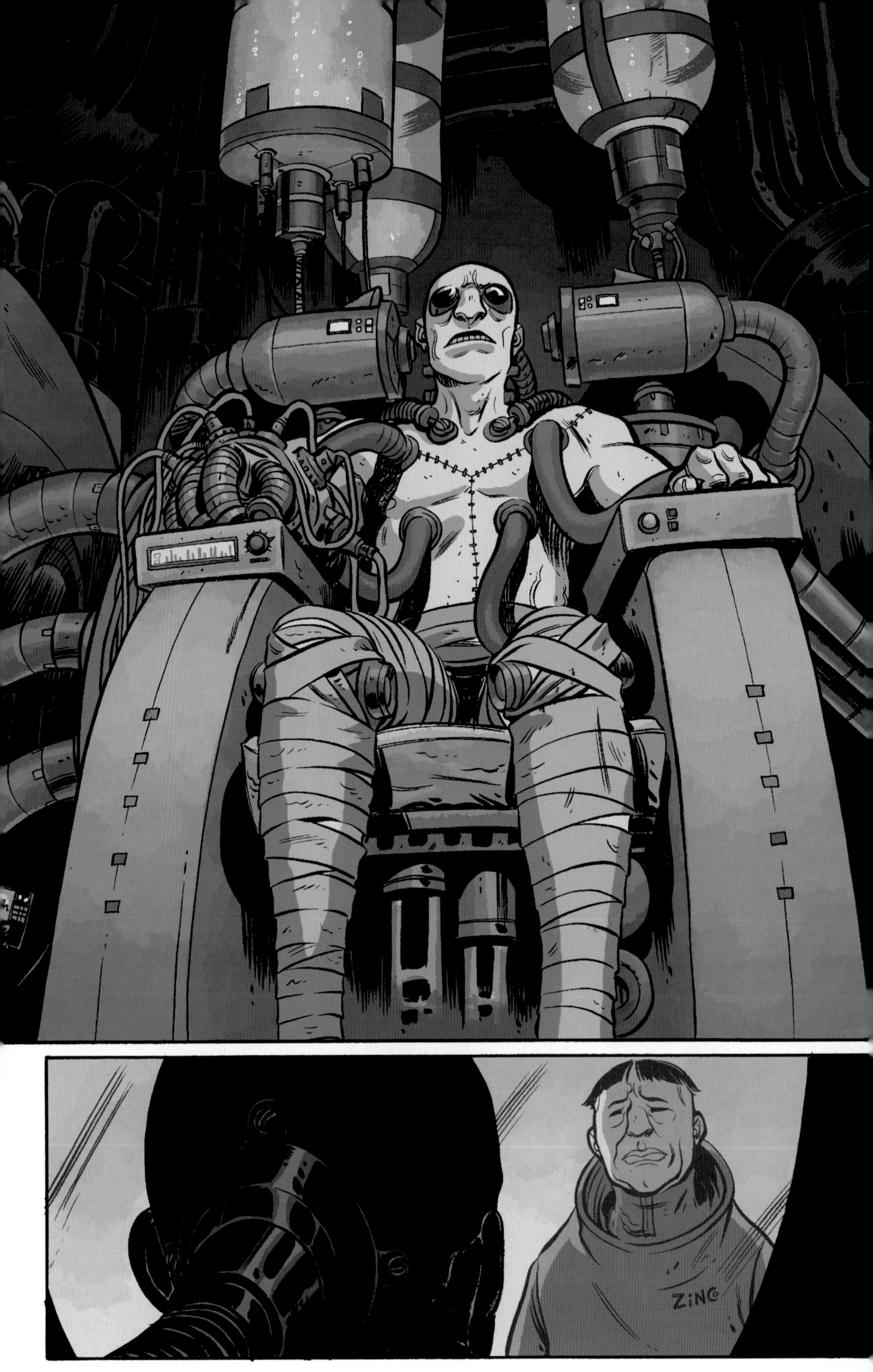
ZING

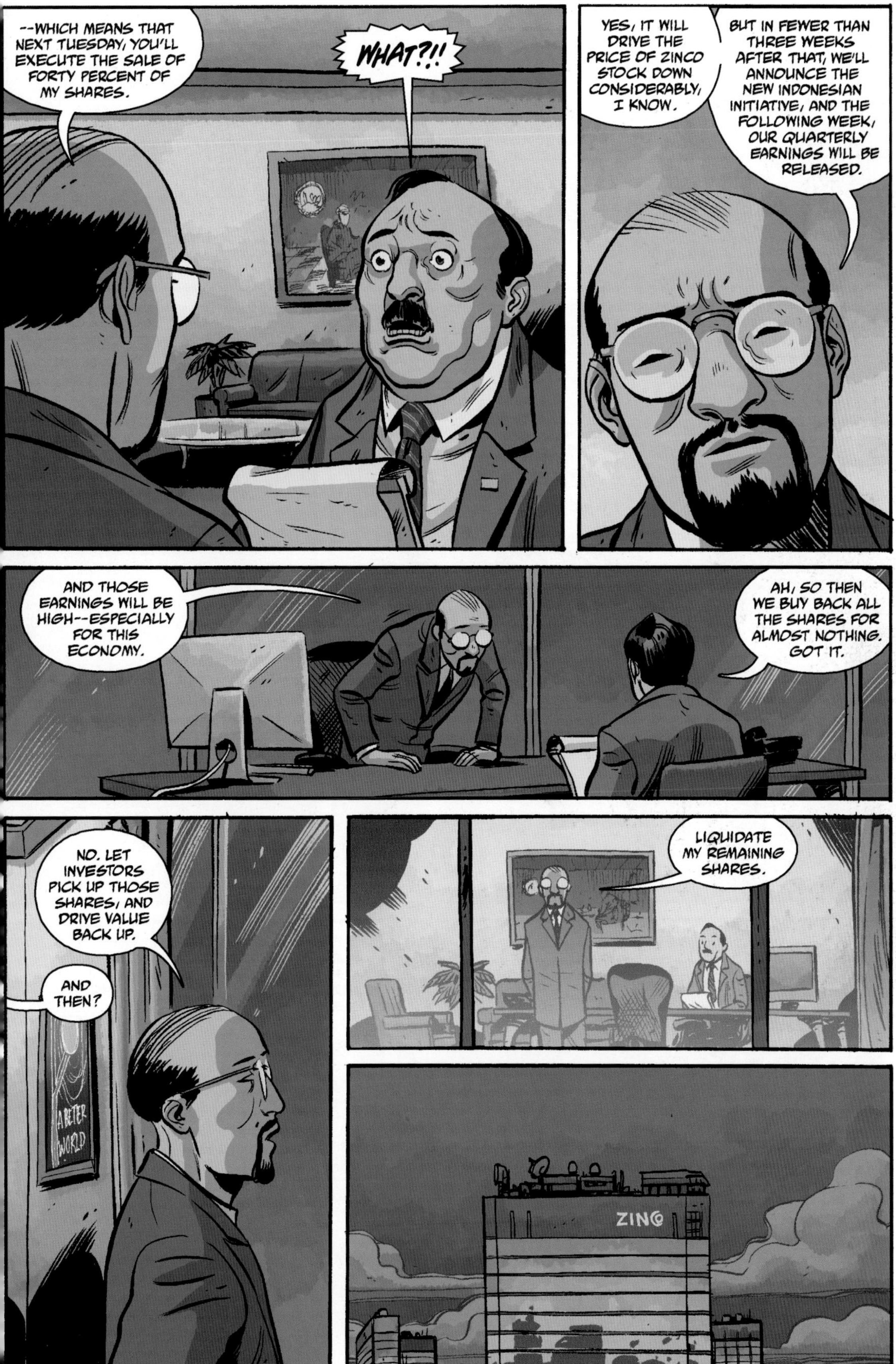

--WHICH MEANS THAT NEXT TUESDAY, YOU'LL EXECUTE THE SALE OF FORTY PERCENT OF MY SHARES.
WHAT?!!
YES, IT WILL DRIVE THE PRICE OF ZINCO STOCK DOWN CONSIDERABLY, I KNOW.
BUT IN FEWER THAN THREE WEEKS AFTER THAT, WE'LL ANNOUNCE THE NEW INDONESIAN INITIATIVE, AND THE FOLLOWING WEEK, OUR QUARTERLY EARNINGS WILL BE RELEASED.
AND THOSE EARNINGS WILL BE HIGH--ESPECIALLY FOR THIS ECONOMY.
AH, SO THEN WE BUY BACK ALL THE SHARES FOR ALMOST NOTHING. GOT IT.
NO. LET INVESTORS PICK UP THOSE SHARES, AND DRIVE VALUE BACK UP.
AND THEN?
A BETTER WORLD
LIQUIDATE MY REMAINING SHARES.
ZINCO

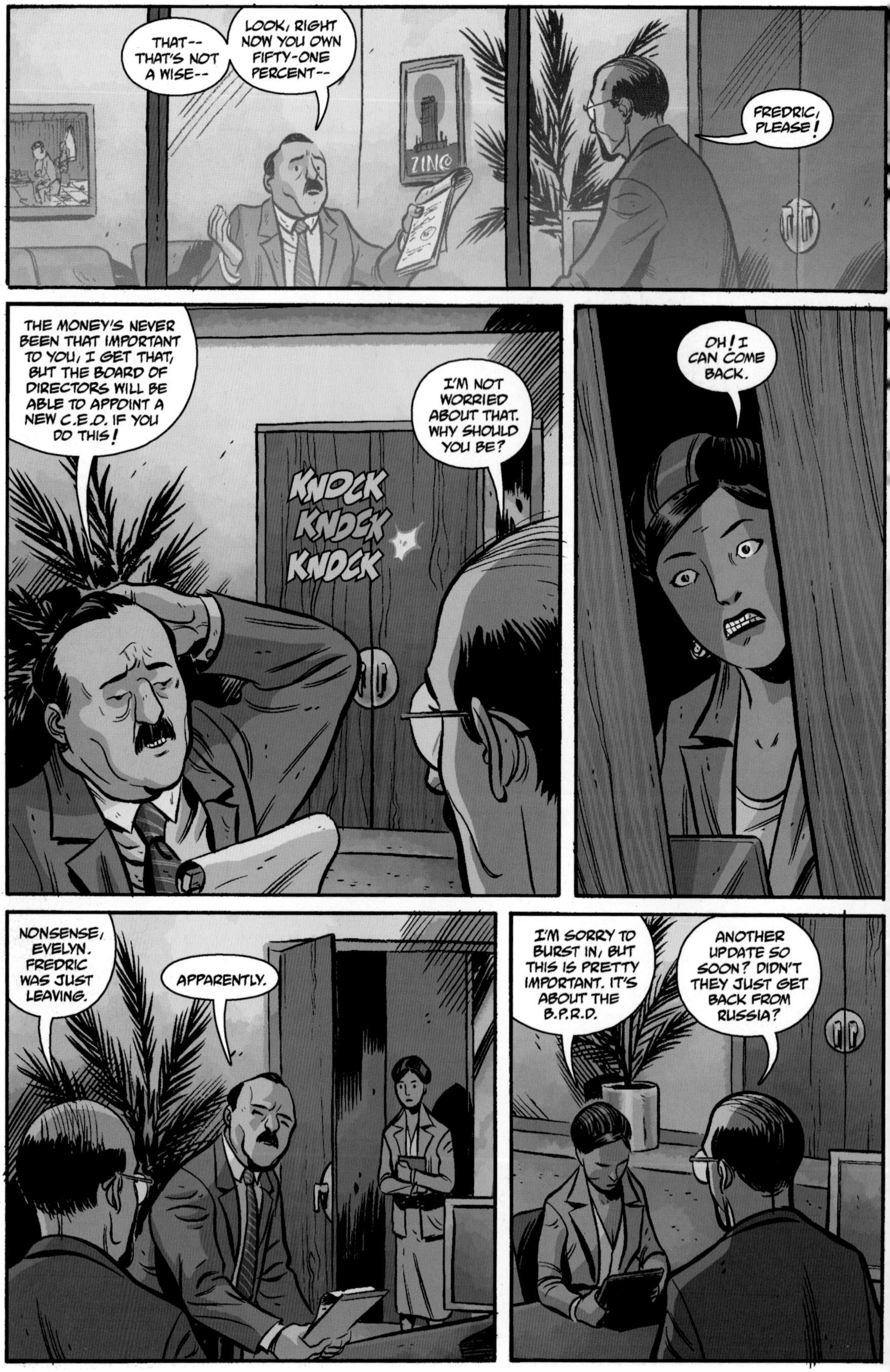
THAT-- THAT'S NOT A WISE--
LOOK, RIGHT NOW YOU OWN FIFTY-ONE PERCENT--
FREDRIC, PLEASE!
THE MONEY'S NEVER BEEN THAT IMPORTANT TO YOU, I GET THAT, BUT THE BOARD OF DIRECTORS WILL BE ABLE TO APPOINT A NEW C.E.O. IF YOU DO THIS!
I'M NOT WORRIED ABOUT THAT. WHY SHOULD YOU BE?
KNOCK KNOCK KNOCK
OH! I CAN COME BACK.
NONSENSE, EVELYN. FREDRIC WAS JUST LEAVING.
APPARENTLY.
I'M SORRY TO BURST IN, BUT THIS IS PRETTY IMPORTANT. IT'S ABOUT THE B.P.R.D.
ANOTHER UPDATE SO SOON? DIDN'T THEY JUST GET BACK FROM RUSSIA?

NOT AN UPDATE EXACTLY.

THE THING IS, NOW THAT THE BUREAU IS PART OF THE U.N., KEEPING TRACK OF WHAT THEY DO TAKES SOME FINESSE.

BUT FOR MANY YEARS, THEY WERE A U.S. GOVERNMENT AGENCY.

AND CLASSIFIED INFORMATION IN THIS COUNTRY SIMPLY ISN'T WHAT IT USED TO BE.

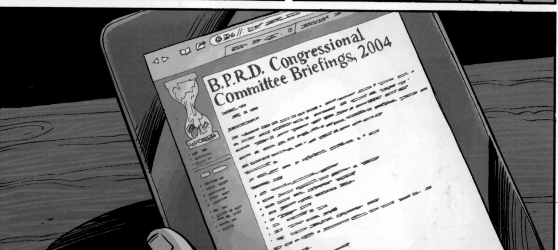

B.P.R.D. Congressional Committee Briefings, 2004

SIR, IF YOU DON'T MIND...WHAT EXACTLY IS YOUR INTEREST IN THIS AGENCY?

RRIINGG

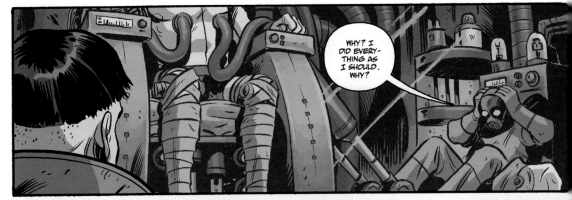

WHY? I DID EVERYTHING AS I SHOULD. WHY?

WHAT IS THIS ALL ABOUT? I THOUGHT EVERYTHING WAS SET.

HERR MARSTEN!

ZINC

I'M SORRY. WE HAD EVERY REASON TO BELIEVE THAT. I'VE SEEN KROENEN WORK MIRACLES IN RAISING THE DEAD.

ONCE I SAW HIM FISH A HEAD OUT OF THE JUNGLES OF SOUTH AMERICA--

YOU'VE TOLD ME THOSE STORIES, BUT WHAT ABOUT *CREATING* LIFE? HE'S DONE THAT, YES?

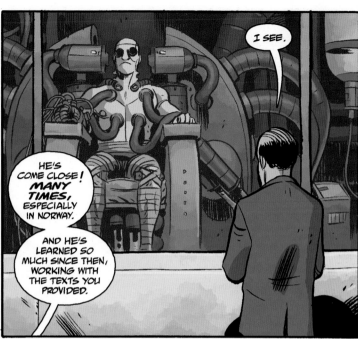

I SEE.

HE'S COME CLOSE! *MANY TIMES,* ESPECIALLY IN NORWAY.

AND HE'S LEARNED SO MUCH SINCE THEN, WORKING WITH THE TEXTS YOU PROVIDED.

WE HAD EVERY REASON TO BELIEVE.

BUT I THINK WE WILL NEED ASSISTANCE--

HERR MARSTEN!

WHAT IS IT?

WHAT ARE YOU THINKING, SIR? WILL--WILL THERE BE PUNISHMENT?

HERR MARSTEN!

MAN, CAN YOU BELIEVE WE HAD THE JUICE TO MAKE IT?!

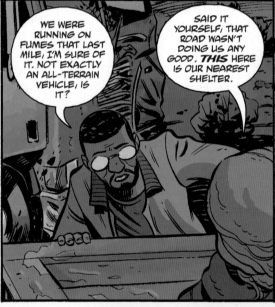

WE WERE RUNNING ON FUMES THAT LAST MILE, I'M SURE OF IT. NOT EXACTLY AN ALL-TERRAIN VEHICLE, IS IT?

SAID IT YOURSELF, THAT ROAD WASN'T DOING US ANY GOOD. *THIS* HERE IS OUR NEAREST SHELTER.

AND, YOU KNOW, MAYBE WE END UP NOT EVEN NEEDIN' IT.

WATCH YOUR STEP, BRUISER.

MAYBE WE LOST THOSE THINGS. CHRIST KNOWS YOU *DROVE* FAST ENOUGH!

UH-UH.

"NOT FAST ENOUGH."

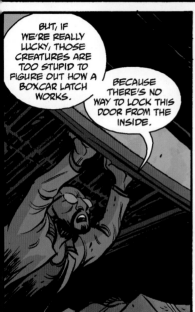

BUT, IF WE'RE REALLY LUCKY, THOSE CREATURES ARE TOO STUPID TO FIGURE OUT HOW A BOXCAR LATCH WORKS.

BECAUSE THERE'S NO WAY TO LOCK THIS DOOR FROM THE INSIDE.

SLAM

CLANK

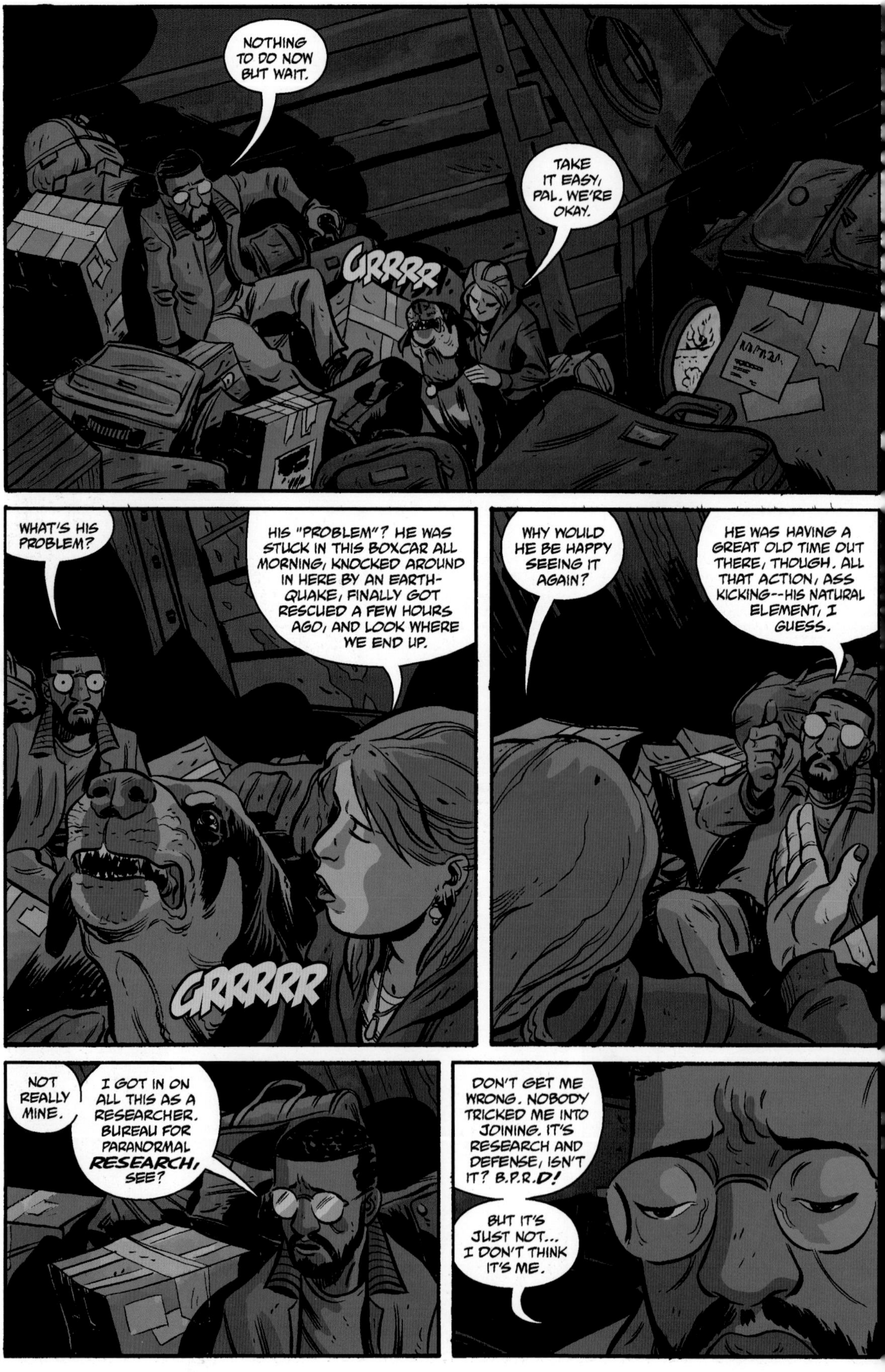

NOTHING TO DO NOW BUT WAIT.
TAKE IT EASY, PAL. WE'RE OKAY.
GRRRR
WHAT'S HIS PROBLEM?
HIS "PROBLEM"? HE WAS STUCK IN THIS BOXCAR ALL MORNING, KNOCKED AROUND IN HERE BY AN EARTH-QUAKE, FINALLY GOT RESCUED A FEW HOURS AGO, AND LOOK WHERE WE END UP.
GRRRRR
WHY WOULD HE BE HAPPY SEEING IT AGAIN?
HE WAS HAVING A GREAT OLD TIME OUT THERE, THOUGH. ALL THAT ACTION, ASS KICKING--HIS NATURAL ELEMENT, I GUESS.
NOT REALLY MINE.
I GOT IN ON ALL THIS AS A RESEARCHER. BUREAU FOR PARANORMAL RESEARCH, SEE?
DON'T GET ME WRONG. NOBODY TRICKED ME INTO JOINING. IT'S RESEARCH AND DEFENSE, ISN'T IT? B.P.R.D!
BUT IT'S JUST NOT... I DON'T THINK IT'S ME.

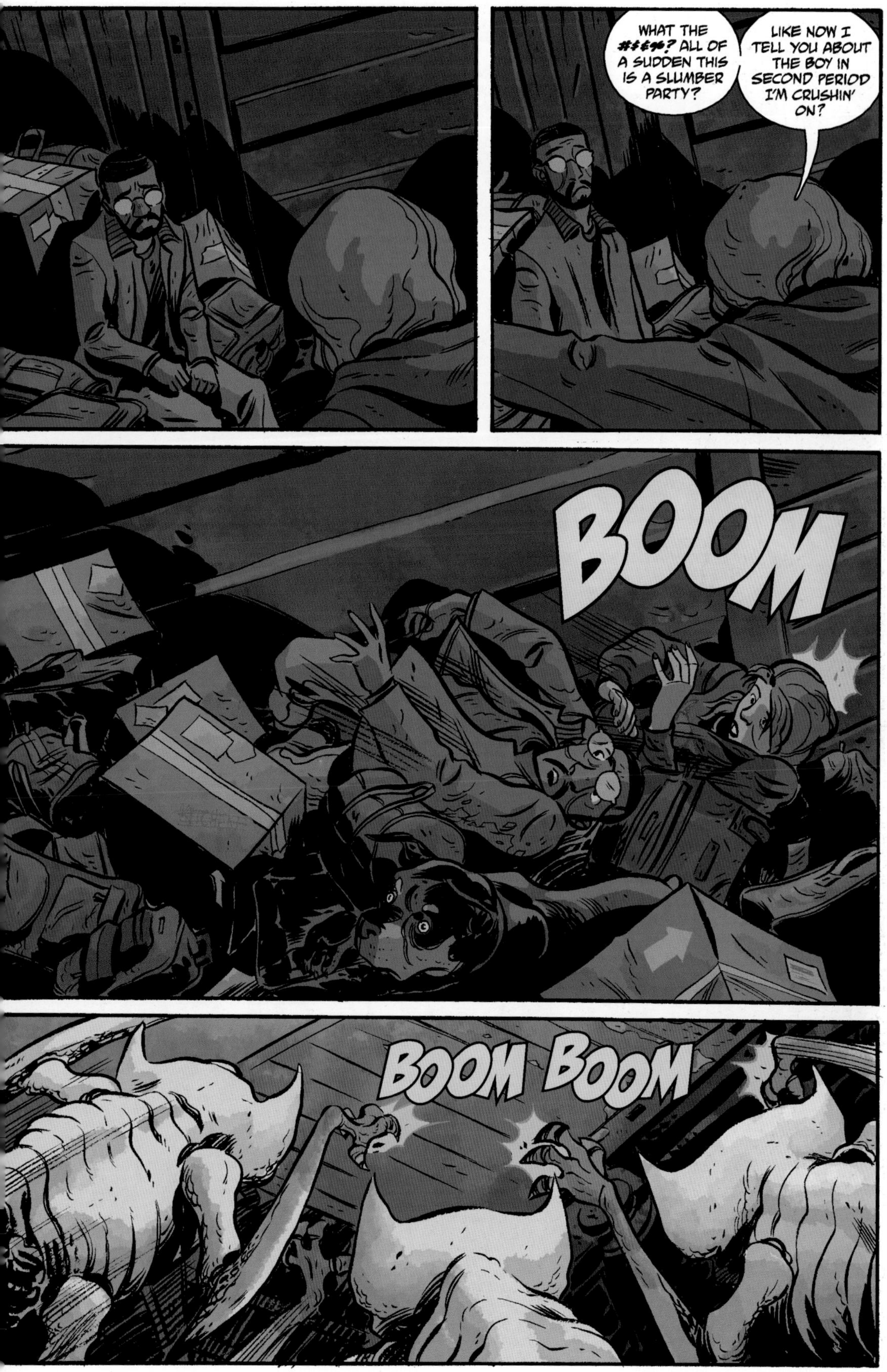
WHAT THE #$&%? ALL OF A SUDDEN THIS IS A SLUMBER PARTY?
LIKE NOW I TELL YOU ABOUT THE BOY IN SECOND PERIOD I'M CRUSHIN' ON?
BOOM
BOOM BOOM

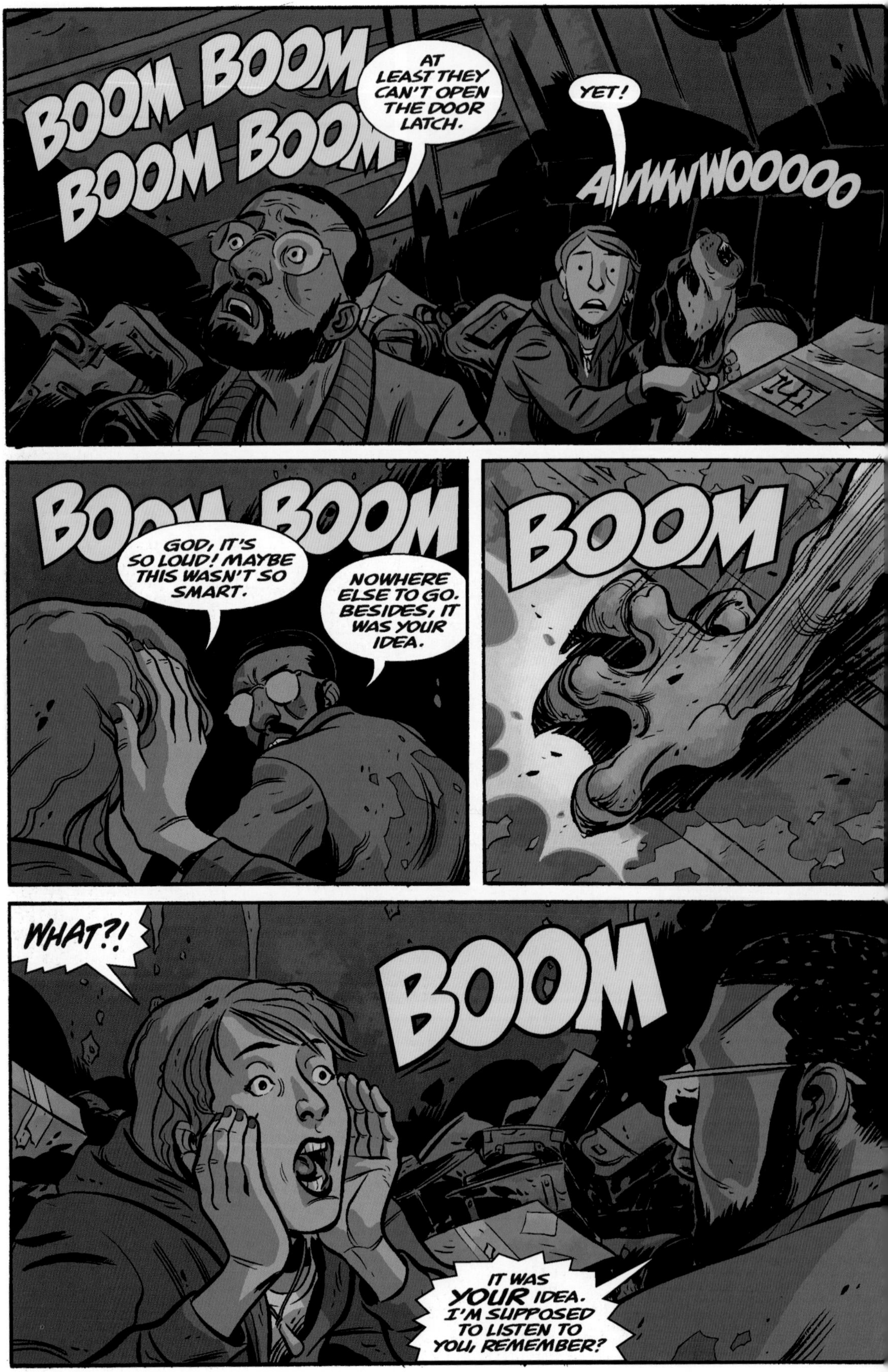

BOOM BOOM
BOOM BOOM
AT LEAST THEY CAN'T OPEN THE DOOR LATCH.
YET!
AWWWOOOOO
BOOM BOOM
GOD, IT'S SO LOUD! MAYBE THIS WASN'T SO SMART.
NOWHERE ELSE TO GO. BESIDES, IT WAS YOUR IDEA.
BOOM
WHAT?!
BOOM
IT WAS YOUR IDEA. I'M SUPPOSED TO LISTEN TO YOU, REMEMBER?

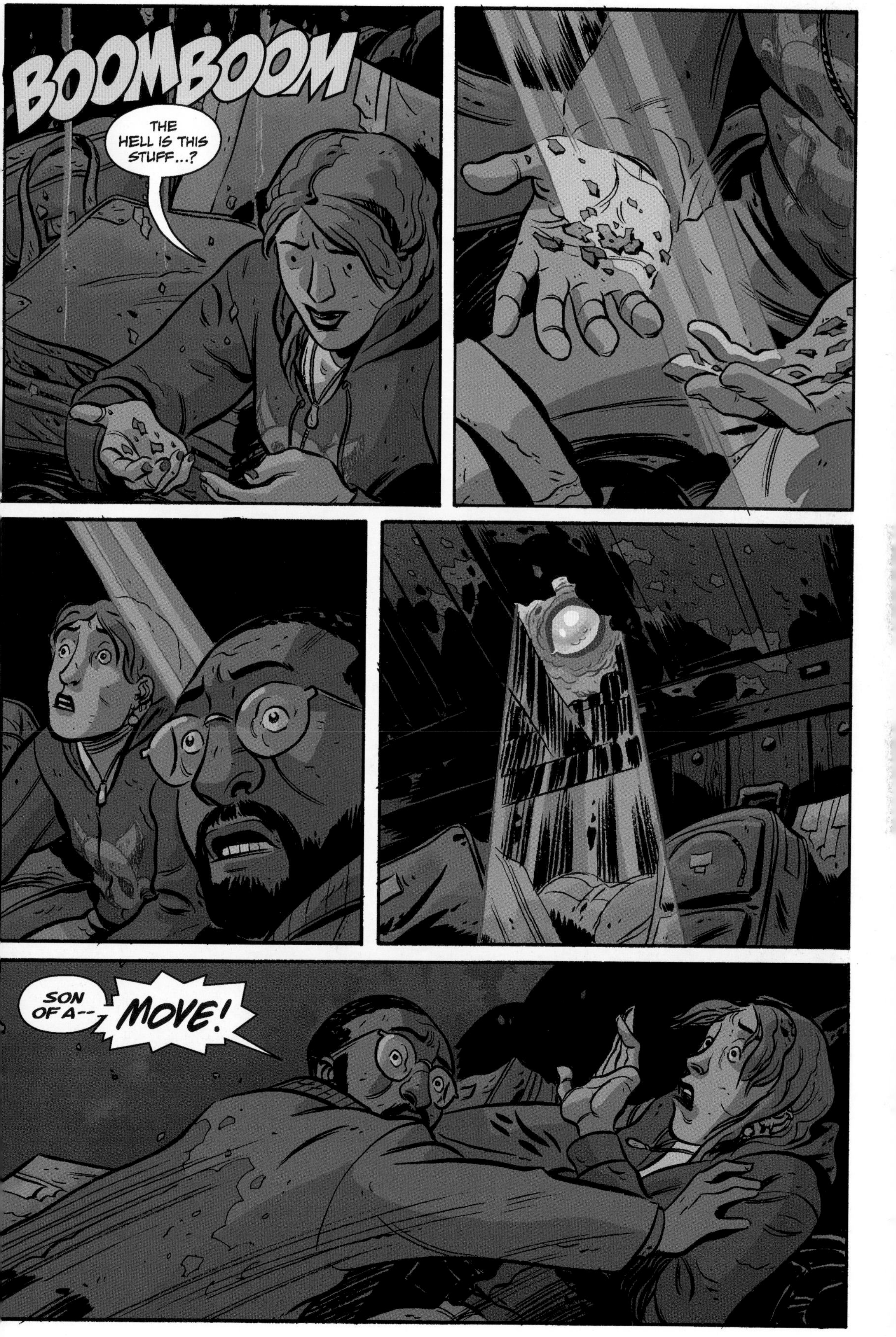
BOOMBOOM
THE HELL IS THIS STUFF...?
SON OF A--
MOVE!

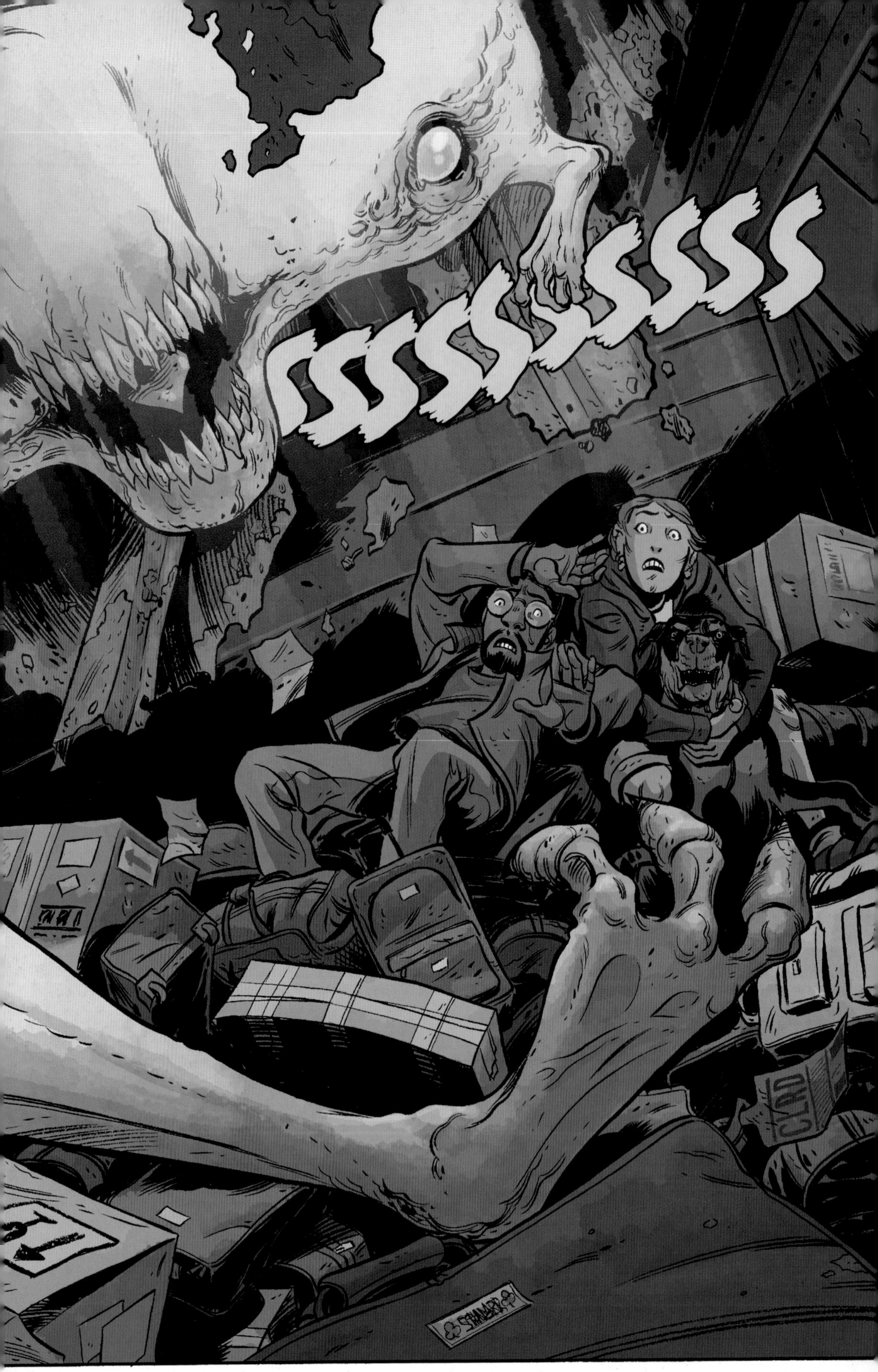

SSSSSSSSSS
CLRD

THE DEVIL'S ENGINE CHAPTER THREE

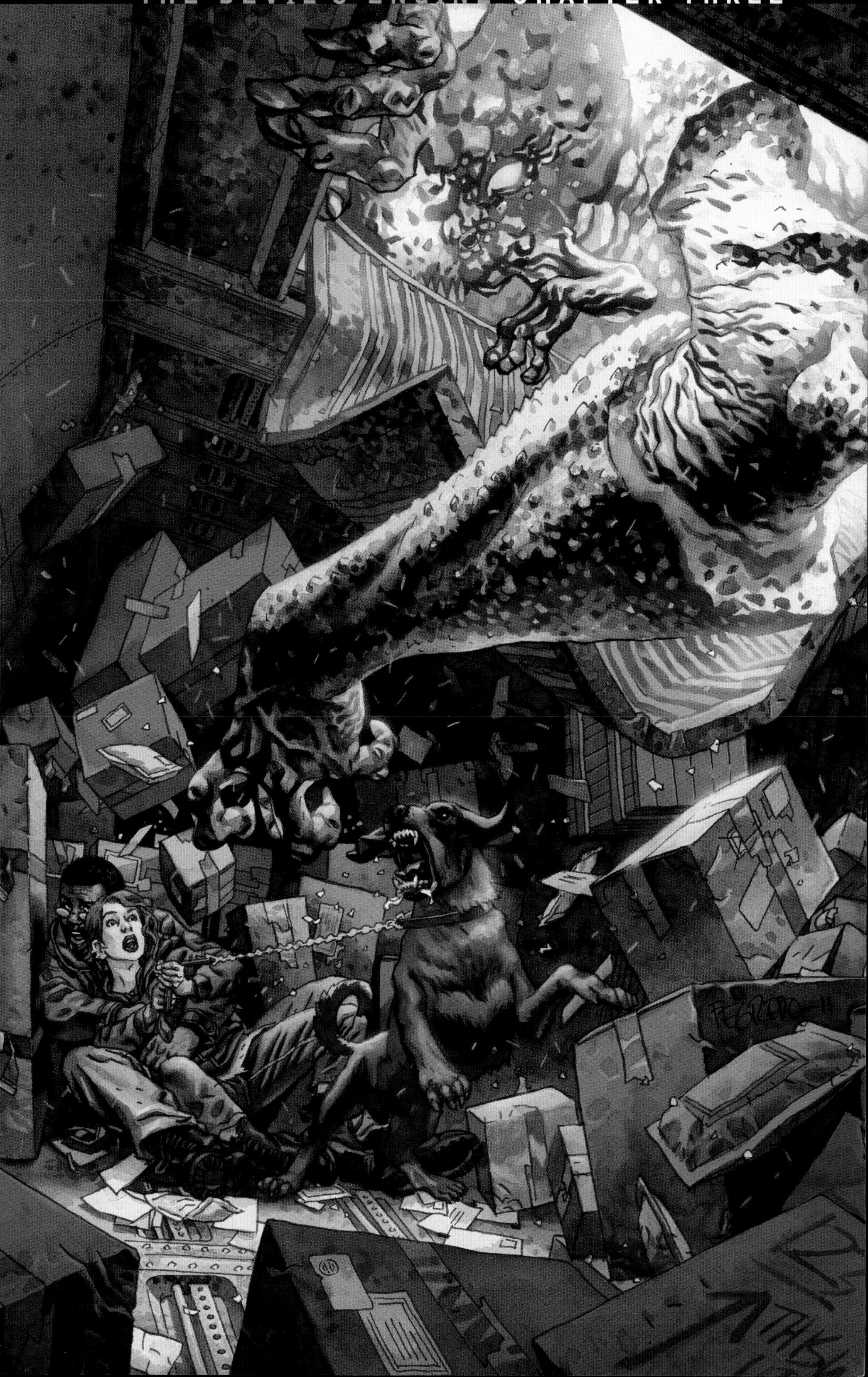

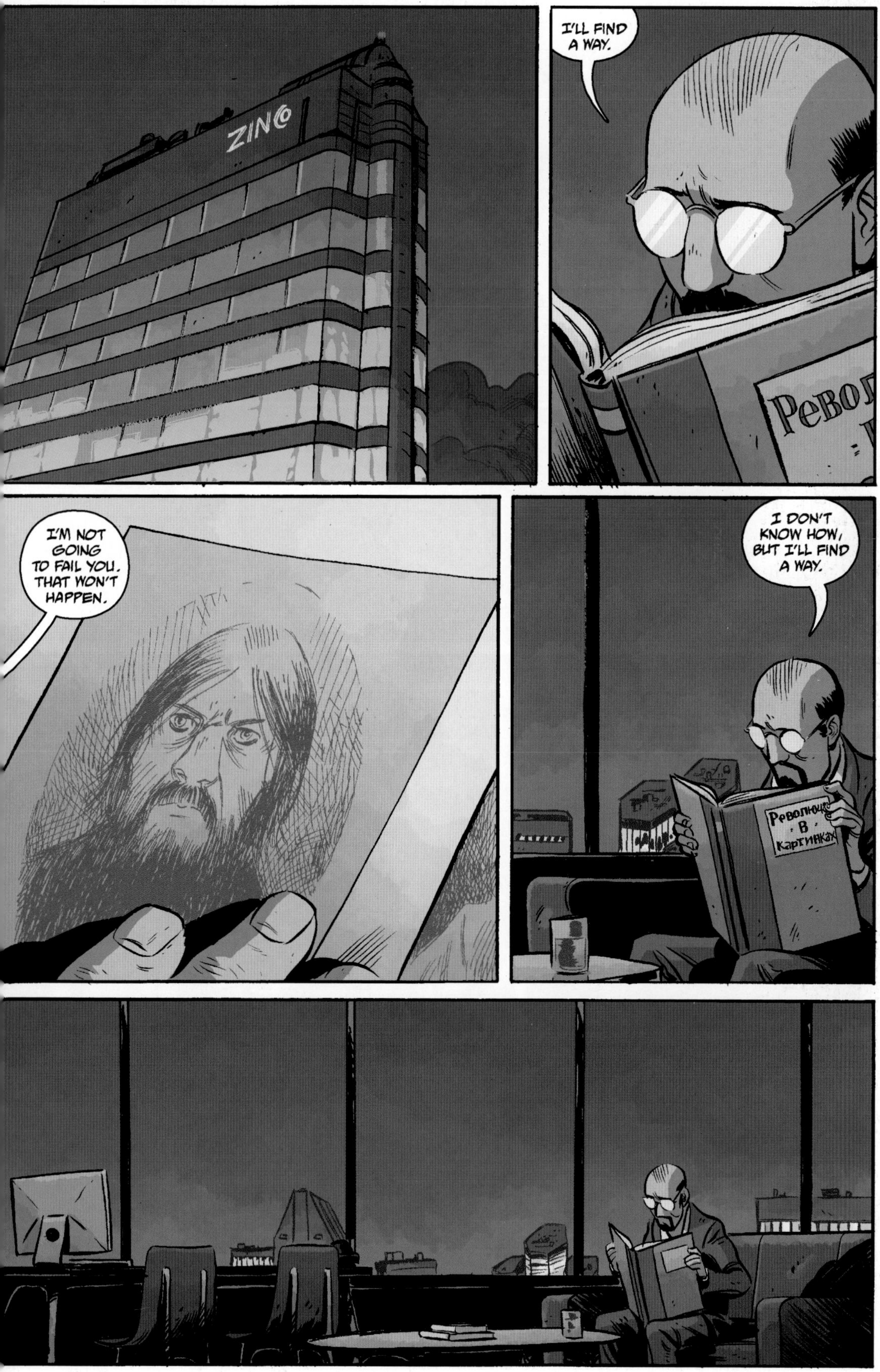
ZINCO
I'LL FIND A WAY.
I'M NOT GOING TO FAIL YOU. THAT WON'T HAPPEN.
I DON'T KNOW HOW, BUT I'LL FIND A WAY.
Револнюця В картинках

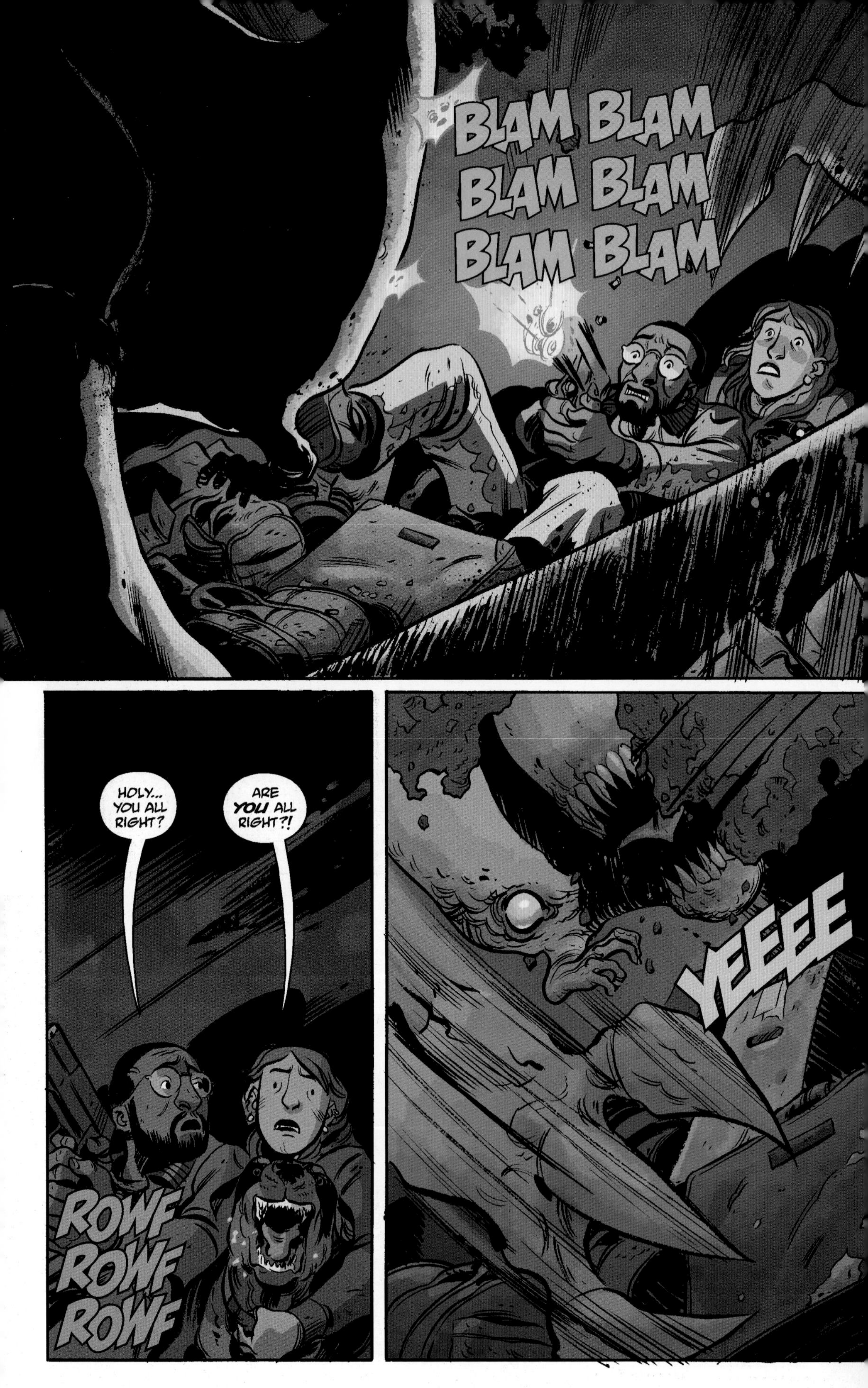
BLAM BLAM
BLAM BLAM
BLAM BLAM
HOLY... YOU ALL RIGHT?
ARE *YOU* ALL RIGHT?!
ROWF
ROWF
ROWF
YEEEE

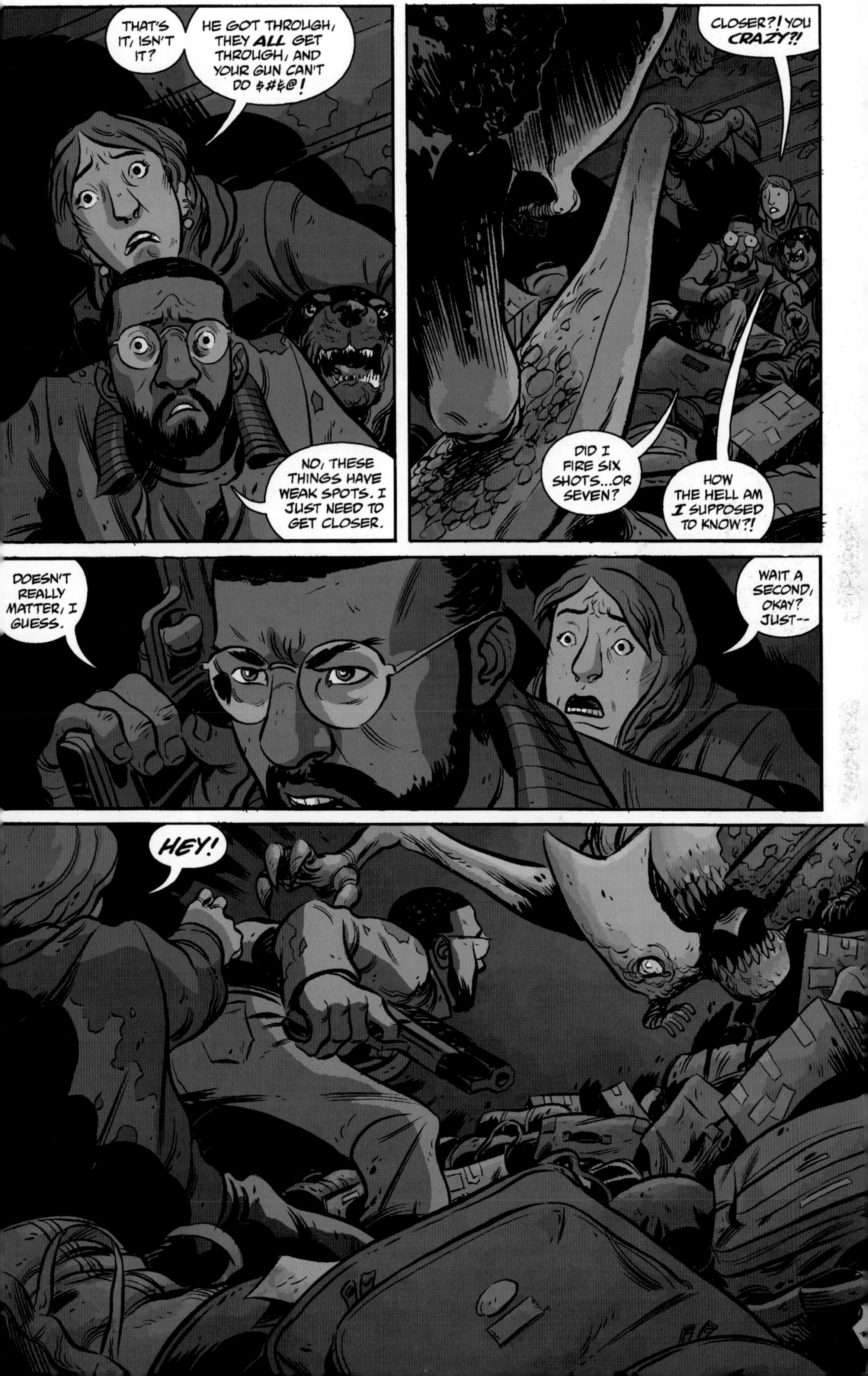
THAT'S IT, ISN'T IT?
HE GOT THROUGH, THEY ALL GET THROUGH, AND YOUR GUN CAN'T DO $#&@!
NO, THESE THINGS HAVE WEAK SPOTS. I JUST NEED TO GET CLOSER.
CLOSER?! YOU CRAZY?!
DID I FIRE SIX SHOTS...OR SEVEN?
HOW THE HELL AM I SUPPOSED TO KNOW?!
DOESN'T REALLY MATTER, I GUESS.
WAIT A SECOND, OKAY? JUST--
HEY!

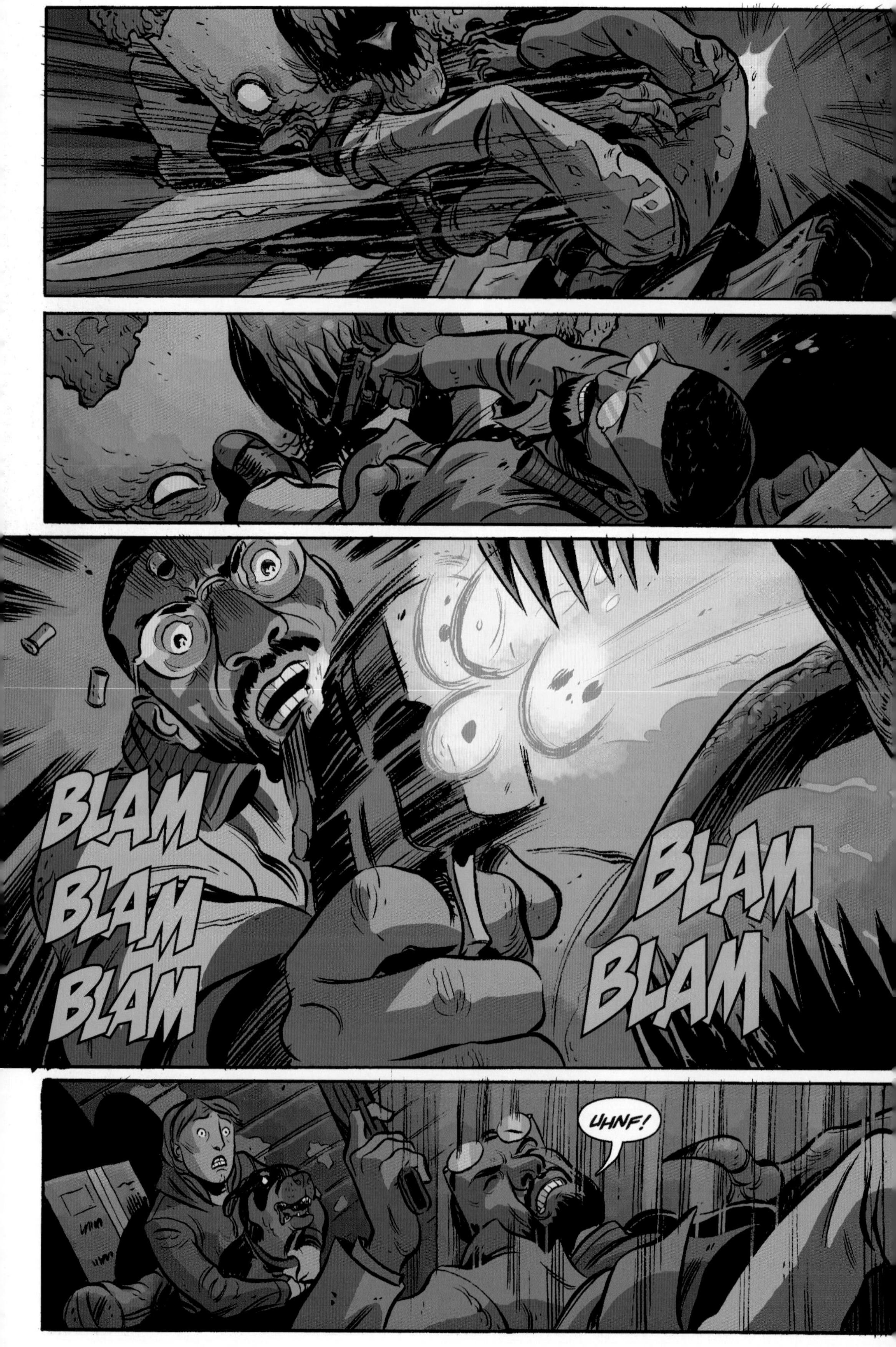
BLAM
BLAM
BLAM
BLAM
BLAM
UHNF!

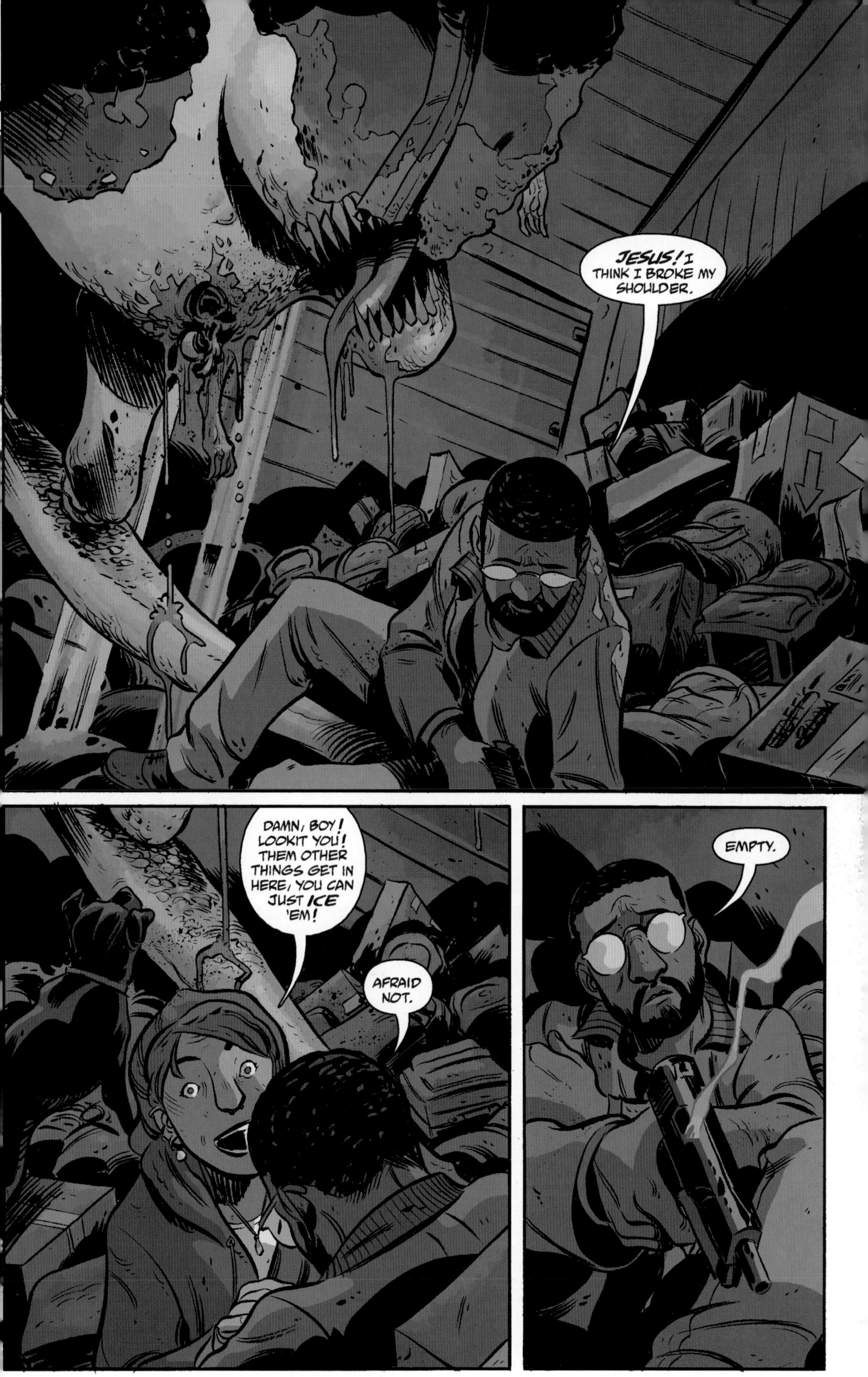
JESUS! I THINK I BROKE MY SHOULDER.
DAMN, BOY! LOOKIT YOU! THEM OTHER THINGS GET IN HERE, YOU CAN JUST ICE 'EM!
AFRAID NOT.
EMPTY.

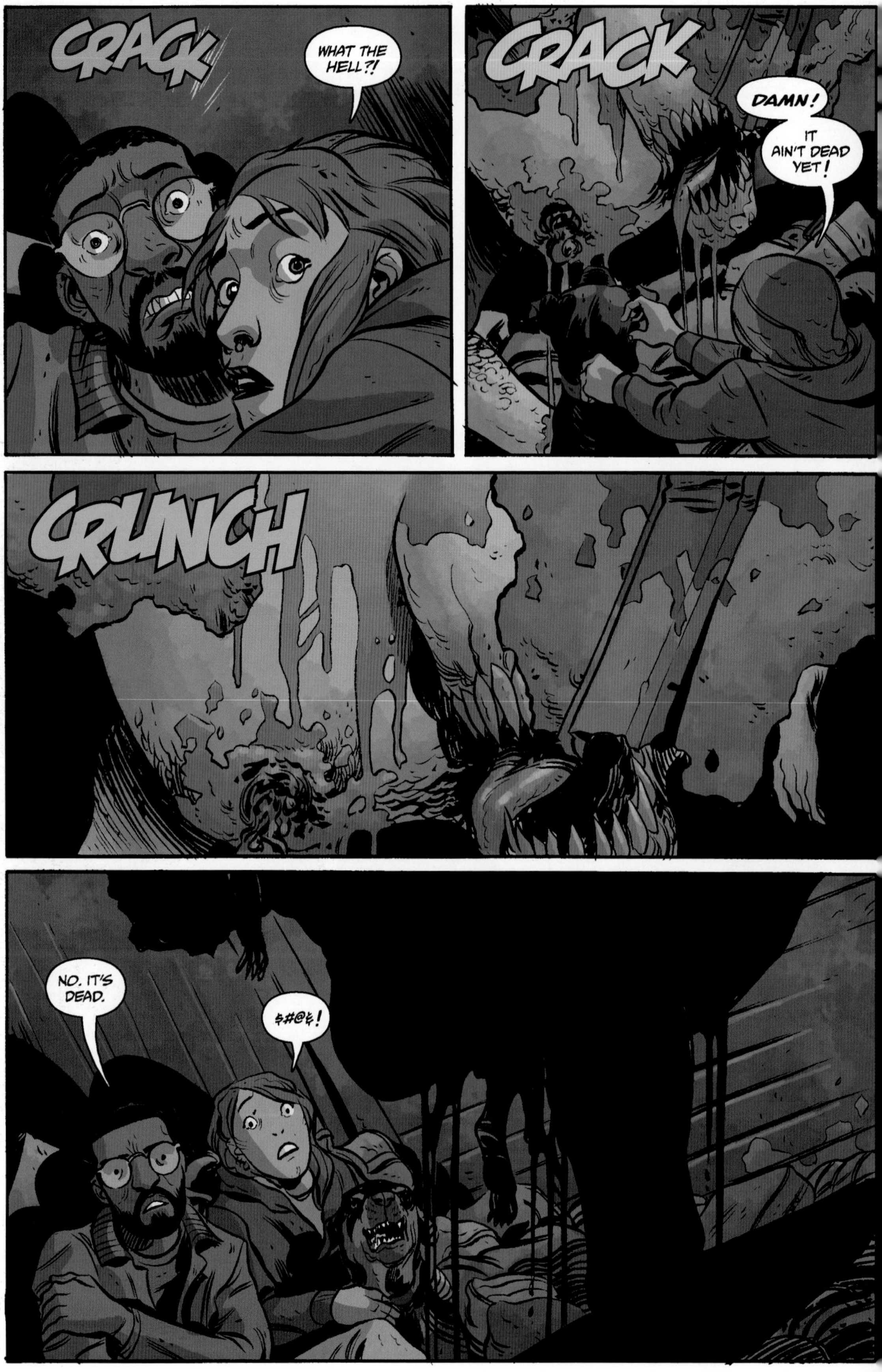
CRACK
WHAT THE HELL?!
CRACK
DAMN!
IT AIN'T DEAD YET!
CRUNCH
NO. IT'S DEAD.
$#@&!

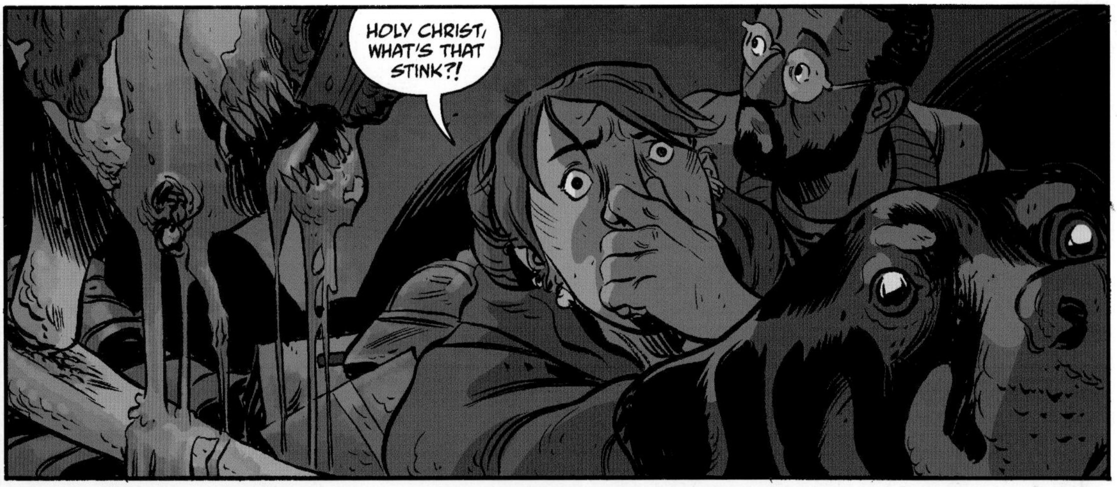
HOLY CHRIST, WHAT'S THAT STINK?!

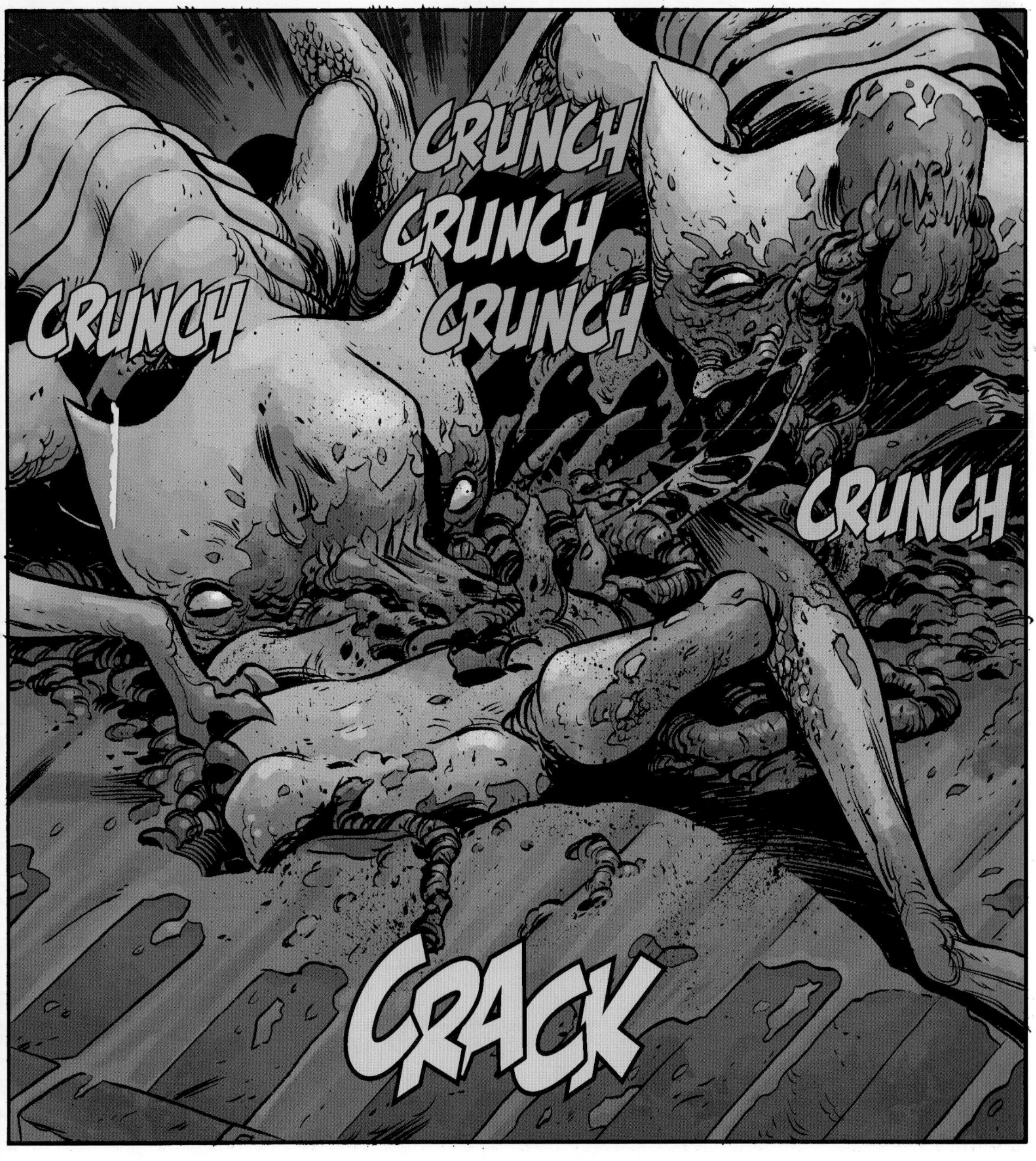
CRUNCH
CRUNCH
CRUNCH
CRUNCH
CRUNCH
CRACK

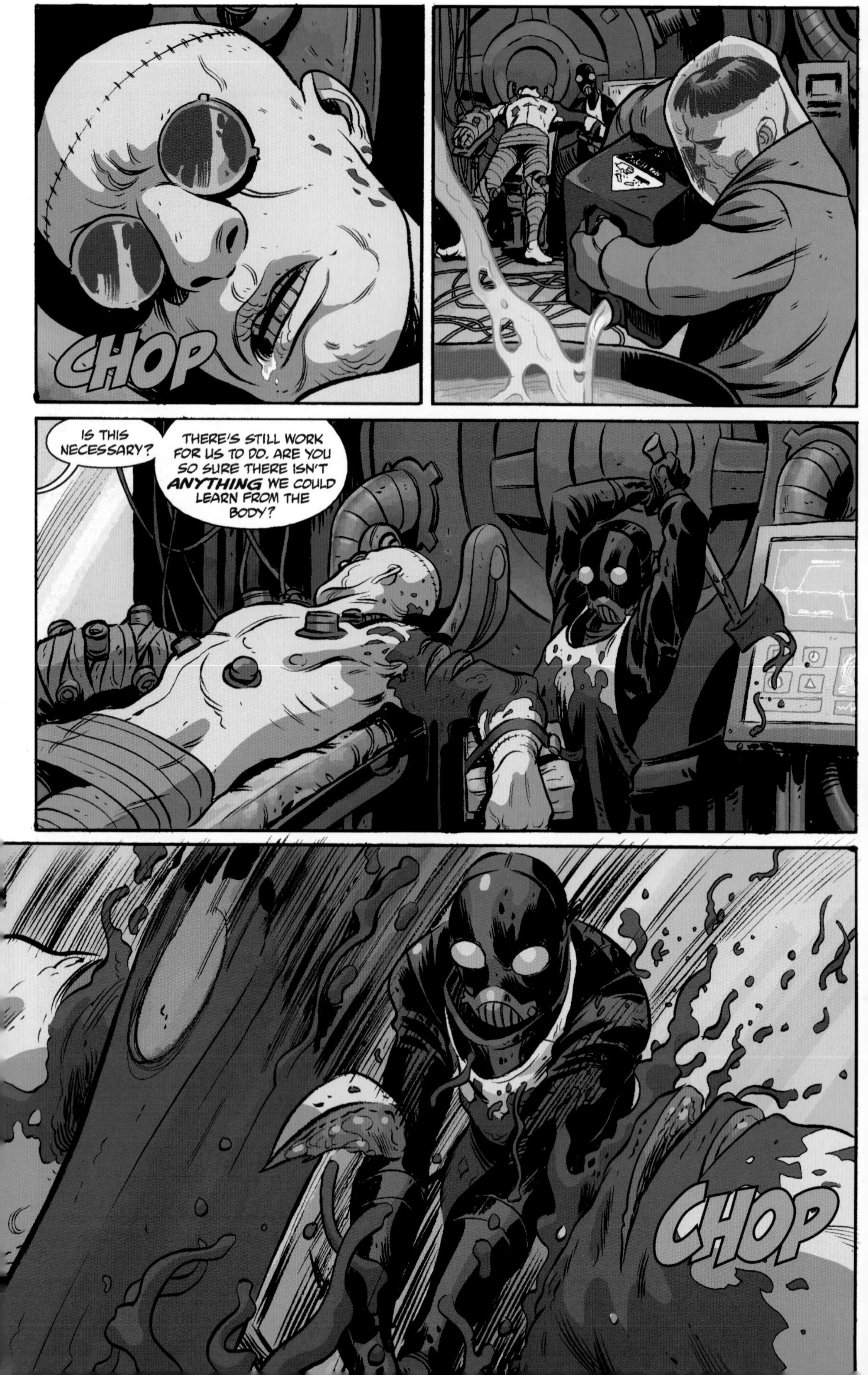
CHOP
IS THIS NECESSARY?
THERE'S STILL WORK FOR US TO DO. ARE YOU SO SURE THERE ISN'T ANYTHING WE COULD LEARN FROM THE BODY?
CHOP

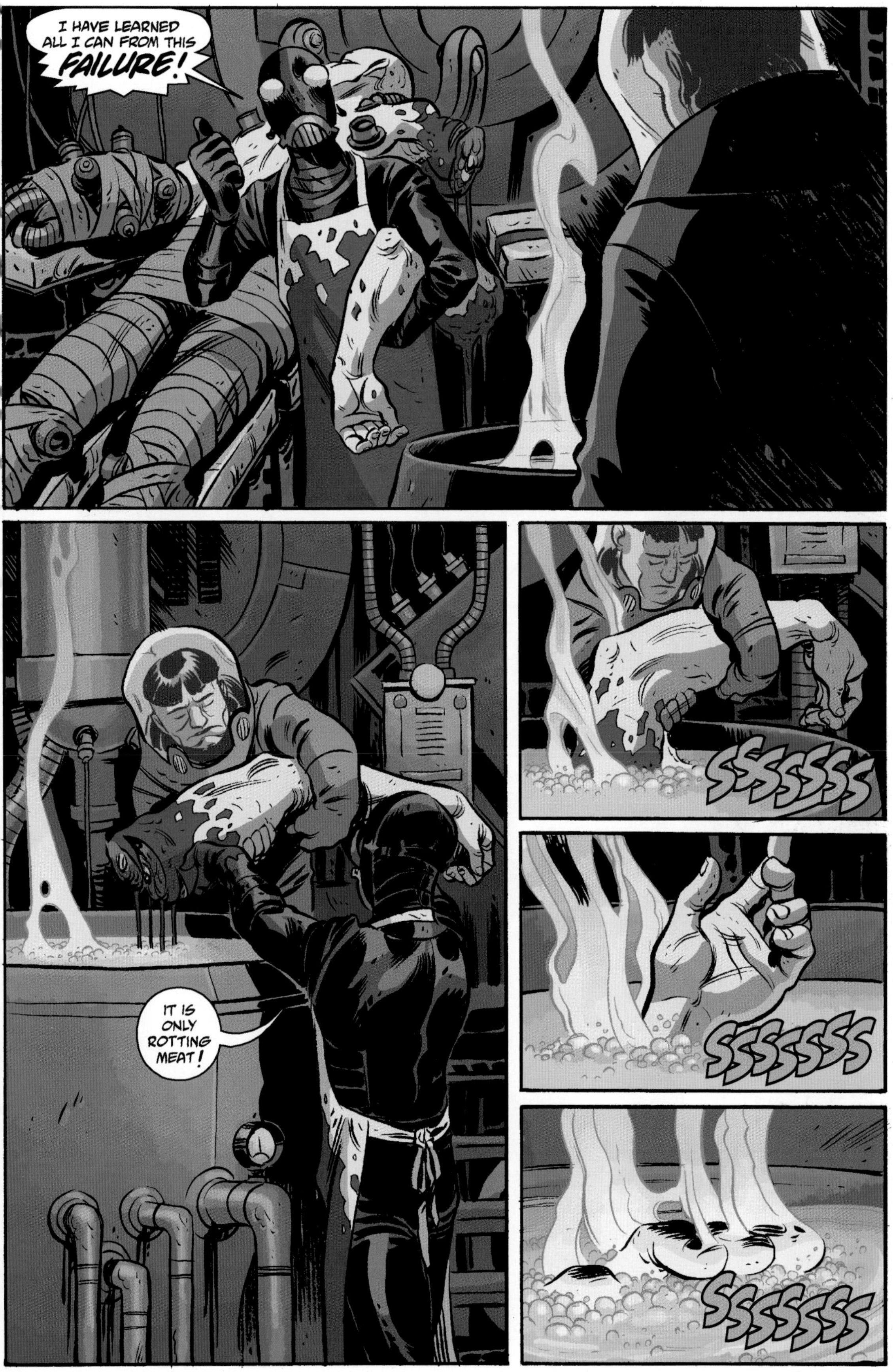
I HAVE LEARNED ALL I CAN FROM THIS FAILURE!
IT IS ONLY ROTTING MEAT!
SSSSSSS
SSSSSSS
SSSSSSS

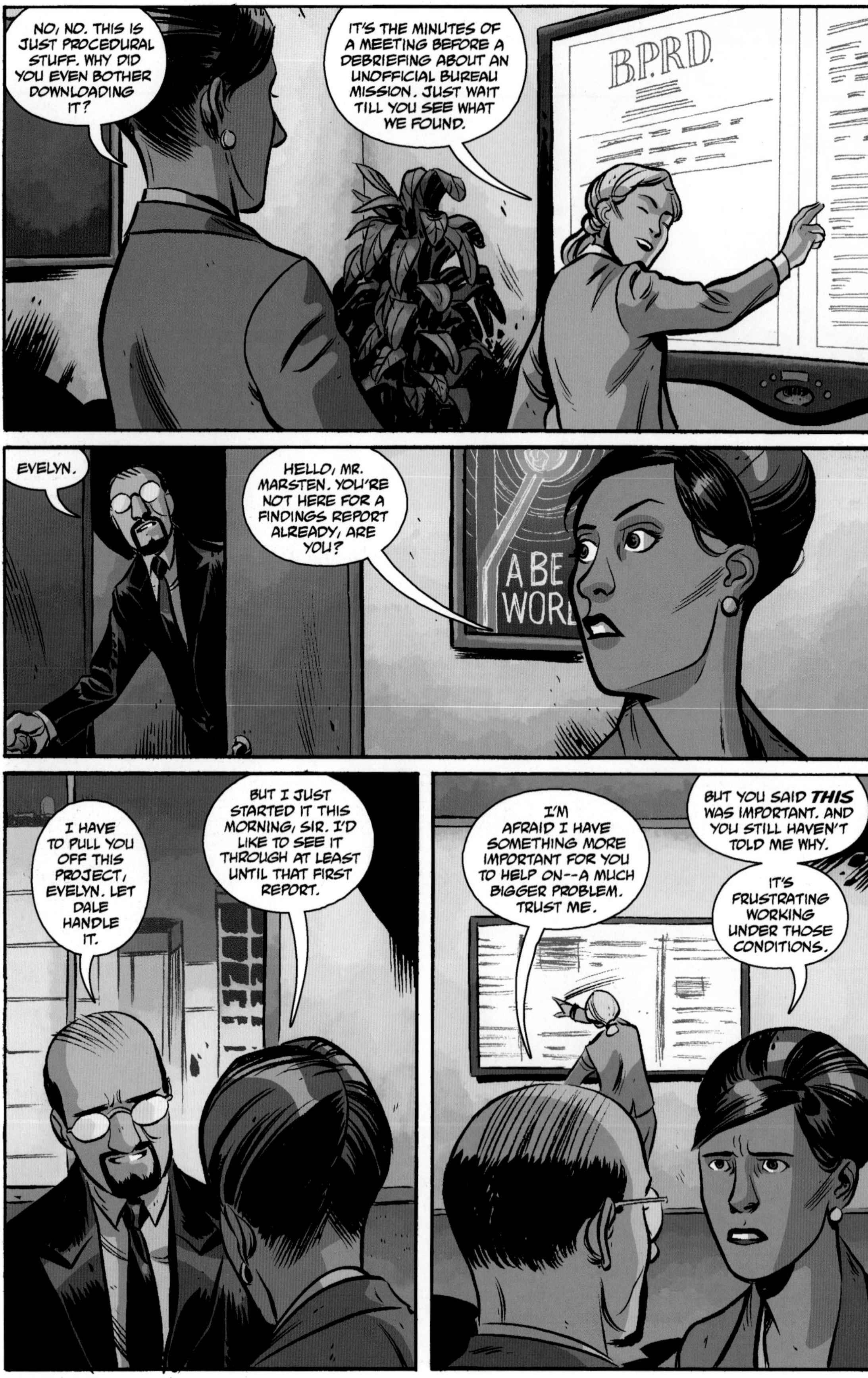
NO, NO. THIS IS JUST PROCEDURAL STUFF. WHY DID YOU EVEN BOTHER DOWNLOADING IT?
IT'S THE MINUTES OF A MEETING BEFORE A DEBRIEFING ABOUT AN UNOFFICIAL BUREAU MISSION. JUST WAIT TILL YOU SEE WHAT WE FOUND.
B.P.R.D.
EVELYN.
HELLO, MR. MARSTEN. YOU'RE NOT HERE FOR A FINDINGS REPORT ALREADY, ARE YOU?
I HAVE TO PULL YOU OFF THIS PROJECT, EVELYN. LET DALE HANDLE IT.
BUT I JUST STARTED IT THIS MORNING, SIR. I'D LIKE TO SEE IT THROUGH AT LEAST UNTIL THAT FIRST REPORT.
I'M AFRAID I HAVE SOMETHING MORE IMPORTANT FOR YOU TO HELP ON--A MUCH BIGGER PROBLEM. TRUST ME.
BUT YOU SAID *THIS* WAS IMPORTANT. AND YOU STILL HAVEN'T TOLD ME WHY.
IT'S FRUSTRATING WORKING UNDER THOSE CONDITIONS.

YES.

YES, I CAN UNDERSTAND THAT, BUT THIS PROBLEM...

IT'S OUR PRIORITY. IT'S VITAL, EVELYN.

I NEED ALL OF OUR BEST MINDS, MY MOST DEDICATED COLLEAGUES WORKING IN CONCERT ON IT.

THE FUTURE THAT WE'VE BEEN TALKING ABOUT, THE MASTER AND...HIS...

SIR?

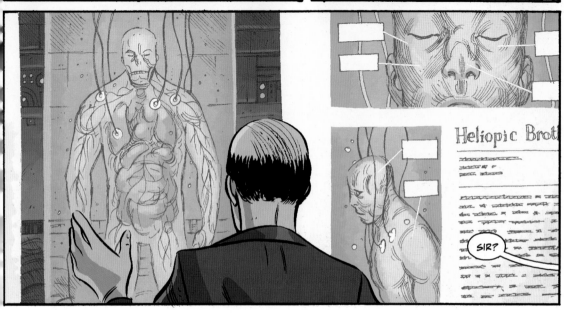

Heliopic Brot

SIR?

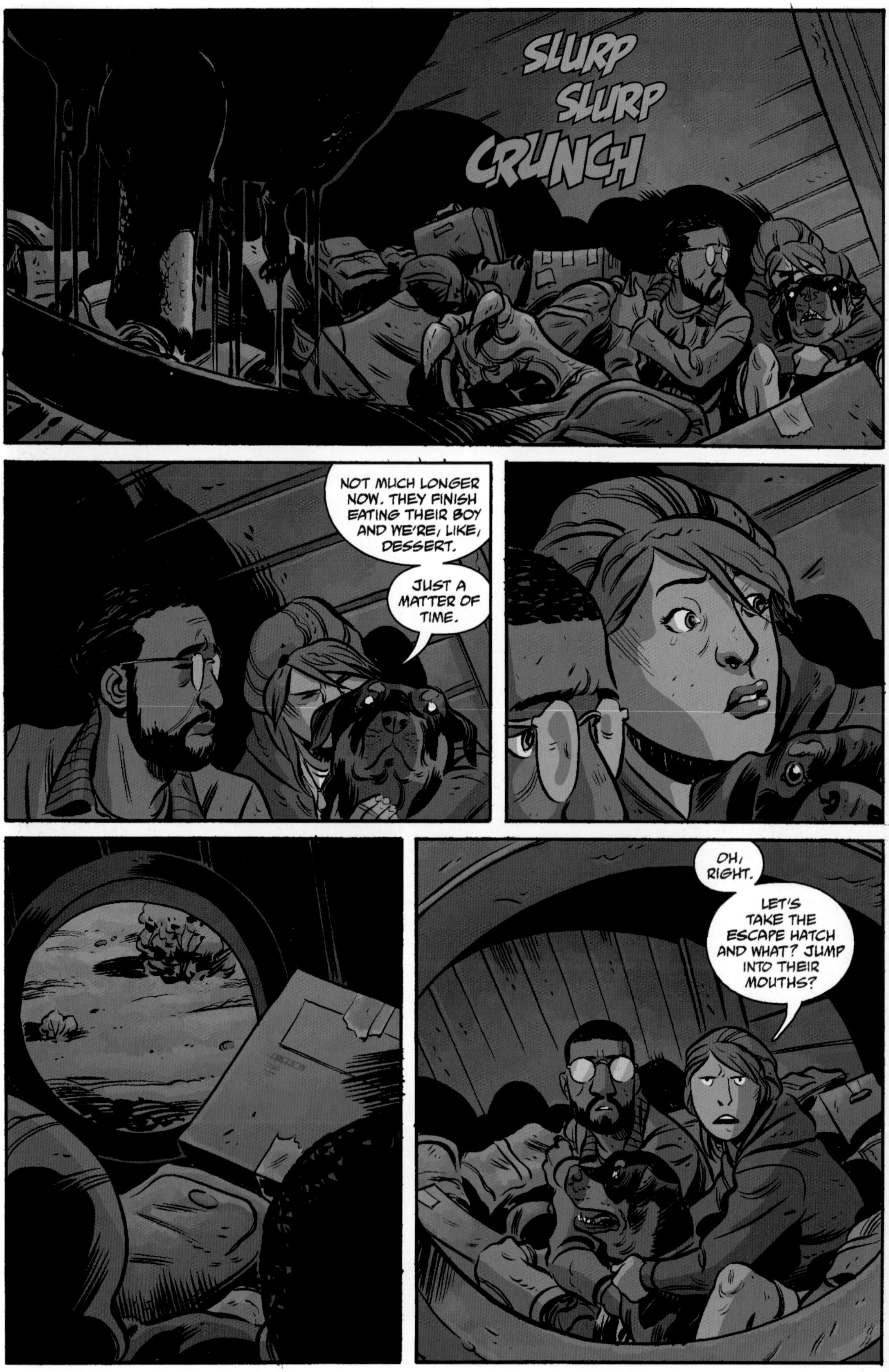
SLURP
SLURP
CRUNCH
NOT MUCH LONGER NOW. THEY FINISH EATING THEIR BOY AND WE'RE, LIKE, DESSERT.
JUST A MATTER OF TIME.
OH, RIGHT.
LET'S TAKE THE ESCAPE HATCH AND WHAT? JUMP INTO THEIR MOUTHS?

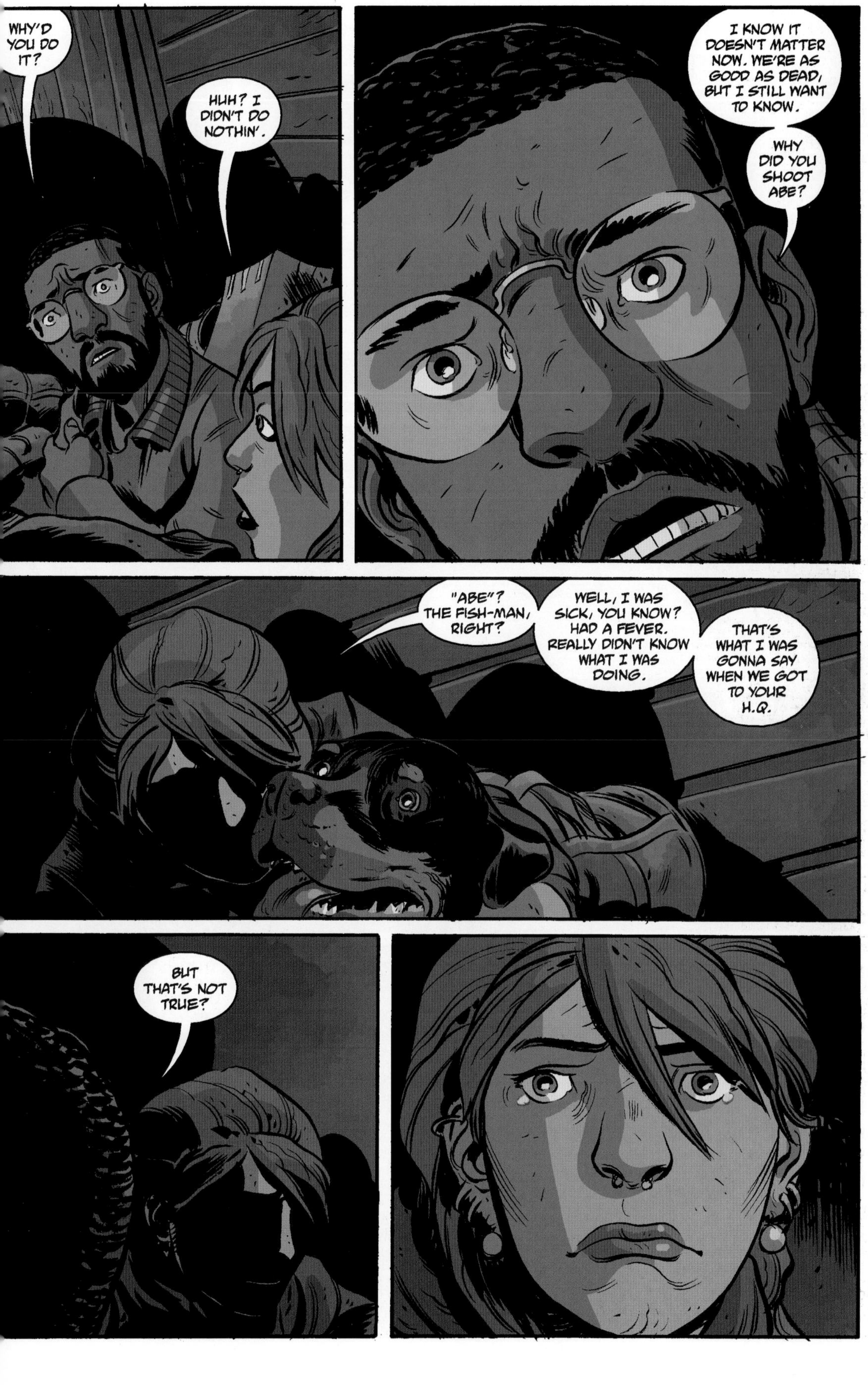
WHY'D YOU DO IT?
HUH? I DIDN'T DO NOTHIN'.
I KNOW IT DOESN'T MATTER NOW. WE'RE AS GOOD AS DEAD, BUT I STILL WANT TO KNOW.
WHY DID YOU SHOOT ABE?
"ABE"? THE FISH-MAN, RIGHT?
WELL, I WAS SICK, YOU KNOW? HAD A FEVER. REALLY DIDN'T KNOW WHAT I WAS DOING.
THAT'S WHAT I WAS GONNA SAY WHEN WE GOT TO YOUR H.Q.
BUT THAT'S NOT TRUE?

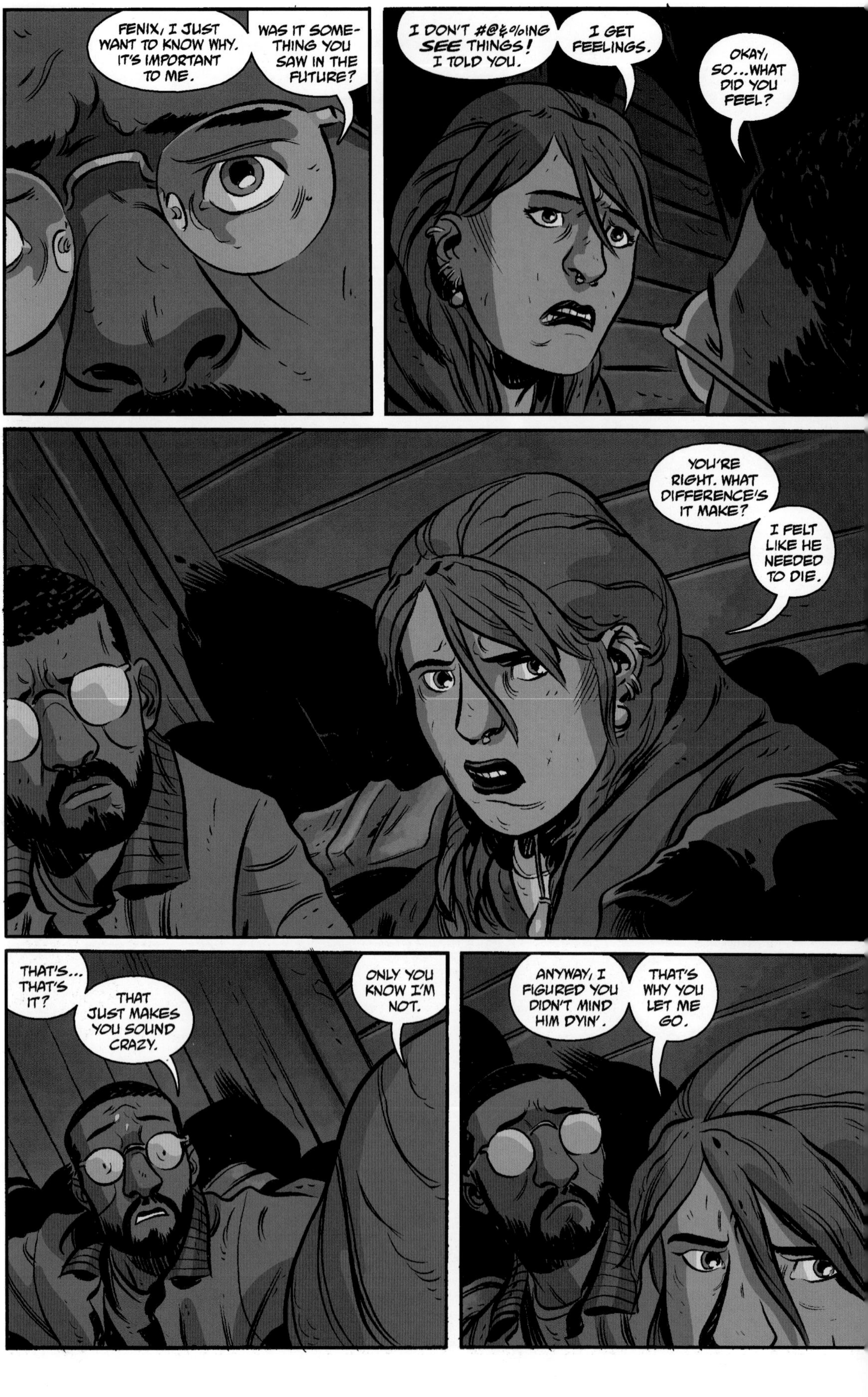
FENIX, I JUST WANT TO KNOW WHY. IT'S IMPORTANT TO ME.
WAS IT SOMETHING YOU SAW IN THE FUTURE?
I DON'T #@&%ING SEE THINGS! I TOLD YOU.
I GET FEELINGS.
OKAY, SO...WHAT DID YOU FEEL?
YOU'RE RIGHT. WHAT DIFFERENCE'S IT MAKE?
I FELT LIKE HE NEEDED TO DIE.
THAT'S... THAT'S IT?
THAT JUST MAKES YOU SOUND CRAZY.
ONLY YOU KNOW I'M NOT.
ANYWAY, I FIGURED YOU DIDN'T MIND HIM DYIN'.
THAT'S WHY YOU LET ME GO.

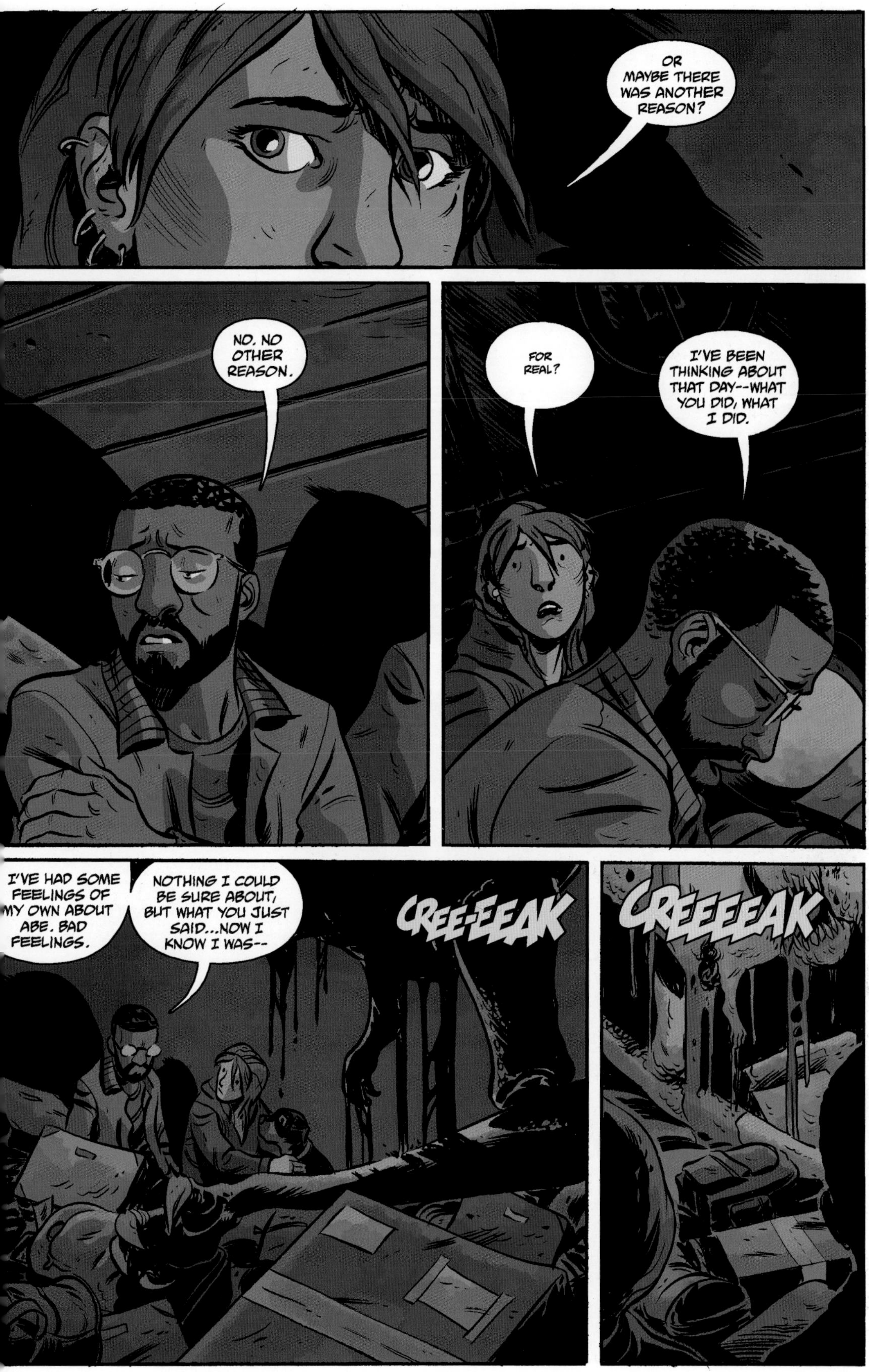
OR MAYBE THERE WAS ANOTHER REASON?
NO. NO OTHER REASON.
FOR REAL?
I'VE BEEN THINKING ABOUT THAT DAY--WHAT YOU DID, WHAT I DID.
I'VE HAD SOME FEELINGS OF MY OWN ABOUT ABE. BAD FEELINGS.
NOTHING I COULD BE SURE ABOUT, BUT WHAT YOU JUST SAID...NOW I KNOW I WAS--
CREE-EEAK
CREEEEAK

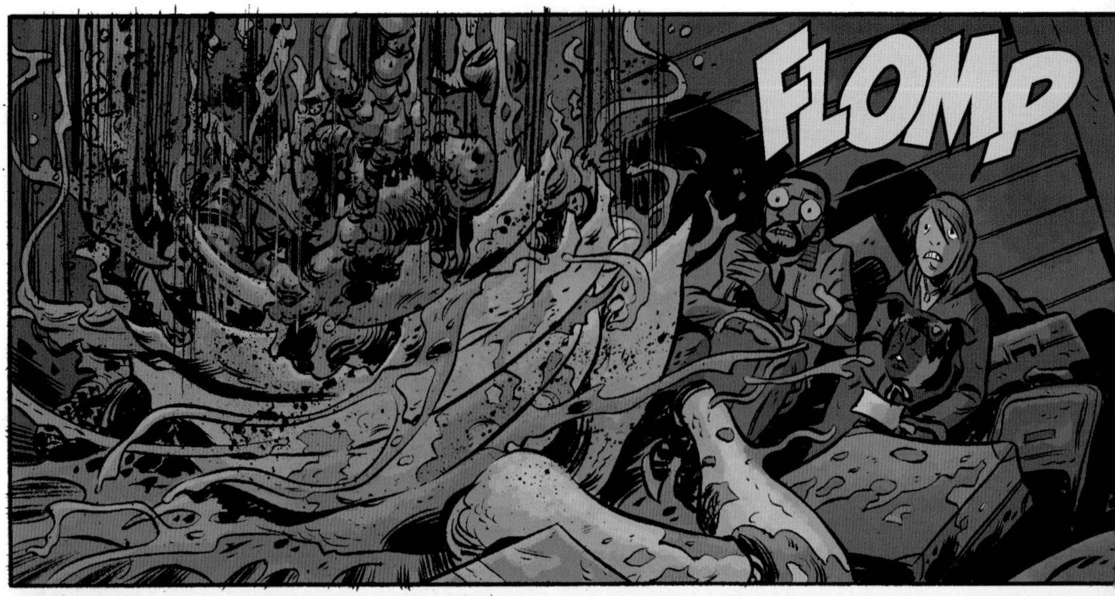
FLOMP

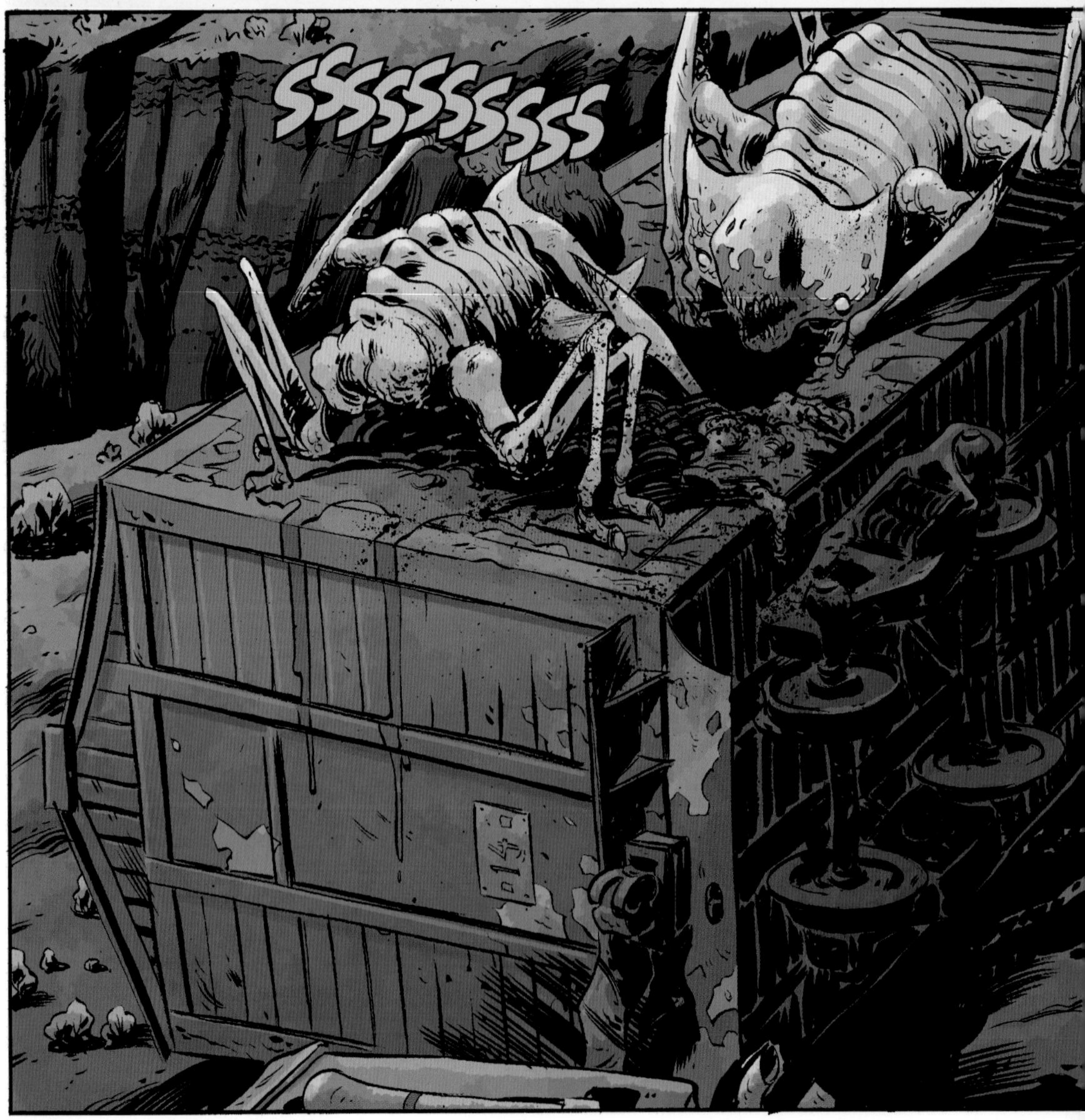
SSSSSSSSS

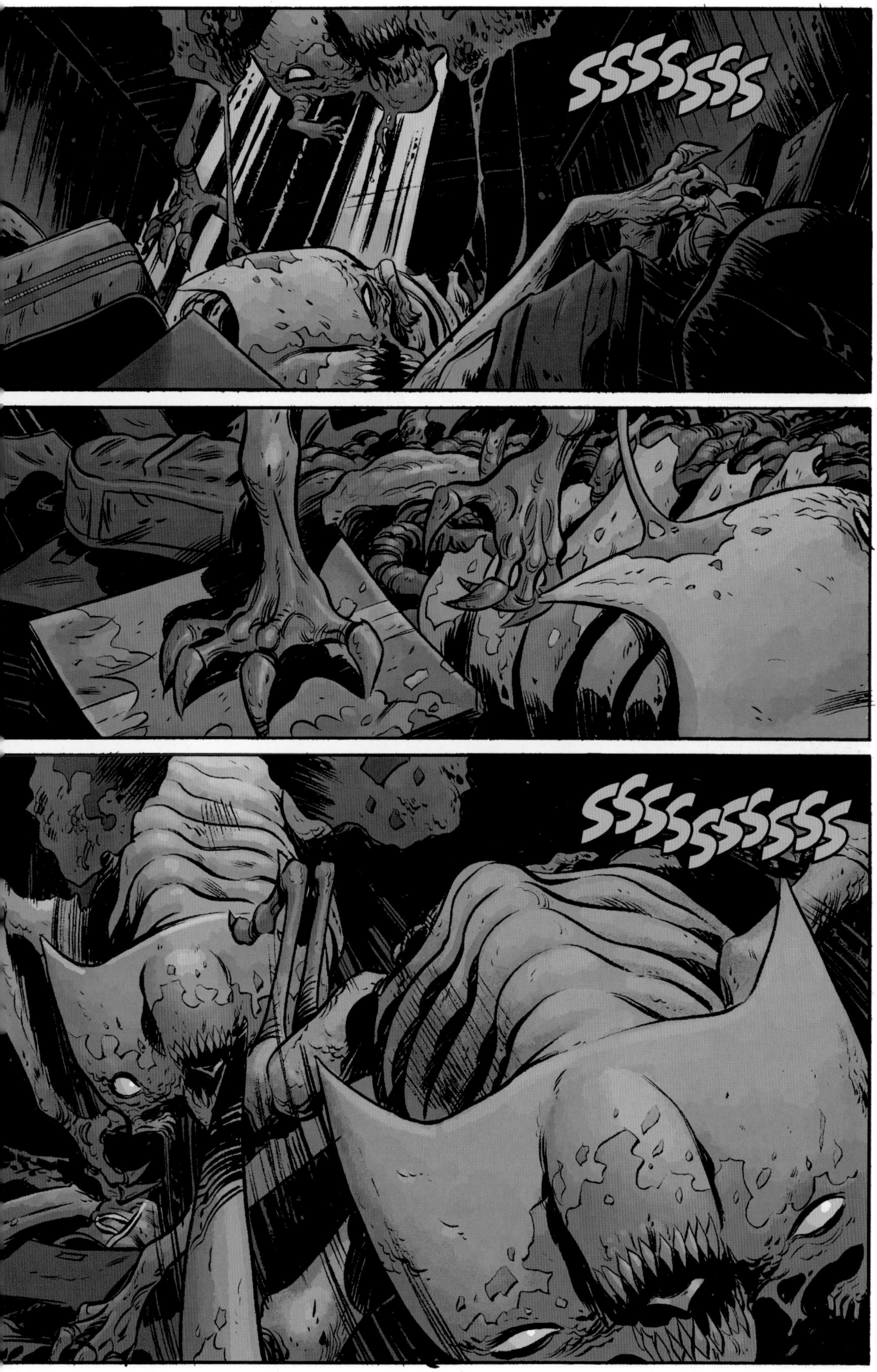
SSSSSSS
SSSSSSSSSS

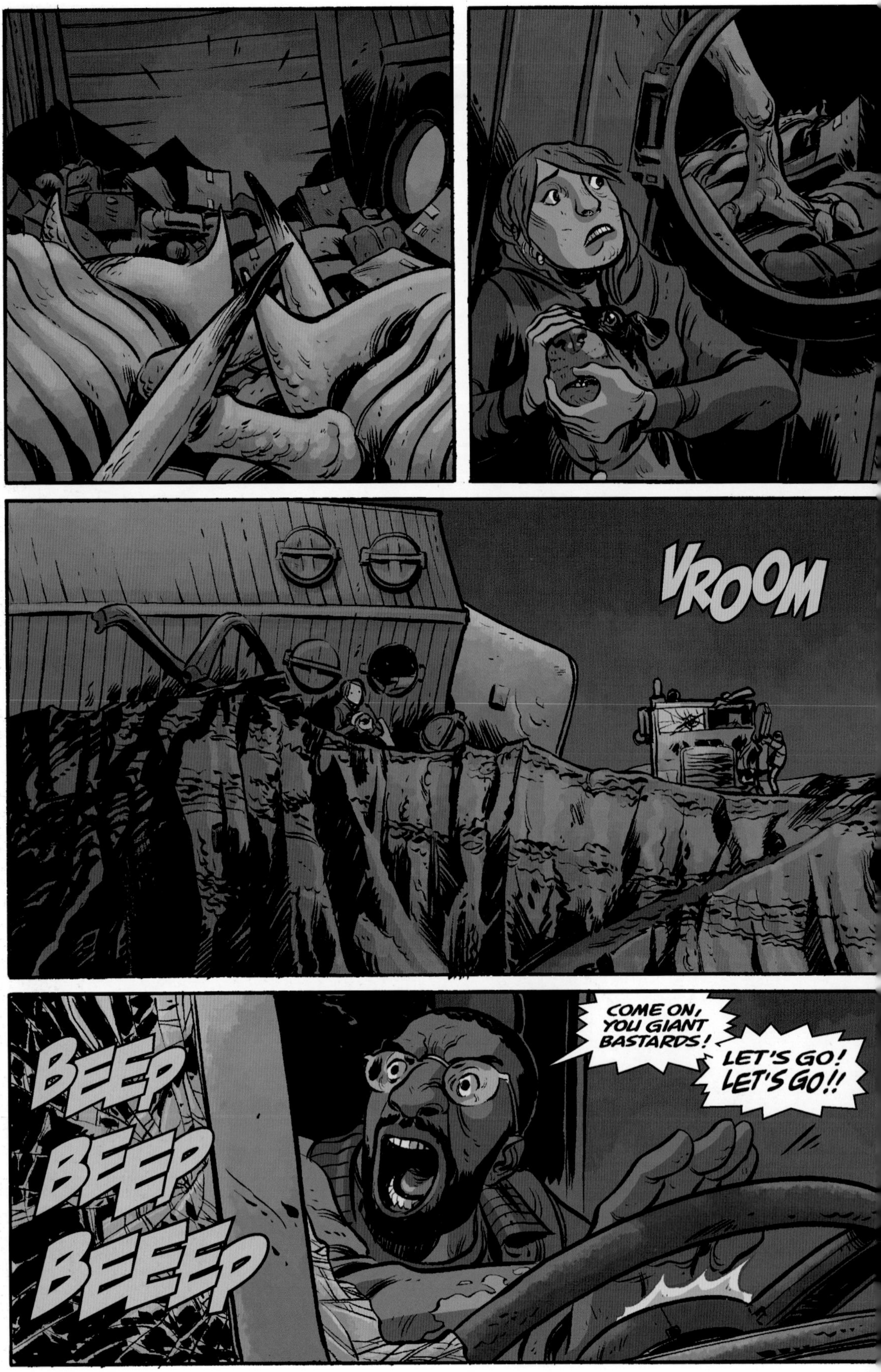
VROOM
BEEP
BEEP
BEEEP
COME ON, YOU GIANT BASTARDS!
LET'S GO! LET'S GO!!

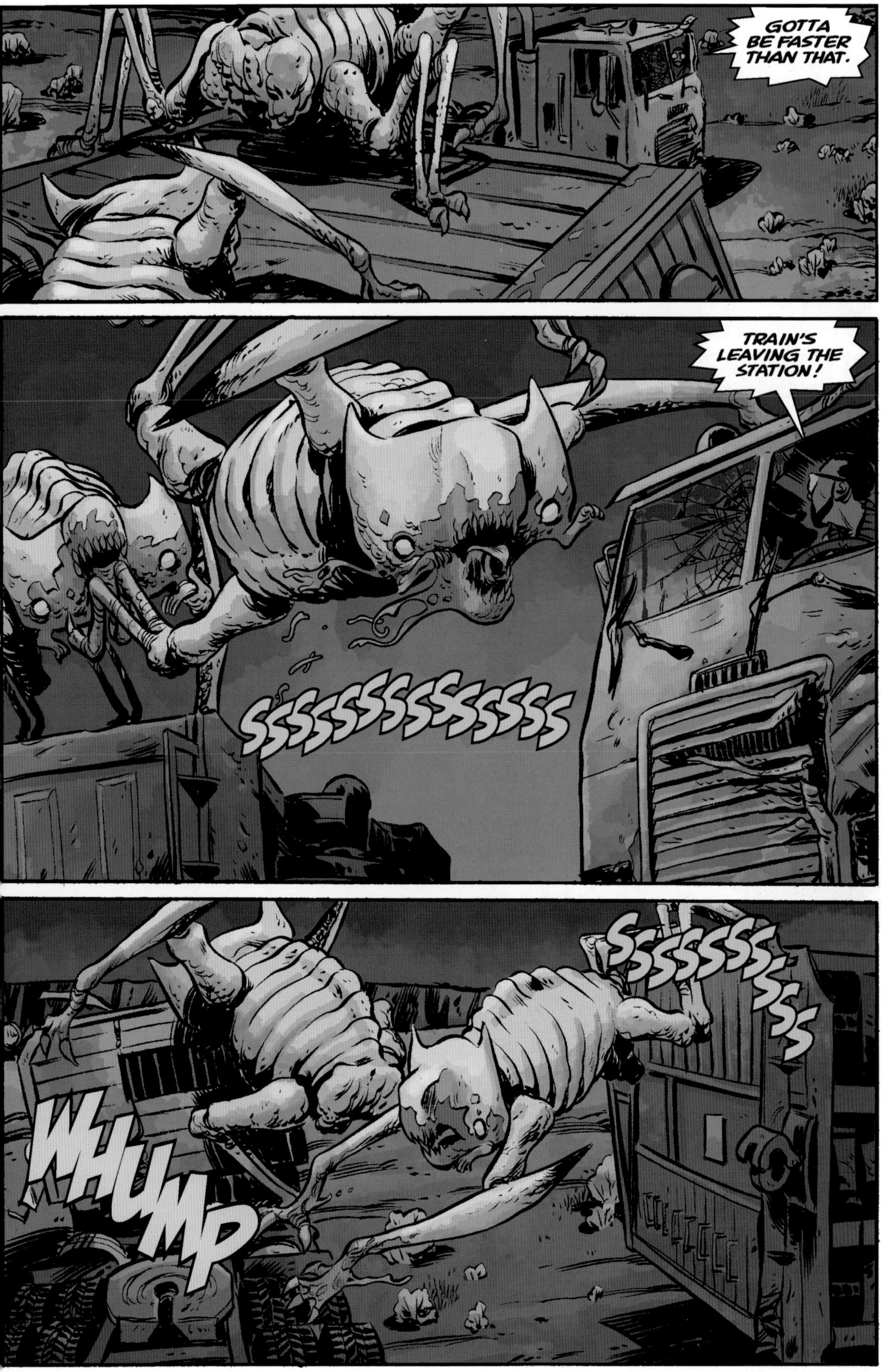
GOTTA BE FASTER THAN THAT.
TRAIN'S LEAVING THE STATION!
SSSSSSSSSSSSSS
SSSSSSSSSS
WHUMP

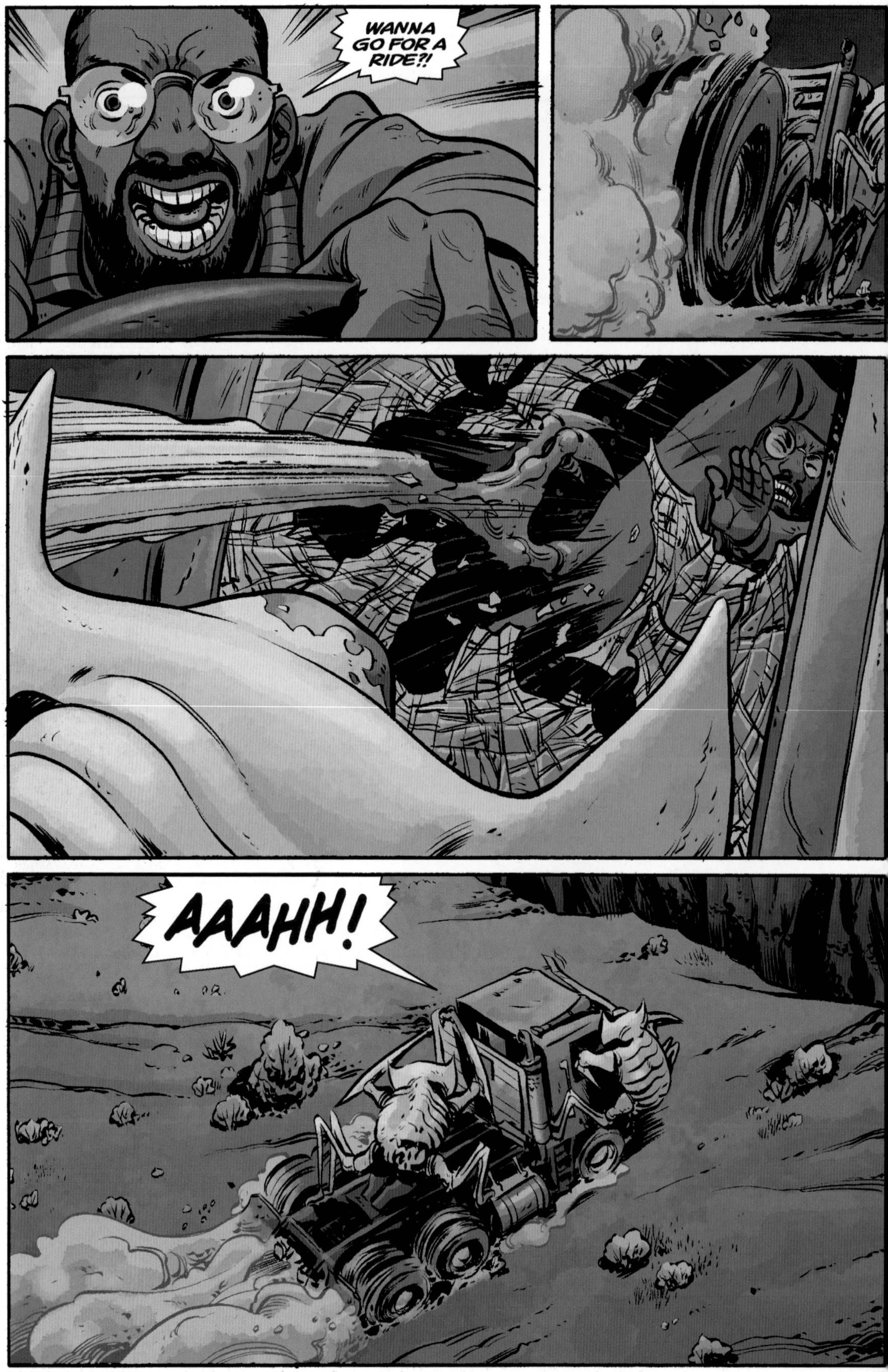
WANNA GO FOR A RIDE?!
AAAHH!

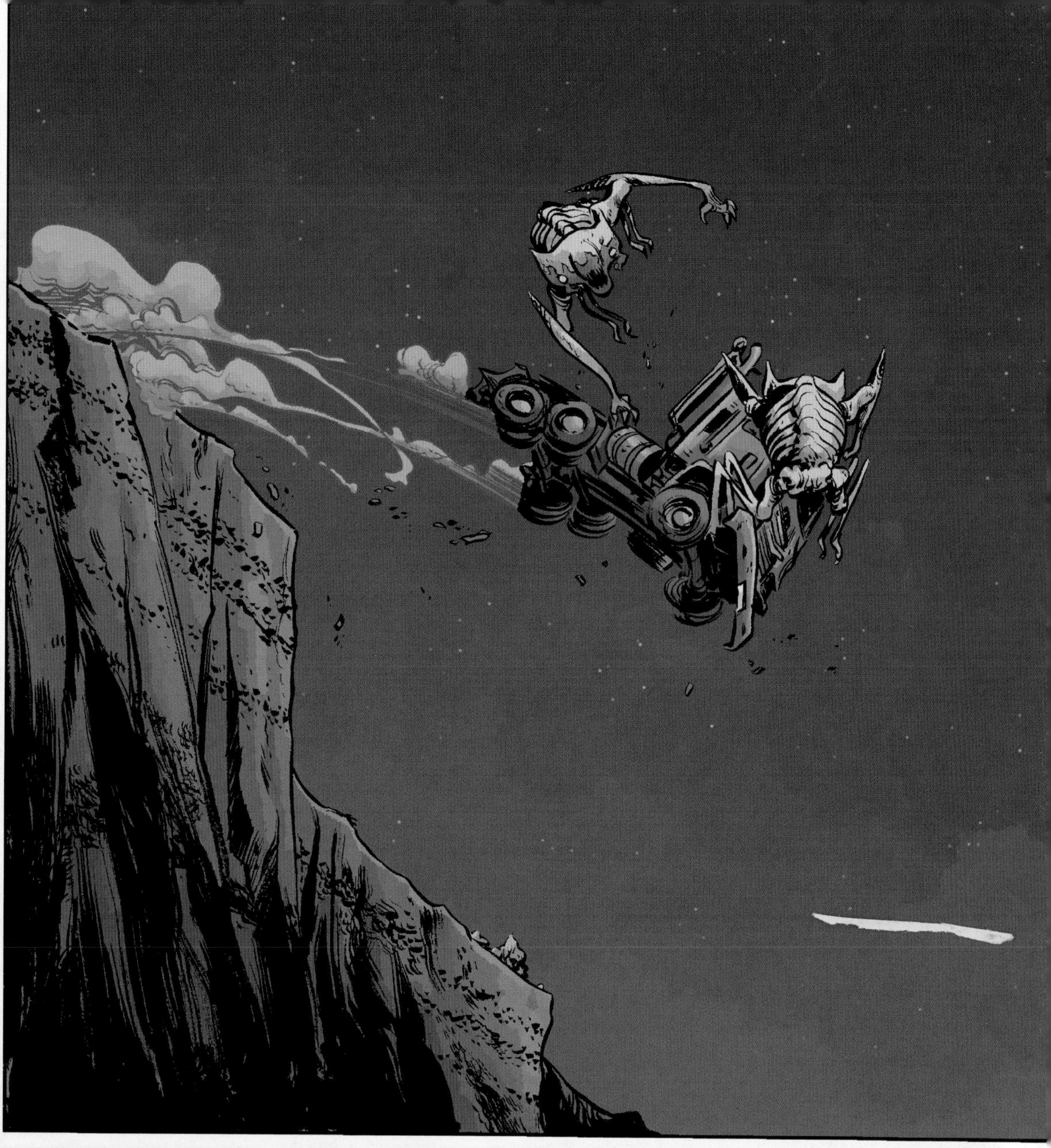

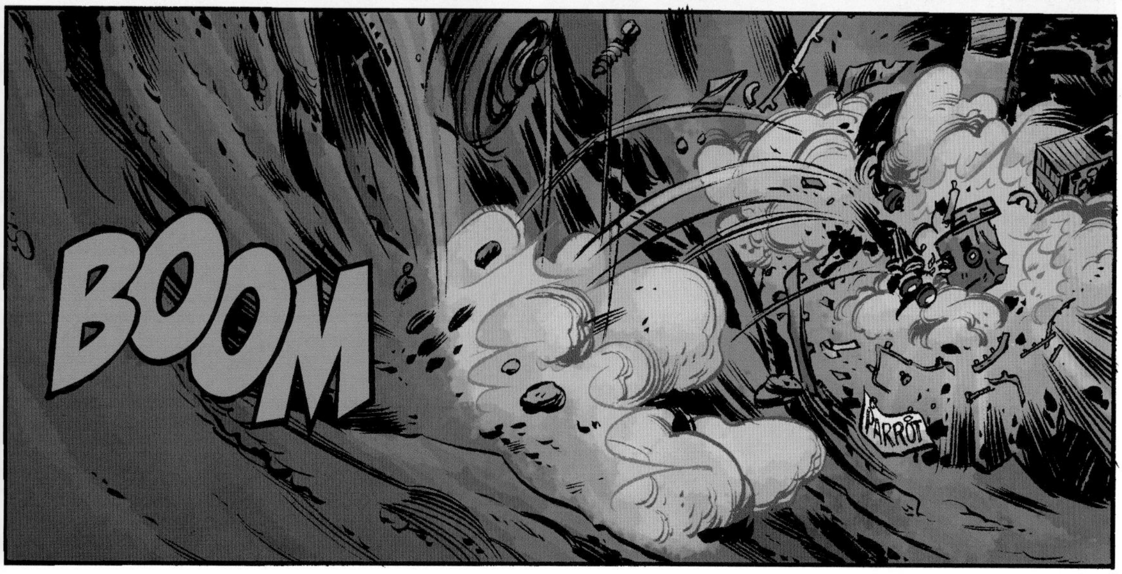
BOOM
PARROT

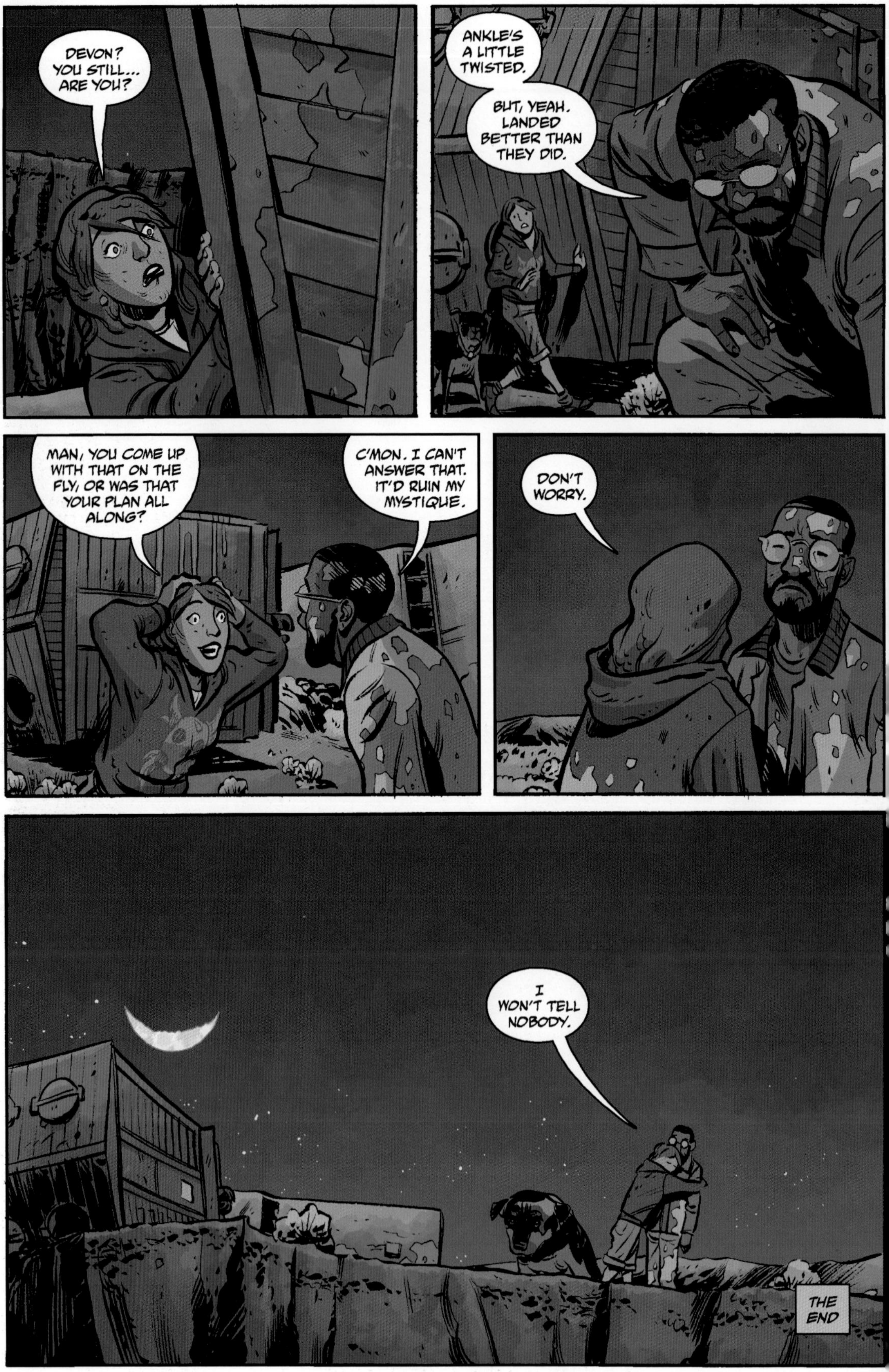
DEVON? YOU STILL... ARE YOU?
ANKLE'S A LITTLE TWISTED.
BUT, YEAH. LANDED BETTER THAN THEY DID.
MAN, YOU COME UP WITH THAT ON THE FLY, OR WAS THAT YOUR PLAN ALL ALONG?
C'MON. I CAN'T ANSWER THAT. IT'D RUIN MY MYSTIQUE.
DON'T WORRY.
I WON'T TELL NOBODY.
THE END

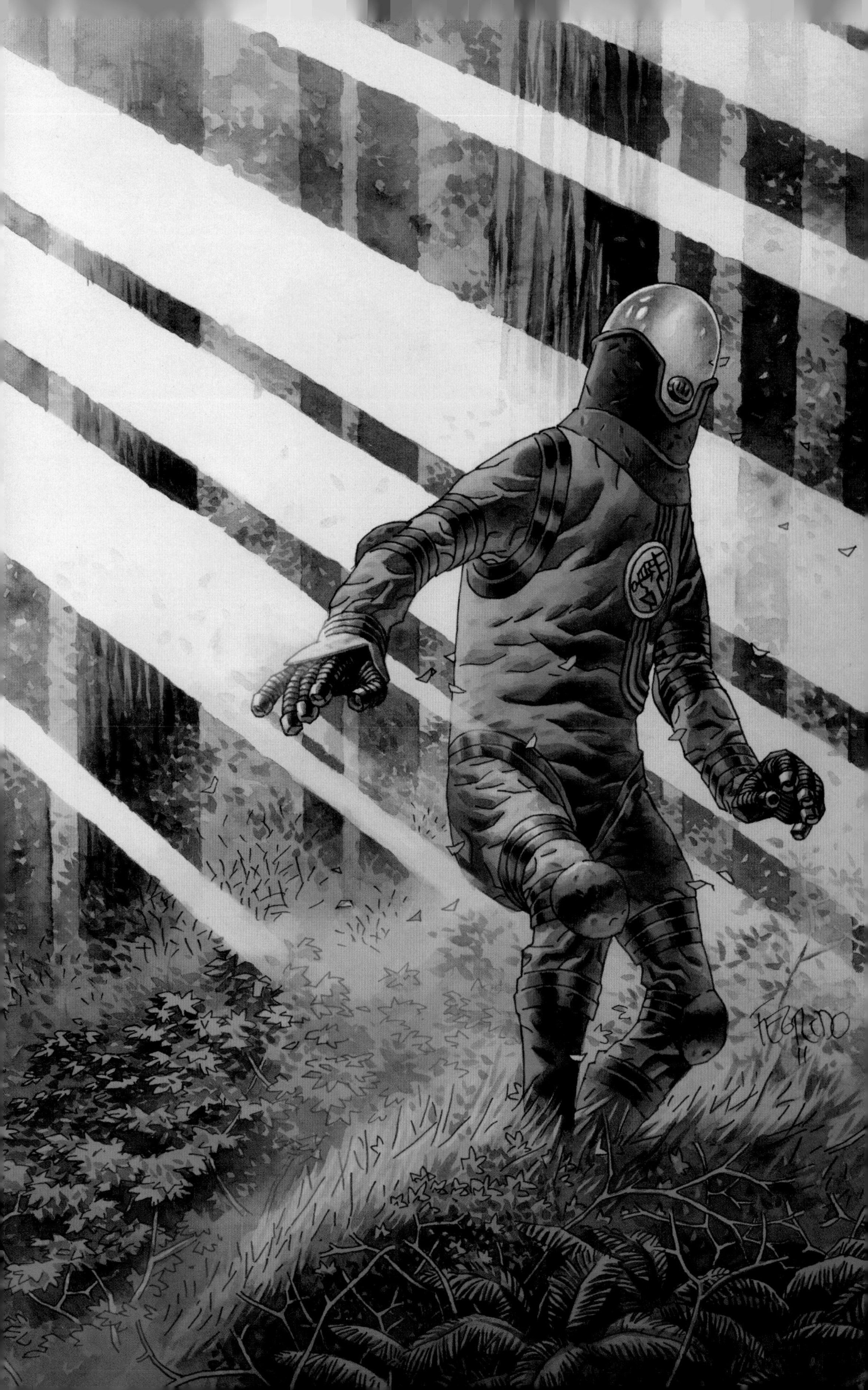

COMMISSARY
HEY, JOHANN.

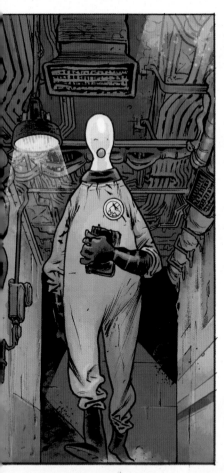

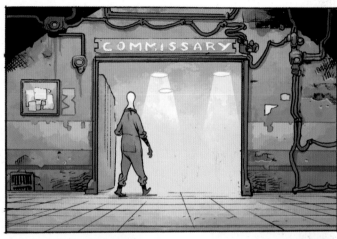

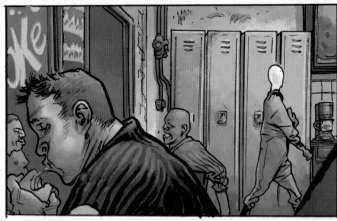

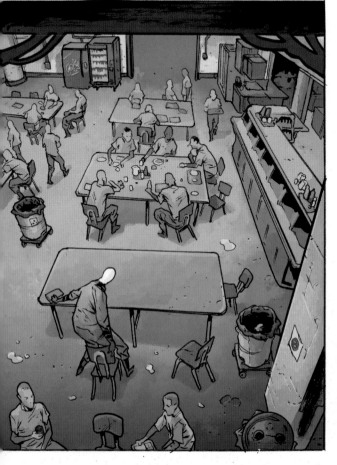

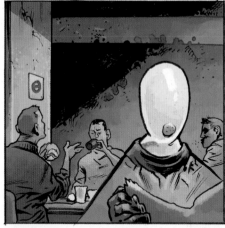

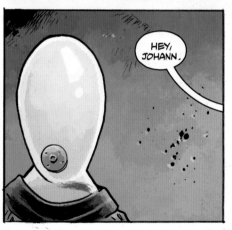

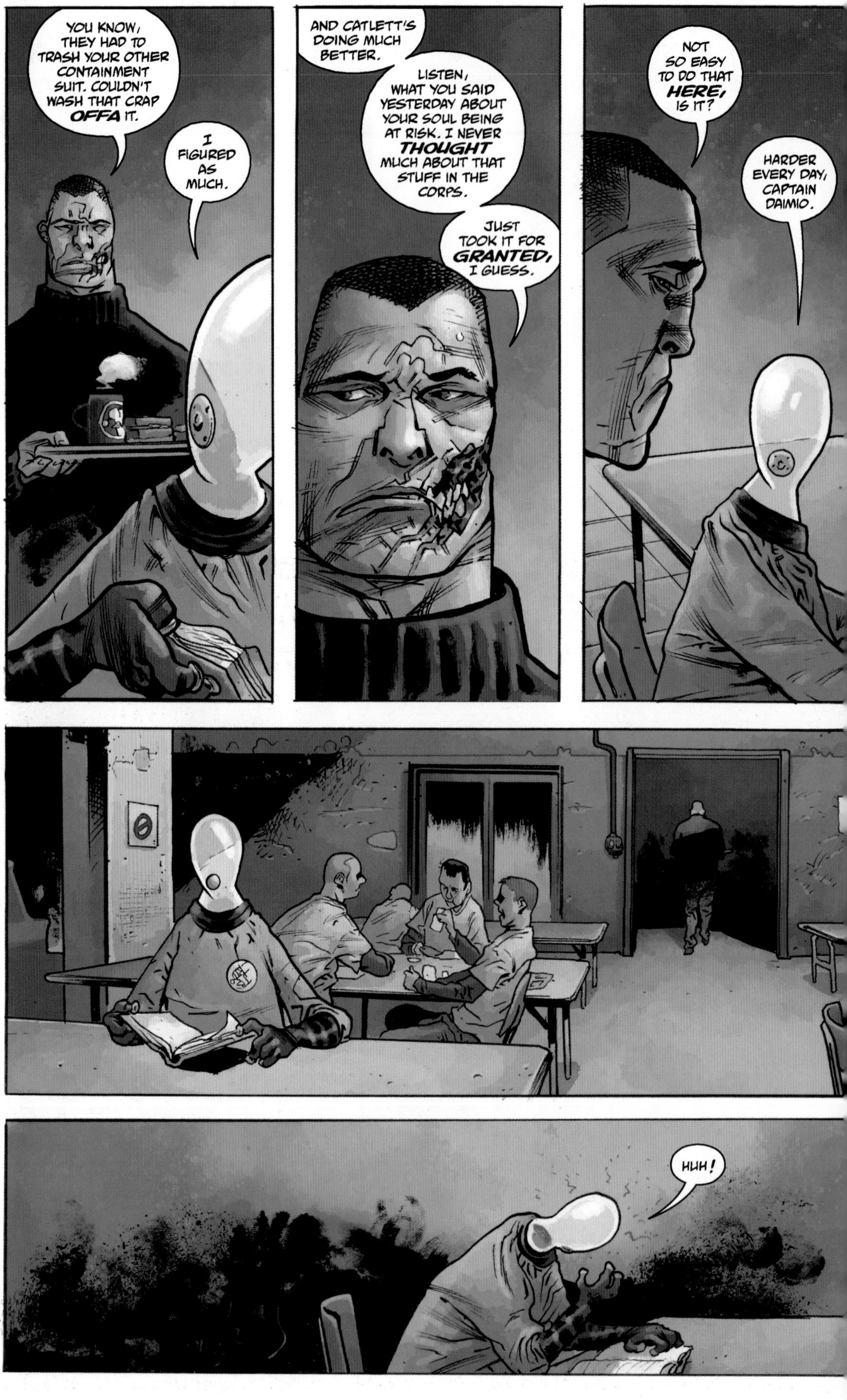
YOU KNOW, THEY HAD TO TRASH YOUR OTHER CONTAINMENT SUIT. COULDN'T WASH THAT CRAP OFFA IT.
I FIGURED AS MUCH.
AND CATLETT'S DOING MUCH BETTER.
LISTEN, WHAT YOU SAID YESTERDAY ABOUT YOUR SOUL BEING AT RISK. I NEVER THOUGHT MUCH ABOUT THAT STUFF IN THE CORPS.
JUST TOOK IT FOR GRANTED, I GUESS.
NOT SO EASY TO DO THAT HERE, IS IT?
HARDER EVERY DAY, CAPTAIN DAIMIO.
HUH!

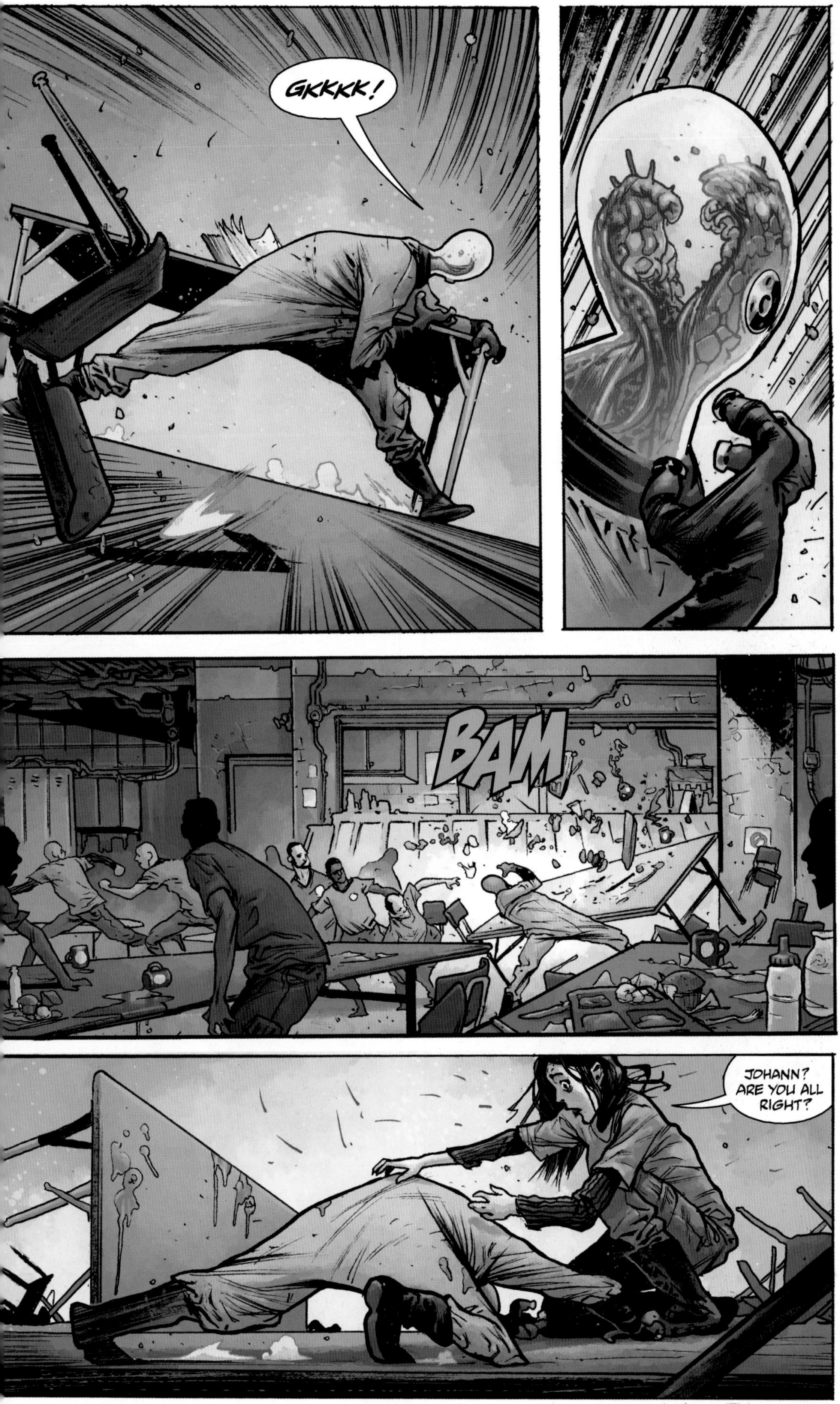
GKKKK!
BAM
JOHANN? ARE YOU ALL RIGHT?

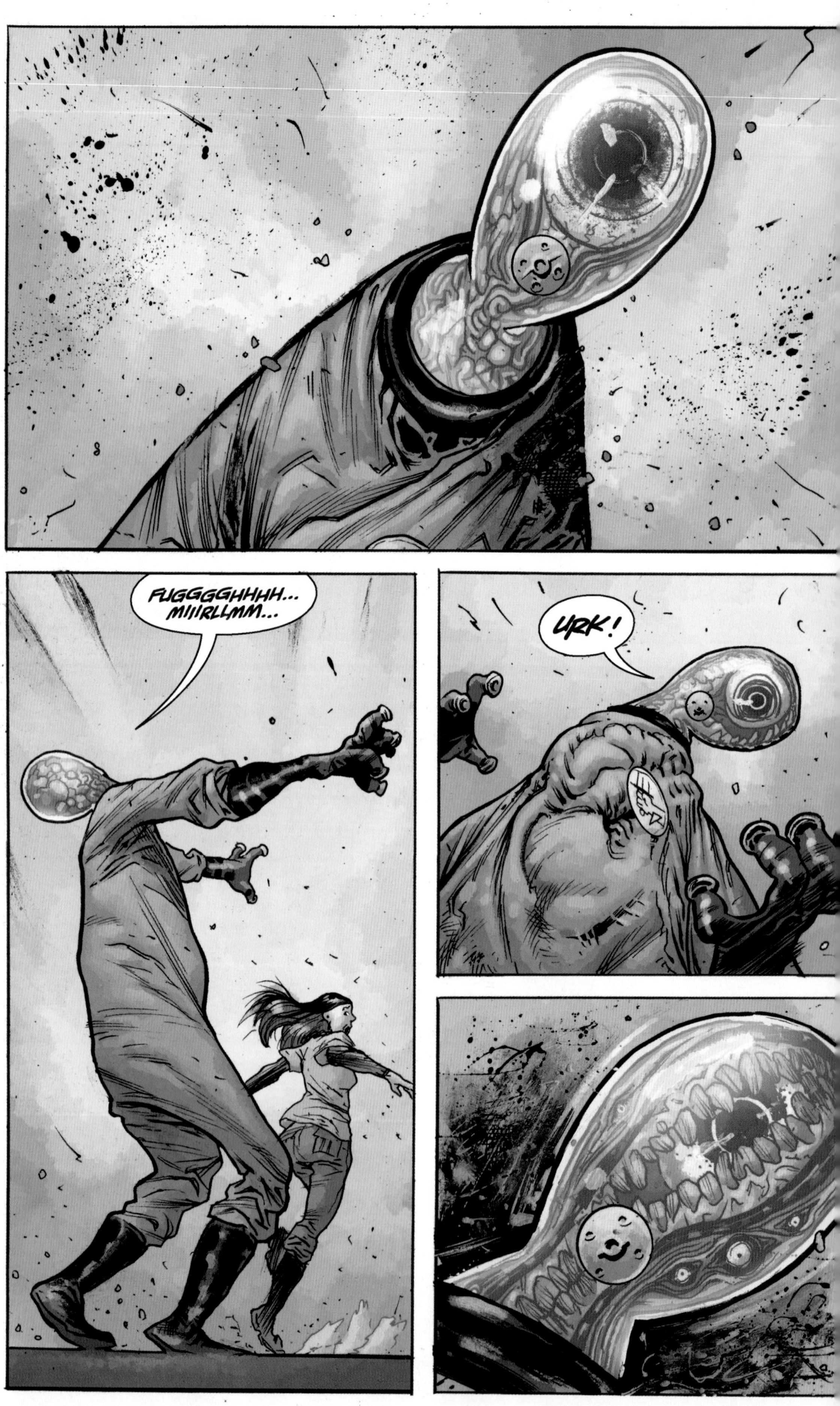
FUGGGGHHHH... MIIIRLLMM...
URK!

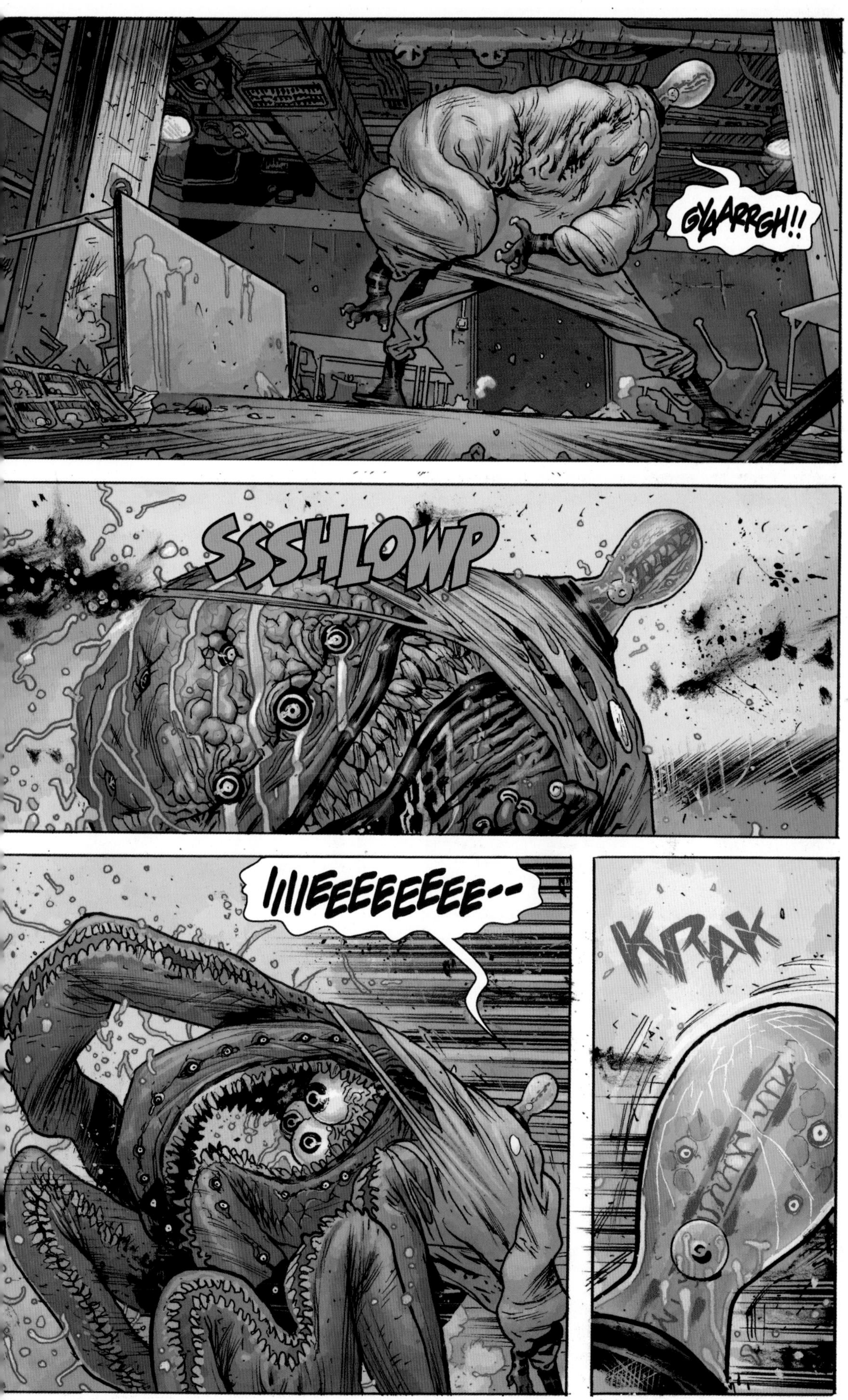
GYAARRGH!!
SSSHLOWP
IIIIIEEEEEEEEE--
KRAK

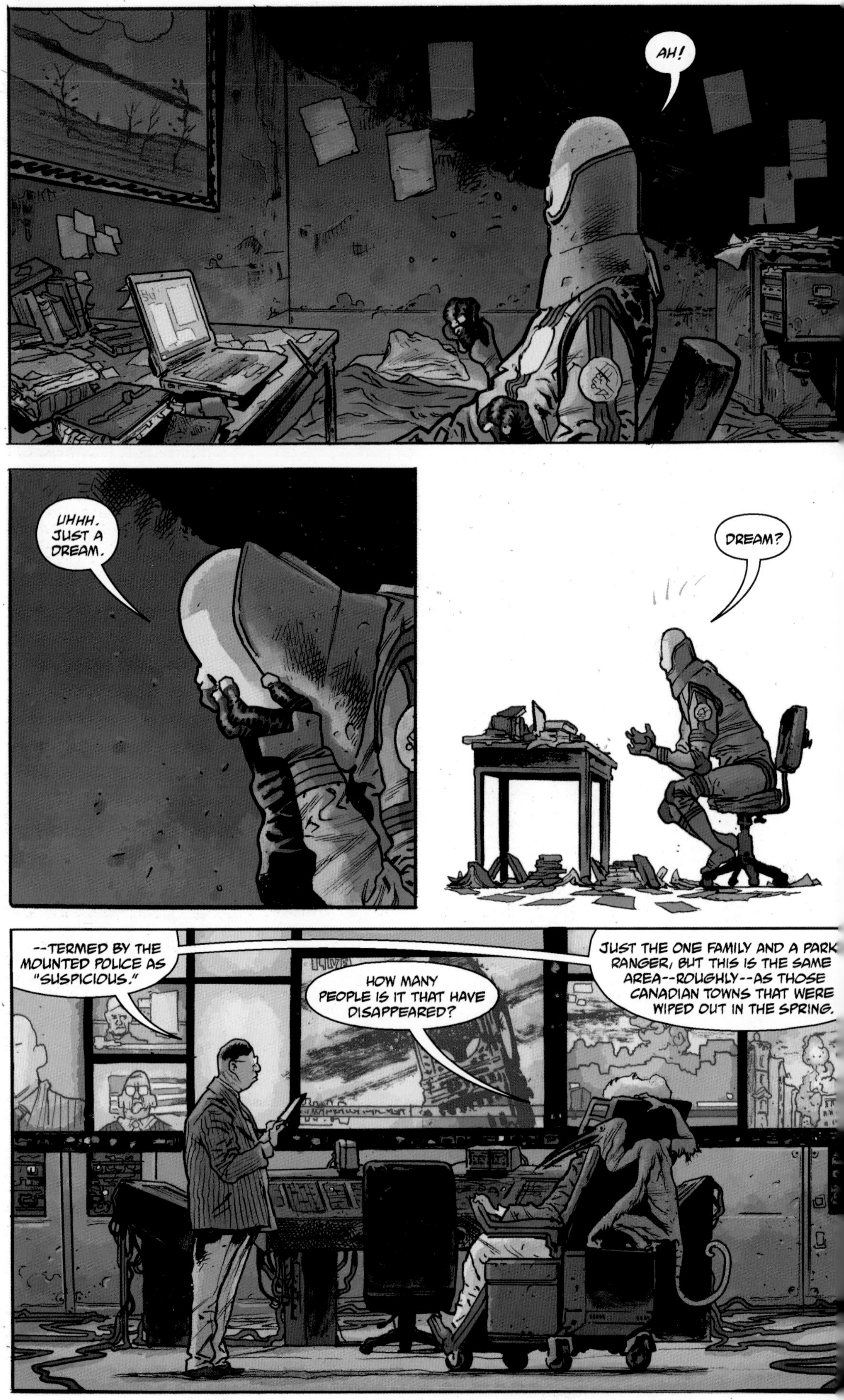
AH!
UHHH. JUST A DREAM.
DREAM?
--TERMED BY THE MOUNTED POLICE AS "SUSPICIOUS."
HOW MANY PEOPLE IS IT THAT HAVE DISAPPEARED?
JUST THE ONE FAMILY AND A PARK RANGER, BUT THIS IS THE SAME AREA--ROUGHLY--AS THOSE CANADIAN TOWNS THAT WERE WIPED OUT IN THE SPRING.

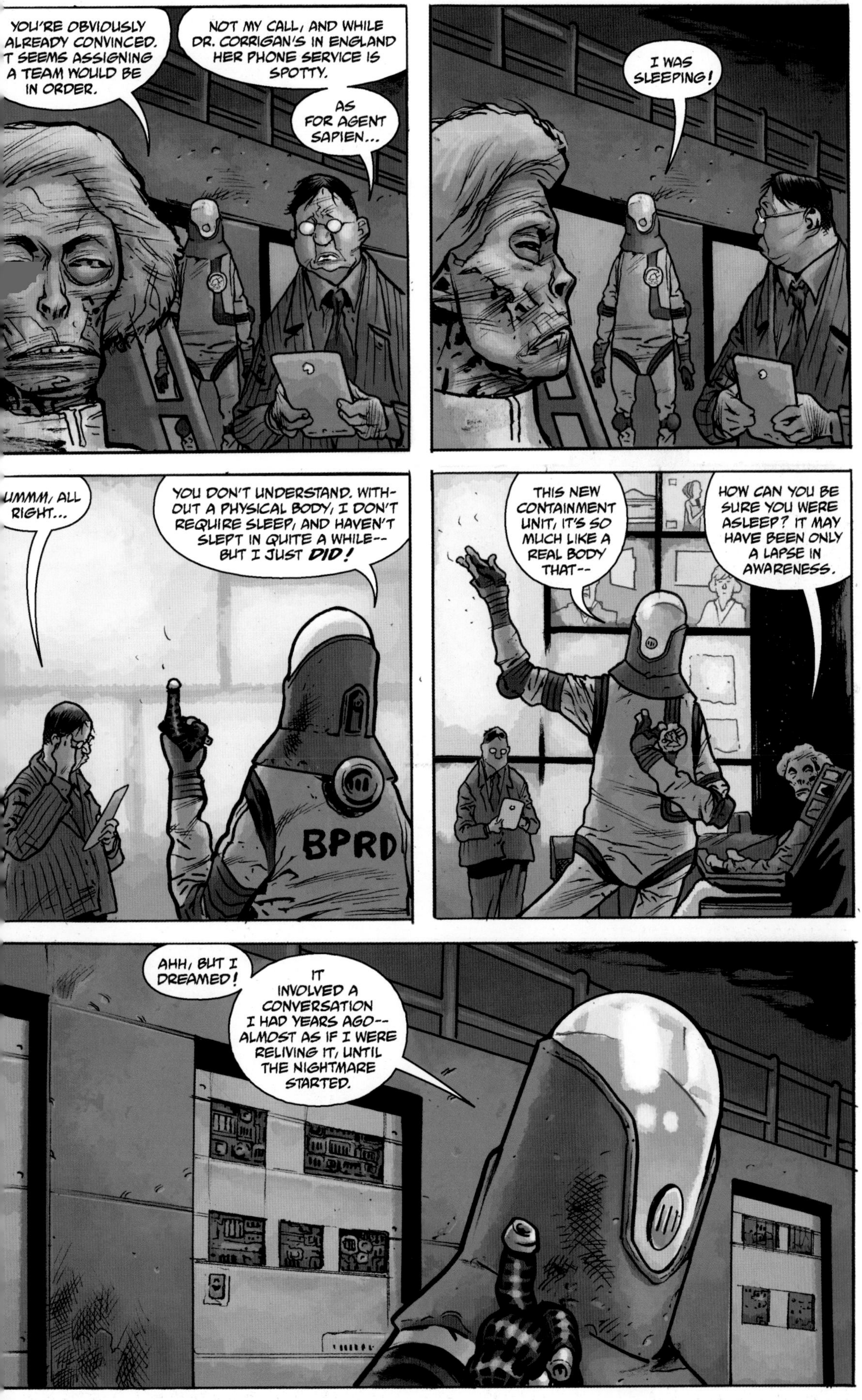
YOU'RE OBVIOUSLY ALREADY CONVINCED. T SEEMS ASSIGNING A TEAM WOULD BE IN ORDER.
NOT MY CALL, AND WHILE DR. CORRIGAN'S IN ENGLAND HER PHONE SERVICE IS SPOTTY.
AS FOR AGENT SAPIEN...
I WAS SLEEPING!
UMMM, ALL RIGHT...
YOU DON'T UNDERSTAND. WITHOUT A PHYSICAL BODY, I DON'T REQUIRE SLEEP, AND HAVEN'T SLEPT IN QUITE A WHILE-- BUT I JUST DID!
BPRD
THIS NEW CONTAINMENT UNIT, IT'S SO MUCH LIKE A REAL BODY THAT--
HOW CAN YOU BE SURE YOU WERE ASLEEP? IT MAY HAVE BEEN ONLY A LAPSE IN AWARENESS.
AHH, BUT I DREAMED!
IT INVOLVED A CONVERSATION I HAD YEARS AGO-- ALMOST AS IF I WERE RELIVING IT, UNTIL THE NIGHTMARE STARTED.

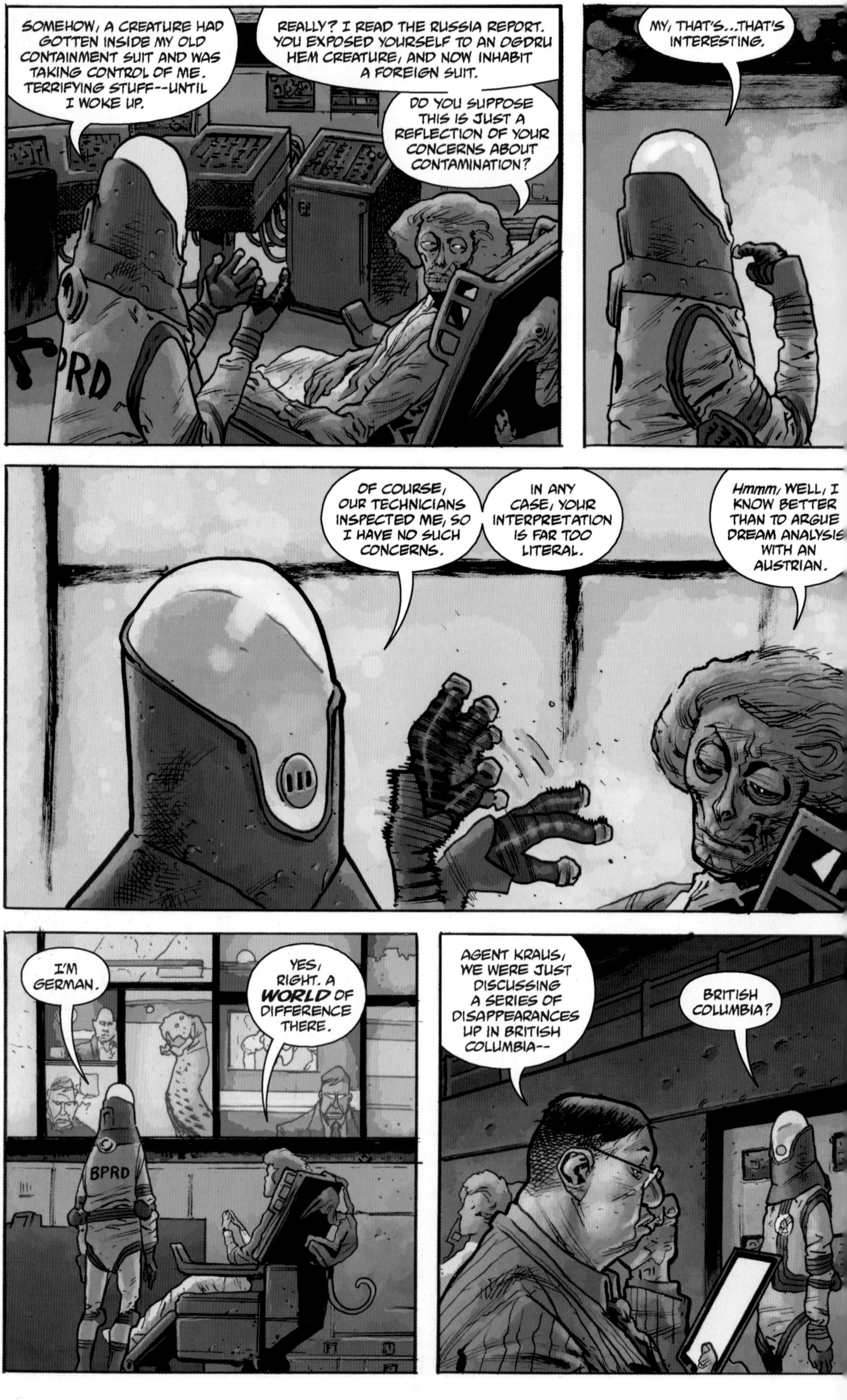
SOMEHOW, A CREATURE HAD GOTTEN INSIDE MY OLD CONTAINMENT SUIT AND WAS TAKING CONTROL OF ME. TERRIFYING STUFF--UNTIL I WOKE UP.
REALLY? I READ THE RUSSIA REPORT. YOU EXPOSED YOURSELF TO AN OGDRU HEM CREATURE, AND NOW INHABIT A FOREIGN SUIT.
DO YOU SUPPOSE THIS IS JUST A REFLECTION OF YOUR CONCERNS ABOUT CONTAMINATION?
MY, THAT'S...THAT'S INTERESTING.
BPRD
OF COURSE, OUR TECHNICIANS INSPECTED ME, SO I HAVE NO SUCH CONCERNS.
IN ANY CASE, YOUR INTERPRETATION IS FAR TOO LITERAL.
Hmmm, WELL, I KNOW BETTER THAN TO ARGUE DREAM ANALYSIS WITH AN AUSTRIAN.
I'M GERMAN.
YES, RIGHT. A WORLD OF DIFFERENCE THERE.
BPRD
AGENT KRAUS, WE WERE JUST DISCUSSING A SERIES OF DISAPPEARANCES UP IN BRITISH COLUMBIA--
BRITISH COLUMBIA?

THAT'S RIGHT. ABOUT AN HOUR AWAY FROM WHERE WE PICKED UP THAT CREATURE THAT AGENT SAPIEN KILLED.

MMMM, I RECALL IT VERY CLEARLY.

"BUT AS AGENT SAPIEN'S NOW IN A COMA..."

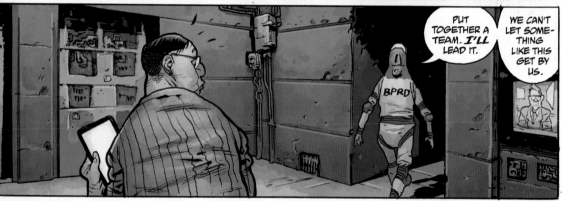

PUT TOGETHER A TEAM. *I'LL* LEAD IT.

WE CAN'T LET SOMETHING LIKE THIS GET BY US.

"CALL ME WHEN THE CREW AND AIRCRAFT HAVE BEEN PREPPED."

AH, HELLO. AGENT GIAROCCO, ISN'T IT?

HI, AGENT KRAUS. THIS YOUR SEAT?

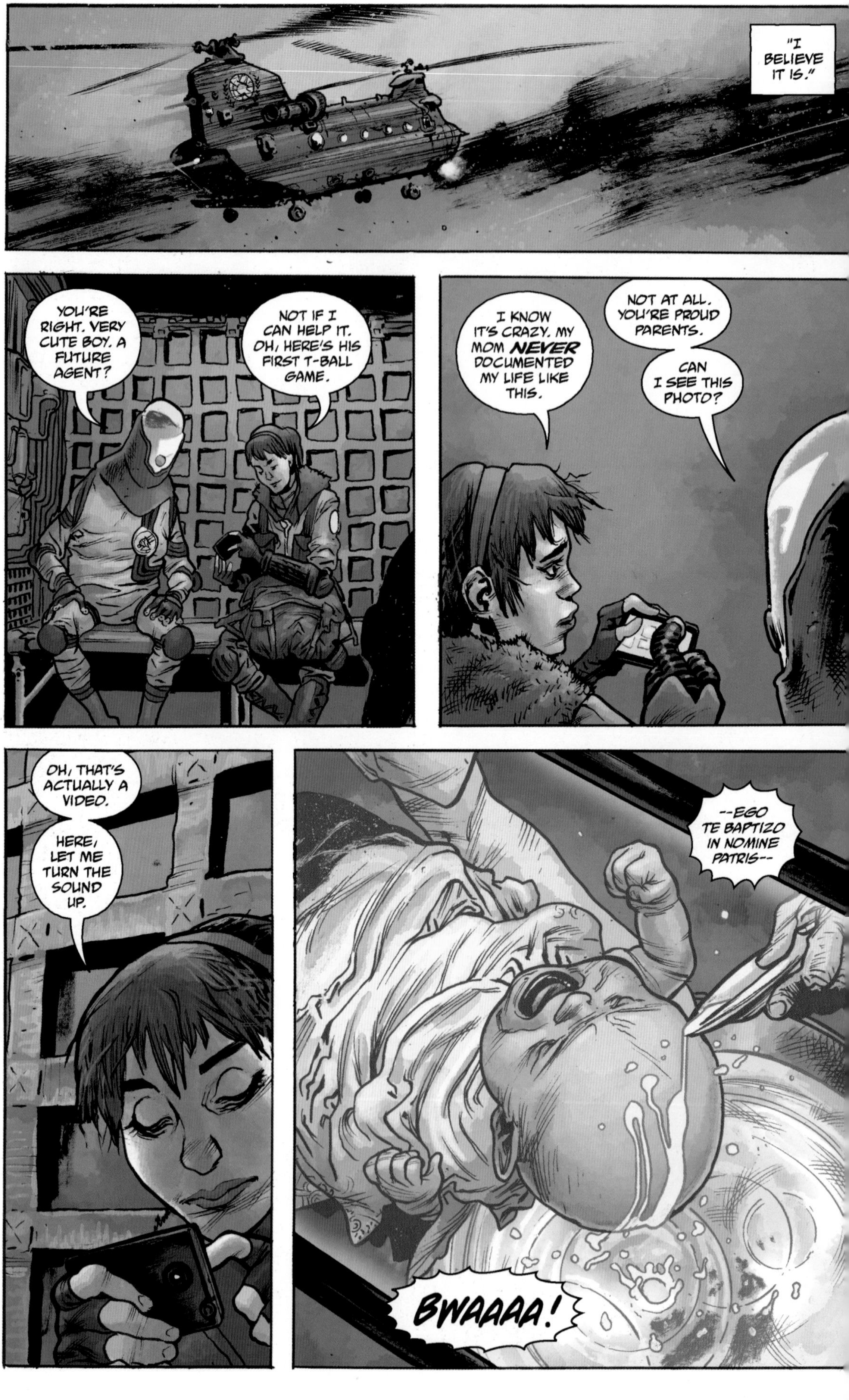
"I BELIEVE IT IS."
YOU'RE RIGHT. VERY CUTE BOY. A FUTURE AGENT?
NOT IF I CAN HELP IT. OH, HERE'S HIS FIRST T-BALL GAME.
I KNOW IT'S CRAZY. MY MOM NEVER DOCUMENTED MY LIFE LIKE THIS.
NOT AT ALL. YOU'RE PROUD PARENTS.
CAN I SEE THIS PHOTO?
OH, THAT'S ACTUALLY A VIDEO.
HERE, LET ME TURN THE SOUND UP.
--EGO TE BAPTIZO IN NOMINE PATRIS--
BWAAAA!

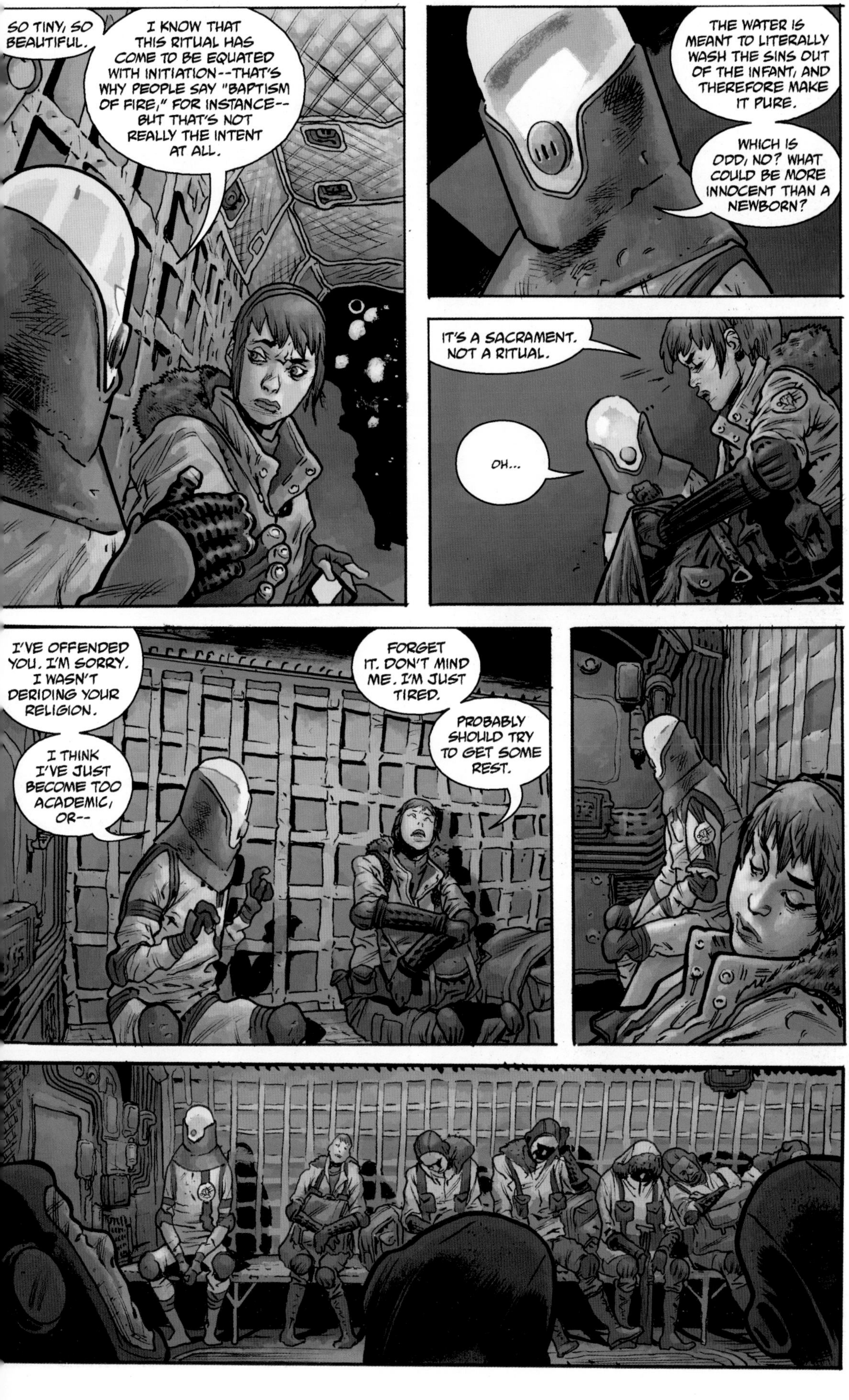
SO TINY, SO BEAUTIFUL.
I KNOW THAT THIS RITUAL HAS COME TO BE EQUATED WITH INITIATION--THAT'S WHY PEOPLE SAY "BAPTISM OF FIRE," FOR INSTANCE--BUT THAT'S NOT REALLY THE INTENT AT ALL.
THE WATER IS MEANT TO LITERALLY WASH THE SINS OUT OF THE INFANT, AND THEREFORE MAKE IT PURE.
WHICH IS ODD, NO? WHAT COULD BE MORE INNOCENT THAN A NEWBORN?
IT'S A SACRAMENT. NOT A RITUAL.
OH...
I'VE OFFENDED YOU. I'M SORRY. I WASN'T DERIDING YOUR RELIGION.
I THINK I'VE JUST BECOME TOO ACADEMIC, OR--
FORGET IT. DON'T MIND ME. I'M JUST TIRED.
PROBABLY SHOULD TRY TO GET SOME REST.

ALL RIGHT, MISS PANYA. IT'S GETTING LATE. I'LL BE TURNING IN.

!

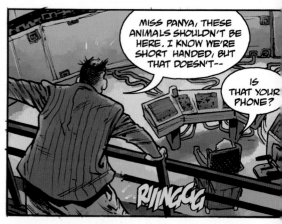

MISS PANYA, THESE ANIMALS SHOULDN'T BE HERE. I KNOW WE'RE SHORT HANDED, BUT THAT DOESN'T--

IS THAT YOUR PHONE?

RIIINGGG

WHAT IS IT?

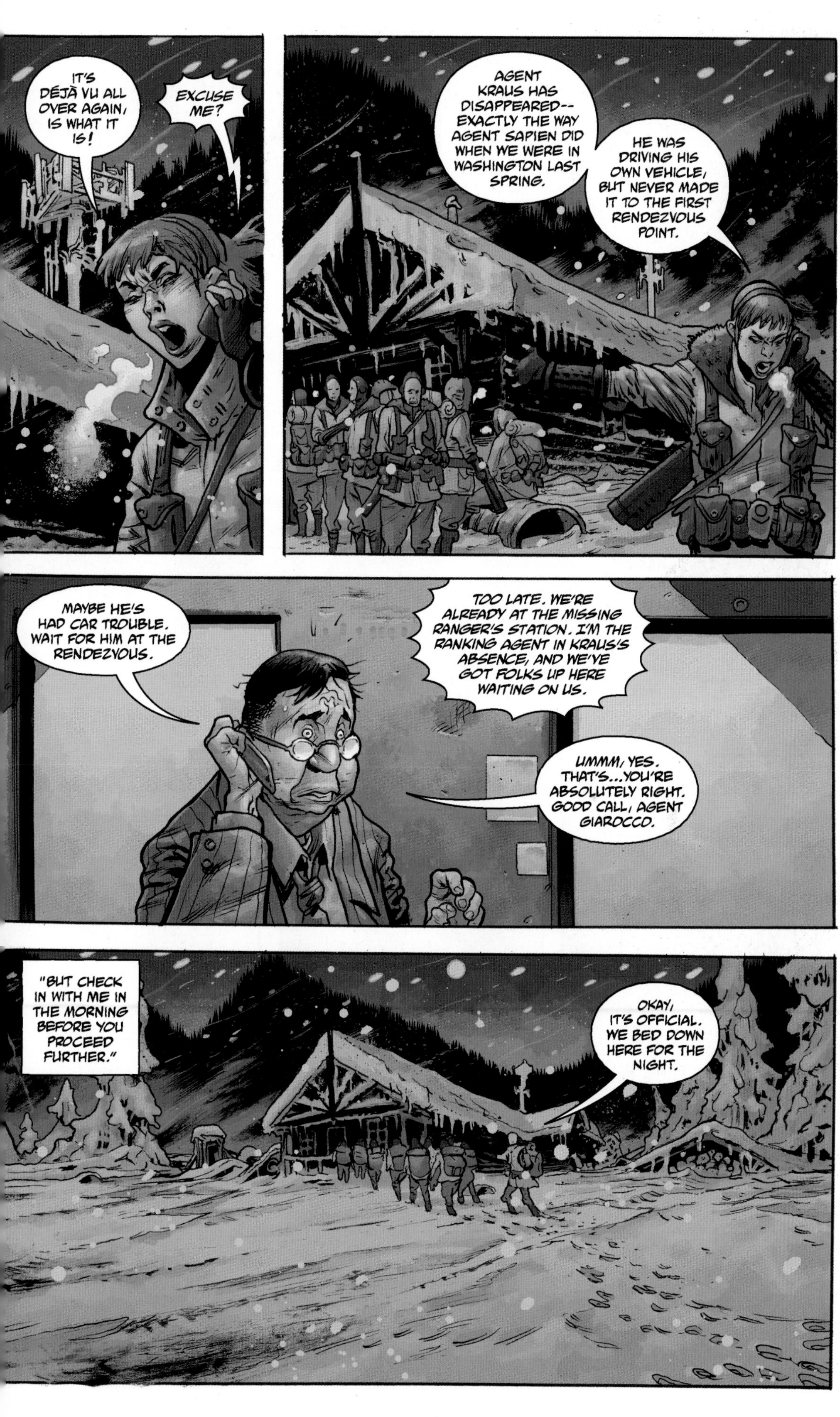

IT'S DÉJÀ VU ALL OVER AGAIN, IS WHAT IT IS!
EXCUSE ME?
AGENT KRAUS HAS DISAPPEARED-- EXACTLY THE WAY AGENT SAPIEN DID WHEN WE WERE IN WASHINGTON LAST SPRING.
HE WAS DRIVING HIS OWN VEHICLE, BUT NEVER MADE IT TO THE FIRST RENDEZVOUS POINT.
MAYBE HE'S HAD CAR TROUBLE. WAIT FOR HIM AT THE RENDEZVOUS.
TOO LATE. WE'RE ALREADY AT THE MISSING RANGER'S STATION. I'M THE RANKING AGENT IN KRAUS'S ABSENCE, AND WE'VE GOT FOLKS UP HERE WAITING ON US.
UMMM, YES. THAT'S...YOU'RE ABSOLUTELY RIGHT. GOOD CALL, AGENT GIAROCCO.
"BUT CHECK IN WITH ME IN THE MORNING BEFORE YOU PROCEED FURTHER."
OKAY, IT'S OFFICIAL. WE BED DOWN HERE FOR THE NIGHT.

THIS IS THE SPOT.

JUST A FEW HUNDRED YARDS FROM WHERE THE B.P.R.D. RECOVERED THE OGDRU HEM CREATURE-- RIGHT WHERE ABE SAID HE KILLED IT.

SO WHEN HE RETURNED HERE WEEKS LATER, USING VACATION TIME, WAS IT TO RELIVE HIS VICTORY?

OR MAYBE ABE CAME BACK TO CANADA FOR THE WILDLIFE.

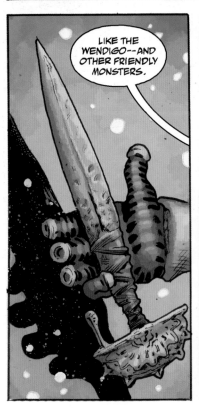

LIKE THE WENDIGO--AND OTHER FRIENDLY MONSTERS.

I DON'T NEED MAPS ANY- MORE, CAPTAIN DAIMIO.

I CAN SMELL YOU.

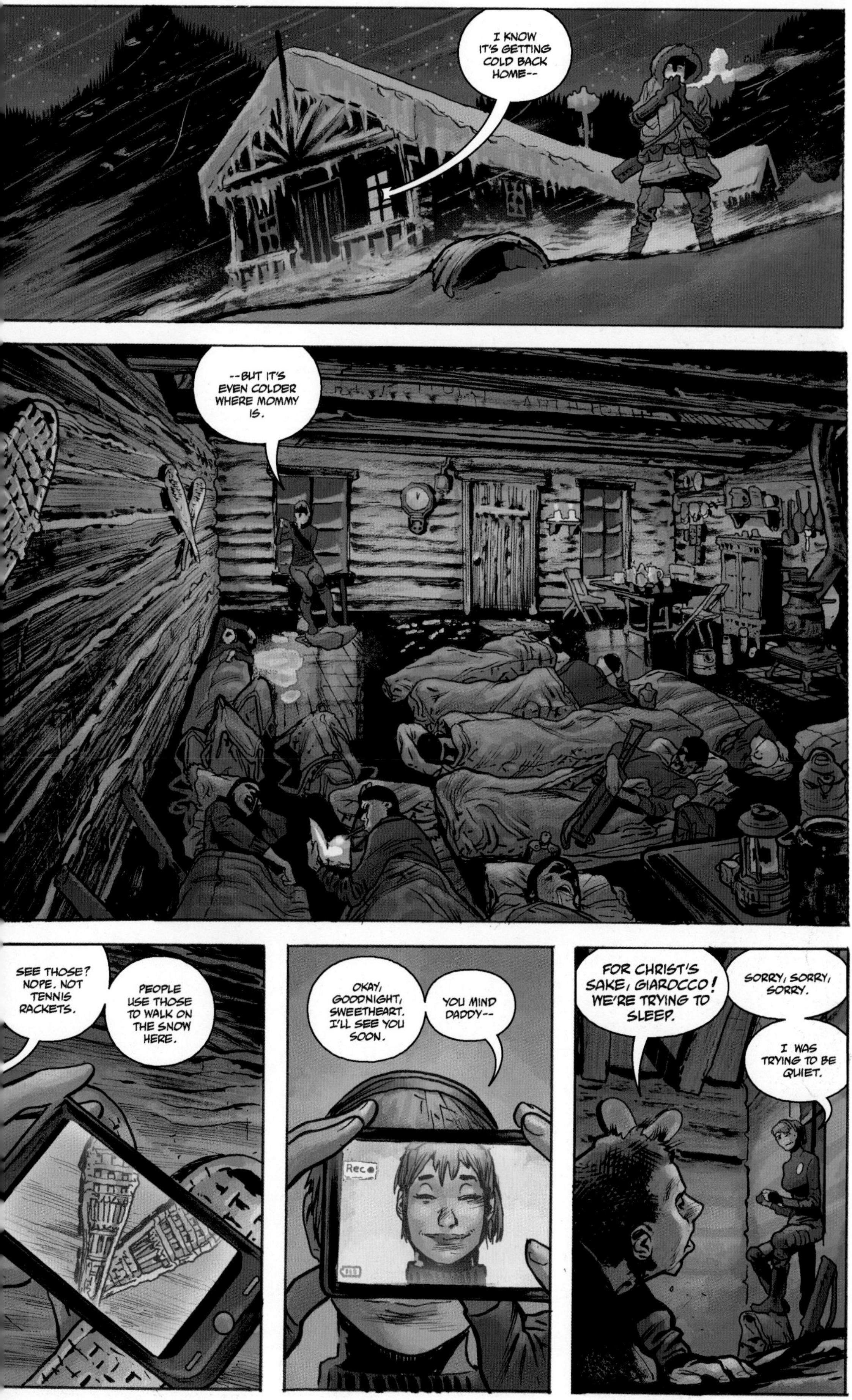
I KNOW IT'S GETTING COLD BACK HOME--
--BUT IT'S EVEN COLDER WHERE MOMMY IS.
SEE THOSE? NOPE. NOT TENNIS RACKETS.
PEOPLE USE THOSE TO WALK ON THE SNOW HERE.
OKAY, GOODNIGHT, SWEETHEART. I'LL SEE YOU SOON.
YOU MIND DADDY--
Rec
FOR CHRIST'S SAKE, GIAROCCO! WE'RE TRYING TO SLEEP.
SORRY, SORRY, SORRY.
I WAS TRYING TO BE QUIET.

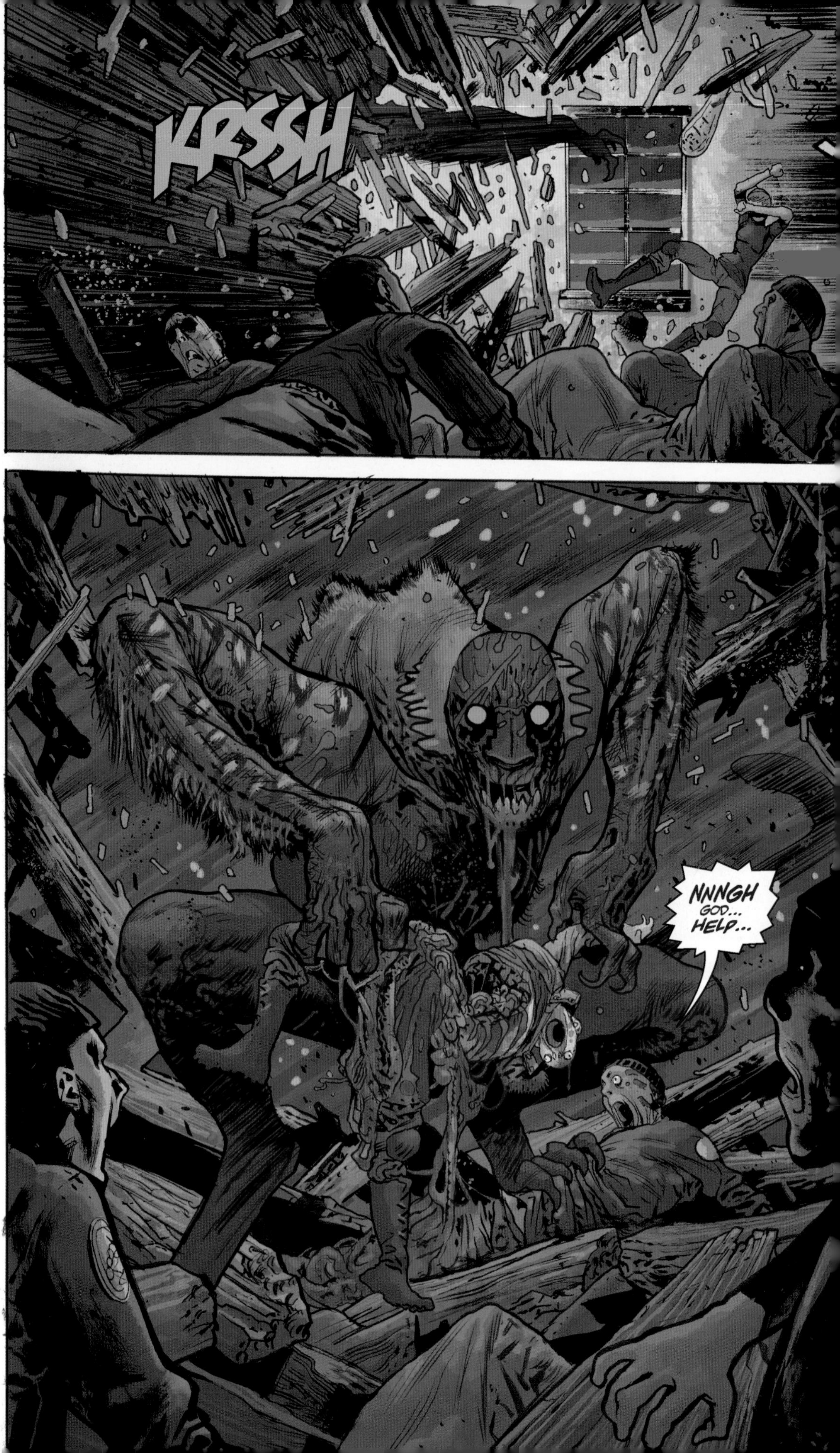
KRSSH
NNNGH GOD... HELP...

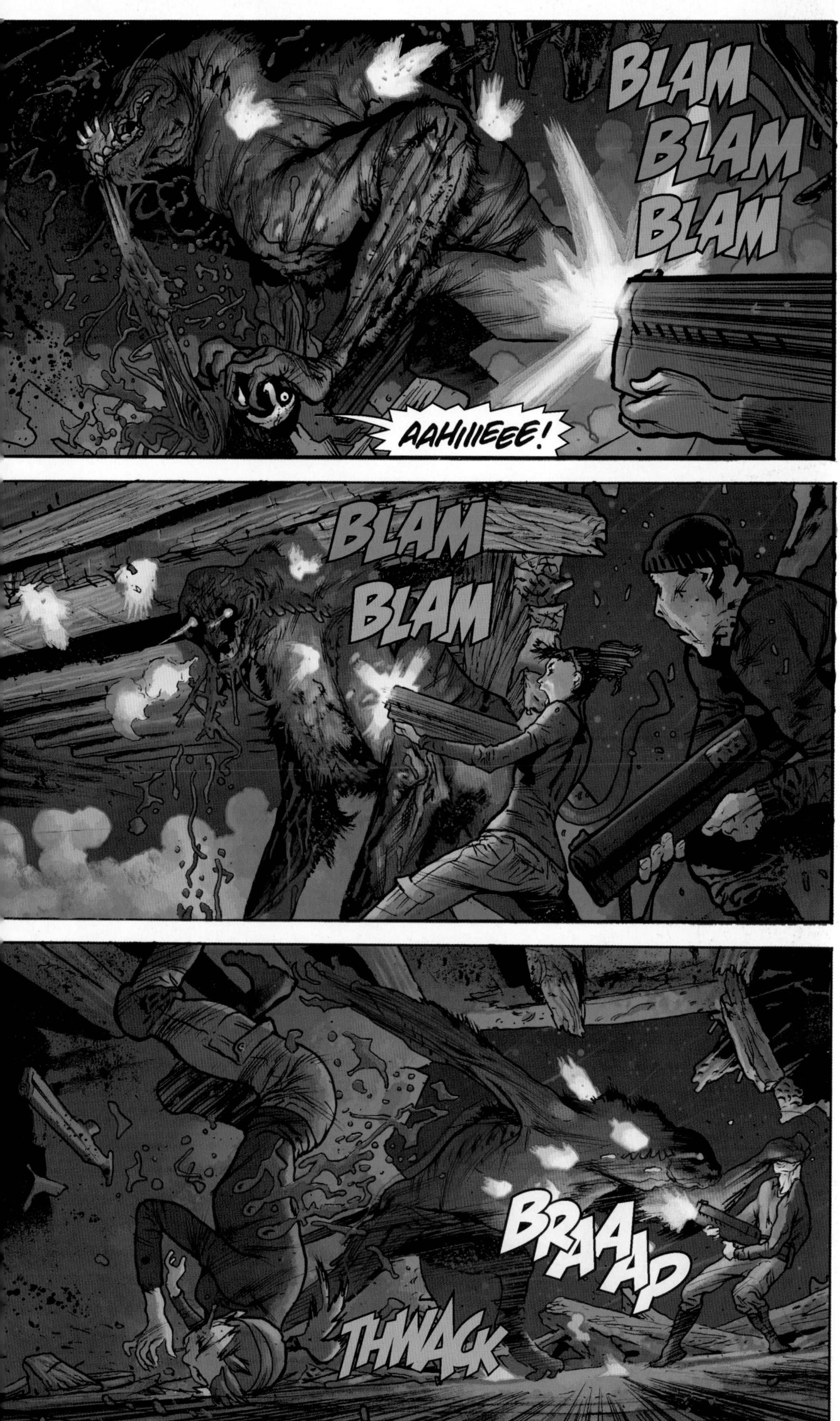
BLAM
BLAM
BLAM
AAHIIIEEE!
BLAM
BLAM
BRAAAP
THWACK

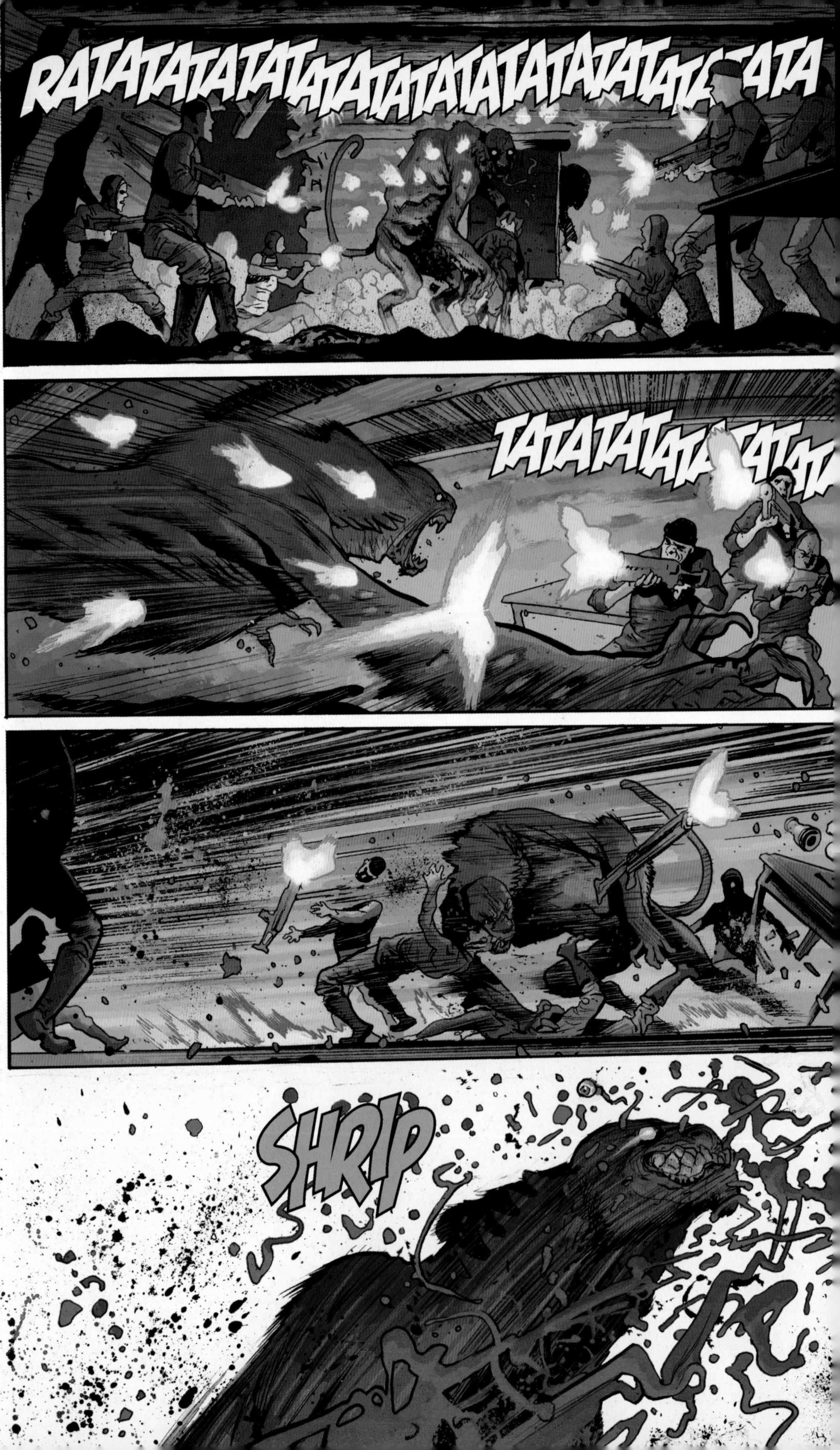
RATATATATATATATATATATATATATATATATATATA
TATATATATATATA
SHRIP

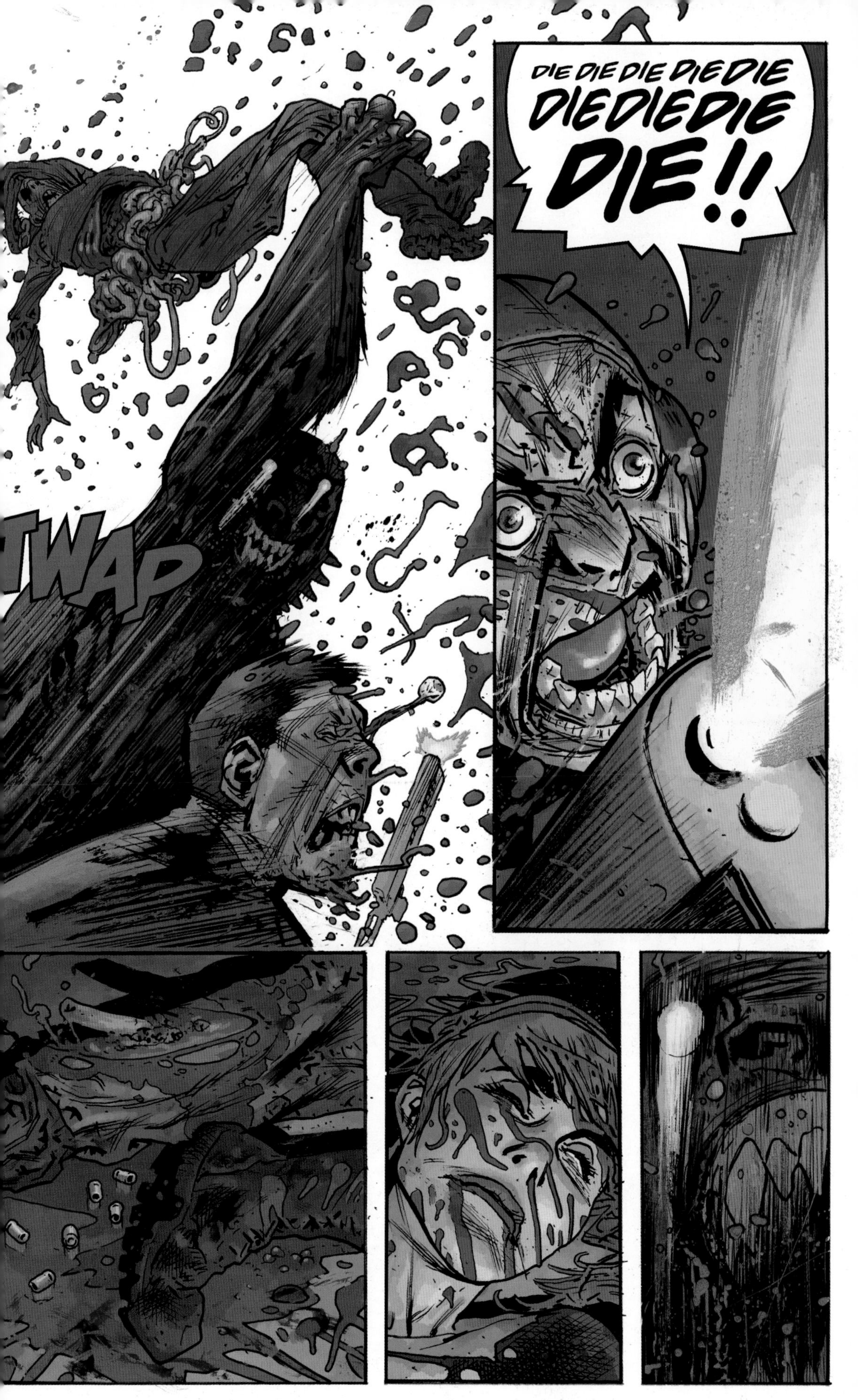
TWAP
DIE DIE DIE DIE DIE
DIE DIE DIE
DIE!!

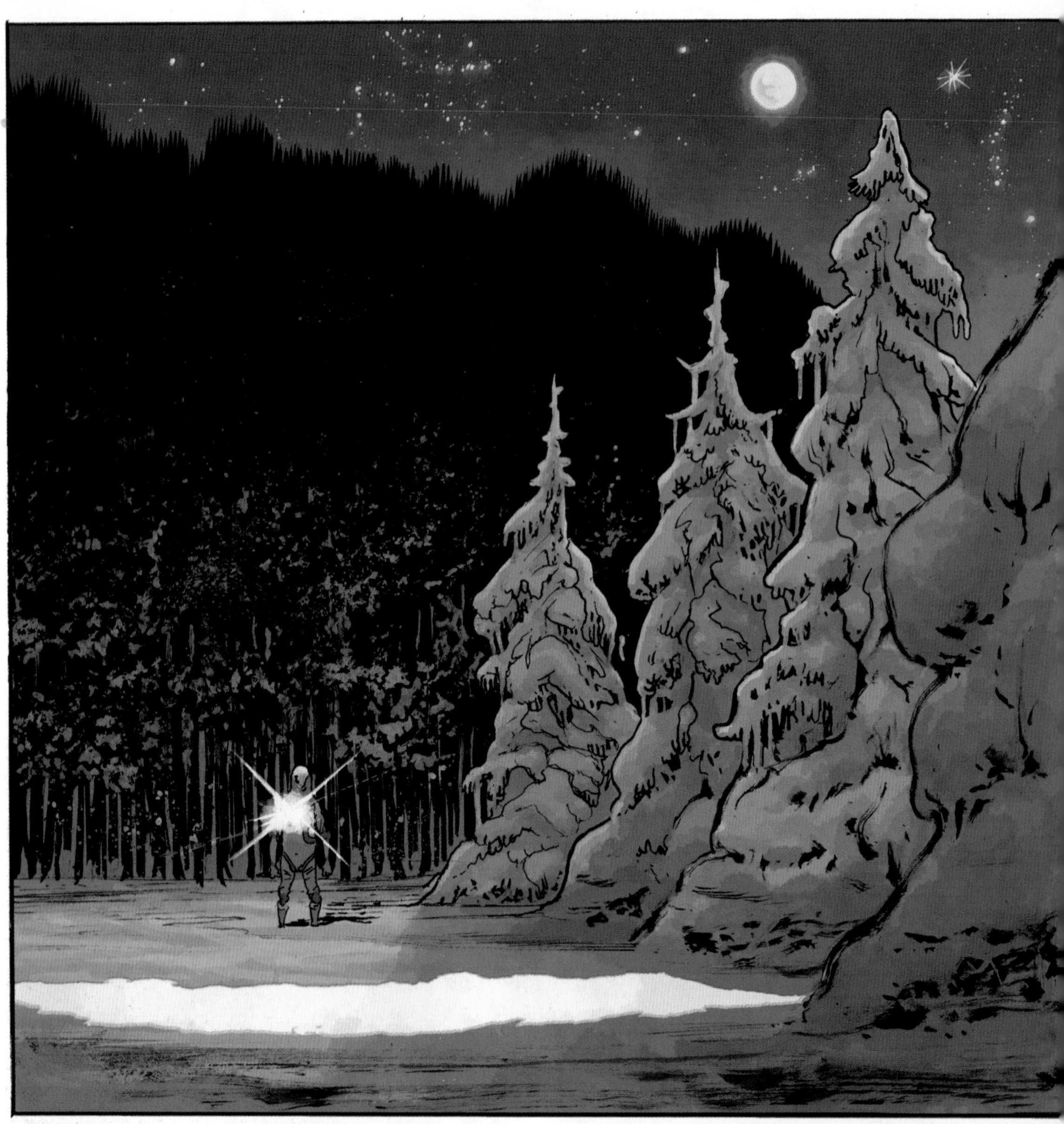

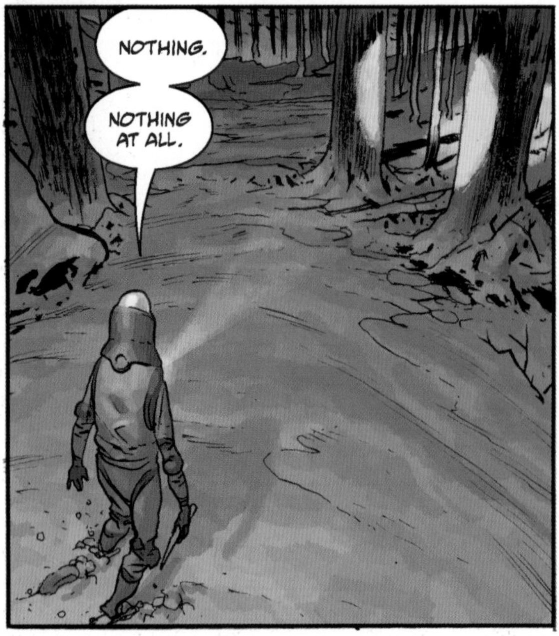
NOTHING.
NOTHING AT ALL.

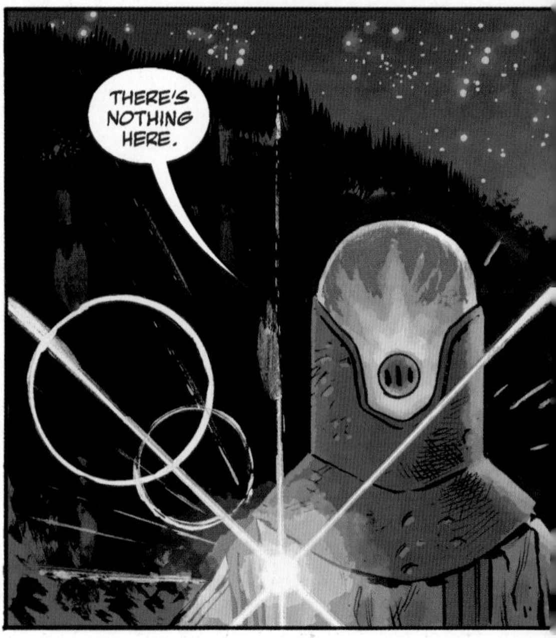
THERE'S NOTHING HERE.

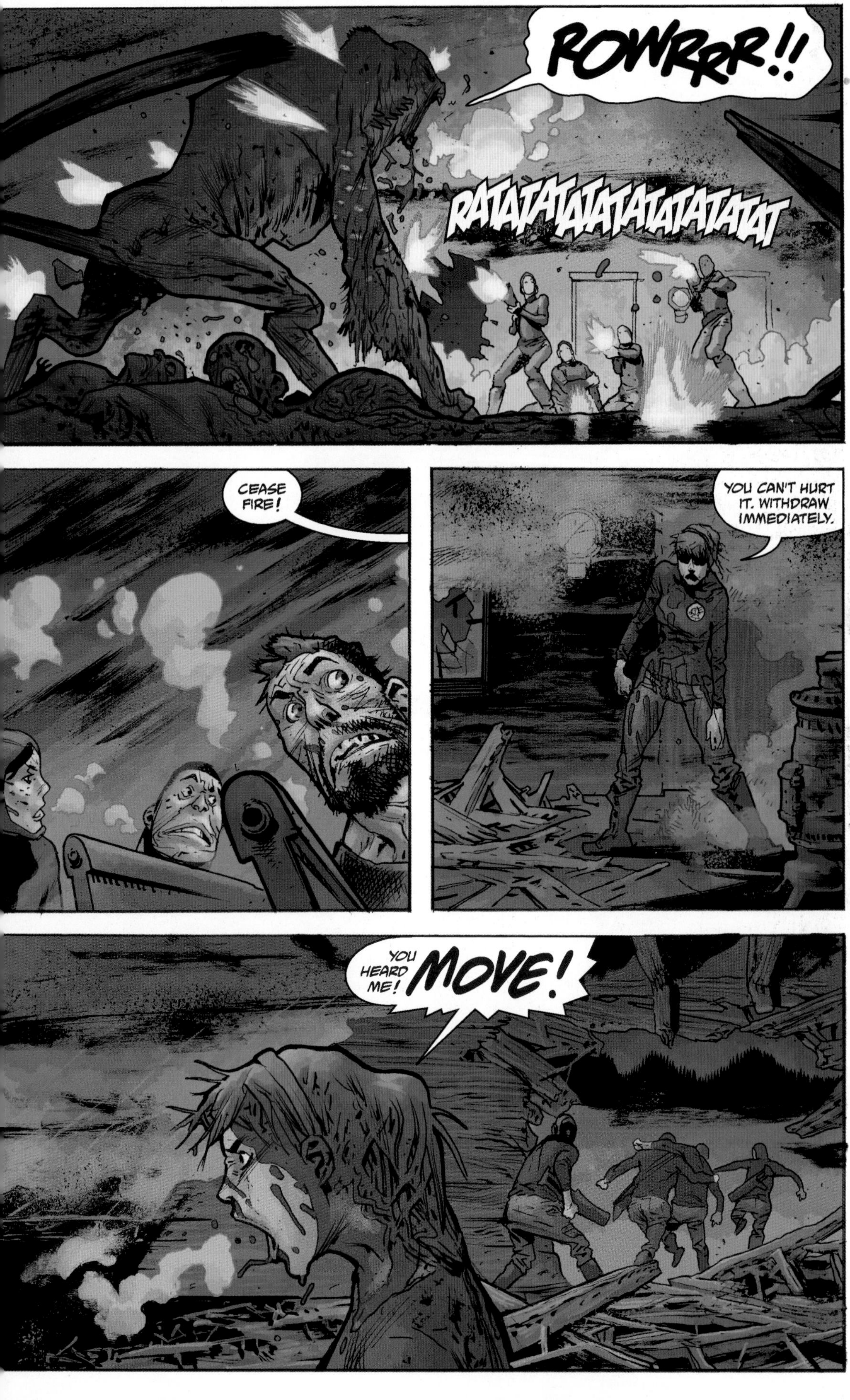
ROWRRR!!
RATATATATATATATATATATAT
CEASE FIRE!
YOU CAN'T HURT IT. WITHDRAW IMMEDIATELY.
YOU HEARD ME! MOVE!

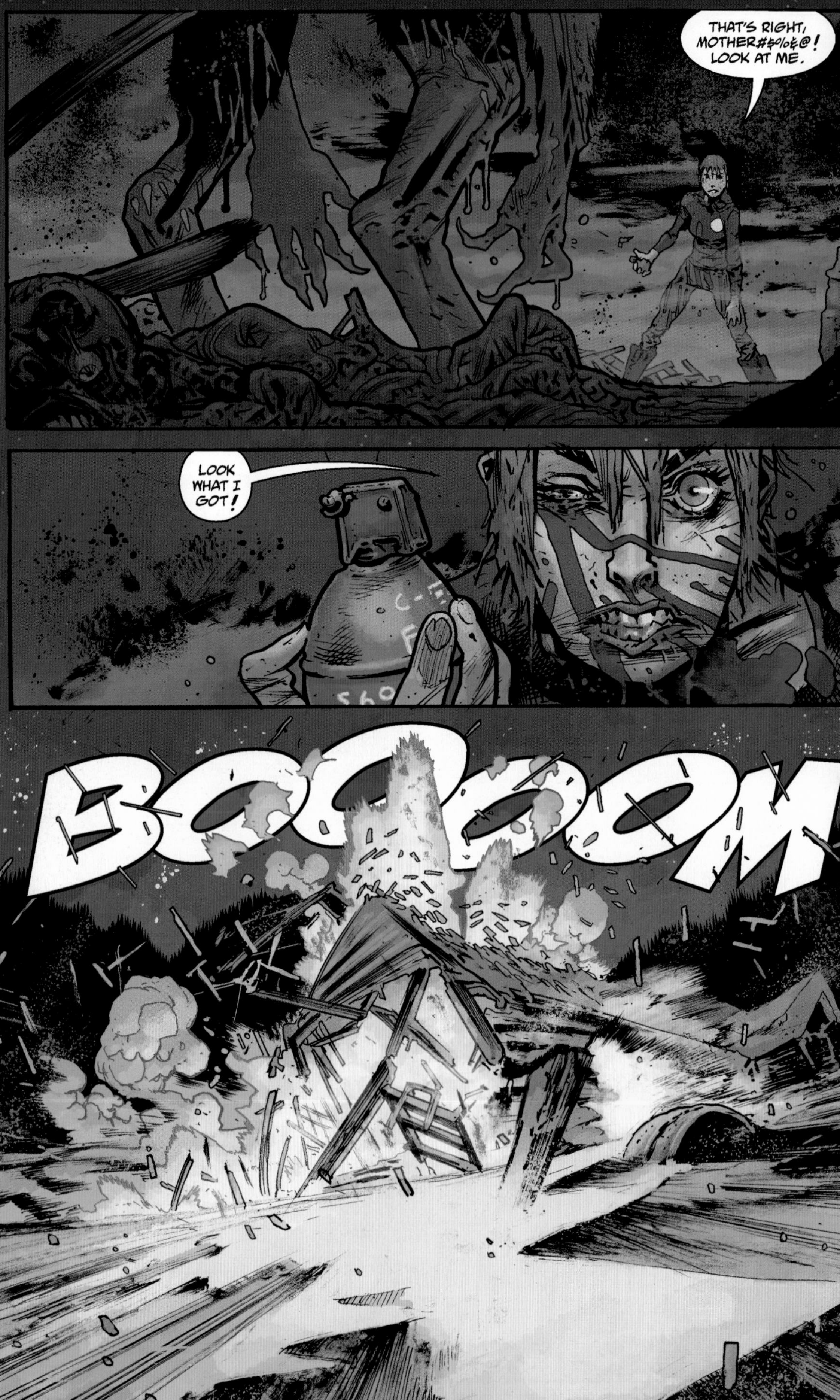
THAT'S RIGHT, MOTHER#$%&@! LOOK AT ME.
LOOK WHAT I GOT!
BOOOOM

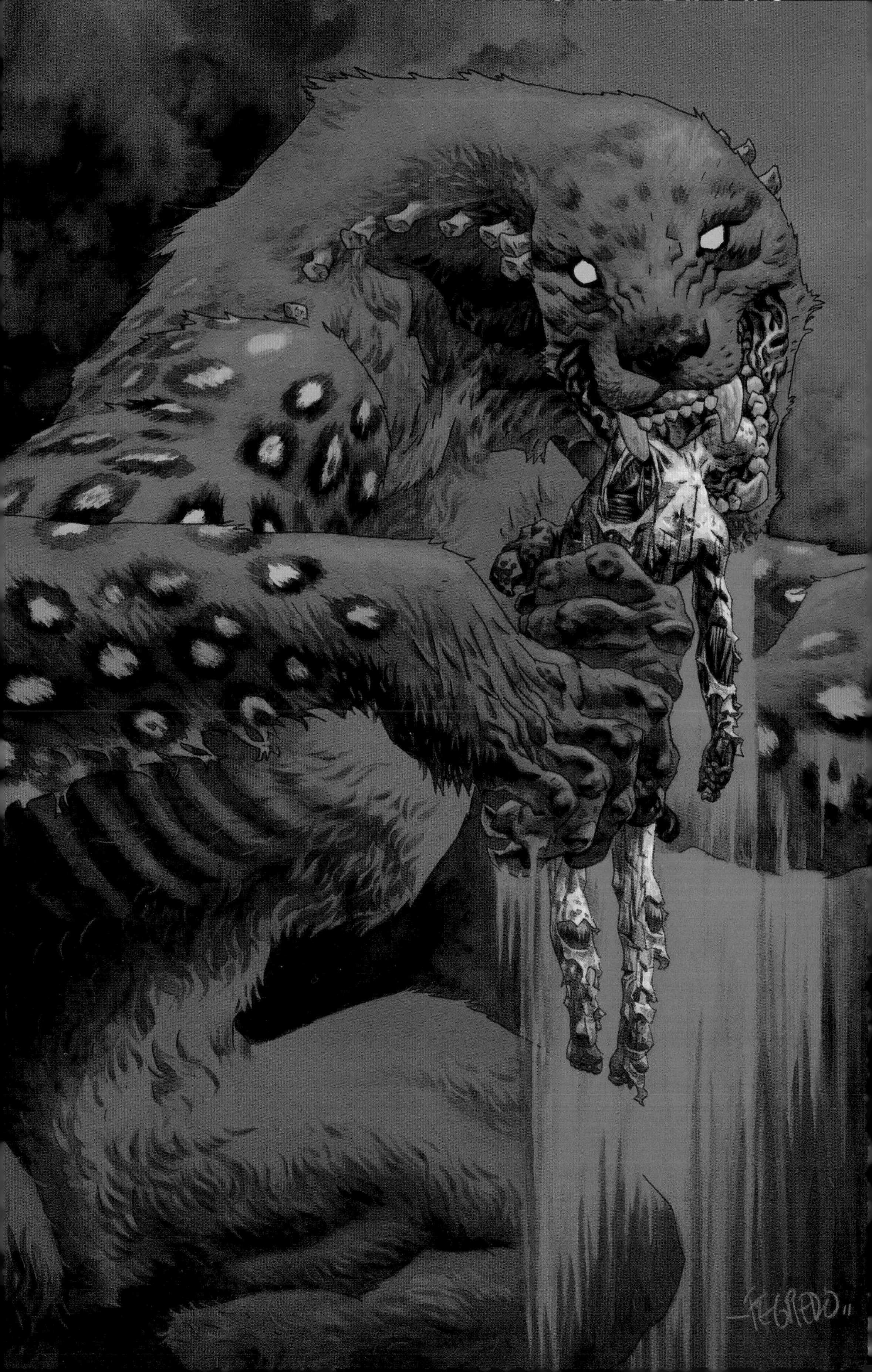
FEGREDO '11

RROWR!

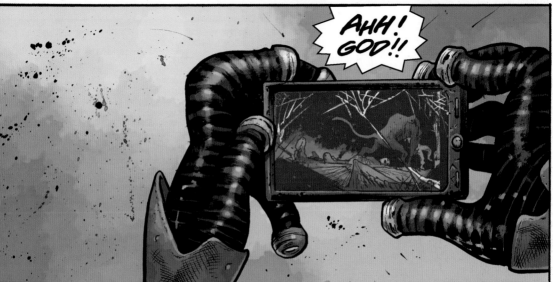

AHH! GOD!!

RROWR!

AHH! GOD!!

I'M SORRY.

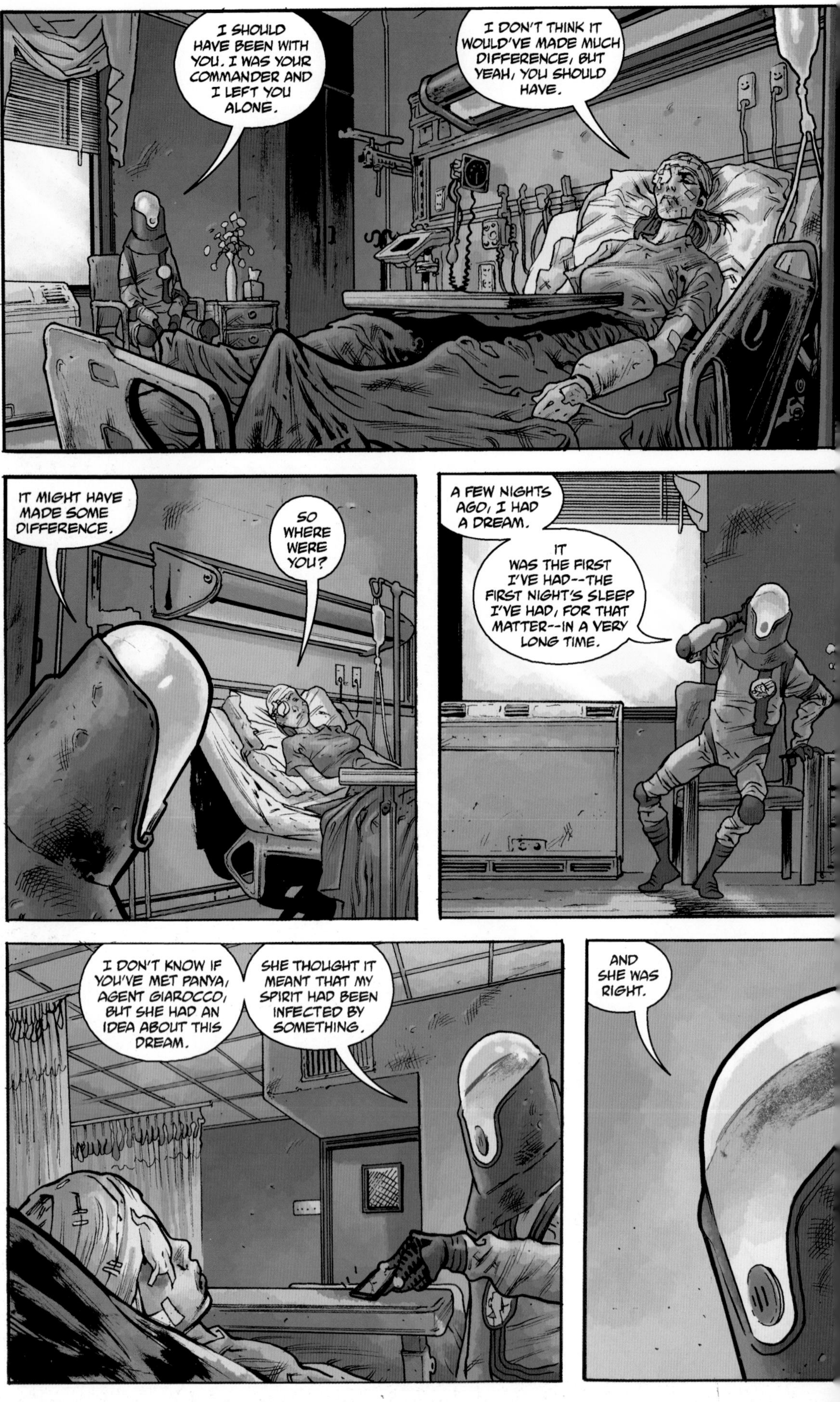
I SHOULD HAVE BEEN WITH YOU. I WAS YOUR COMMANDER AND I LEFT YOU ALONE.
I DON'T THINK IT WOULD'VE MADE MUCH DIFFERENCE, BUT YEAH, YOU SHOULD HAVE.
IT MIGHT HAVE MADE SOME DIFFERENCE.
SO WHERE WERE YOU?
A FEW NIGHTS AGO, I HAD A DREAM.
IT WAS THE FIRST I'VE HAD--THE FIRST NIGHT'S SLEEP I'VE HAD, FOR THAT MATTER--IN A VERY LONG TIME.
I DON'T KNOW IF YOU'VE MET PANYA, AGENT GIAROCCO, BUT SHE HAD AN IDEA ABOUT THIS DREAM.
SHE THOUGHT IT MEANT THAT MY SPIRIT HAD BEEN INFECTED BY SOMETHING.
AND SHE WAS RIGHT.

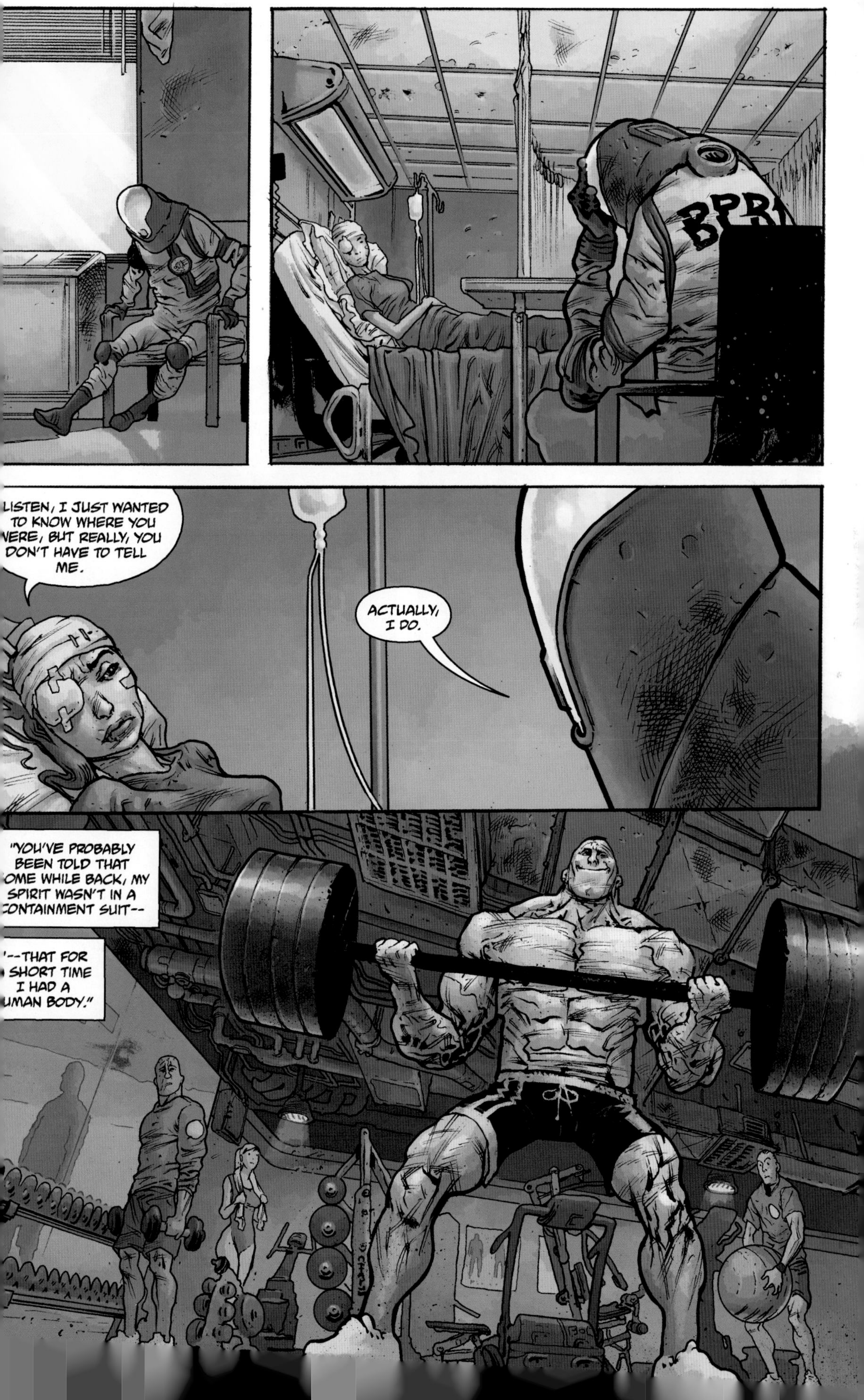
LISTEN, I JUST WANTED TO KNOW WHERE YOU WERE, BUT REALLY, YOU DON'T HAVE TO TELL ME.
ACTUALLY, I DO.
"YOU'VE PROBABLY BEEN TOLD THAT SOME WHILE BACK, MY SPIRIT WASN'T IN A CONTAINMENT SUIT--
"--THAT FOR A SHORT TIME I HAD A HUMAN BODY."

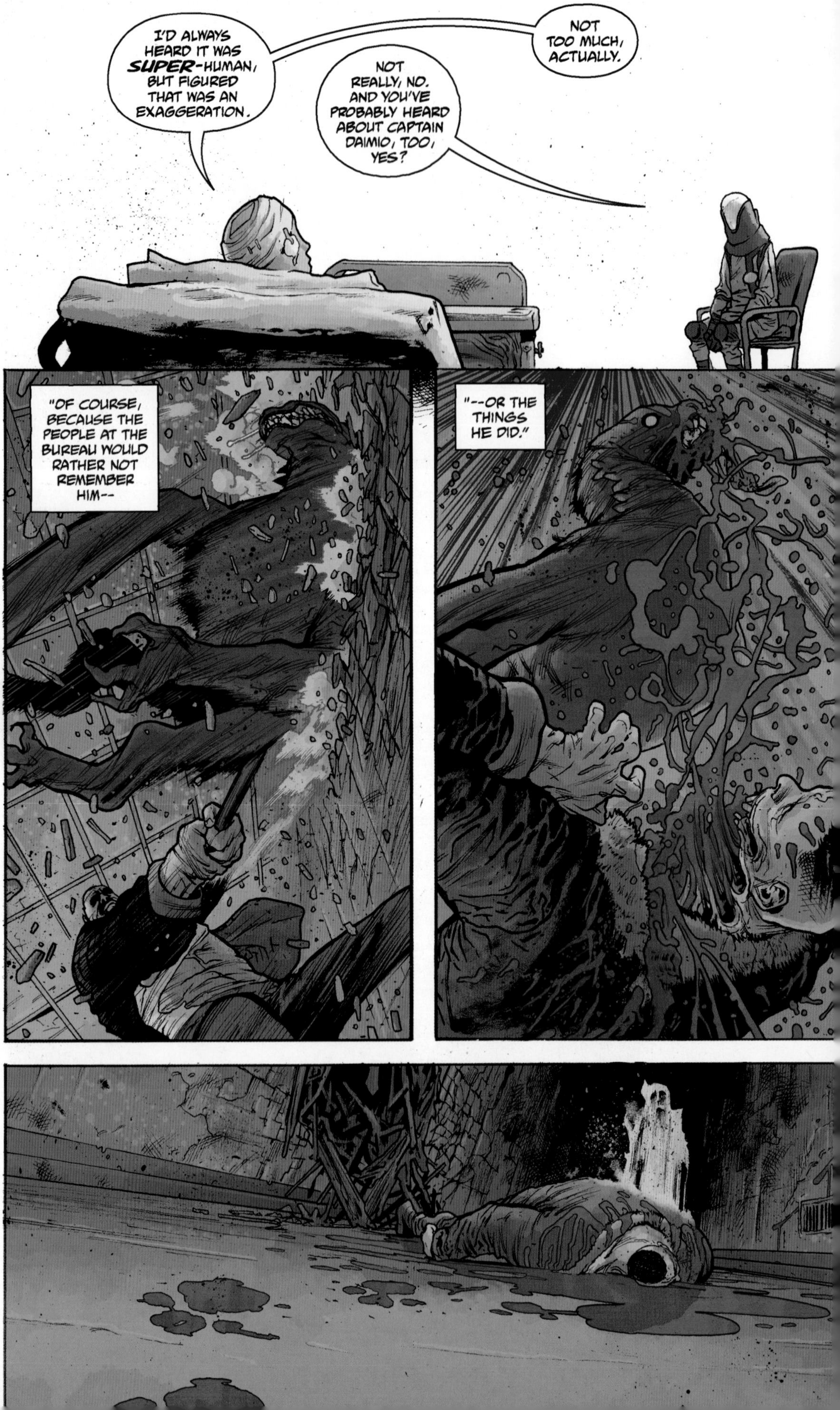
I'D ALWAYS HEARD IT WAS SUPER-HUMAN, BUT FIGURED THAT WAS AN EXAGGERATION.
NOT TOO MUCH, ACTUALLY.
NOT REALLY, NO. AND YOU'VE PROBABLY HEARD ABOUT CAPTAIN DAIMIO, TOO, YES?
"OF COURSE, BECAUSE THE PEOPLE AT THE BUREAU WOULD RATHER NOT REMEMBER HIM--
"--OR THE THINGS HE DID."

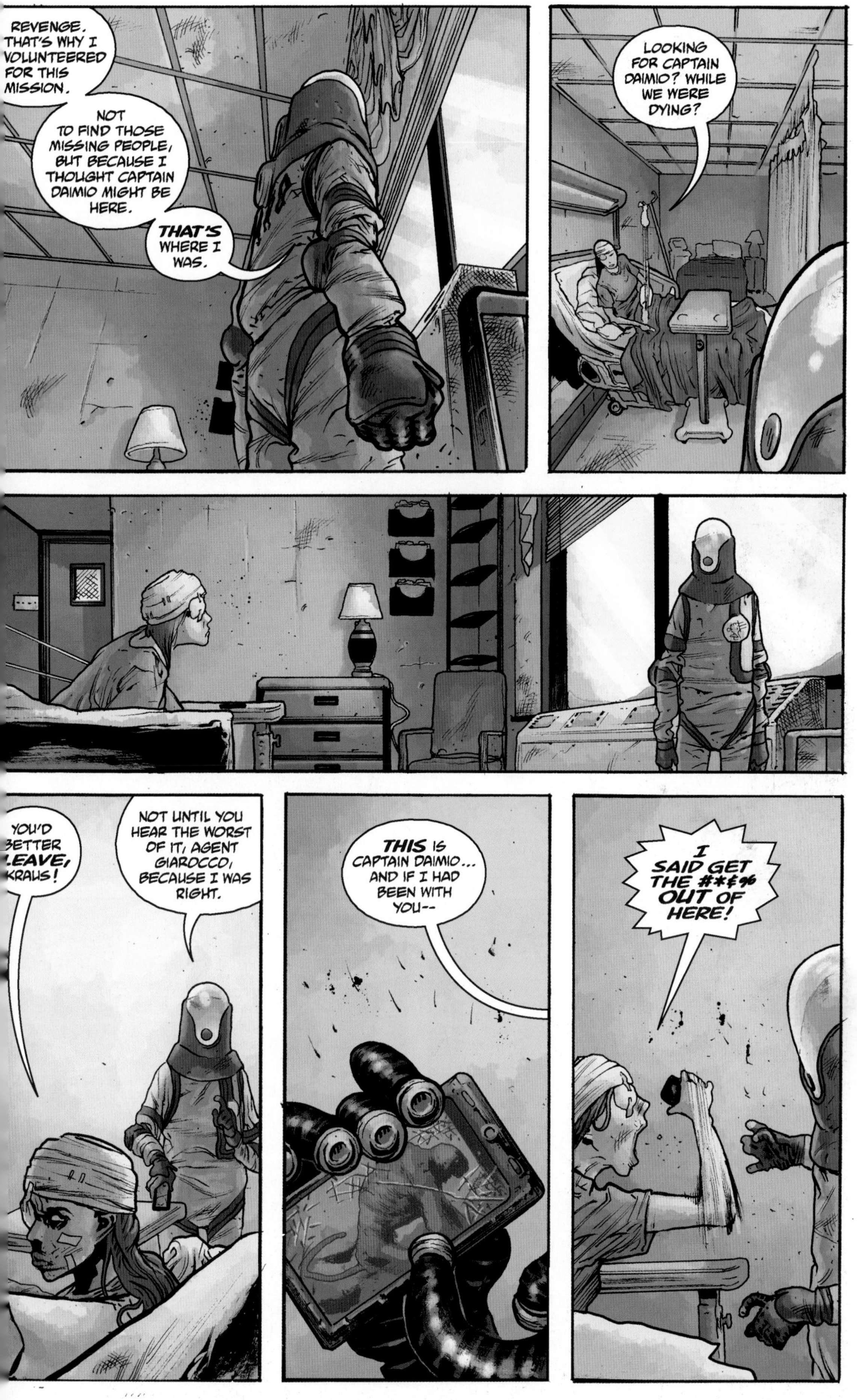
REVENGE. THAT'S WHY I VOLUNTEERED FOR THIS MISSION.
NOT TO FIND THOSE MISSING PEOPLE, BUT BECAUSE I THOUGHT CAPTAIN DAIMIO MIGHT BE HERE.
THAT'S WHERE I WAS.
LOOKING FOR CAPTAIN DAIMIO? WHILE WE WERE DYING?
YOU'D BETTER LEAVE, KRAUS!
NOT UNTIL YOU HEAR THE WORST OF IT, AGENT GIAROCCO, BECAUSE I WAS RIGHT.
THIS IS CAPTAIN DAIMIO... AND IF I HAD BEEN WITH YOU--
I SAID GET THE #*$% OUT OF HERE!

I'M FILING A **REPORT** ABOUT THIS! YOU HEAR ME?!

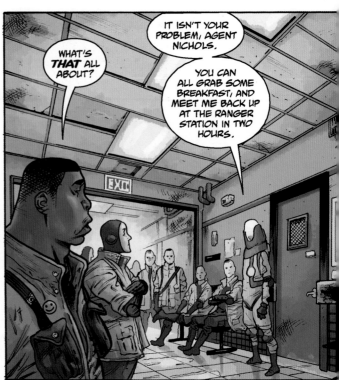

WHAT'S **THAT** ALL ABOUT?

IT ISN'T YOUR PROBLEM, AGENT NICHOLS.

YOU CAN ALL GRAB SOME BREAKFAST, AND MEET ME BACK UP AT THE RANGER STATION IN TWO HOURS.

"WE'VE STILL GOT A MISSION."

HELL NOW, THAT'S A LOT OF BLOOD. GUESS CARLA FRAGGED HIS ASS **GOOD.**

I DOUBT VERY MUCH THAT'S THE CREATURE'S BLOOD.

EVEN WHEN WOUNDED, HE CAN HEAL VERY QUICKLY.

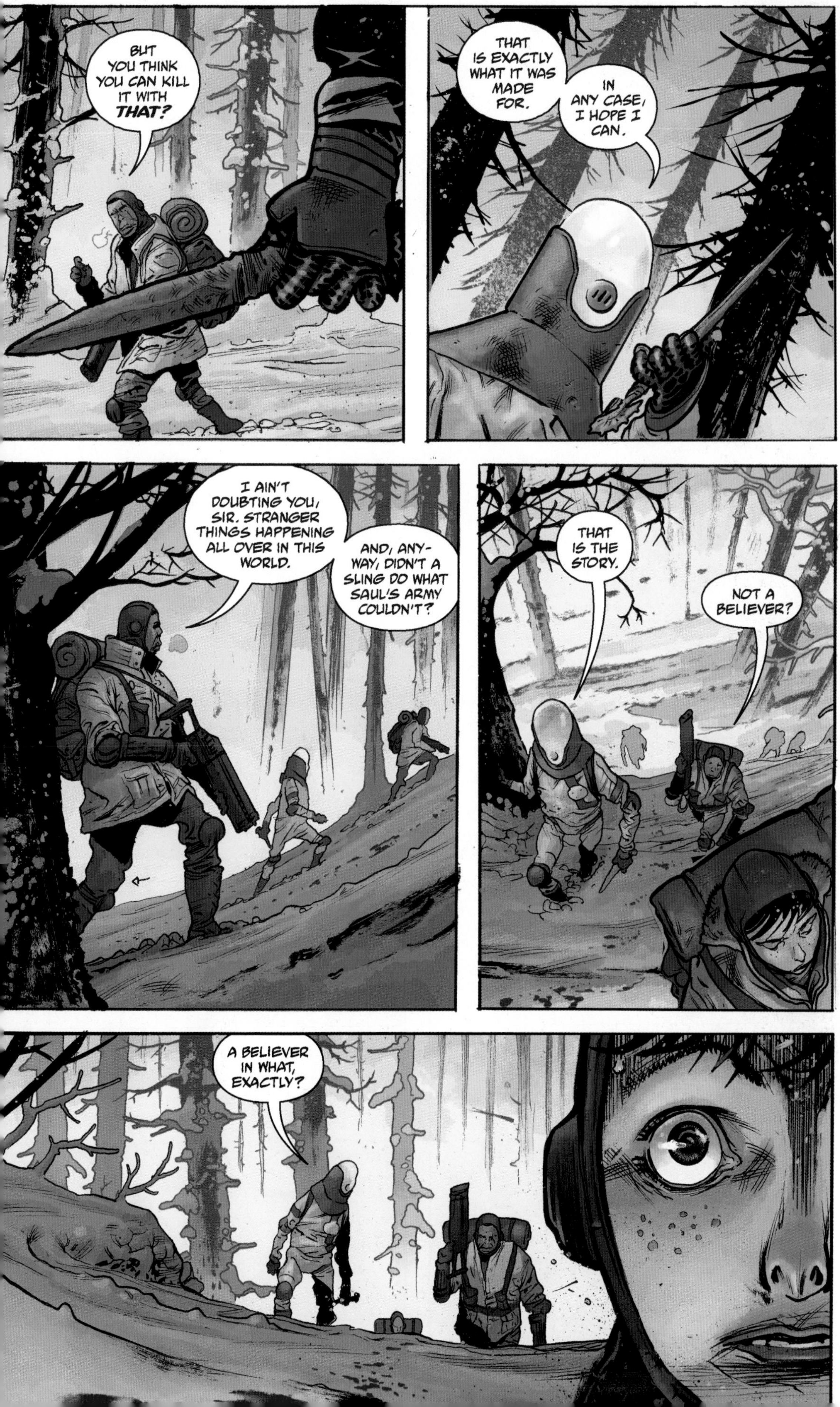
BUT YOU THINK YOU CAN KILL IT WITH THAT?
THAT IS EXACTLY WHAT IT WAS MADE FOR.
IN ANY CASE, I HOPE I CAN.
I AIN'T DOUBTING YOU, SIR. STRANGER THINGS HAPPENING ALL OVER IN THIS WORLD.
AND, ANY-WAY, DIDN'T A SLING DO WHAT SAUL'S ARMY COULDN'T?
THAT IS THE STORY.
NOT A BELIEVER?
A BELIEVER IN WHAT, EXACTLY?

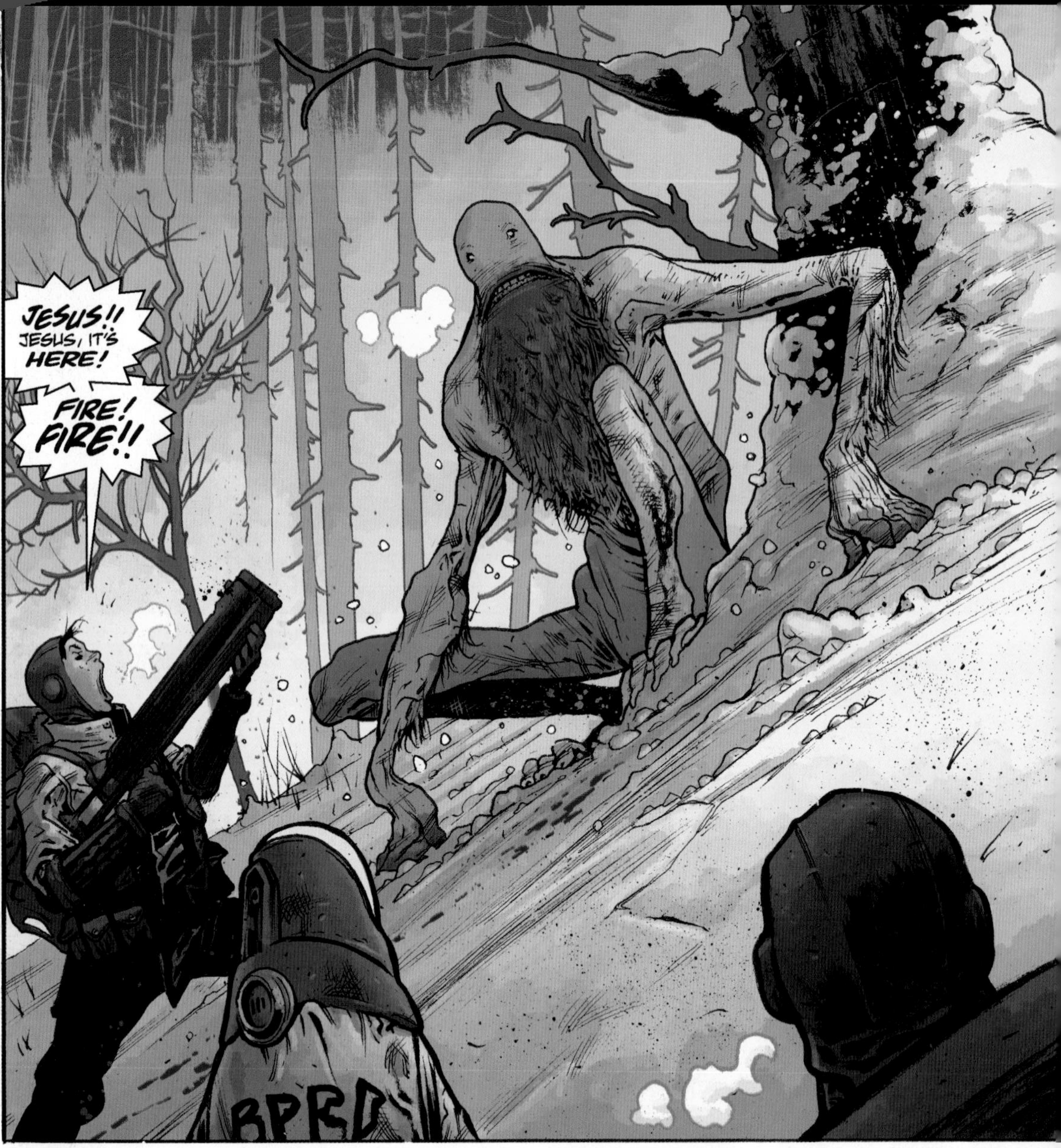
JESUS!! JESUS, IT'S HERE!
FIRE! FIRE!!
BPRD

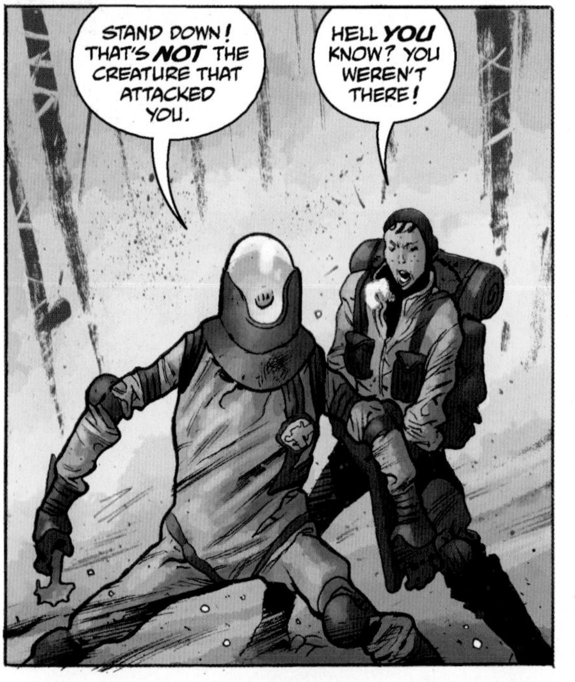
STAND DOWN! THAT'S NOT THE CREATURE THAT ATTACKED YOU.
HELL YOU KNOW? YOU WEREN'T THERE!

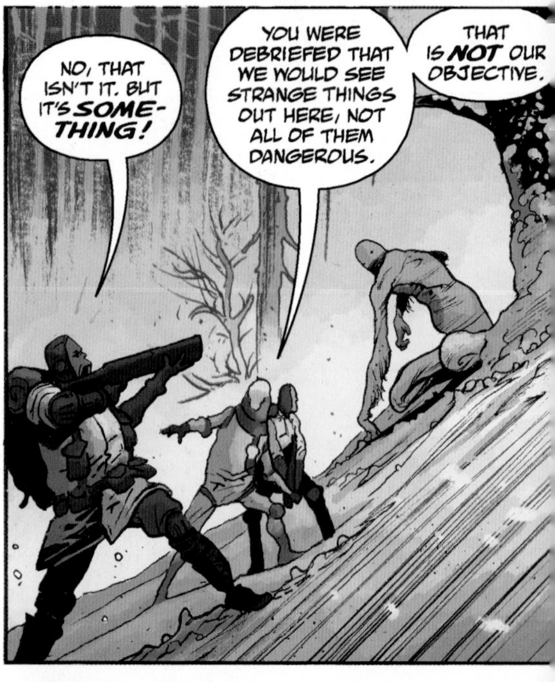
NO, THAT ISN'T IT. BUT IT'S SOME-THING!
YOU WERE DEBRIEFED THAT WE WOULD SEE STRANGE THINGS OUT HERE, NOT ALL OF THEM DANGEROUS.
THAT IS NOT OUR OBJECTIVE.

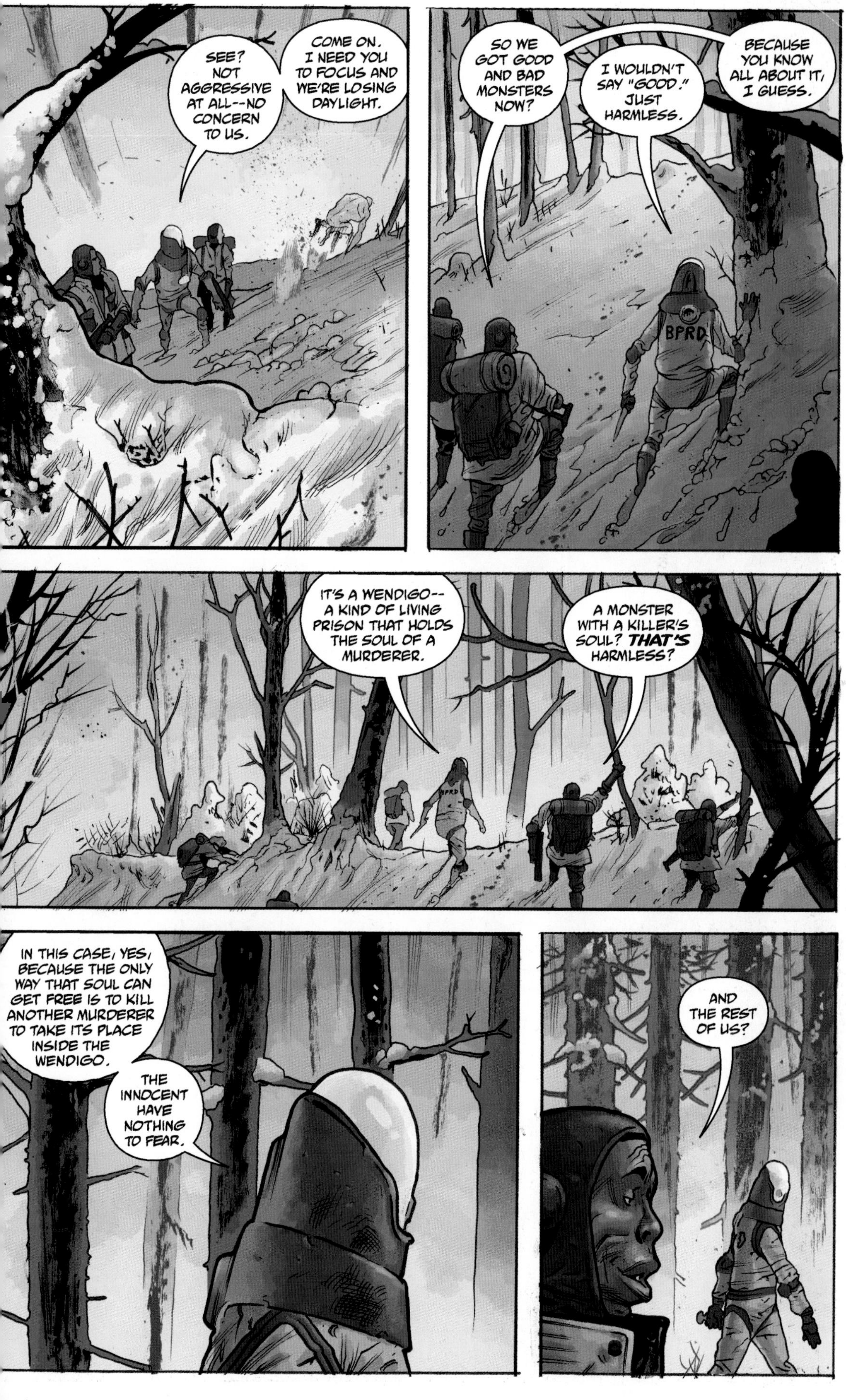
SEE? NOT AGGRESSIVE AT ALL--NO CONCERN TO US.
COME ON. I NEED YOU TO FOCUS AND WE'RE LOSING DAYLIGHT.
SO WE GOT GOOD AND BAD MONSTERS NOW?
I WOULDN'T SAY "GOOD." JUST HARMLESS.
BECAUSE YOU KNOW ALL ABOUT IT, I GUESS.
BPRD
IT'S A WENDIGO-- A KIND OF LIVING PRISON THAT HOLDS THE SOUL OF A MURDERER.
A MONSTER WITH A KILLER'S SOUL? ***THAT'S*** HARMLESS?
BPRD
IN THIS CASE, YES, BECAUSE THE ONLY WAY THAT SOUL CAN GET FREE IS TO KILL ANOTHER MURDERER TO TAKE ITS PLACE INSIDE THE WENDIGO.
THE INNOCENT HAVE NOTHING TO FEAR.
AND THE REST OF US?

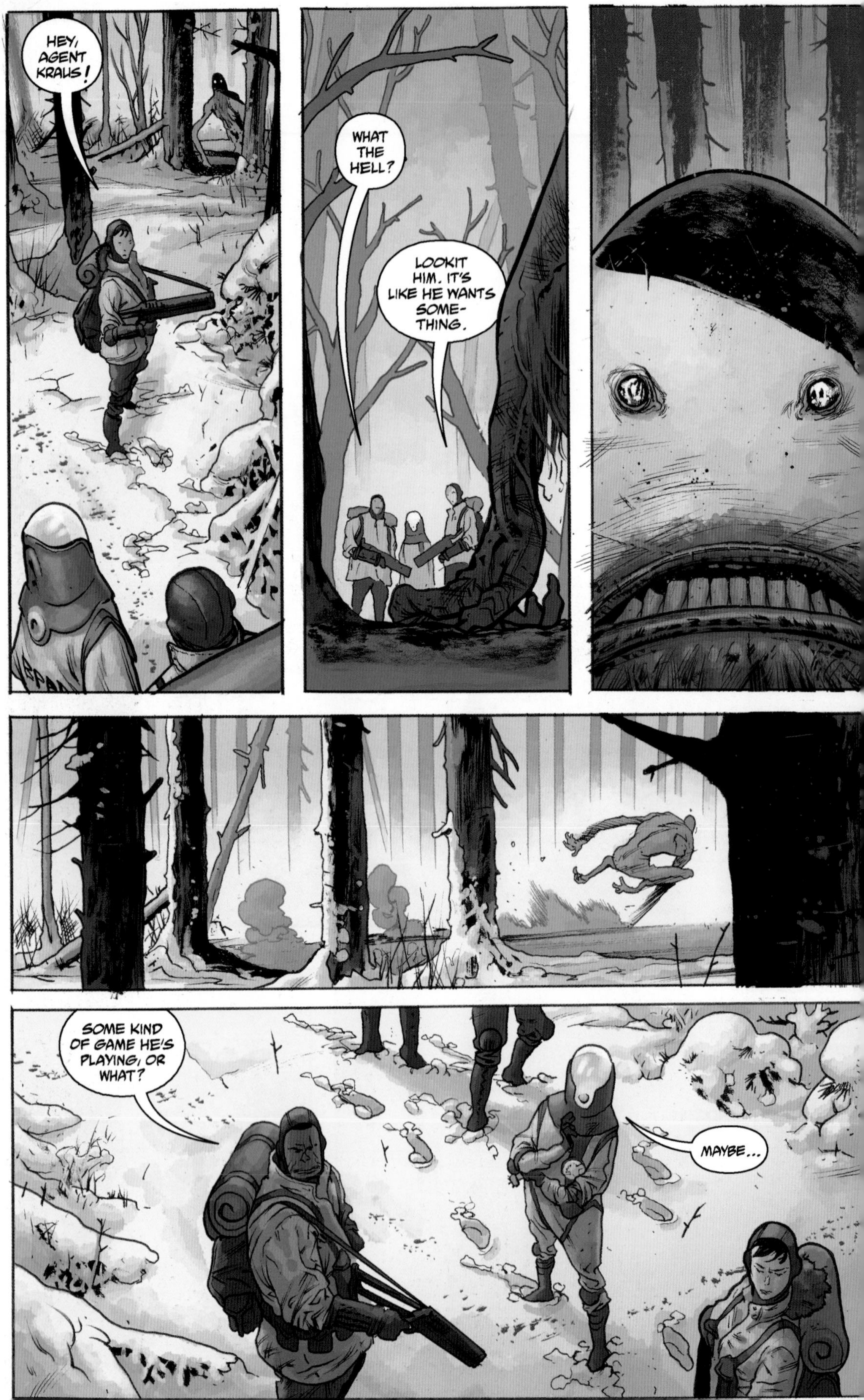
HEY, AGENT KRAUS!
WHAT THE HELL?
LOOKIT HIM. IT'S LIKE HE WANTS SOME-THING.
SOME KIND OF GAME HE'S PLAYING, OR WHAT?
MAYBE...

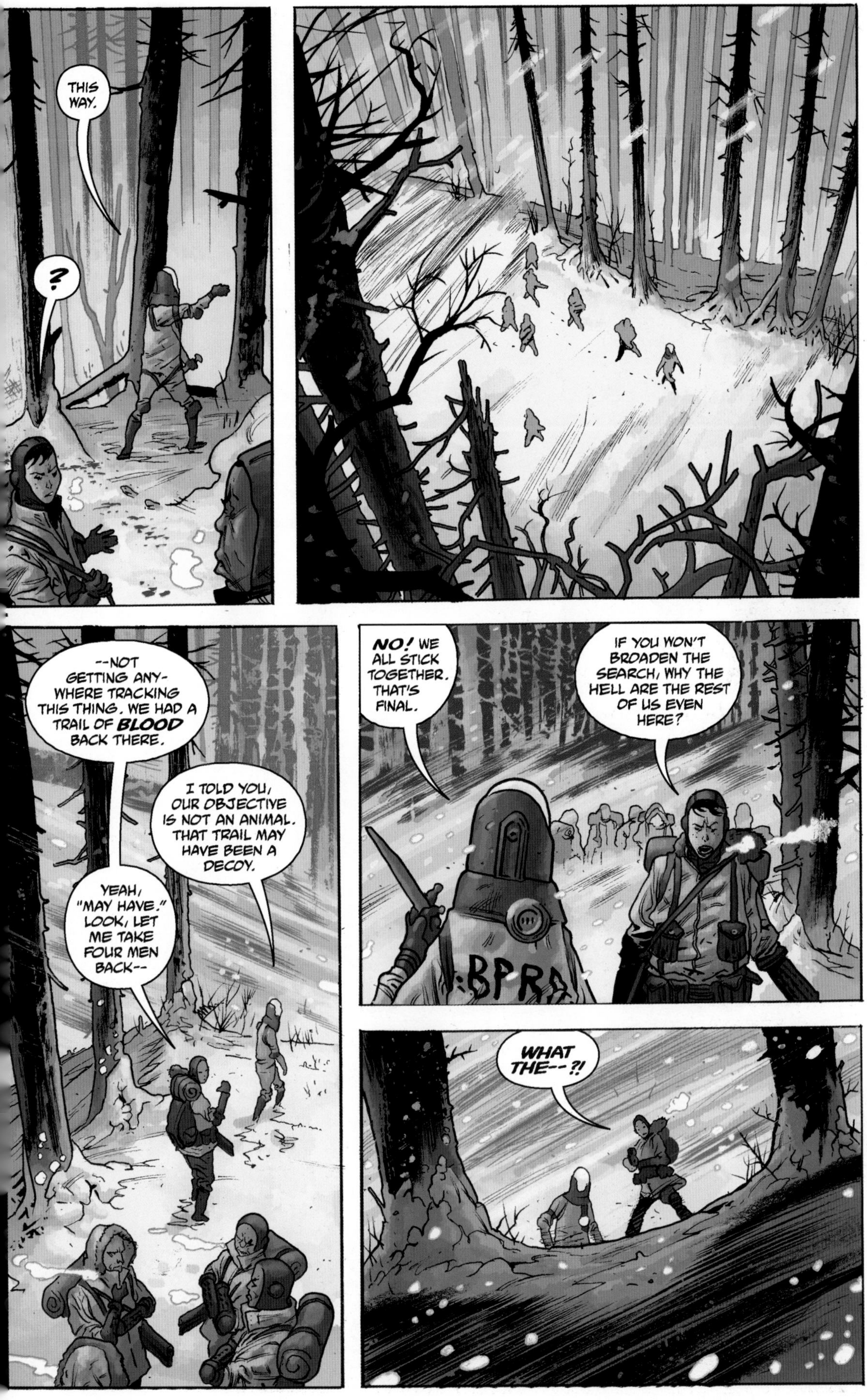
THIS WAY.
?
--NOT GETTING ANYWHERE TRACKING THIS THING. WE HAD A TRAIL OF BLOOD BACK THERE.
I TOLD YOU, OUR OBJECTIVE IS NOT AN ANIMAL. THAT TRAIL MAY HAVE BEEN A DECOY.
YEAH, "MAY HAVE." LOOK, LET ME TAKE FOUR MEN BACK--
NO! WE ALL STICK TOGETHER. THAT'S FINAL.
IF YOU WON'T BROADEN THE SEARCH, WHY THE HELL ARE THE REST OF US EVEN HERE?
BPRD
WHAT THE--?!

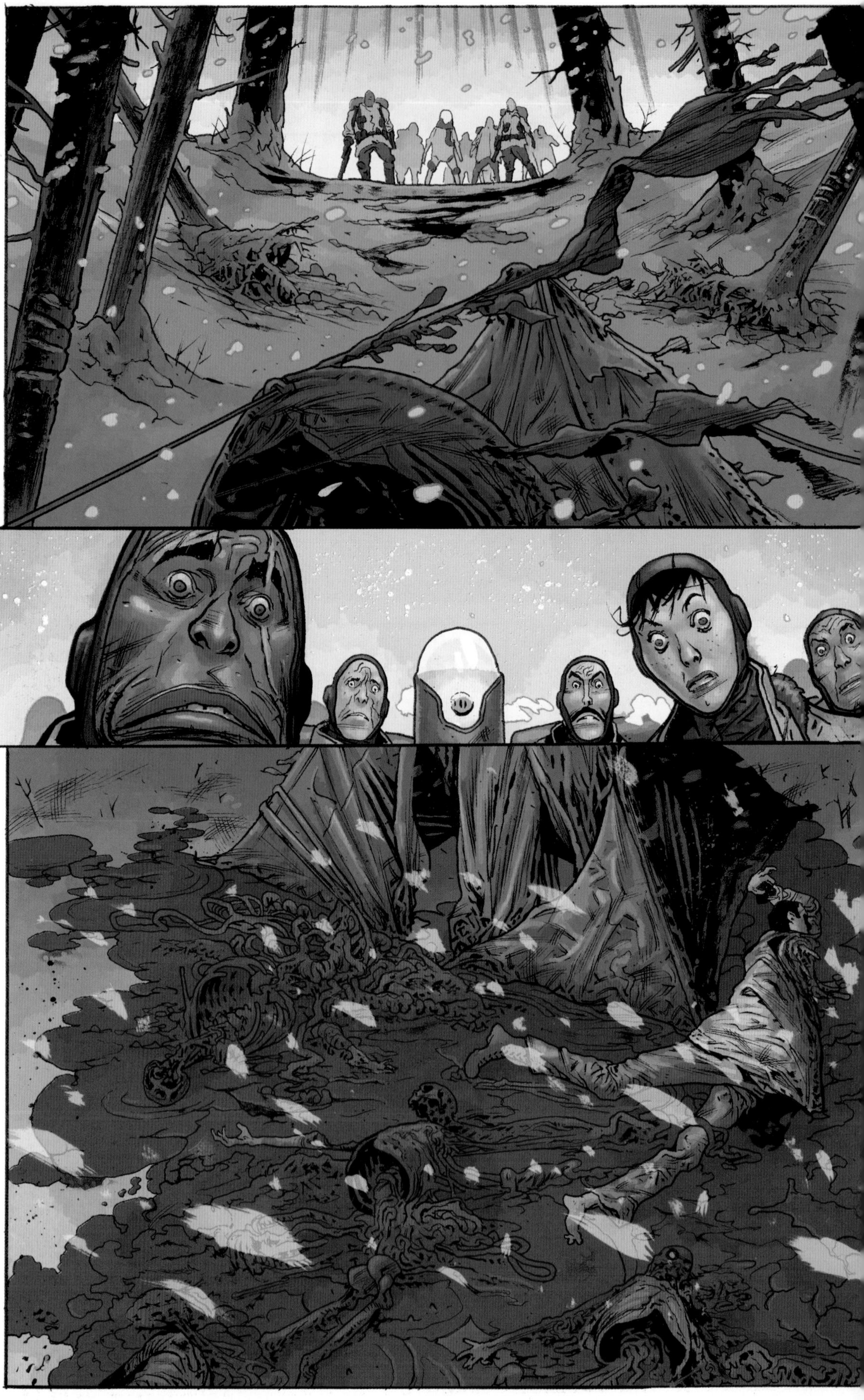

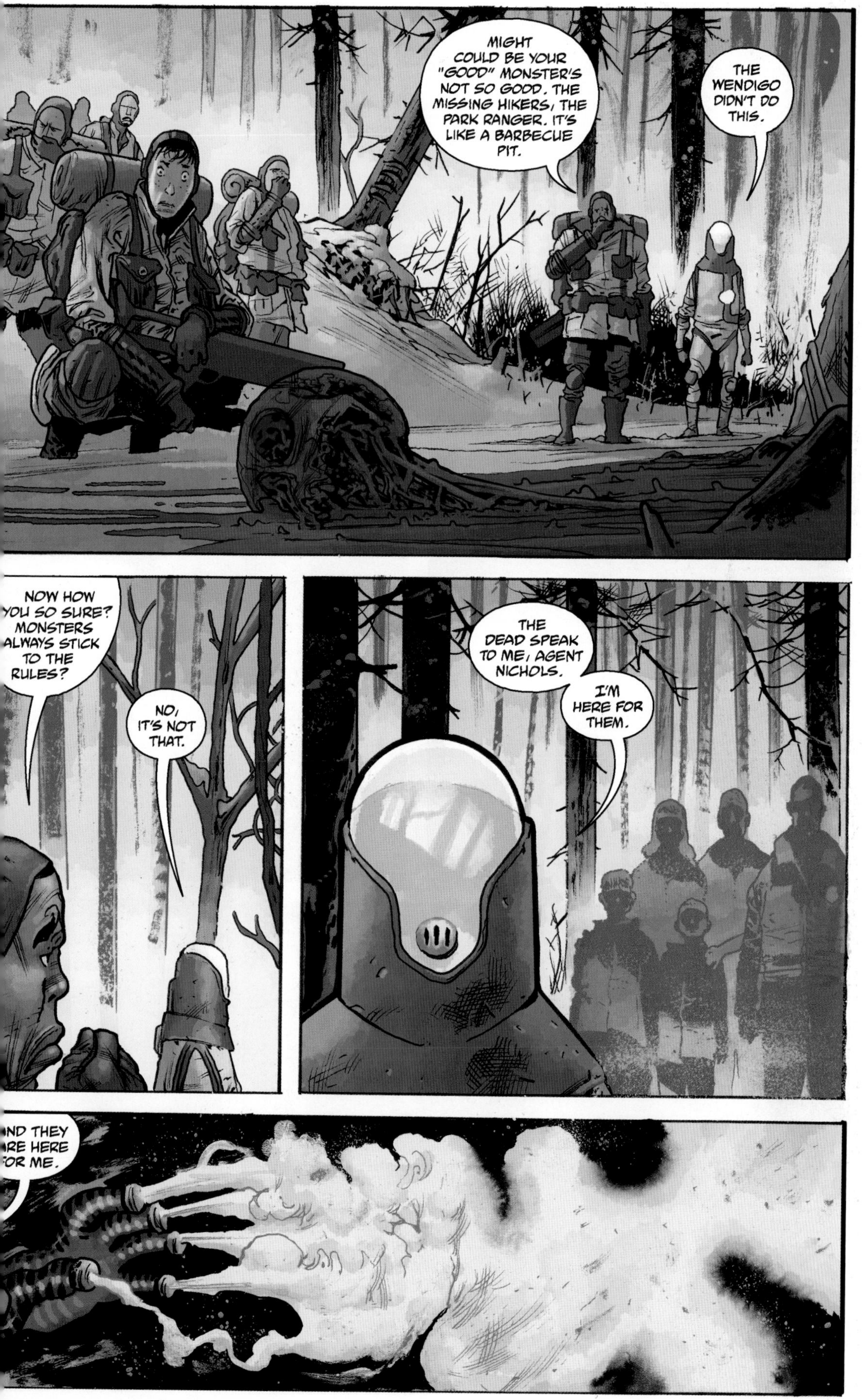
MIGHT COULD BE YOUR "GOOD" MONSTER'S NOT SO GOOD. THE MISSING HIKERS, THE PARK RANGER. IT'S LIKE A BARBECUE PIT.
THE WENDIGO DIDN'T DO THIS.
NOW HOW YOU SO SURE? MONSTERS ALWAYS STICK TO THE RULES?
NO, IT'S NOT THAT.
THE DEAD SPEAK TO ME, AGENT NICHOLS.
I'M HERE FOR THEM.
ND THEY RE HERE FOR ME.

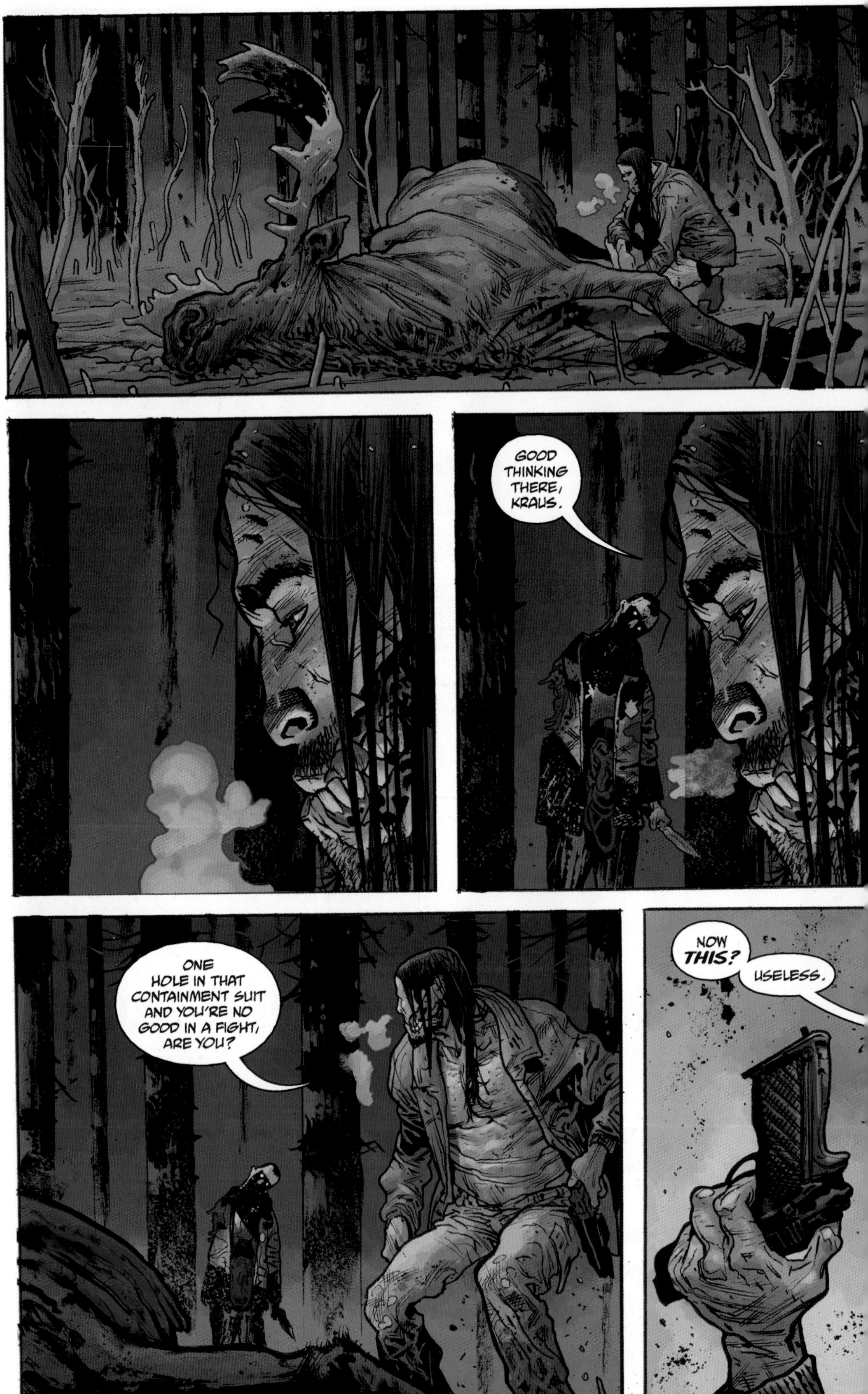

GOOD THINKING THERE, KRAUS.
ONE HOLE IN THAT CONTAINMENT SUIT AND YOU'RE NO GOOD IN A FIGHT, ARE YOU?
NOW THIS?
USELESS.

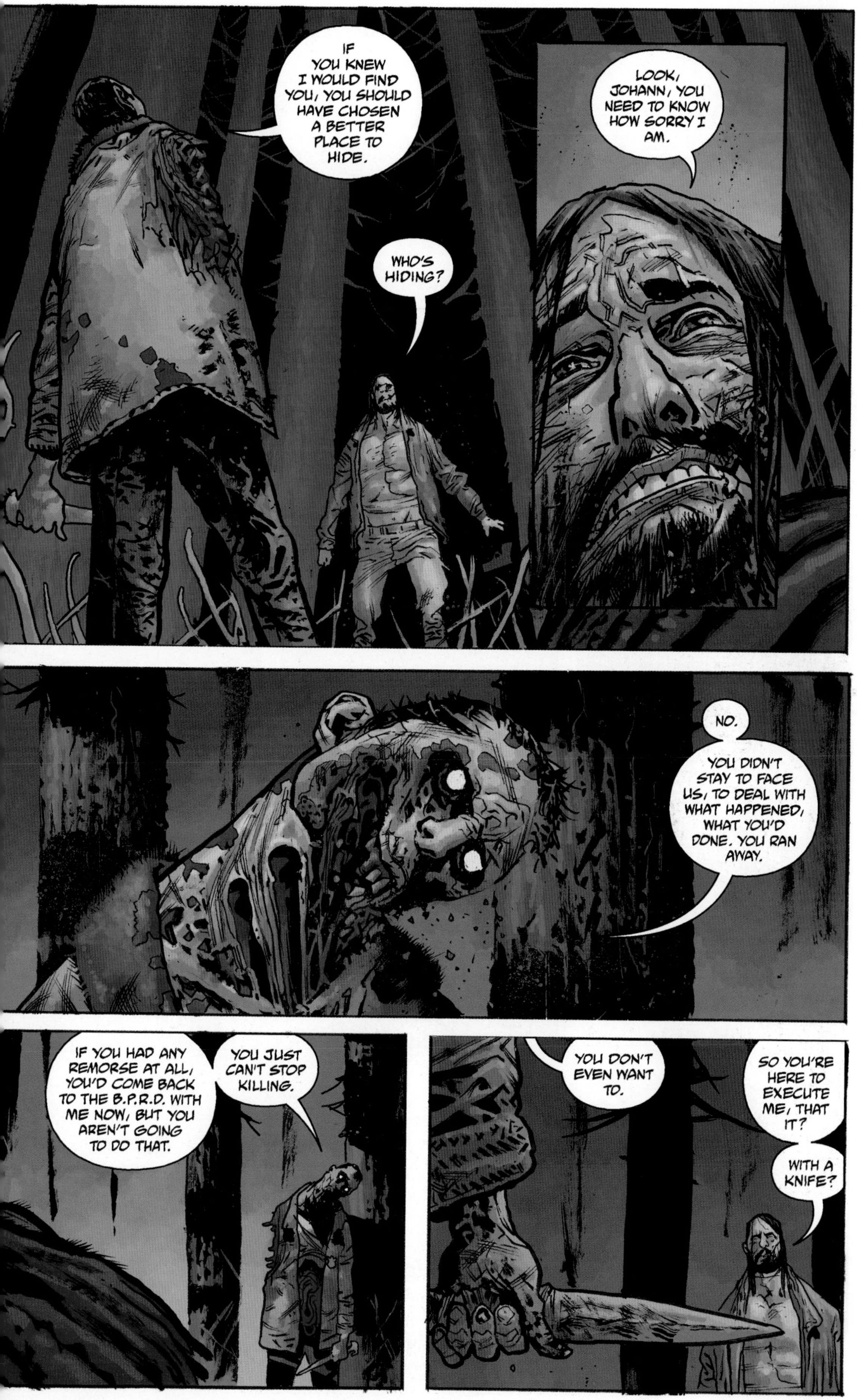
IF YOU KNEW I WOULD FIND YOU, YOU SHOULD HAVE CHOSEN A BETTER PLACE TO HIDE.
WHO'S HIDING?
LOOK, JOHANN, YOU NEED TO KNOW HOW SORRY I AM.
NO.
YOU DIDN'T STAY TO FACE US, TO DEAL WITH WHAT HAPPENED, WHAT YOU'D DONE. YOU RAN AWAY.
IF YOU HAD ANY REMORSE AT ALL, YOU'D COME BACK TO THE B.P.R.D. WITH ME NOW, BUT YOU AREN'T GOING TO DO THAT.
YOU JUST CAN'T STOP KILLING.
YOU DON'T EVEN WANT TO.
SO YOU'RE HERE TO EXECUTE ME, THAT IT?
WITH A KNIFE?

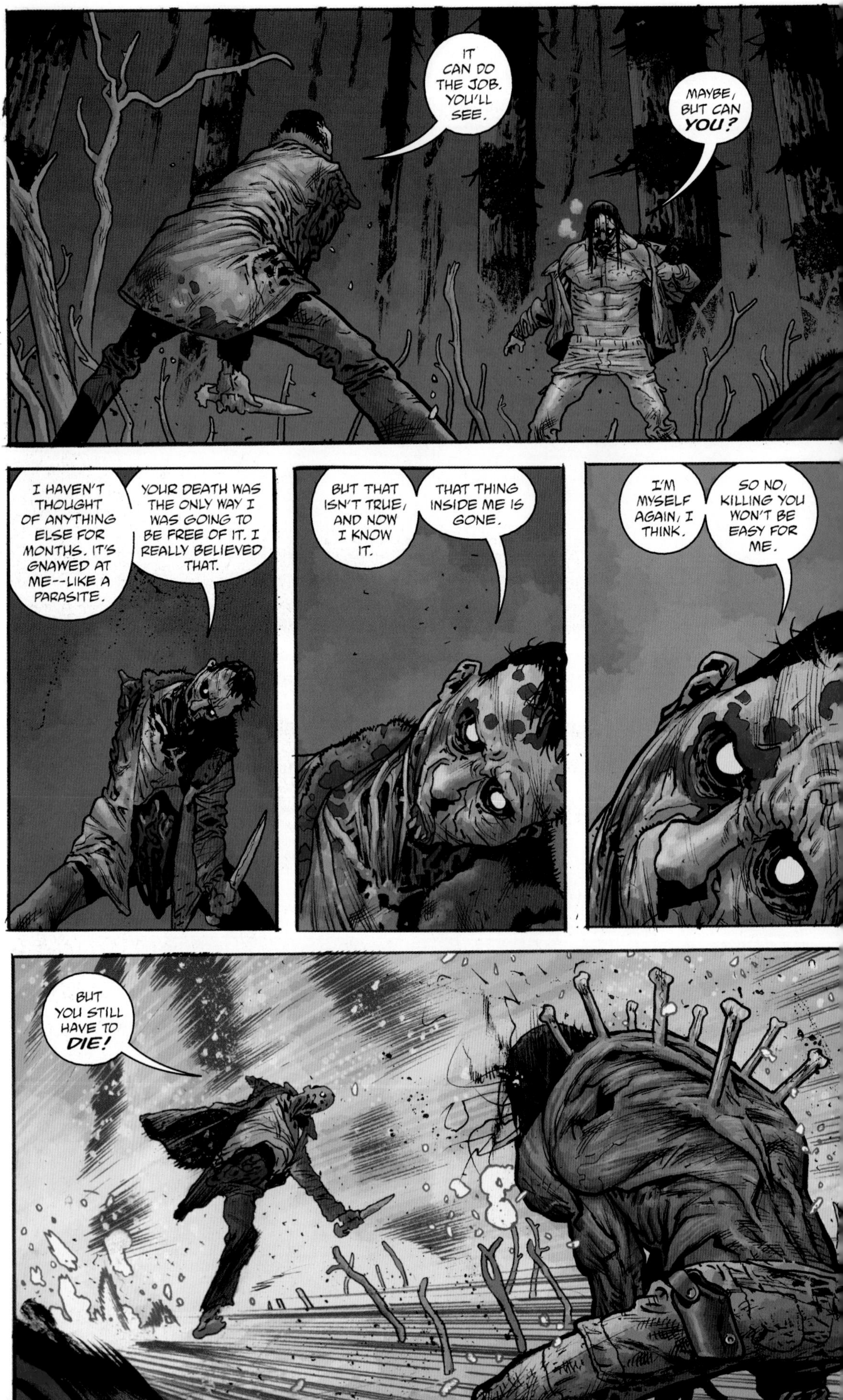

IT CAN DO THE JOB. YOU'LL SEE.
MAYBE, BUT CAN **YOU?**
I HAVEN'T THOUGHT OF ANYTHING ELSE FOR MONTHS. IT'S GNAWED AT ME--LIKE A PARASITE.
YOUR DEATH WAS THE ONLY WAY I WAS GOING TO BE FREE OF IT. I REALLY BELIEVED THAT.
BUT THAT ISN'T TRUE, AND NOW I KNOW IT.
THAT THING INSIDE ME IS GONE.
I'M MYSELF AGAIN, I THINK.
SO NO, KILLING YOU WON'T BE EASY FOR ME.
BUT YOU STILL HAVE TO **DIE!**

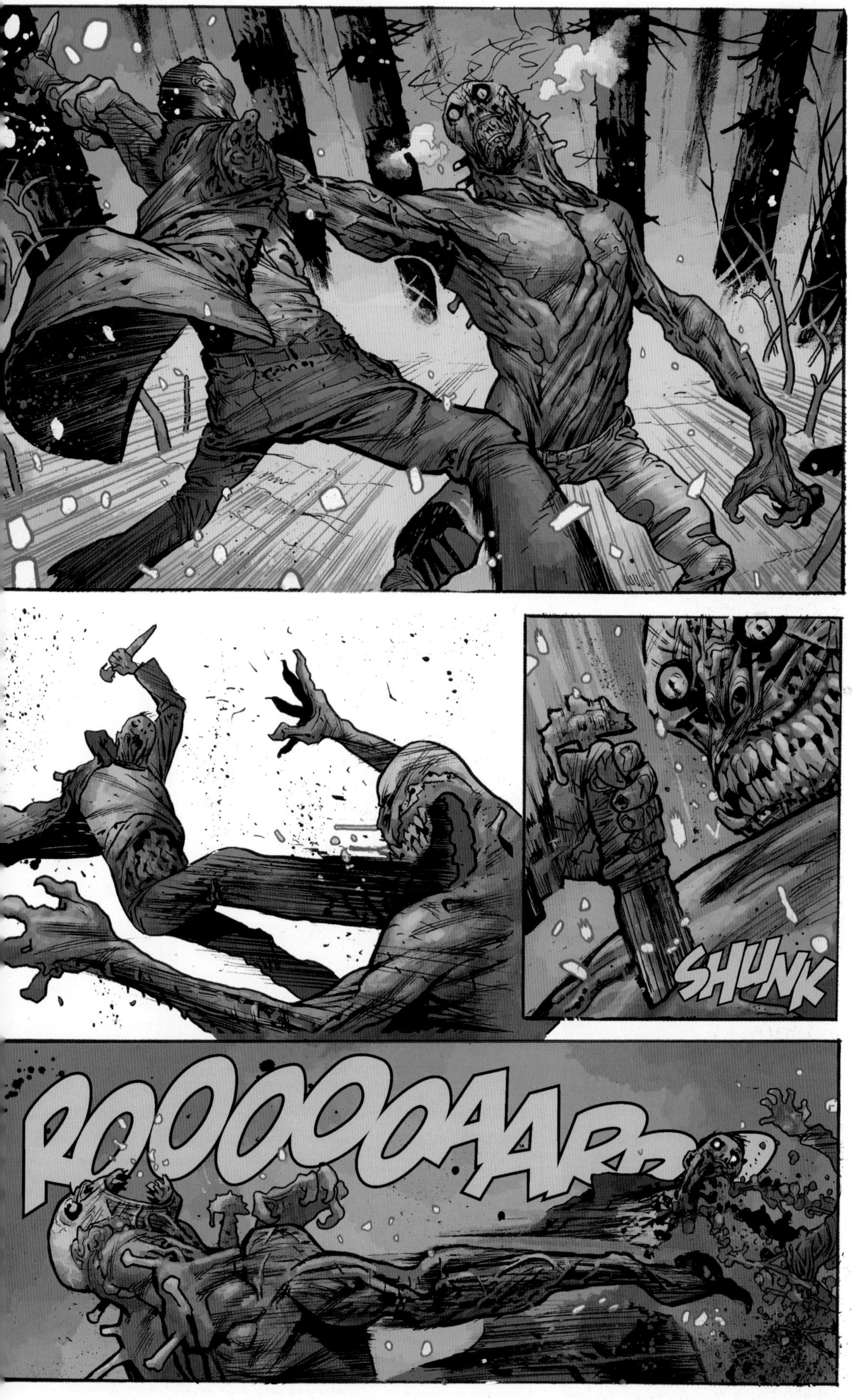
SHUNK
ROOOOOAAR

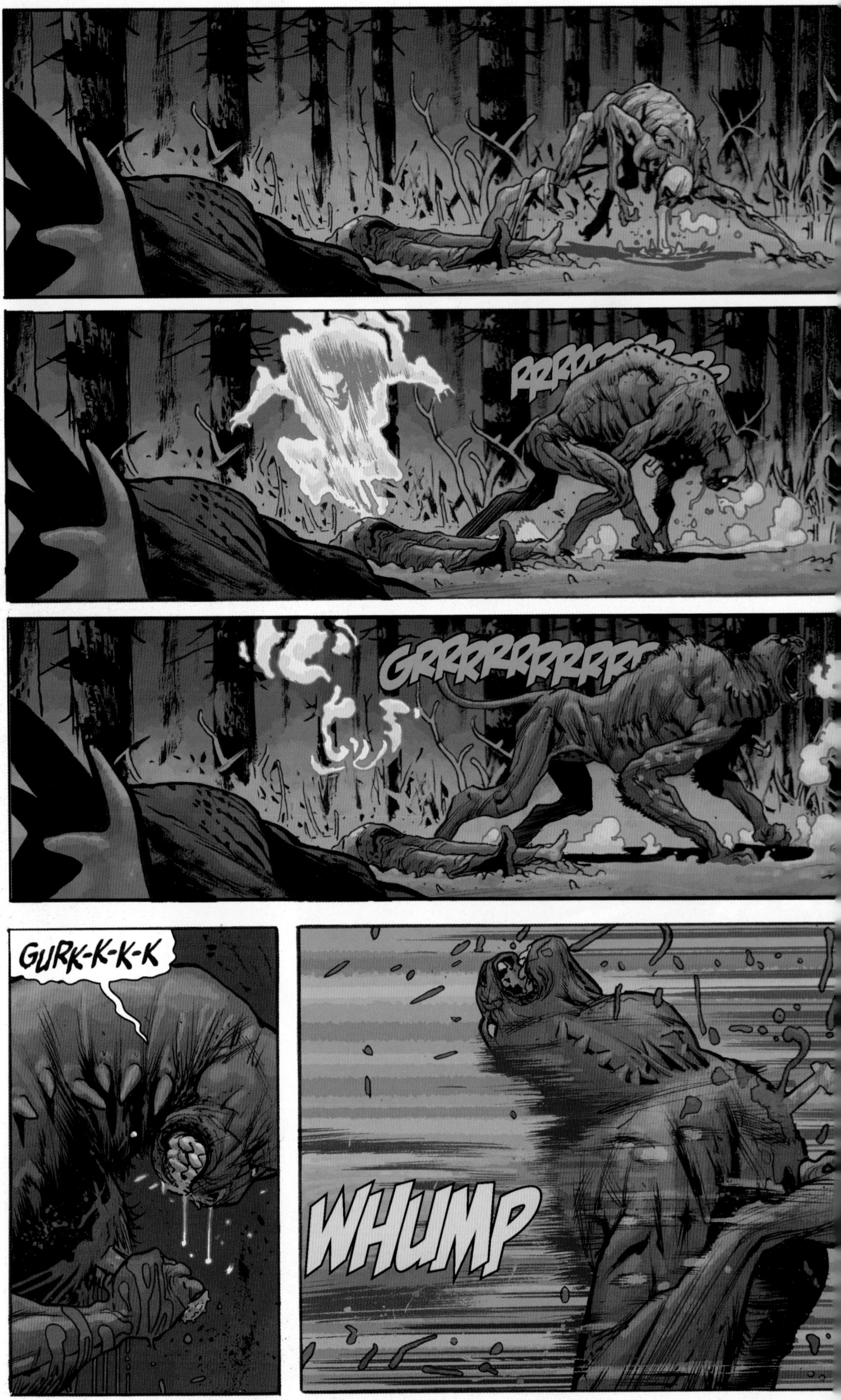

RRRRRRRRRRR
GRRRRRRRRRR
GURK-K-K-K
WHUMP

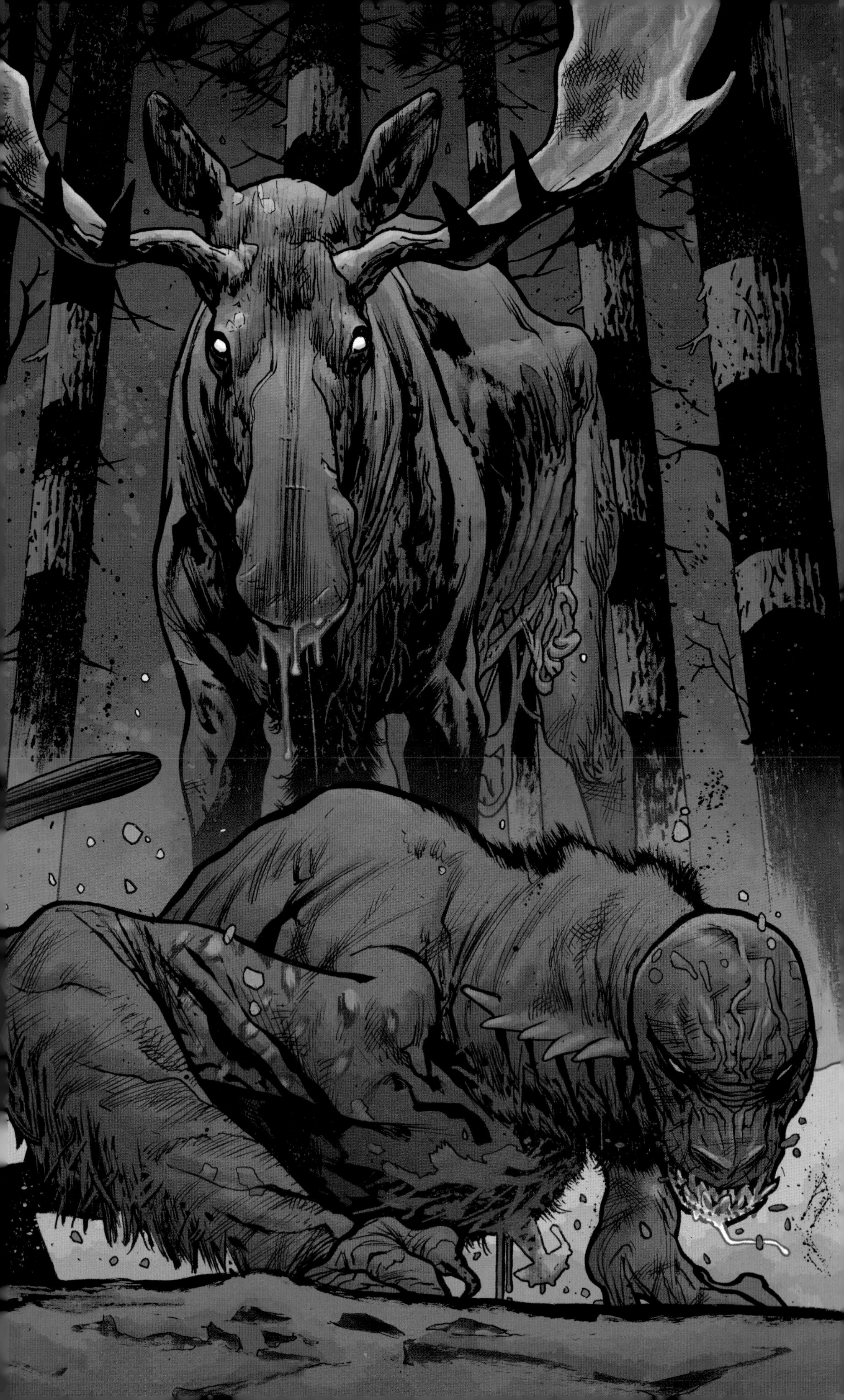

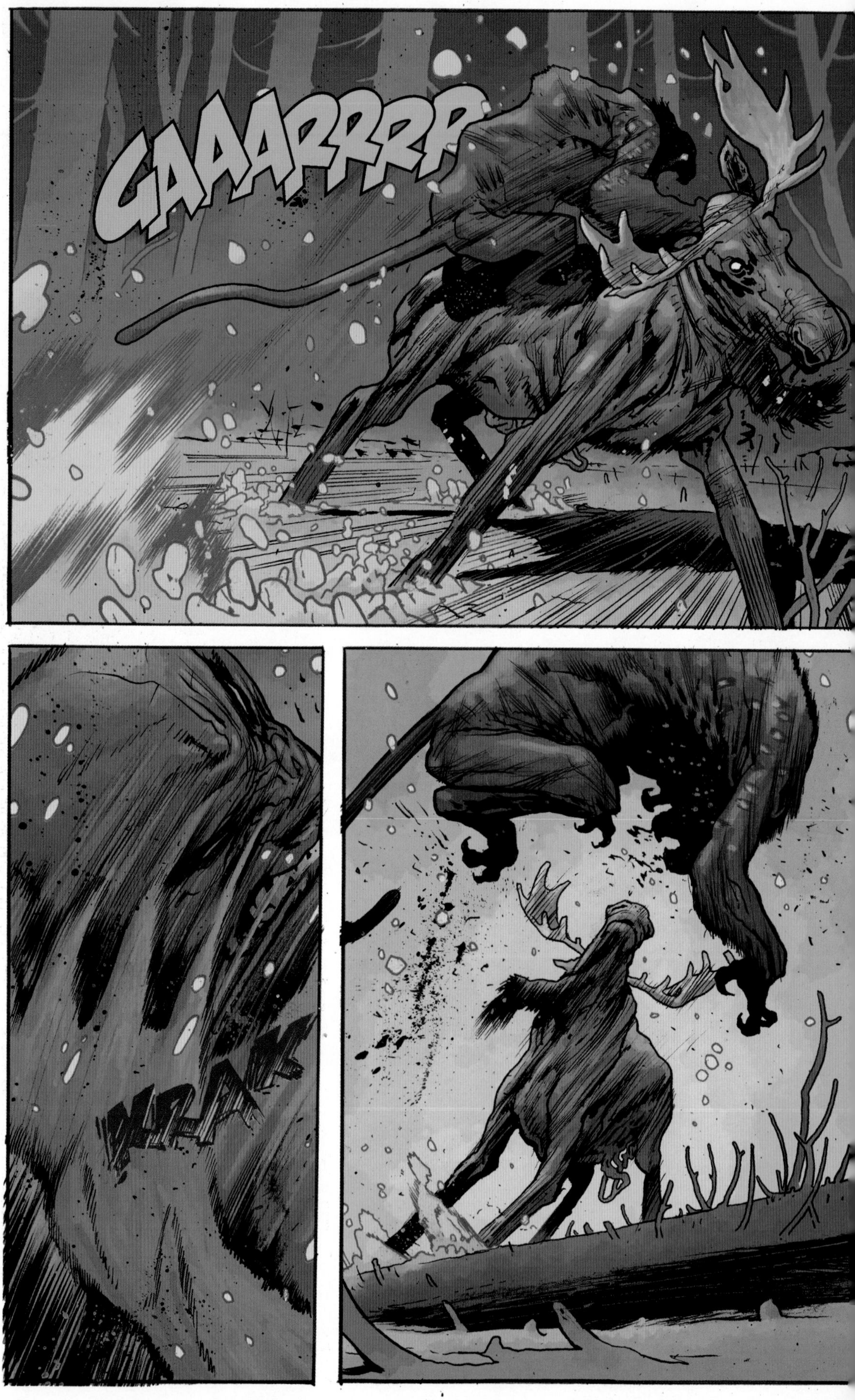
GAAARRRR

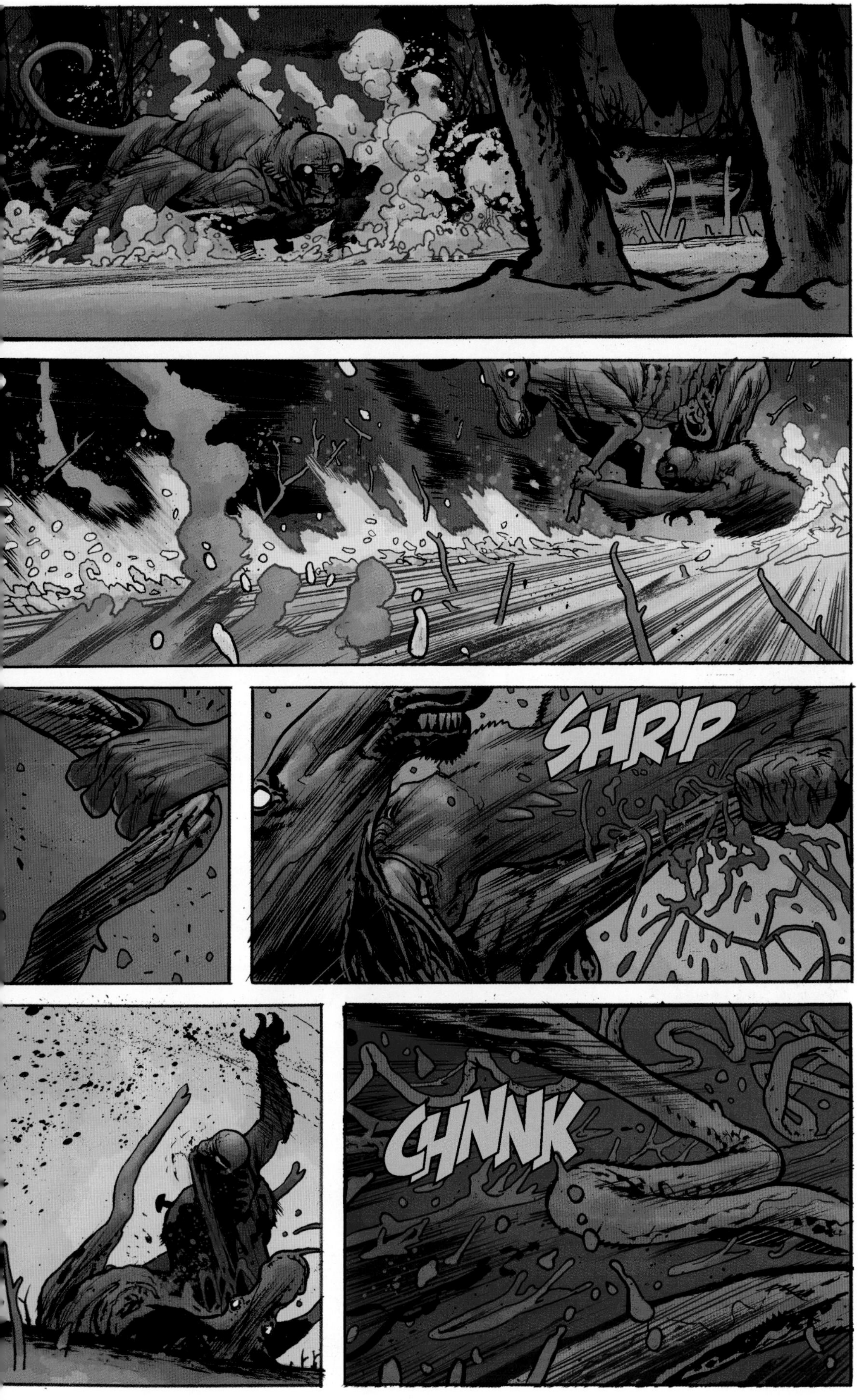
SHRIP
CHNNK

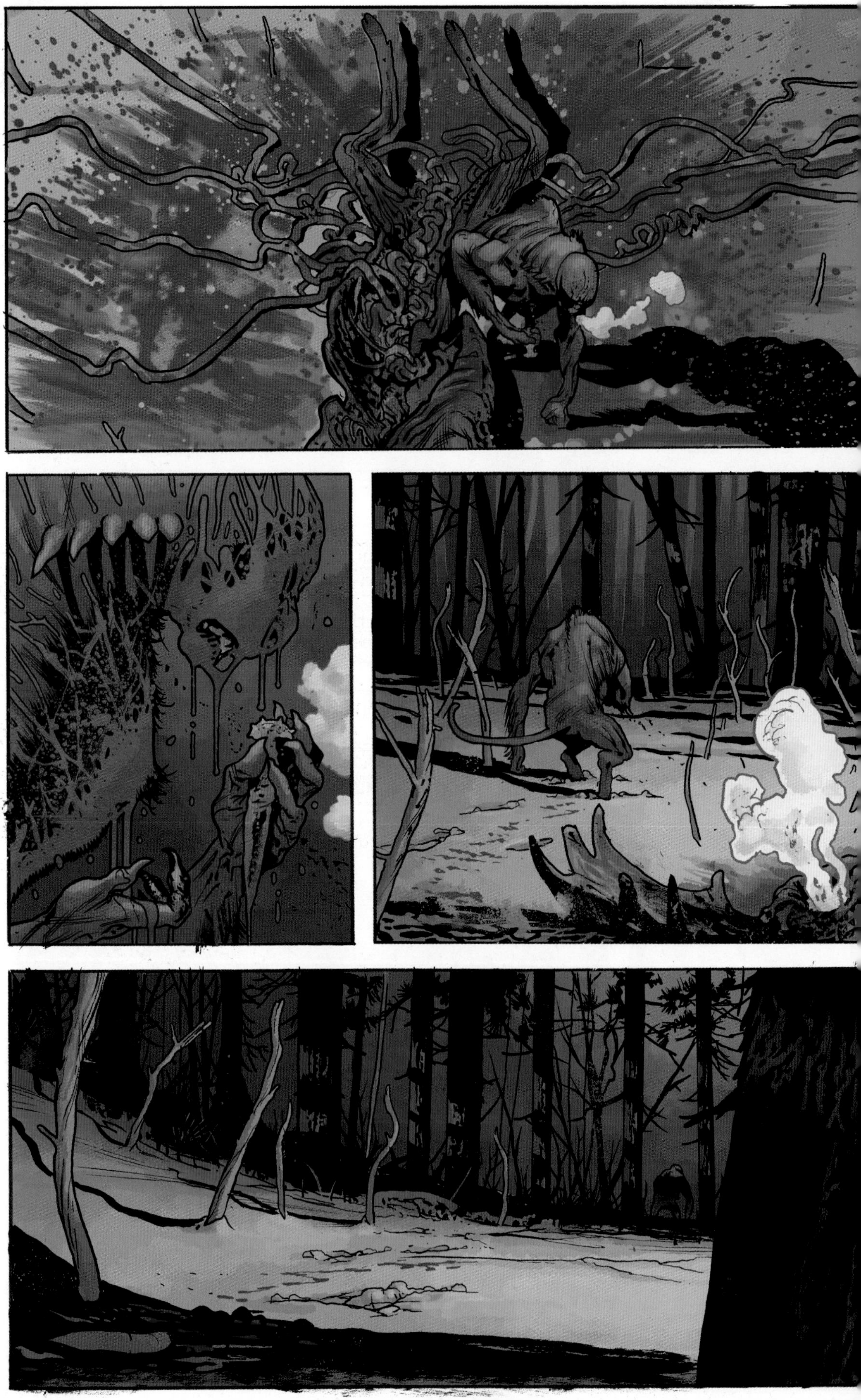

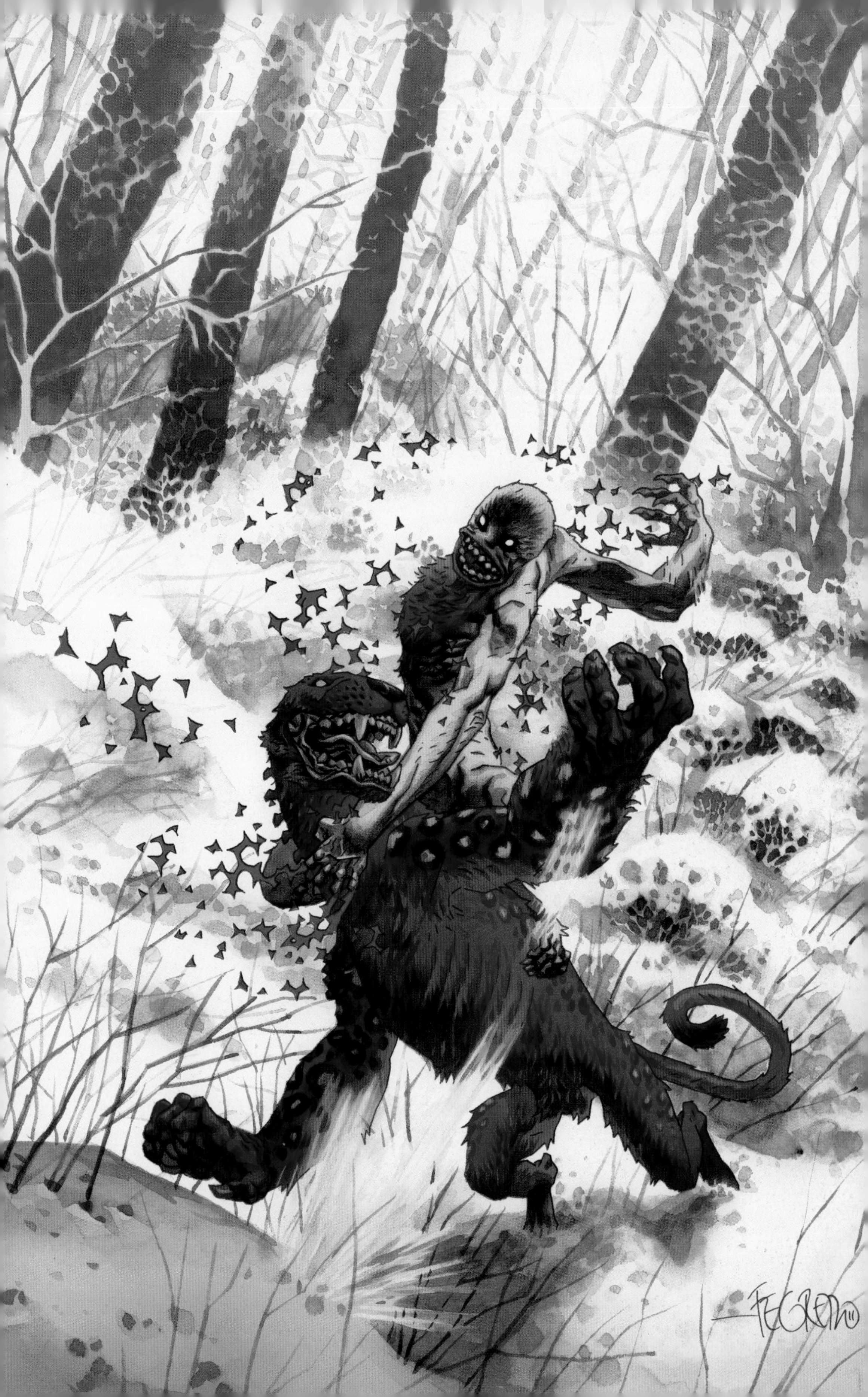

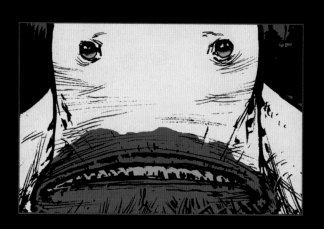

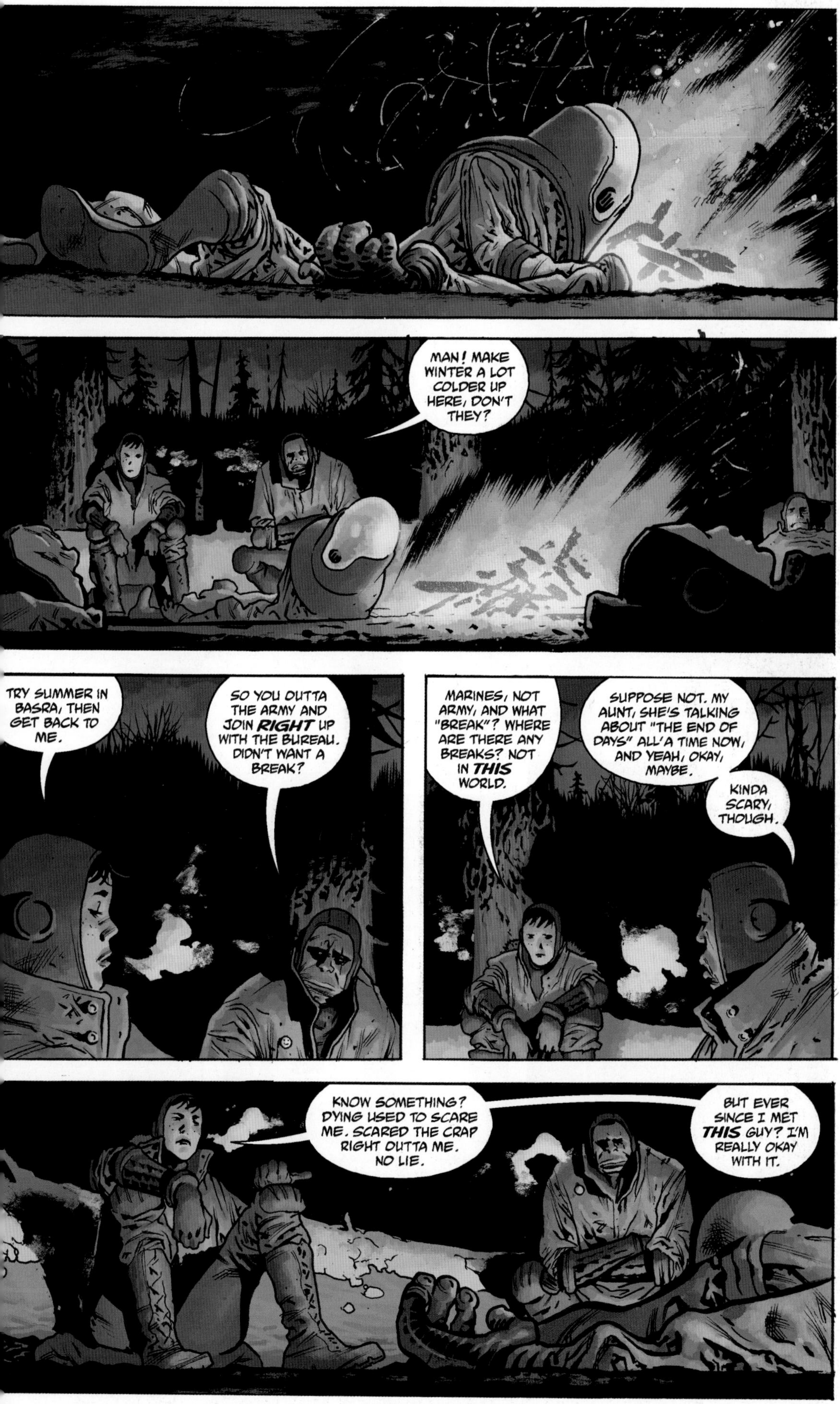
MAN! MAKE WINTER A LOT COLDER UP HERE, DON'T THEY?
TRY SUMMER IN BASRA, THEN GET BACK TO ME.
SO YOU OUTTA THE ARMY AND JOIN RIGHT UP WITH THE BUREAU. DIDN'T WANT A BREAK?
MARINES, NOT ARMY, AND WHAT "BREAK"? WHERE ARE THERE ANY BREAKS? NOT IN THIS WORLD.
SUPPOSE NOT. MY AUNT, SHE'S TALKING ABOUT "THE END OF DAYS" ALL'A TIME NOW, AND YEAH, OKAY, MAYBE.
KINDA SCARY, THOUGH.
KNOW SOMETHING? DYING USED TO SCARE ME. SCARED THE CRAP RIGHT OUTTA ME. NO LIE.
BUT EVER SINCE I MET THIS GUY? I'M REALLY OKAY WITH IT.

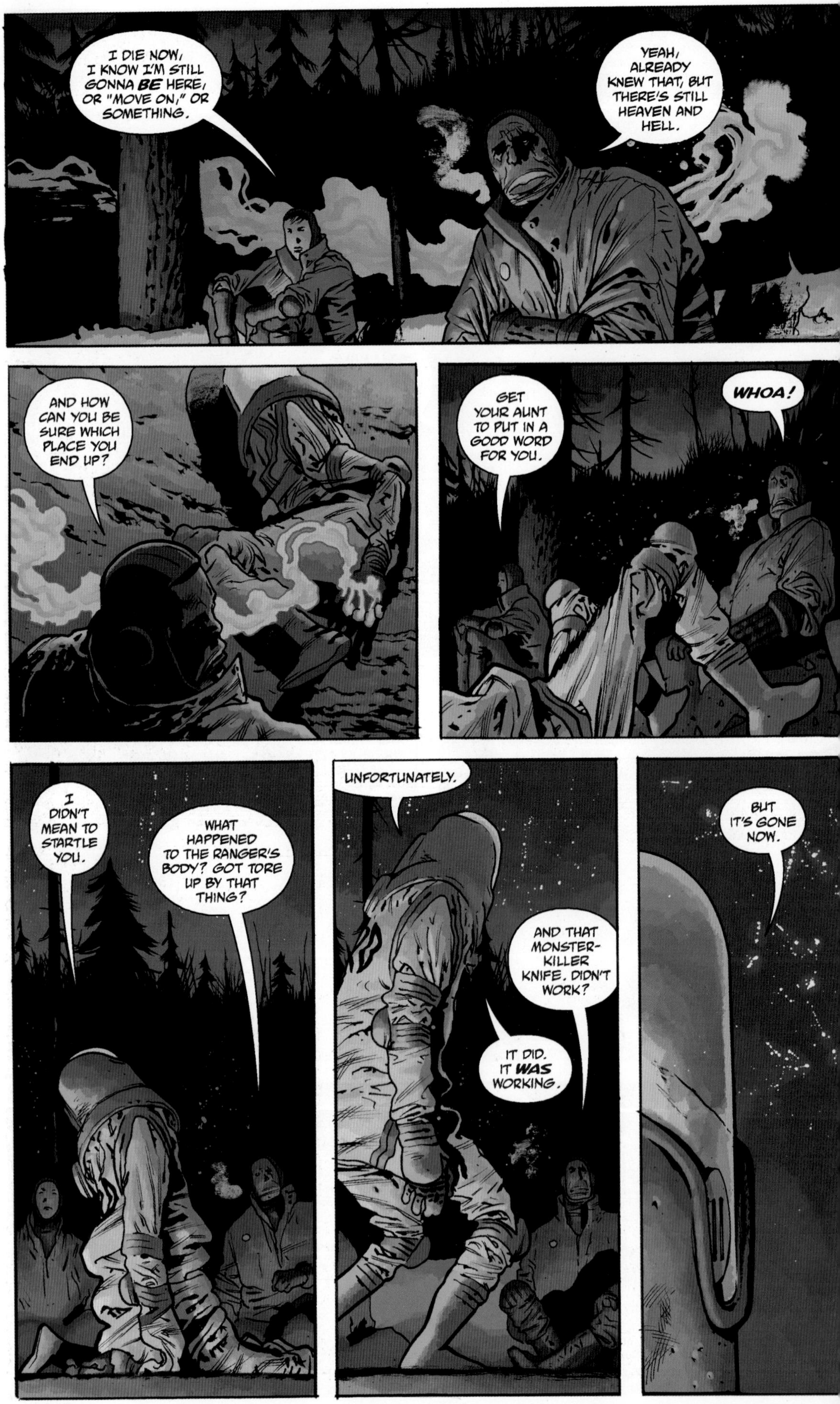
I DIE NOW, I KNOW I'M STILL GONNA **BE** HERE, OR "MOVE ON," OR SOMETHING.
YEAH, ALREADY KNEW THAT, BUT THERE'S STILL HEAVEN AND HELL.
AND HOW CAN YOU BE SURE WHICH PLACE YOU END UP?
GET YOUR AUNT TO PUT IN A GOOD WORD FOR YOU.
WHOA!
I DIDN'T MEAN TO STARTLE YOU.
WHAT HAPPENED TO THE RANGER'S BODY? GOT TORE UP BY THAT THING?
UNFORTUNATELY.
AND THAT MONSTER-KILLER KNIFE. DIDN'T WORK?
IT DID. IT **WAS** WORKING.
BUT IT'S GONE NOW.

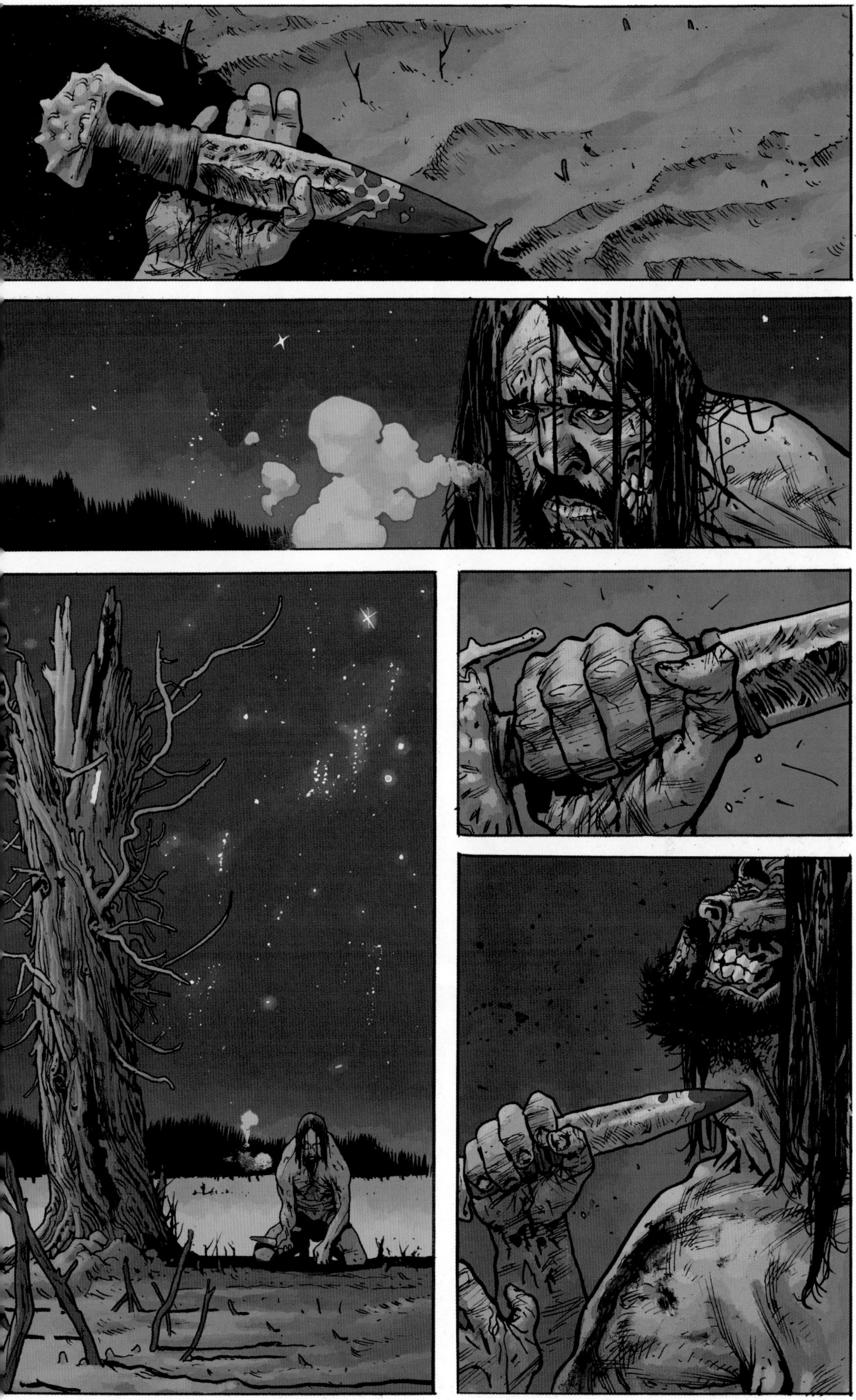

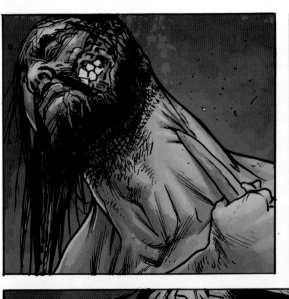

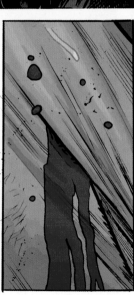

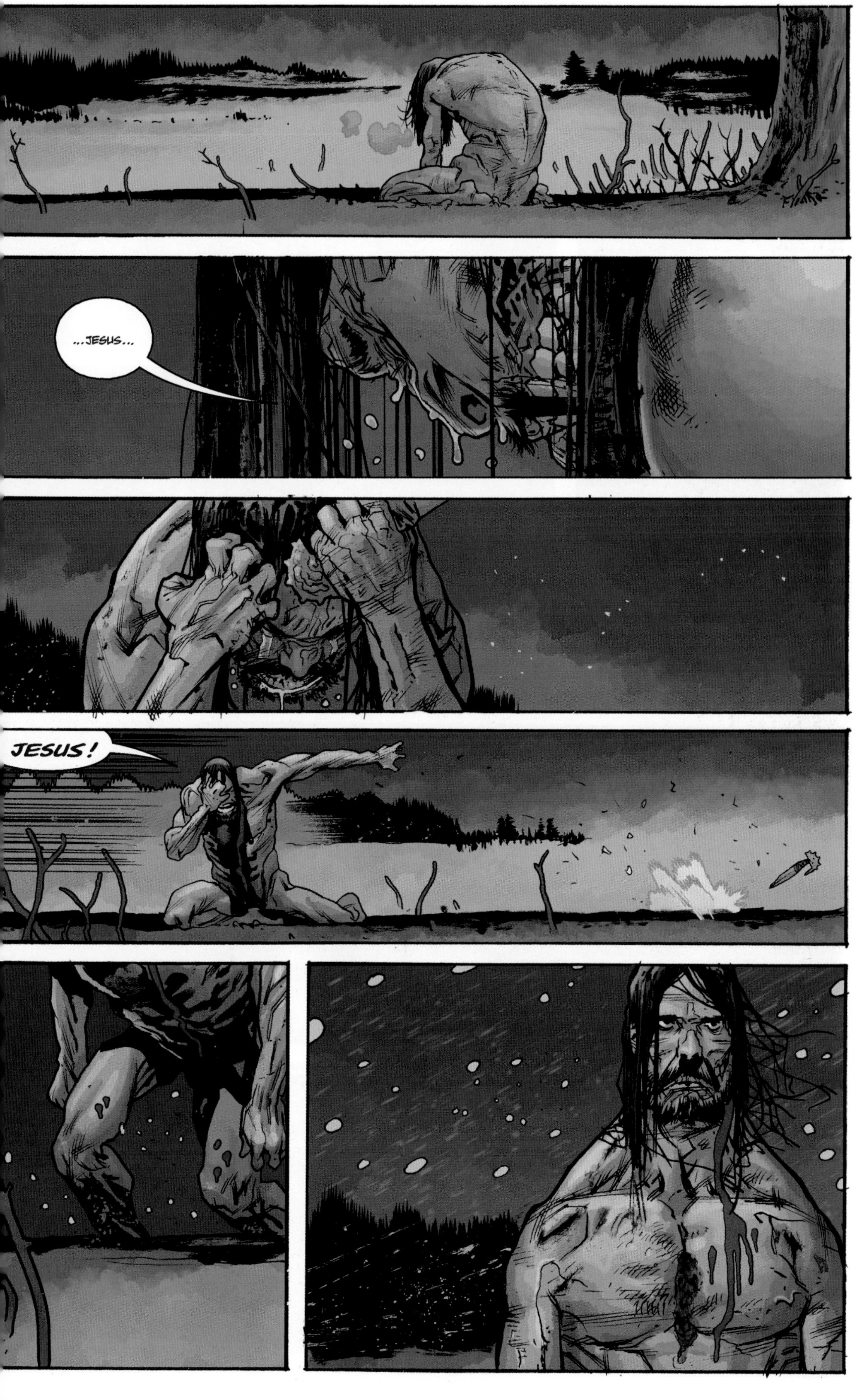
...JESUS...
JESUS!

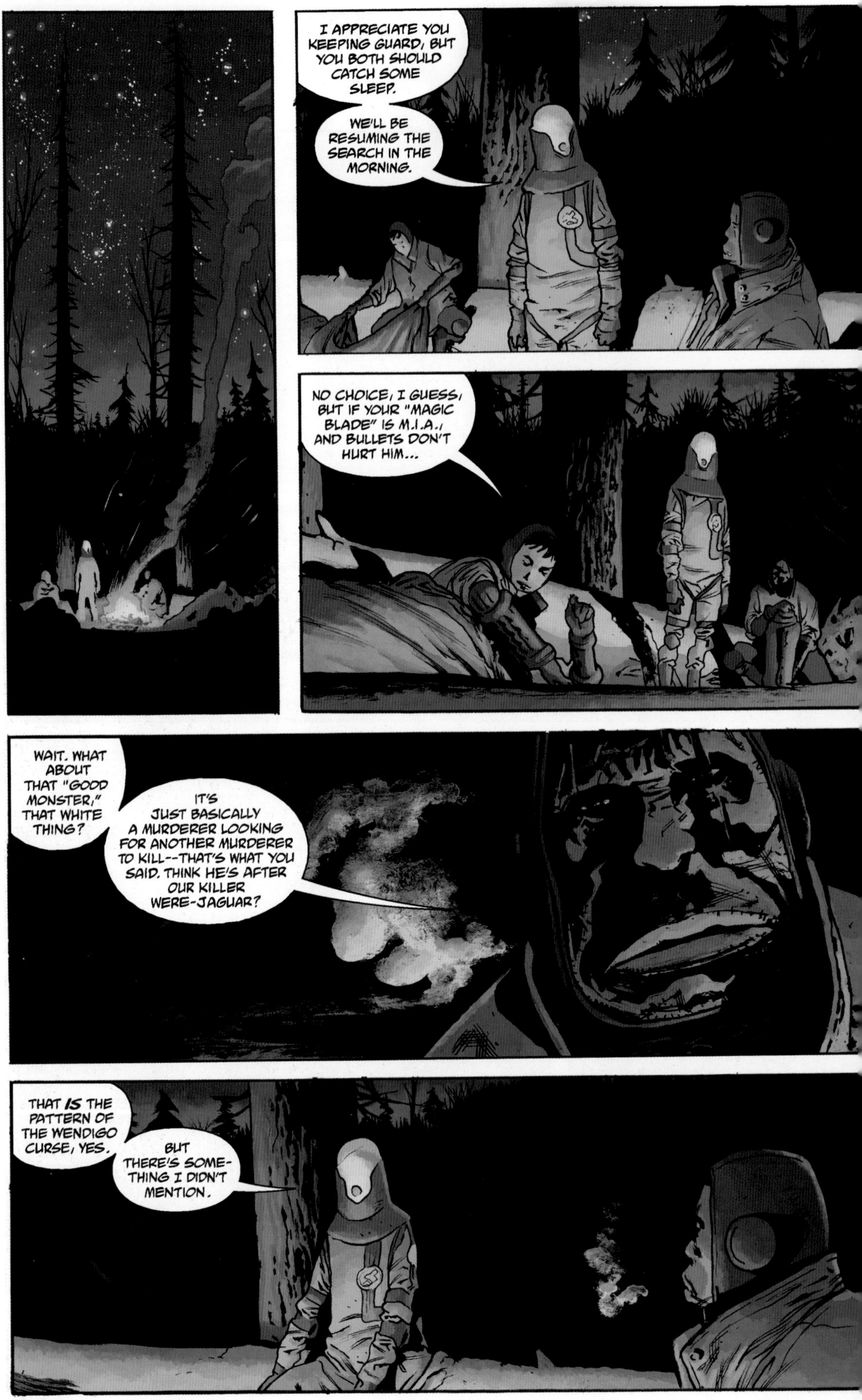
I APPRECIATE YOU KEEPING GUARD, BUT YOU BOTH SHOULD CATCH SOME SLEEP.
WE'LL BE RESUMING THE SEARCH IN THE MORNING.
NO CHOICE, I GUESS, BUT IF YOUR "MAGIC BLADE" IS M.I.A., AND BULLETS DON'T HURT HIM...
WAIT. WHAT ABOUT THAT "GOOD MONSTER," THAT WHITE THING?
IT'S JUST BASICALLY A MURDERER LOOKING FOR ANOTHER MURDERER TO KILL--THAT'S WHAT YOU SAID. THINK HE'S AFTER OUR KILLER WERE-JAGUAR?
THAT *IS* THE PATTERN OF THE WENDIGO CURSE, YES.
BUT THERE'S SOME-THING I DIDN'T MENTION.

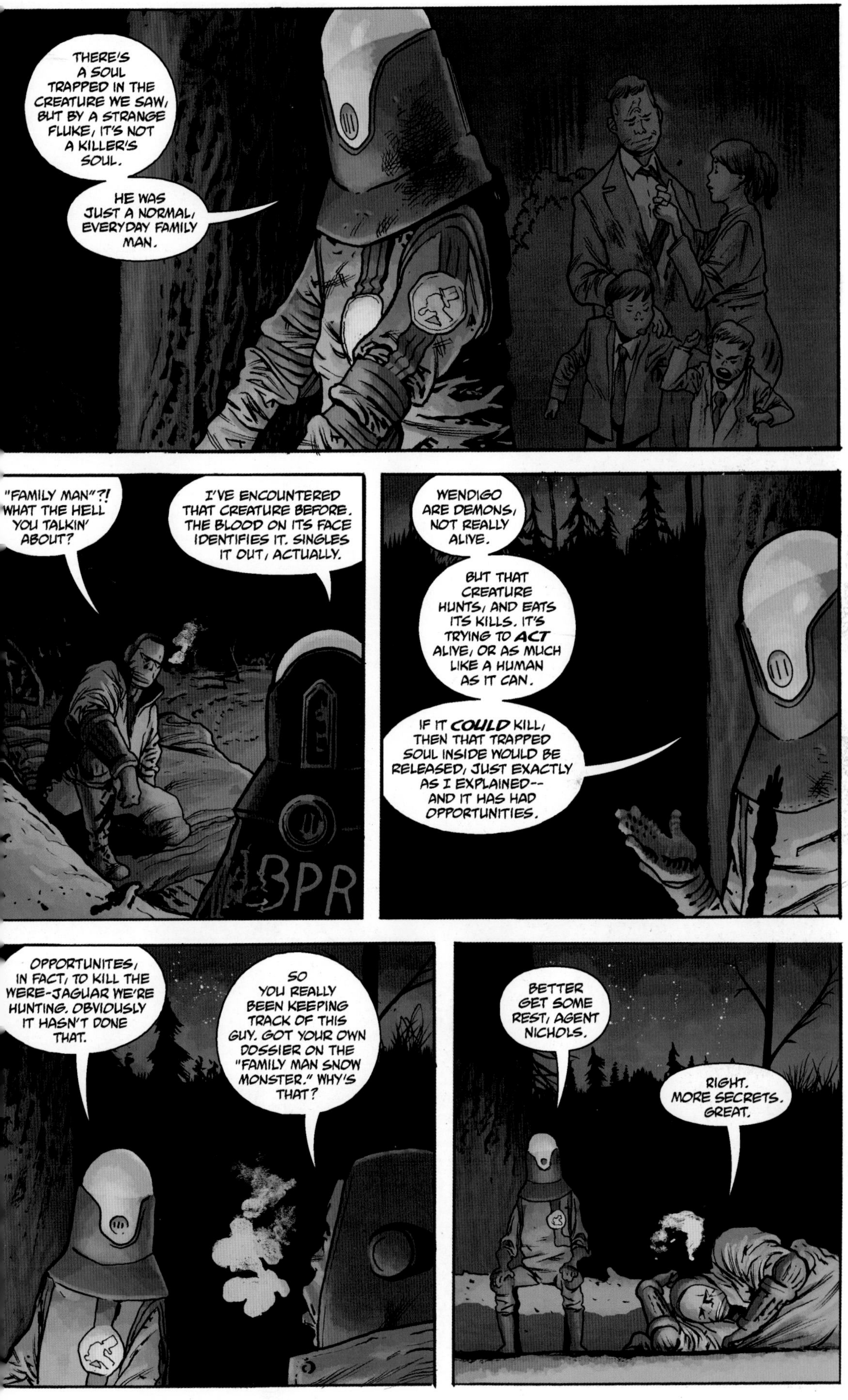
THERE'S A SOUL TRAPPED IN THE CREATURE WE SAW, BUT BY A STRANGE FLUKE, IT'S NOT A KILLER'S SOUL.
HE WAS JUST A NORMAL, EVERYDAY FAMILY MAN.
"FAMILY MAN"?! WHAT THE HELL YOU TALKIN' ABOUT?
I'VE ENCOUNTERED THAT CREATURE BEFORE. THE BLOOD ON ITS FACE IDENTIFIES IT. SINGLES IT OUT, ACTUALLY.
BPR
WENDIGO ARE DEMONS, NOT REALLY ALIVE.
BUT THAT CREATURE HUNTS, AND EATS ITS KILLS. IT'S TRYING TO ACT ALIVE, OR AS MUCH LIKE A HUMAN AS IT CAN.
IF IT COULD KILL, THEN THAT TRAPPED SOUL INSIDE WOULD BE RELEASED, JUST EXACTLY AS I EXPLAINED-- AND IT HAS HAD OPPORTUNITIES.
OPPORTUNITES, IN FACT, TO KILL THE WERE-JAGUAR WE'RE HUNTING. OBVIOUSLY IT HASN'T DONE THAT.
SO YOU REALLY BEEN KEEPING TRACK OF THIS GUY. GOT YOUR OWN DOSSIER ON THE "FAMILY MAN SNOW MONSTER." WHY'S THAT?
BETTER GET SOME REST, AGENT NICHOLS.
RIGHT. MORE SECRETS. GREAT.

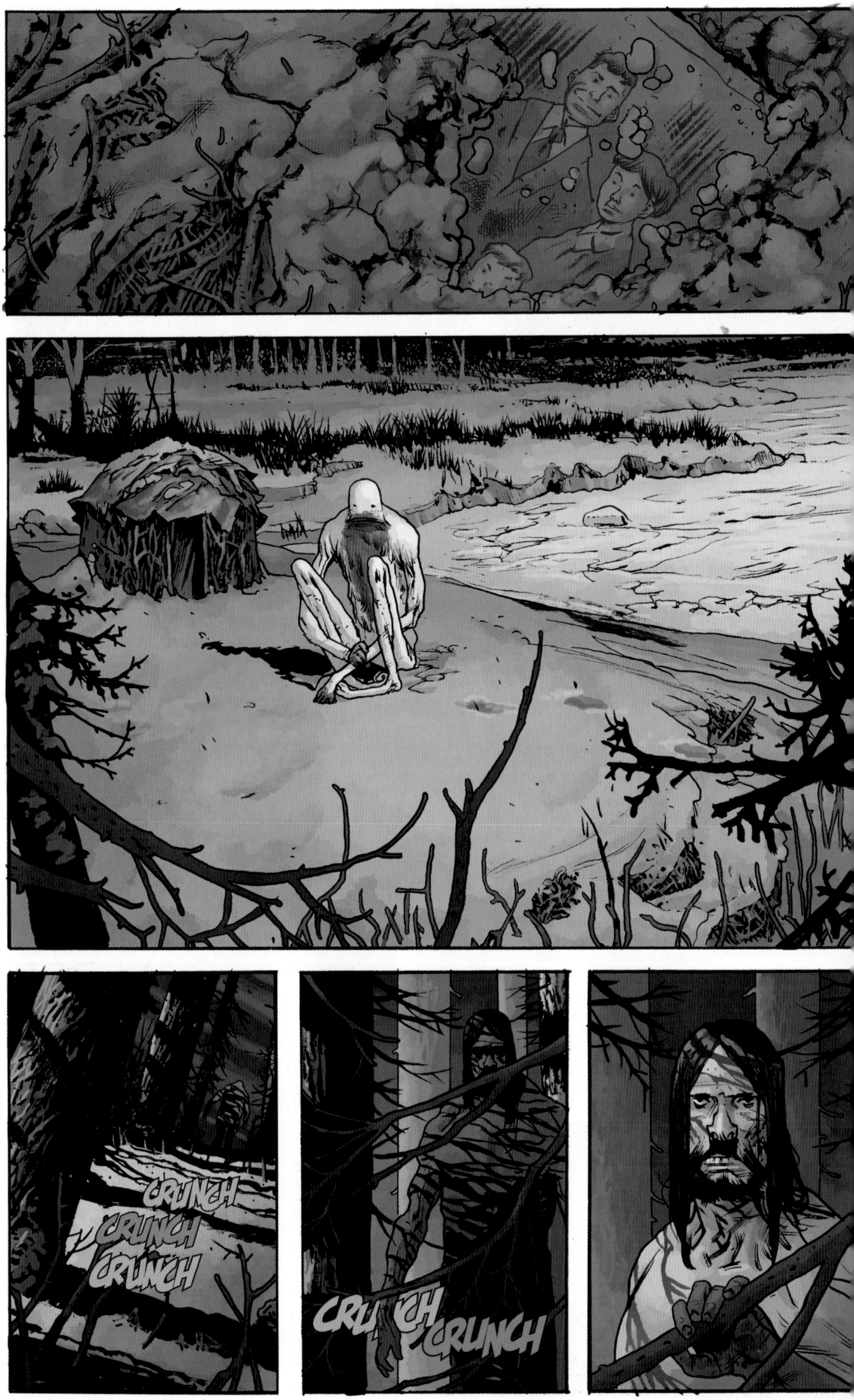
CRUNCH
CRUNCH
CRUNCH
CRUNCH
CRUNCH

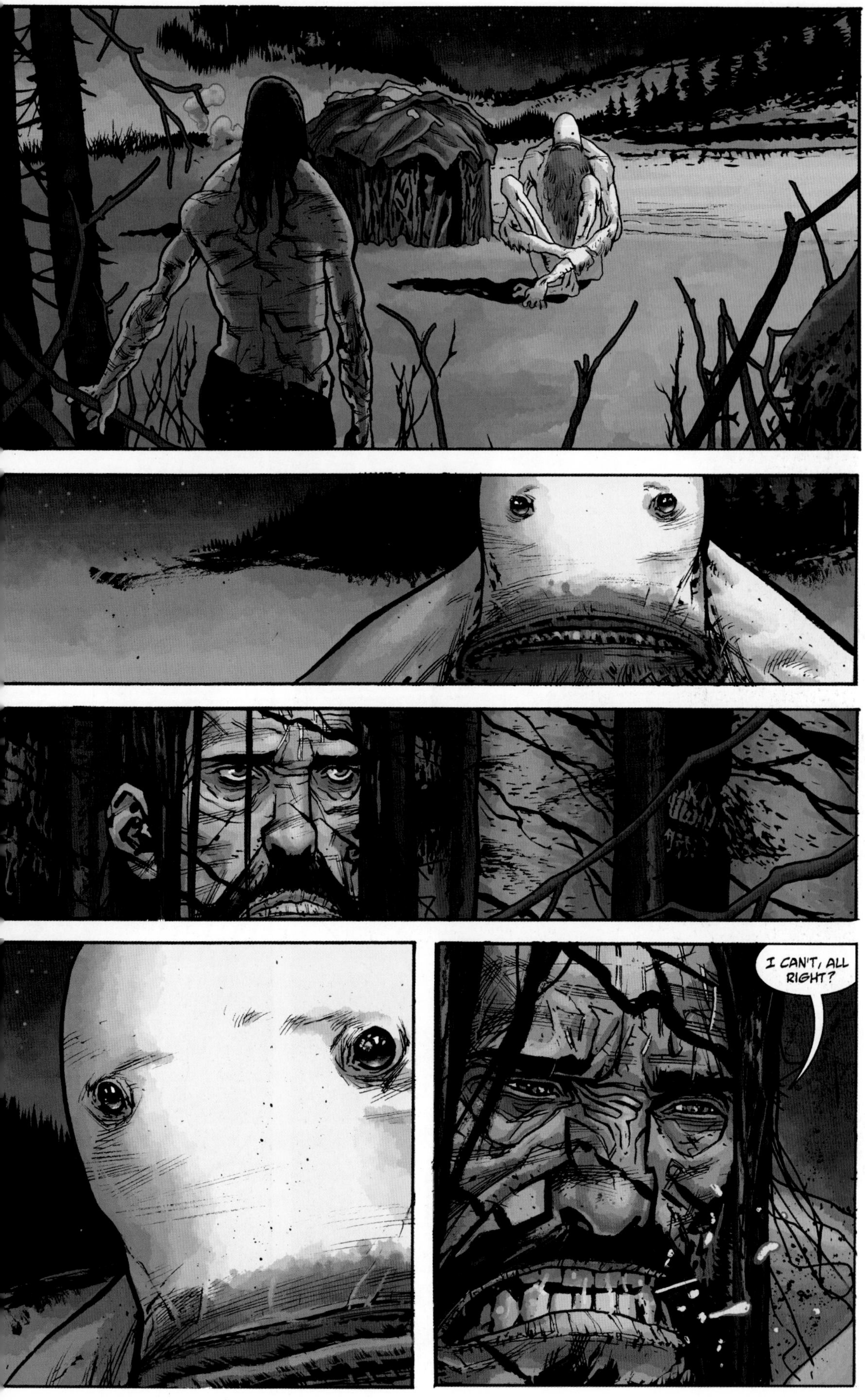
I CAN'T, ALL RIGHT?

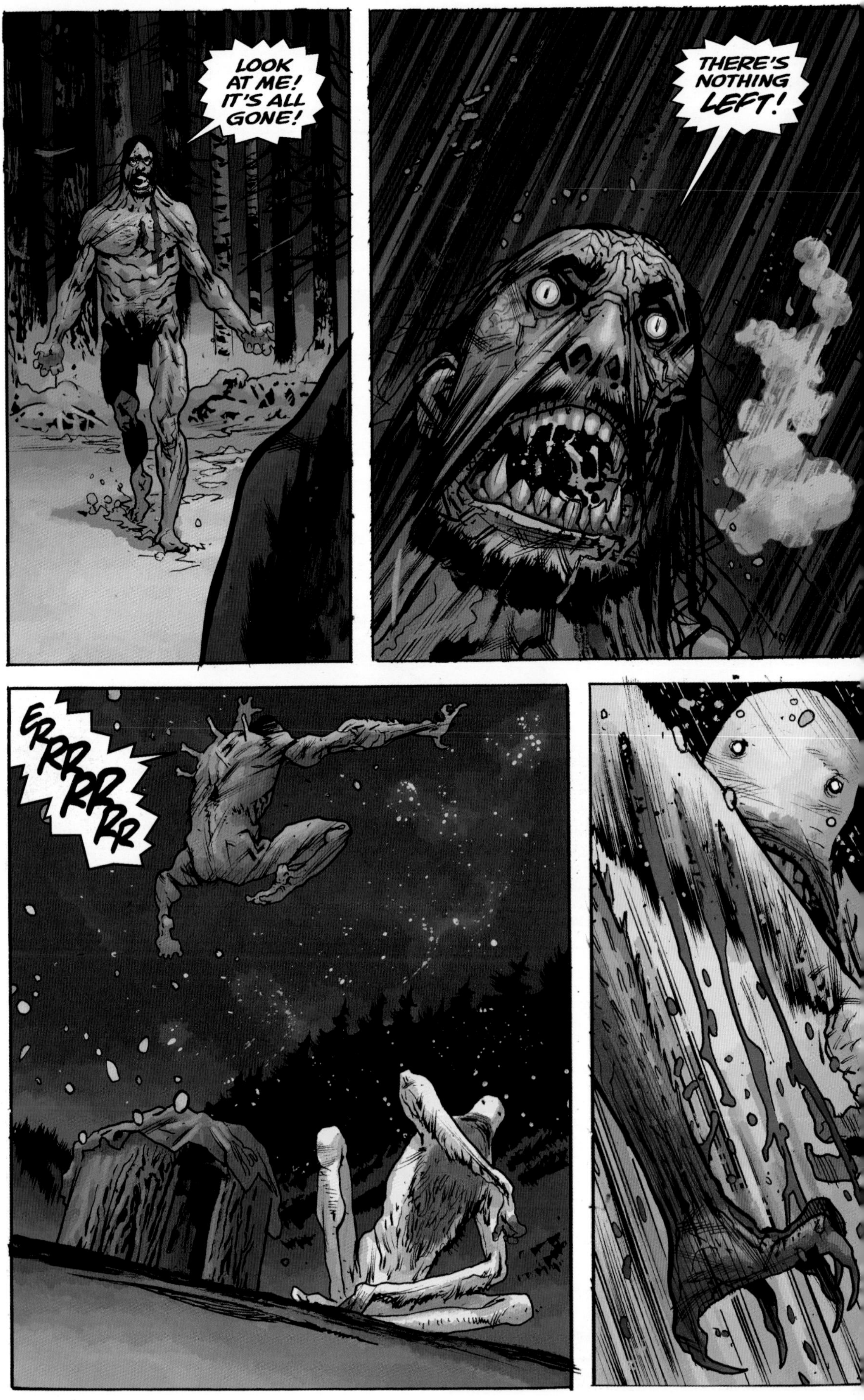
LOOK AT ME! IT'S ALL GONE!
THERE'S NOTHING LEFT!
ERRRRRRRRR

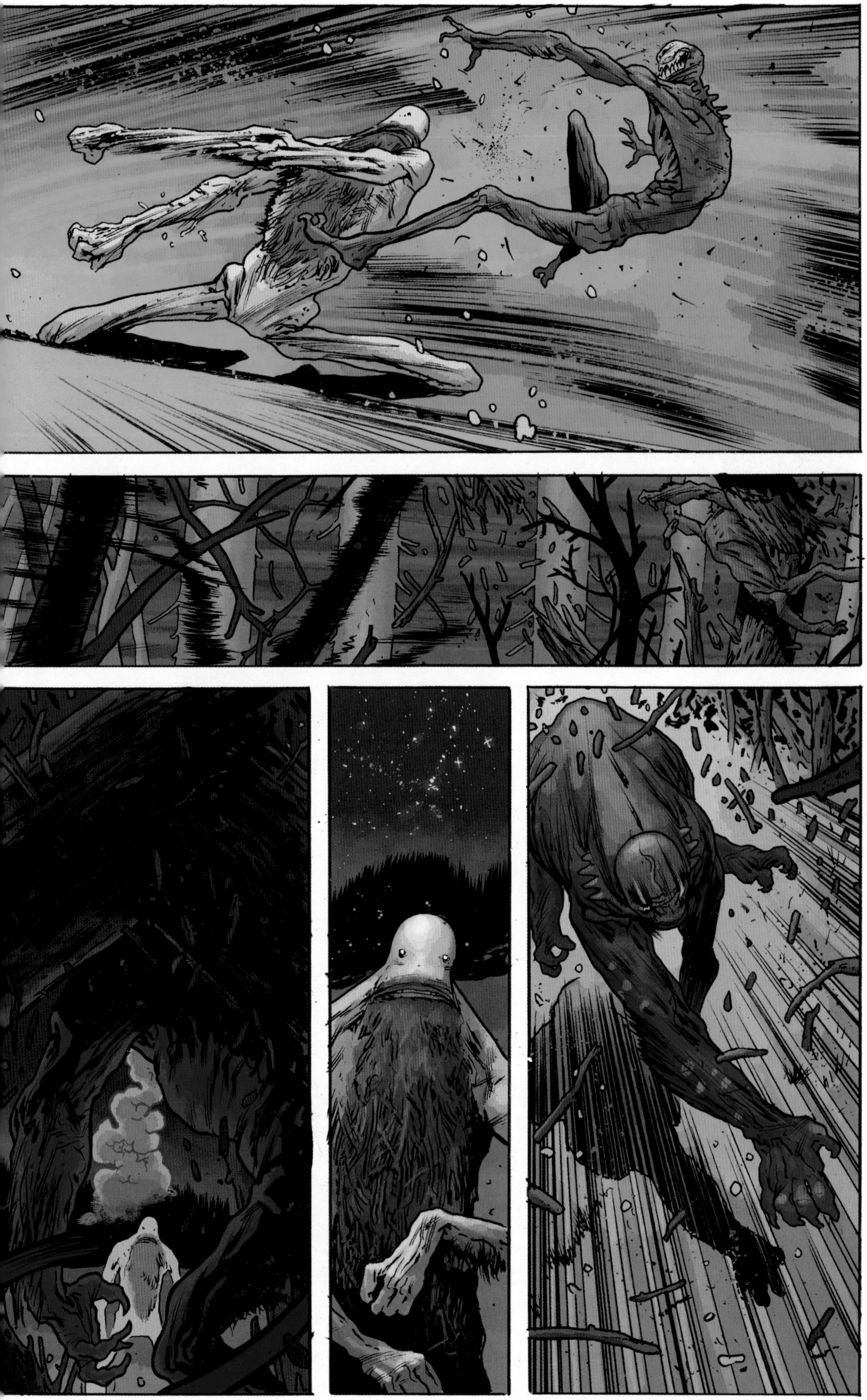

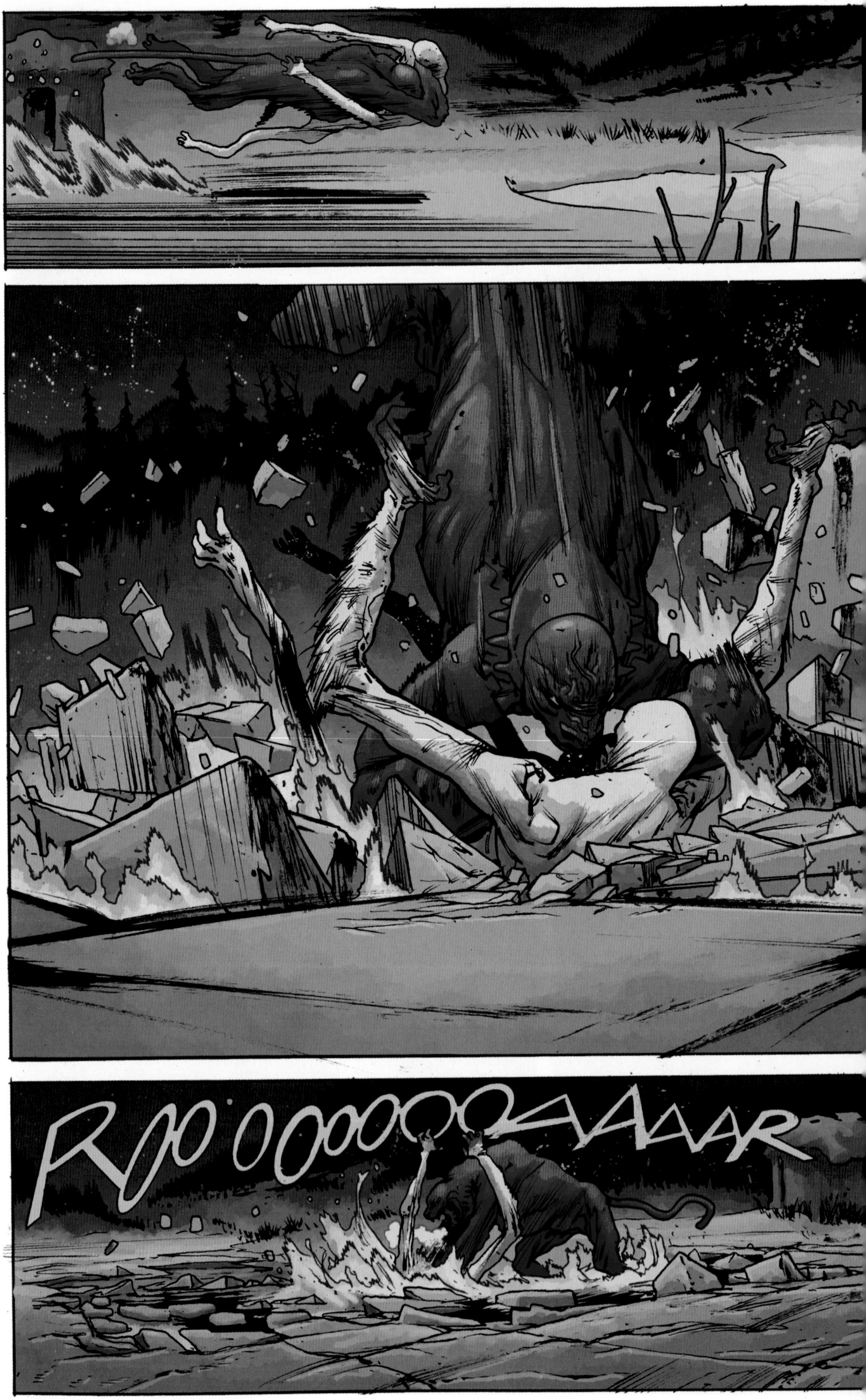
ROOOOOOOOAAAR

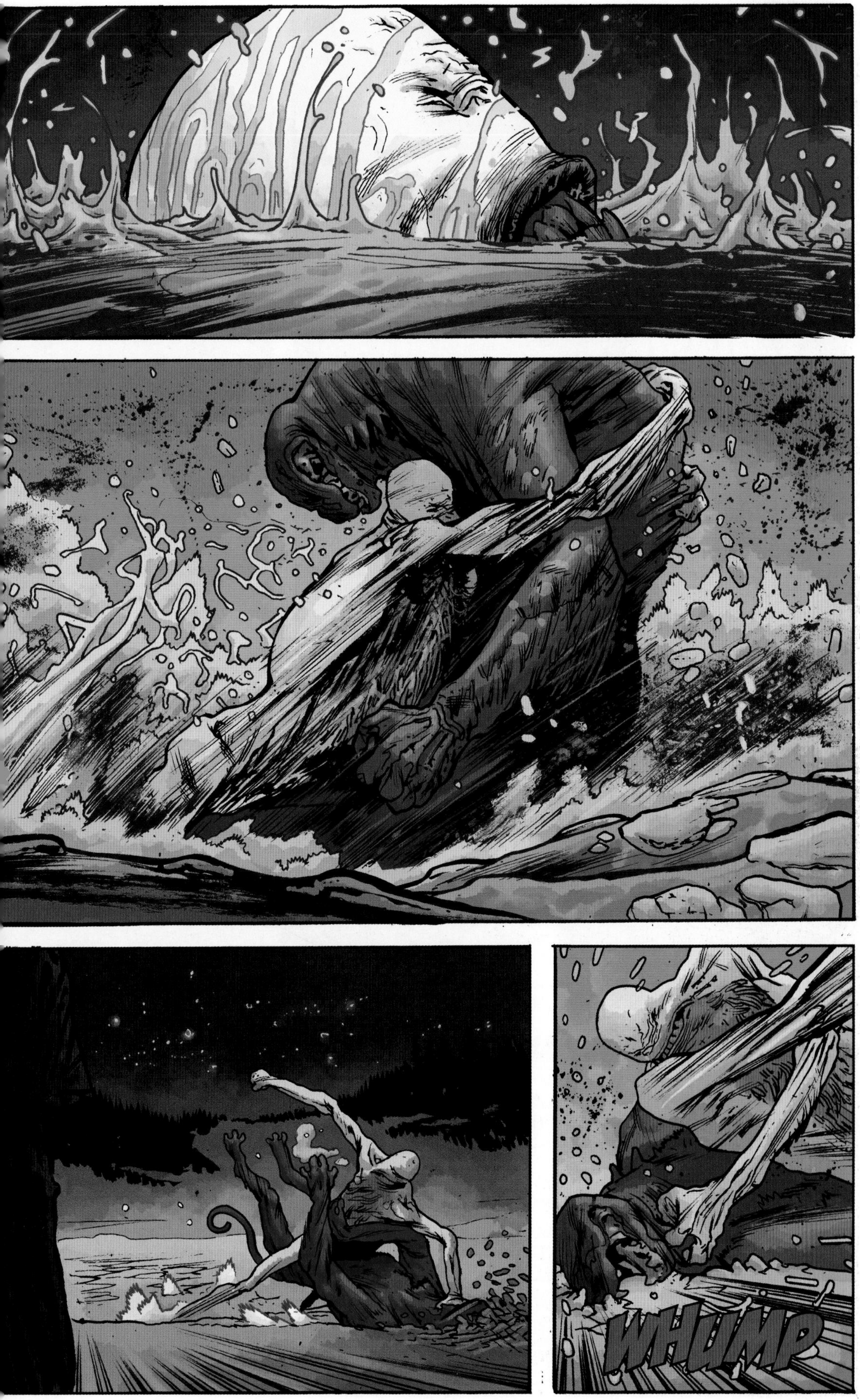
WHUMP

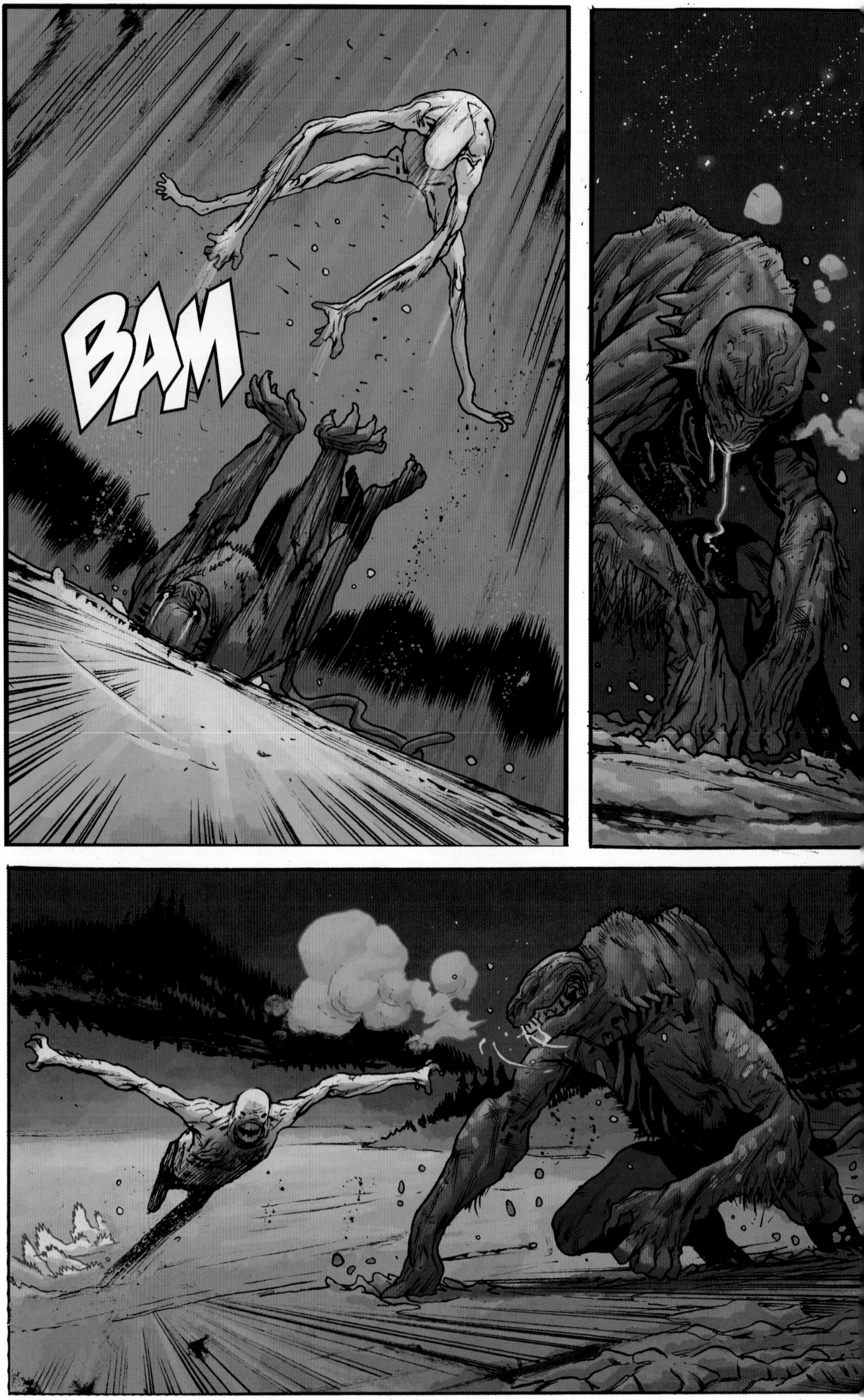
BAM

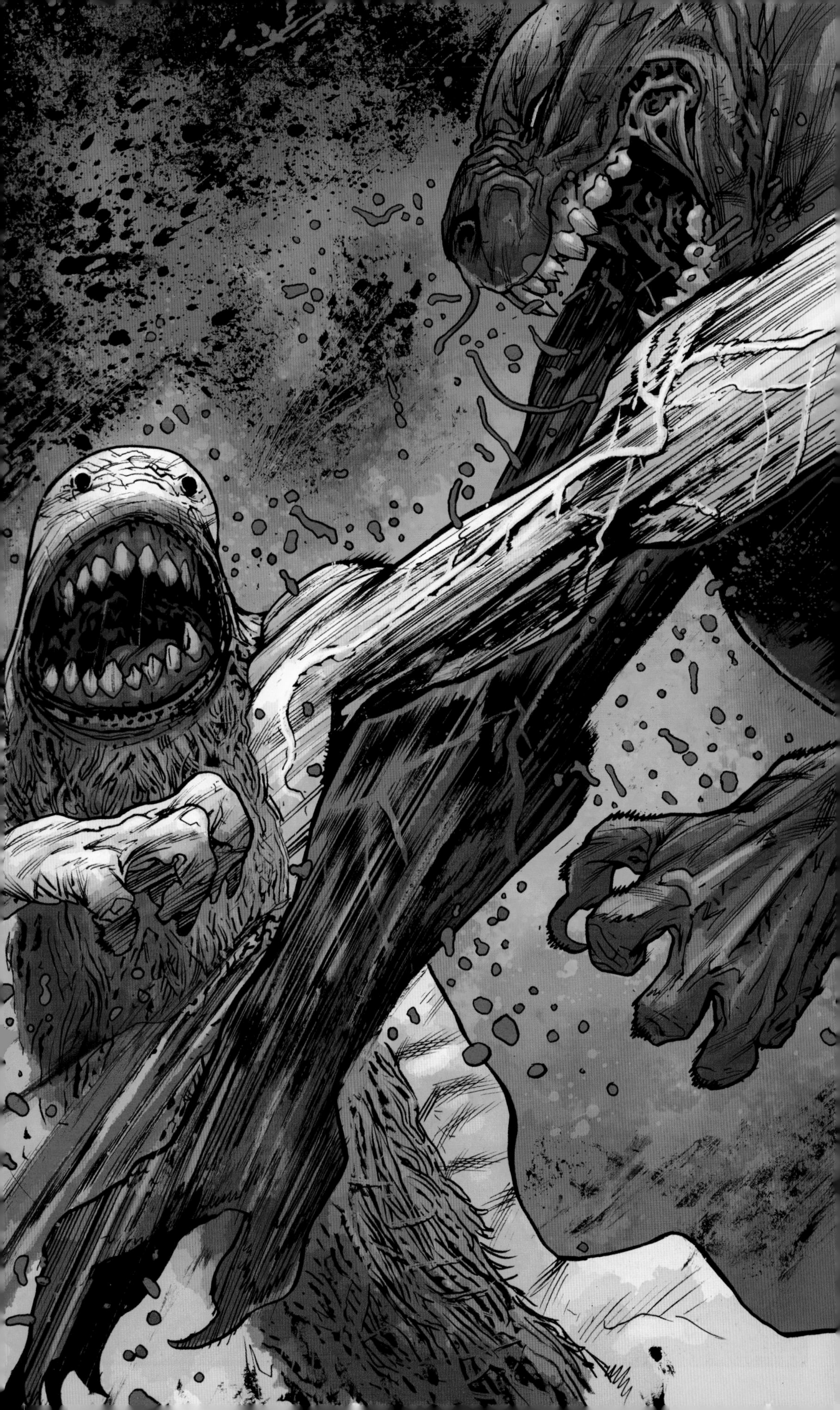

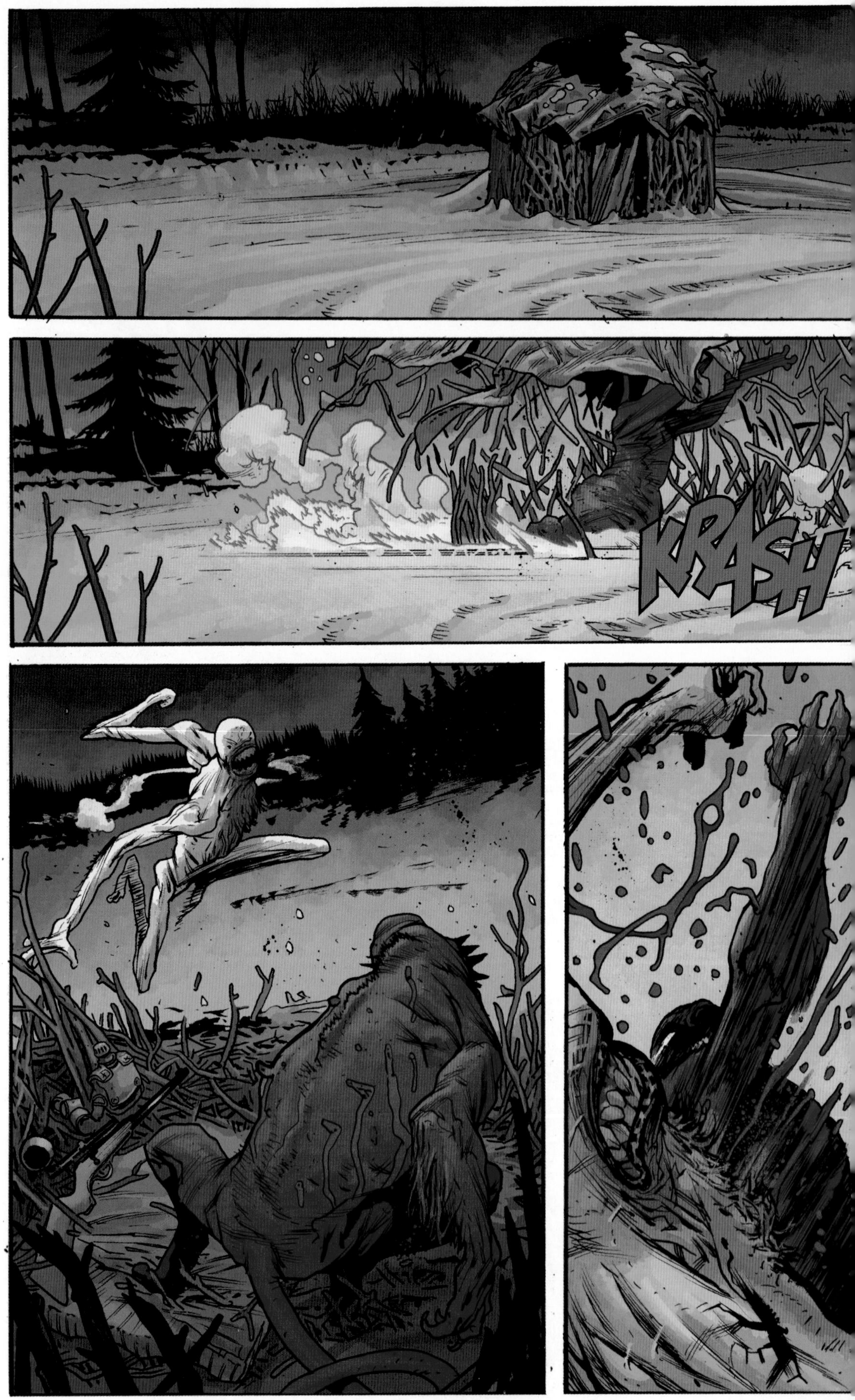
KRASH

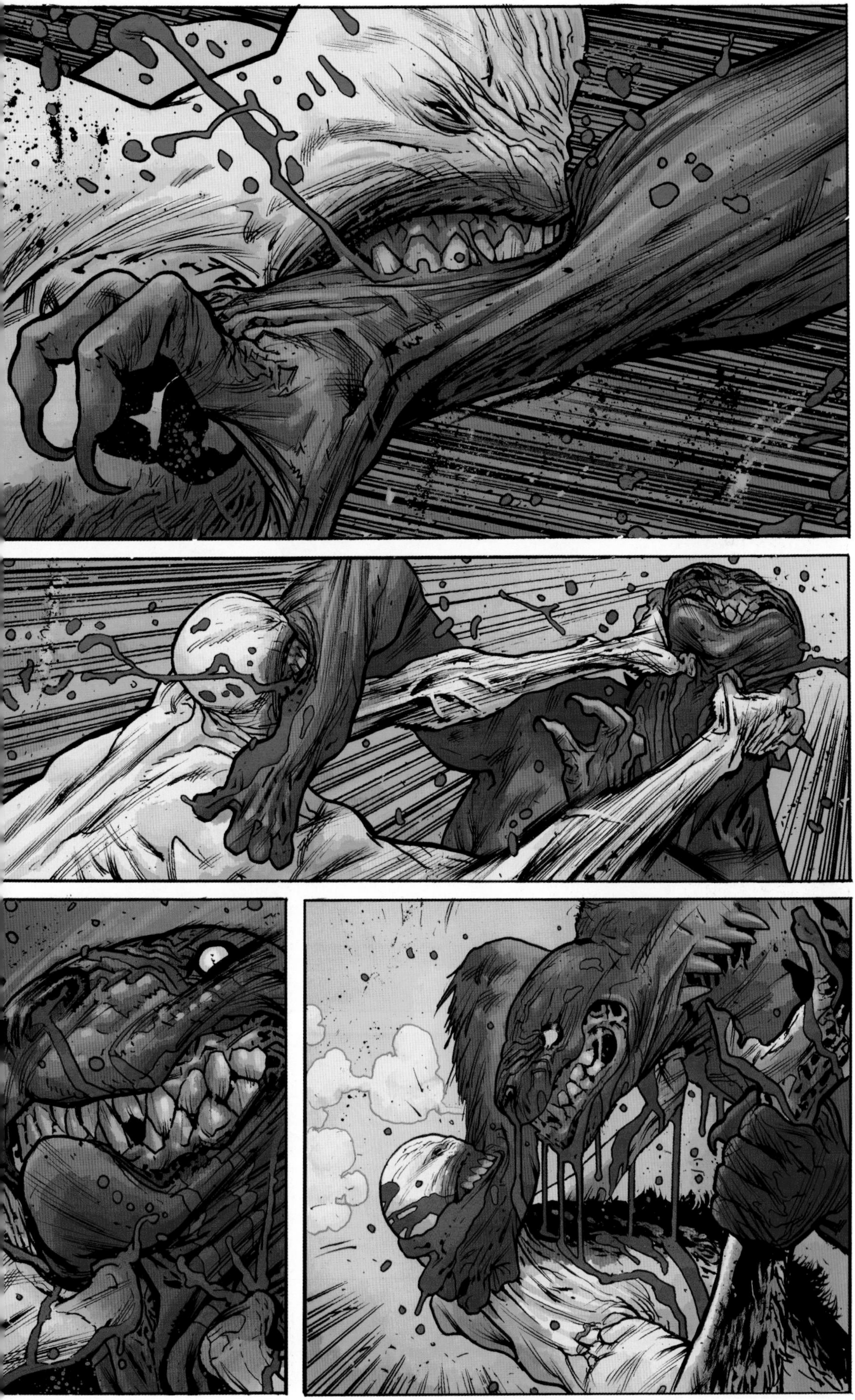

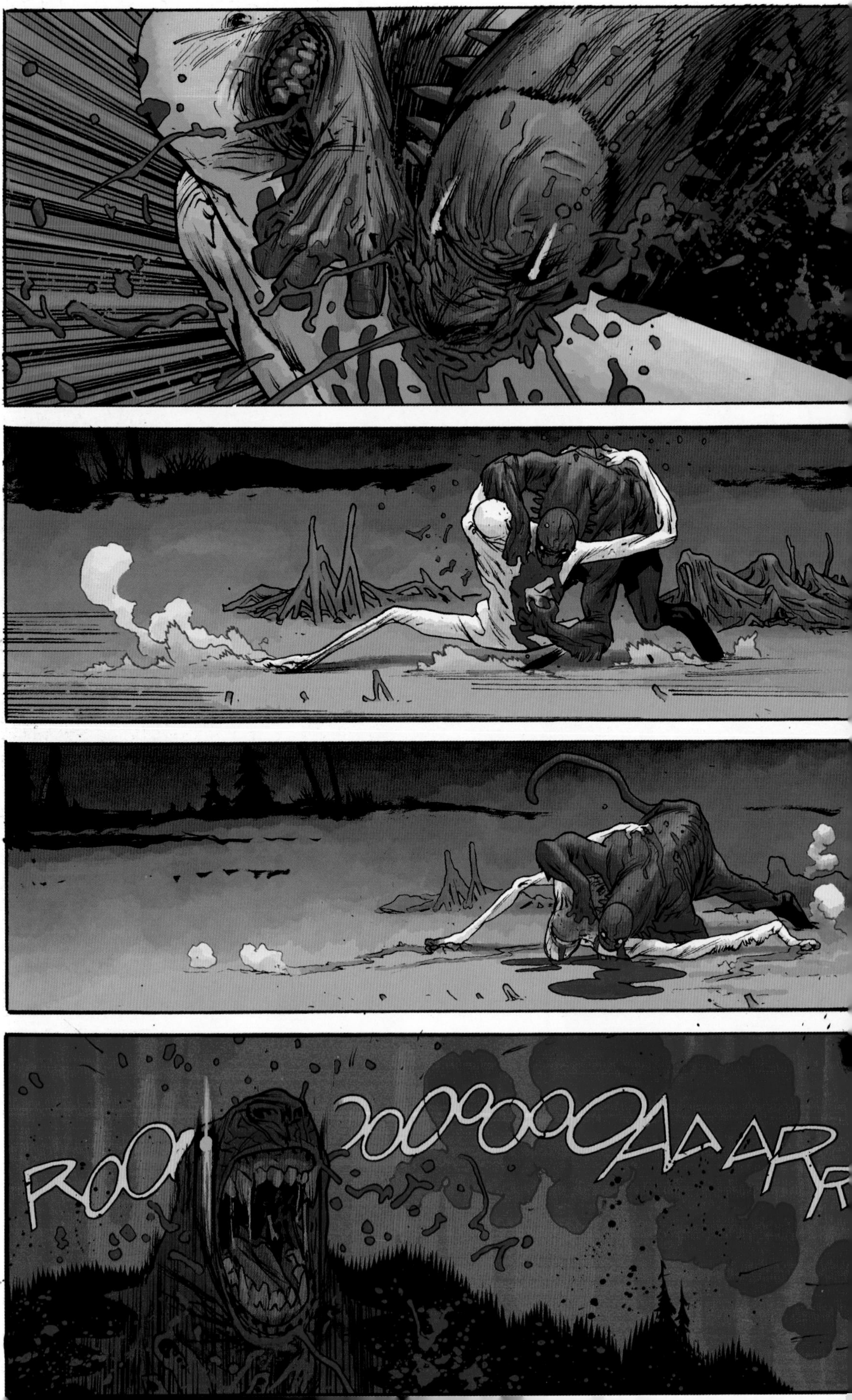
ROOOOOOOOOOOAAARR

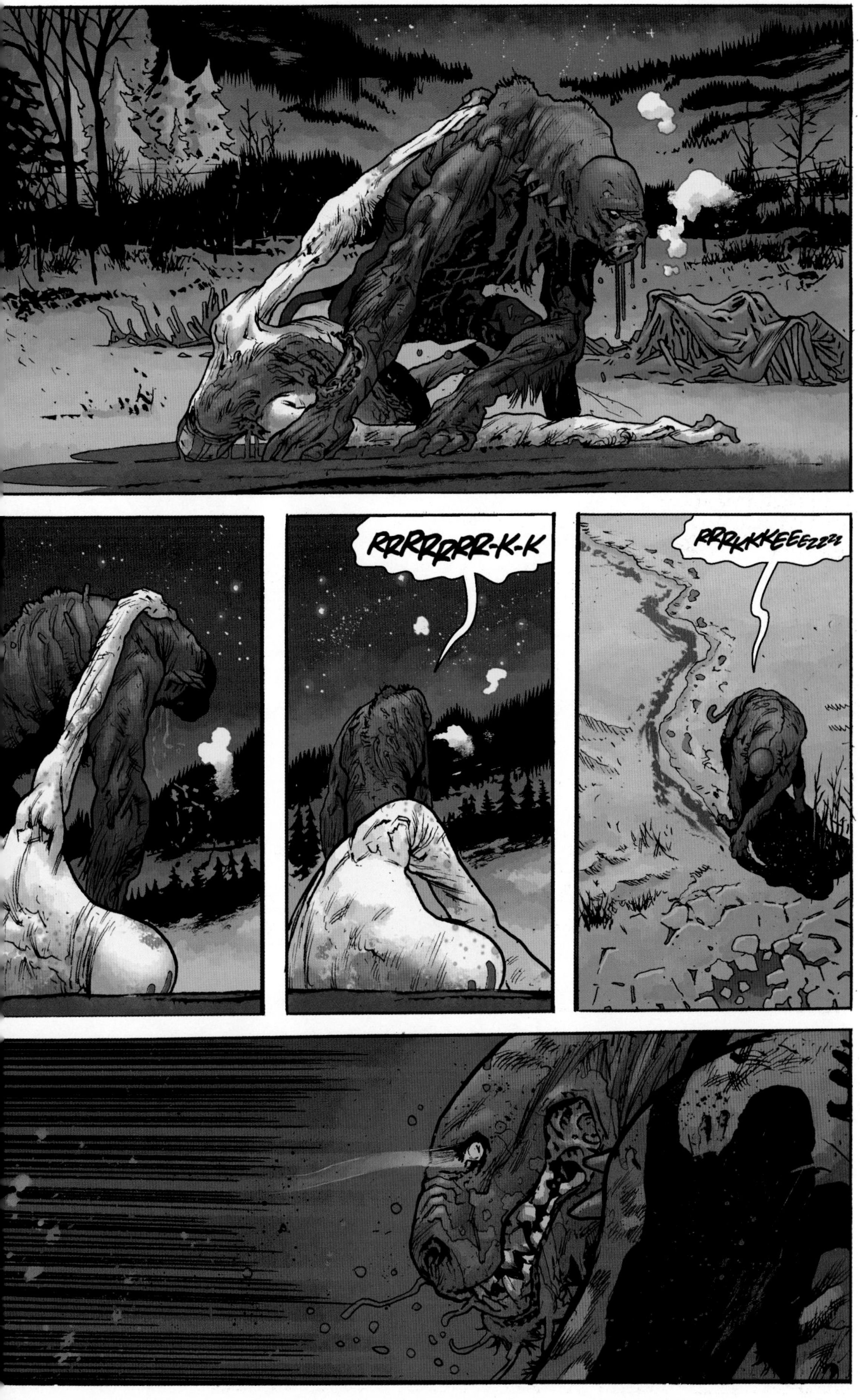
RRRRRRRR-K-K
RRRKKKEEEzzzz

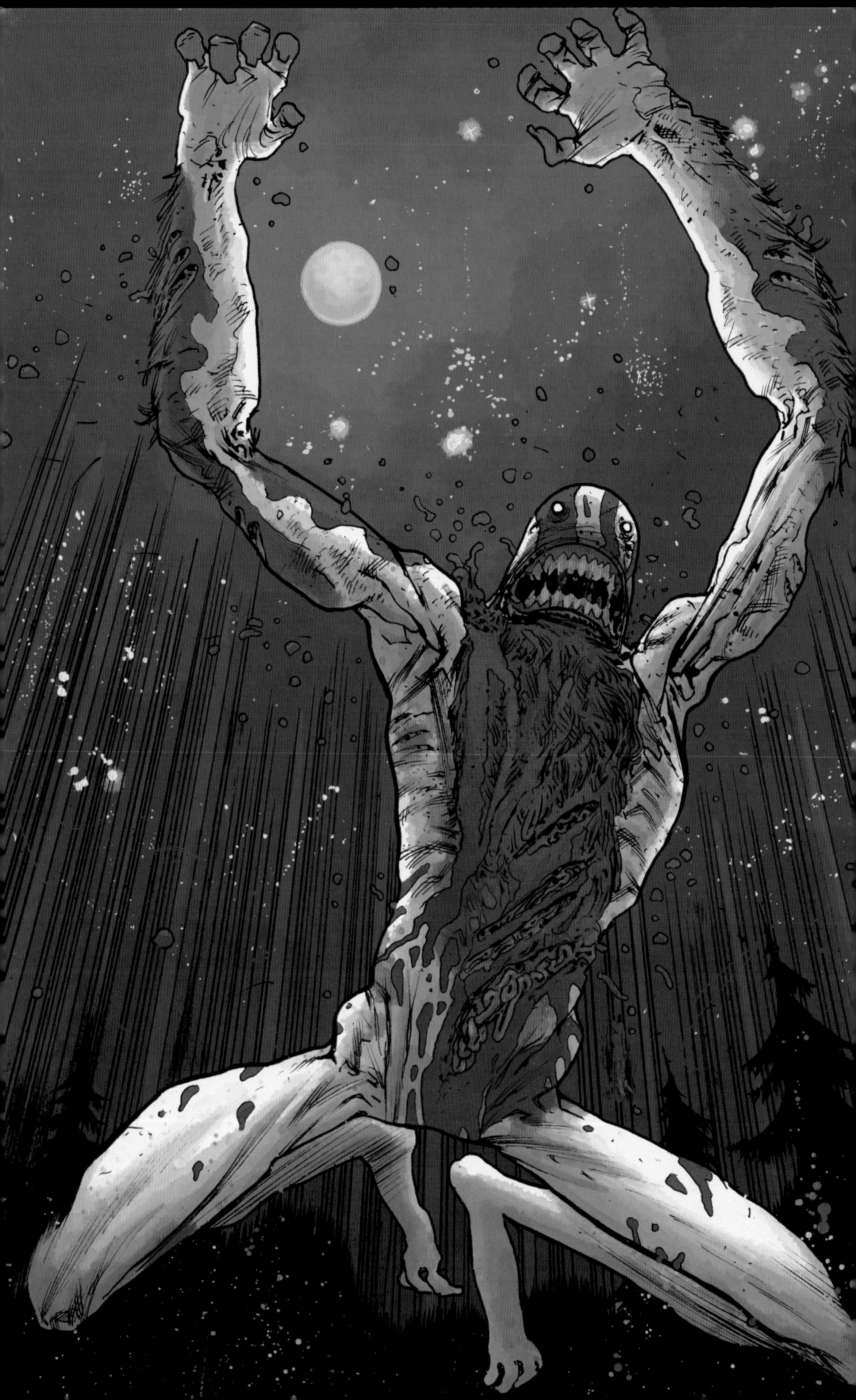

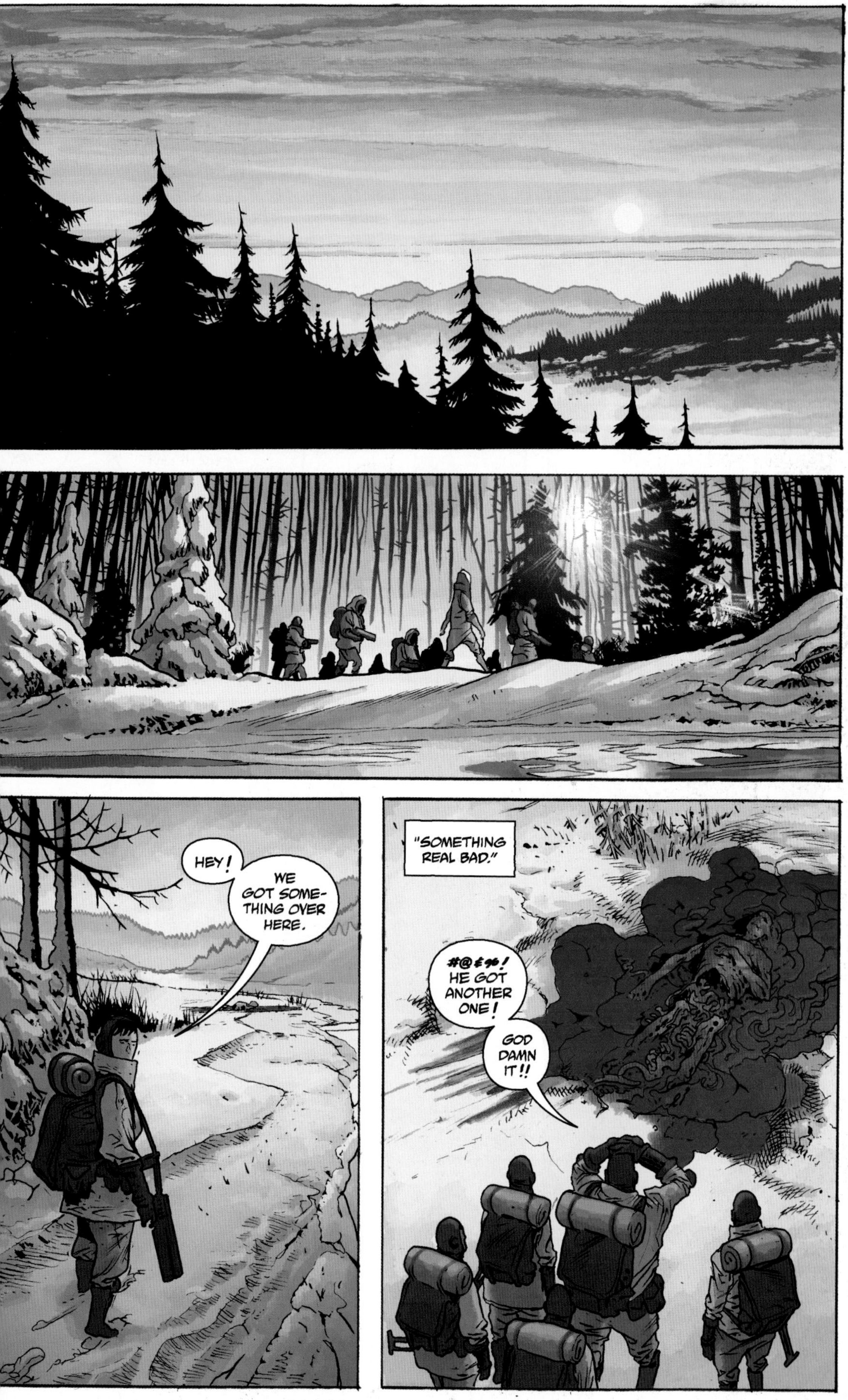
HEY!
WE GOT SOME-THING OVER HERE.
"SOMETHING REAL BAD."
#@£%! HE GOT ANOTHER ONE!
GOD DAMN IT!!

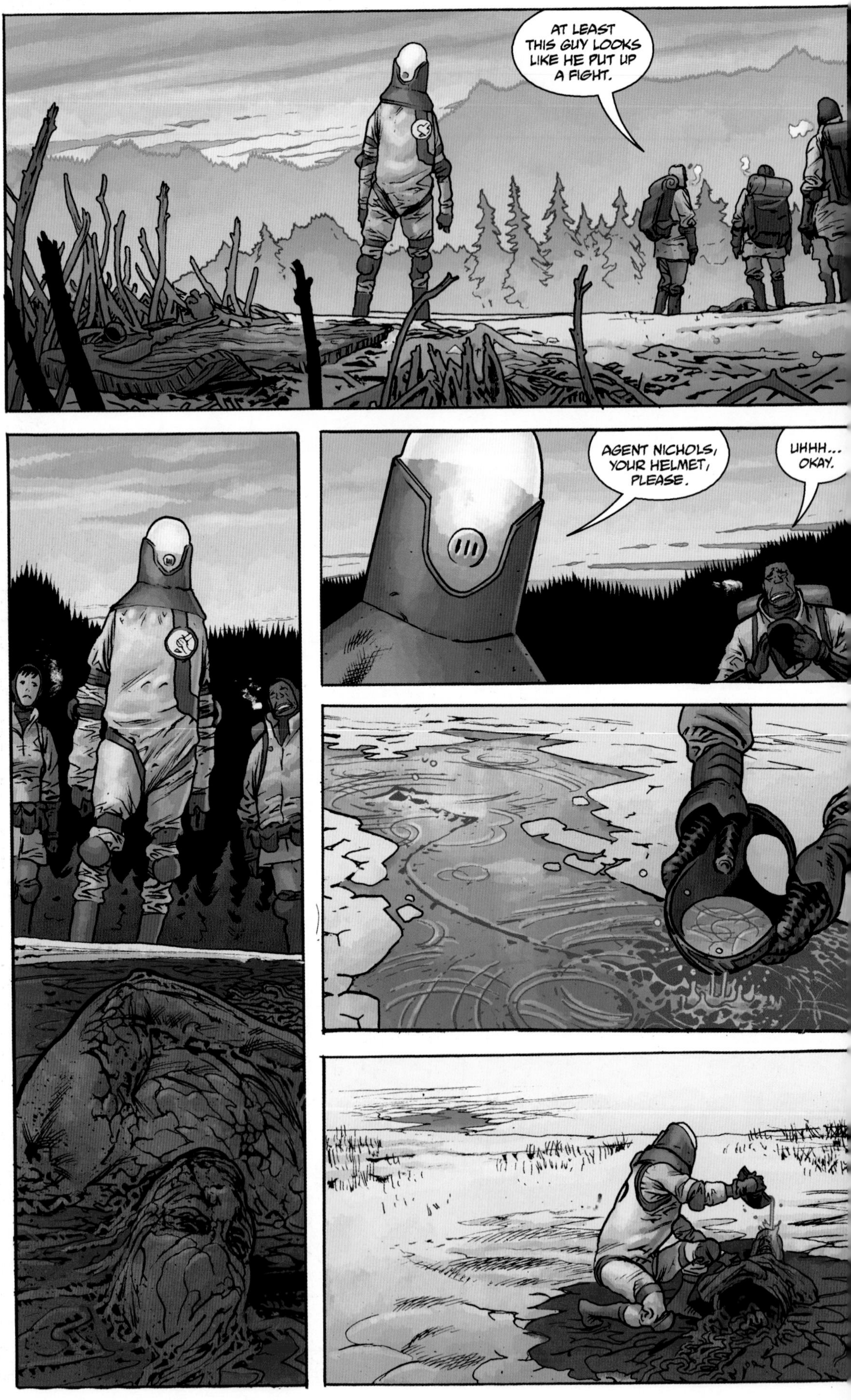
AT LEAST THIS GUY LOOKS LIKE HE PUT UP A FIGHT.
AGENT NICHOLS, YOUR HELMET, PLEASE.
UHHH... OKAY.

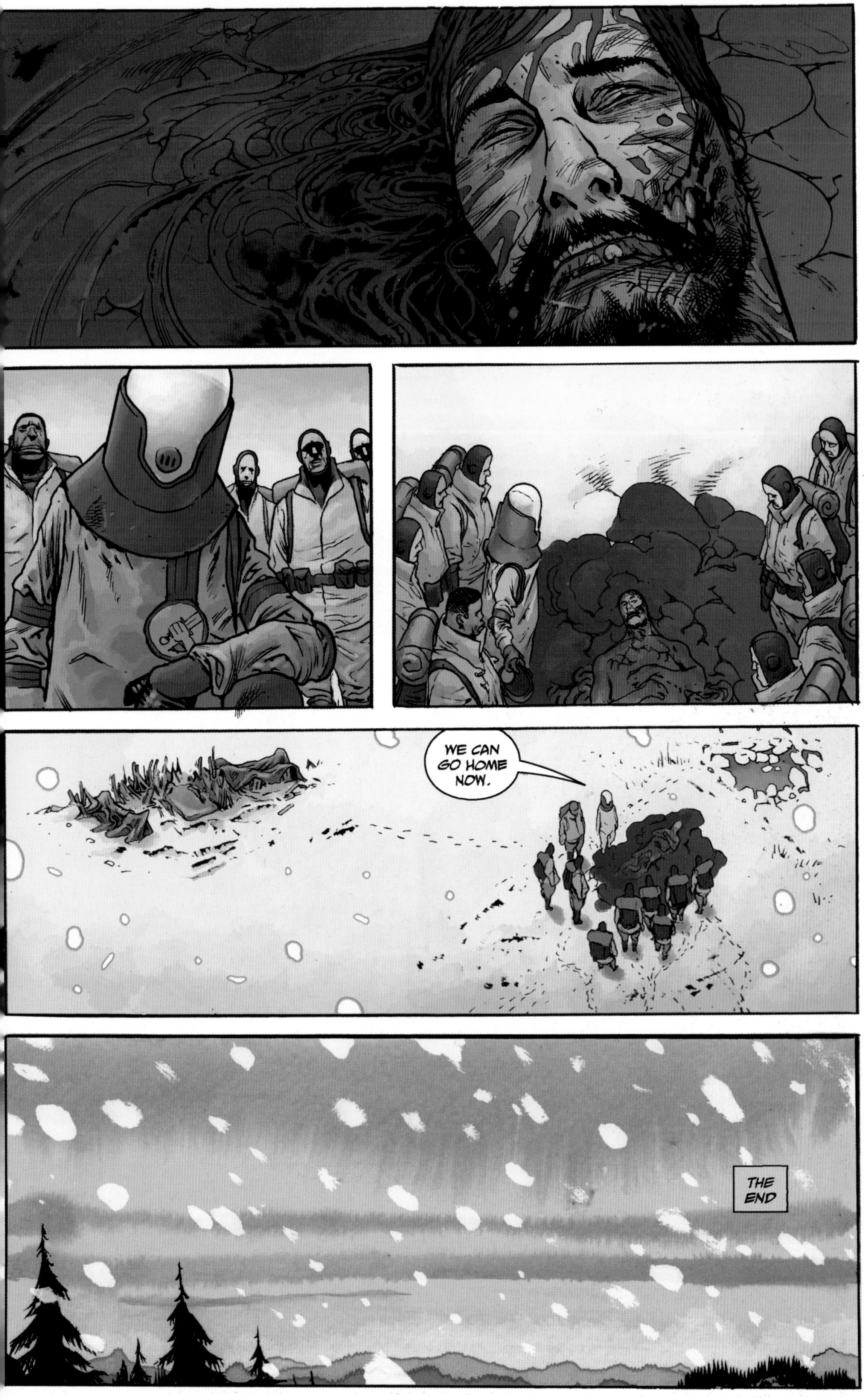
WE CAN GO HOME NOW.
THE END

B.P.R.D.™

SKETCHBOOK

Notes by Scott Allie

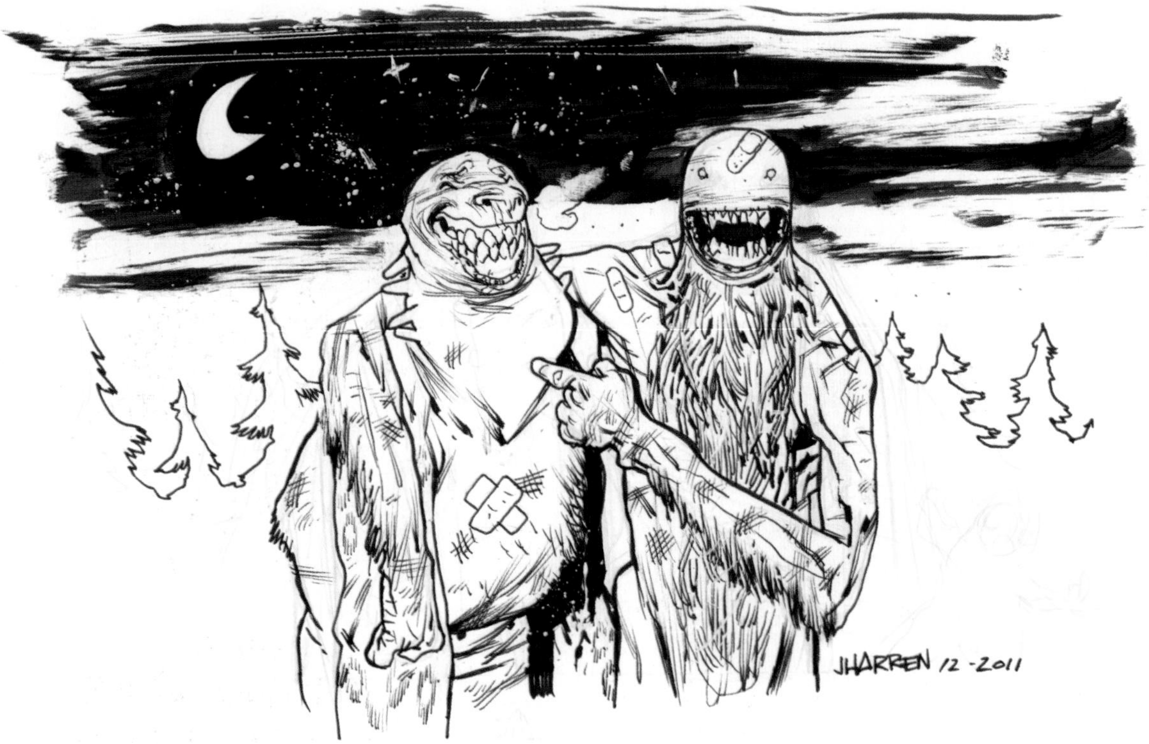
JHARREN 12-2011

James Harren did a short *Abe Sapien* series before *The Long Death*, but if nothing else, the fights between the monsters have earned him a permanent spot on the series.

Duncan Fegredo provided covers for the series, fresh off *Hellboy: The Storm and the Fury*, where he and Mike killed the character who launched all these books. We asked Duncan to design the artificial man that the Nazi scientists try to animate for Zinco Corporation. Duncan's first attempt was based on a loose outline from John.

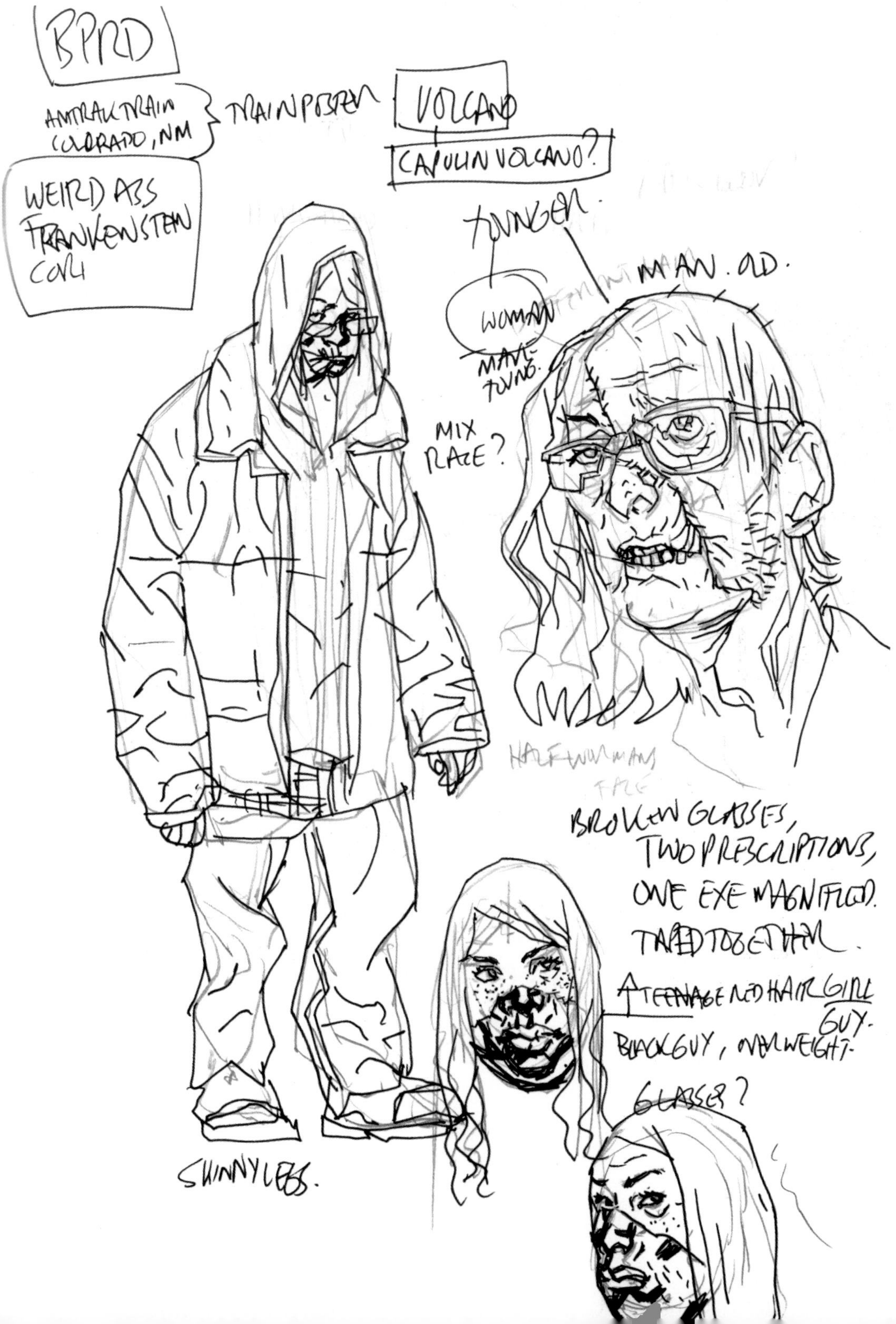
BPRD
AMTRAK TRAIN
COLORADO, NM
TRAIN POSTER
VOLCANO
CAPULIN VOLCANO?
WEIRD ASS
FRANKENSTEIN
GIRL
YOUNGER.
WOMAN
MAN. OLD.
MALE.
YOUNG.
MIX
RACE?
BROKEN GLASSES,
TWO PRESCRIPTIONS,
ONE EYE MAGNIFIED.
TAPED TOGETHER.
A TEENAGE RED HAIR GIRL
GUY.
BLACK GUY, OVERWEIGHT.
GLASSES?
SKINNY LEGS.

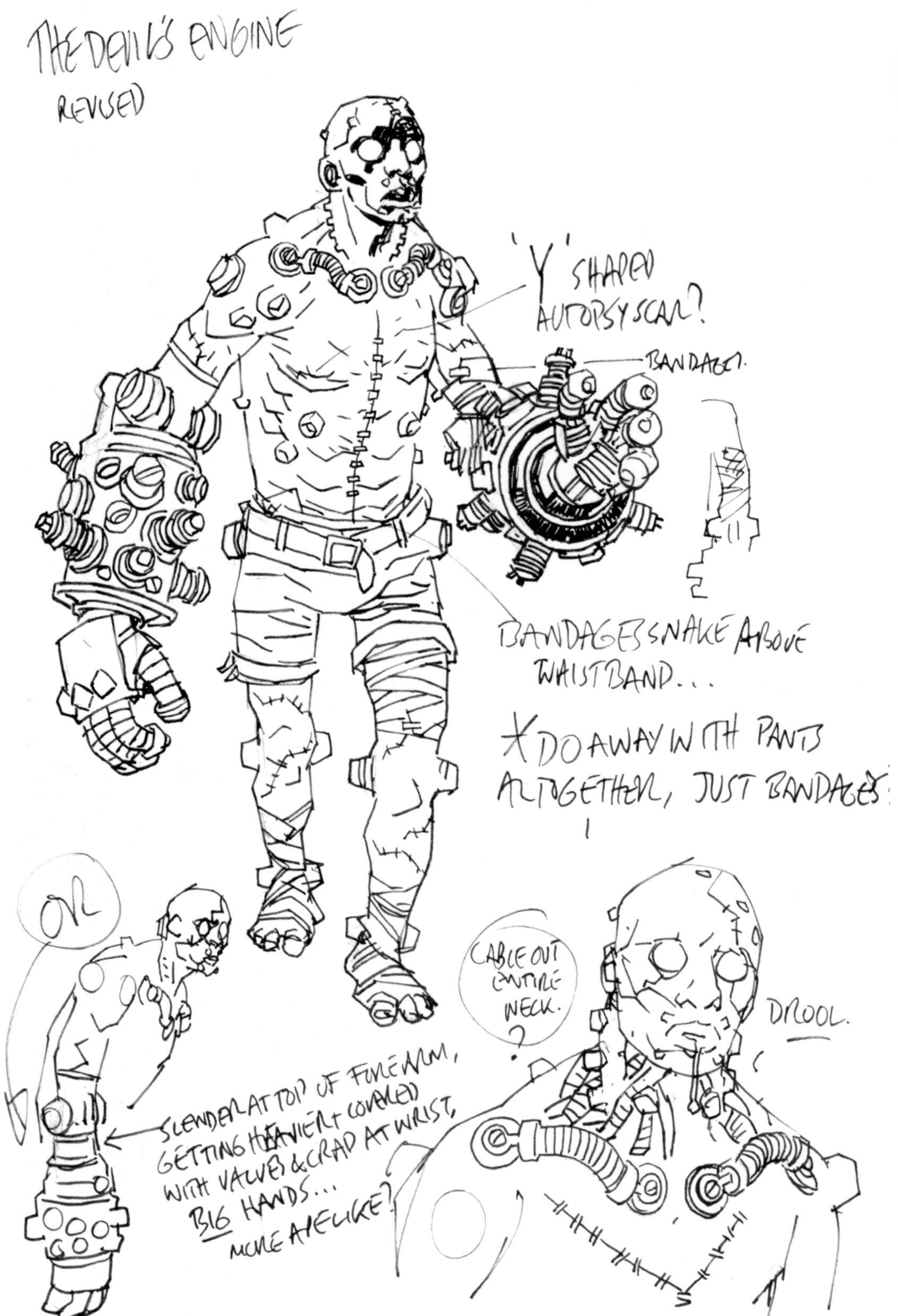
THE DEVIL'S ENGINE
REVISED
'Y' SHAPED AUTOPSY SCAR?
BANDAGES.
BANDAGES SNAKE ABOVE WAISTBAND...
* DO AWAY WITH PANTS ALTOGETHER, JUST BANDAGES!
OR
CABLE OUT ENTIRE NECK. ?
DROOL.
SLENDER AT TOP OF FOREARM, GETTING HEAVIER + COVERED WITH VALVES & CRAP AT WRIST, BIG HANDS... MORE APELIKE?

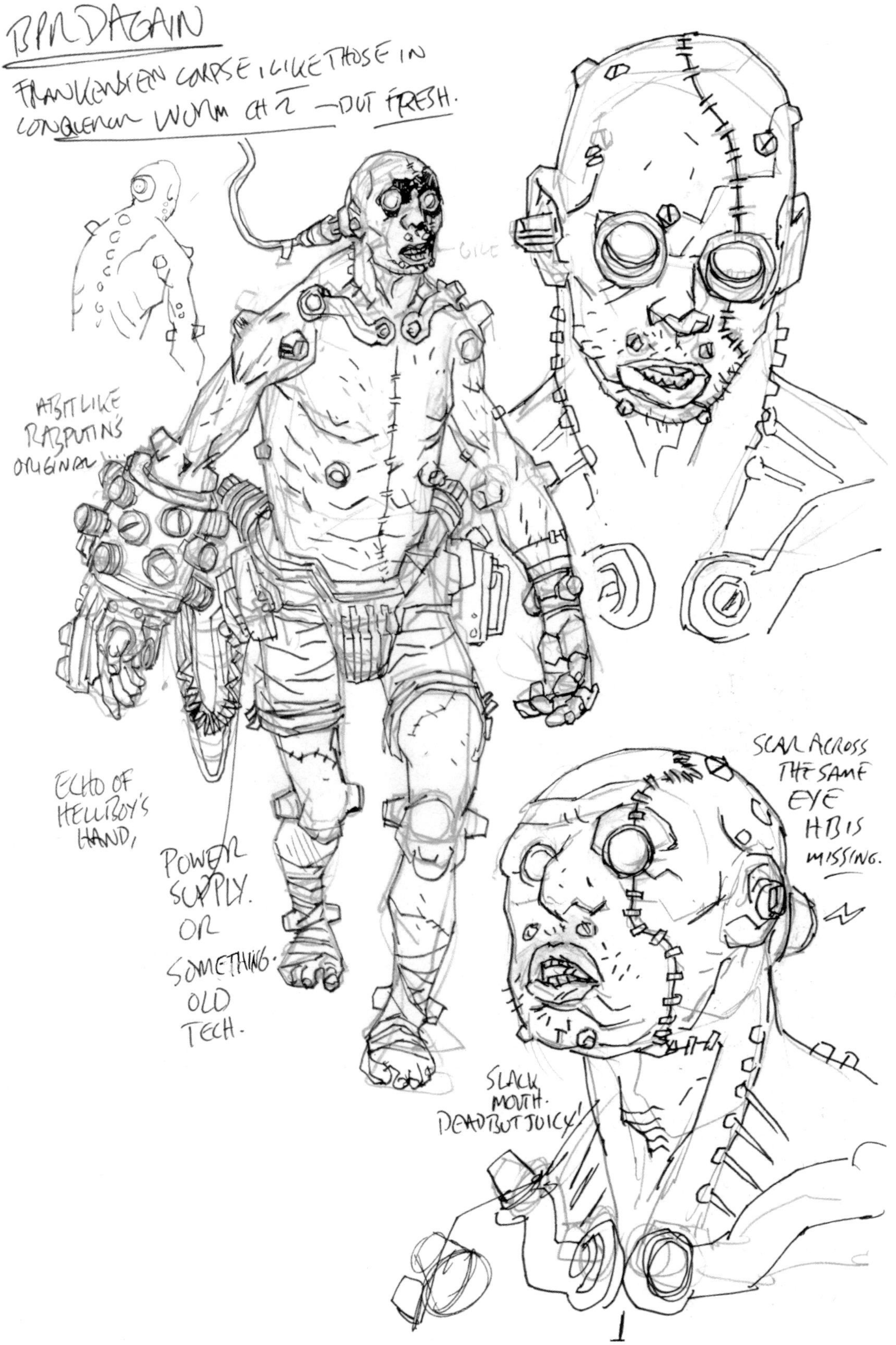
BPRD AGAIN
FRANKENSTEIN CORPSE, LIKE THOSE IN CONQUEROR WORM CH 2 —BUT FRESH.
A BIT LIKE RASPUTIN'S ORIGINAL....
ECHO OF HELLBOY'S HAND,
POWER SUPPLY. OR SOMETHING. OLD TECH.
SCAR ACROSS THE SAME EYE HB IS MISSING.
SLACK MOUTH. DEAD BUT JUICY!

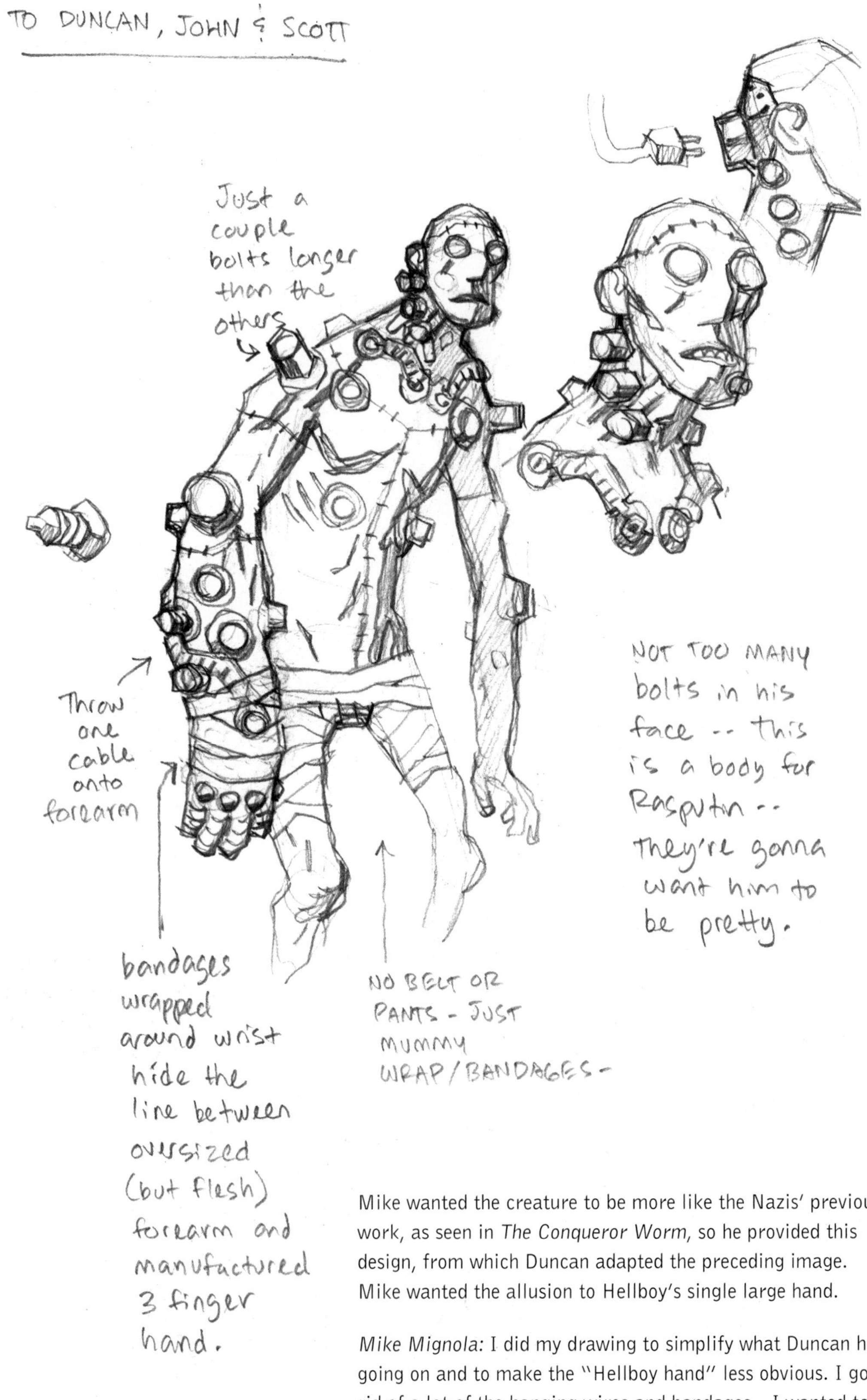
TO DUNCAN, JOHN & SCOTT
Just a couple bolts longer than the others
Throw one cable onto forearm
NOT TOO MANY bolts in his face -- this is a body for Rasputin -- They're gonna want him to be pretty.
bandages wrapped around wrist hide the line between oversized (but flesh) forearm and manufactured 3 finger hand.
NO BELT OR PANTS - JUST MUMMY WRAP/BANDAGES -

Mike wanted the creature to be more like the Nazis' previous work, as seen in *The Conqueror Worm*, so he provided this design, from which Duncan adapted the preceding image. Mike wanted the allusion to Hellboy's single large hand.

Mike Mignola: I did my drawing to simplify what Duncan had going on and to make the "Hellboy hand" less obvious. I got rid of a lot of the hanging wires and bandages—I wanted to hide the transition from flesh to machine.

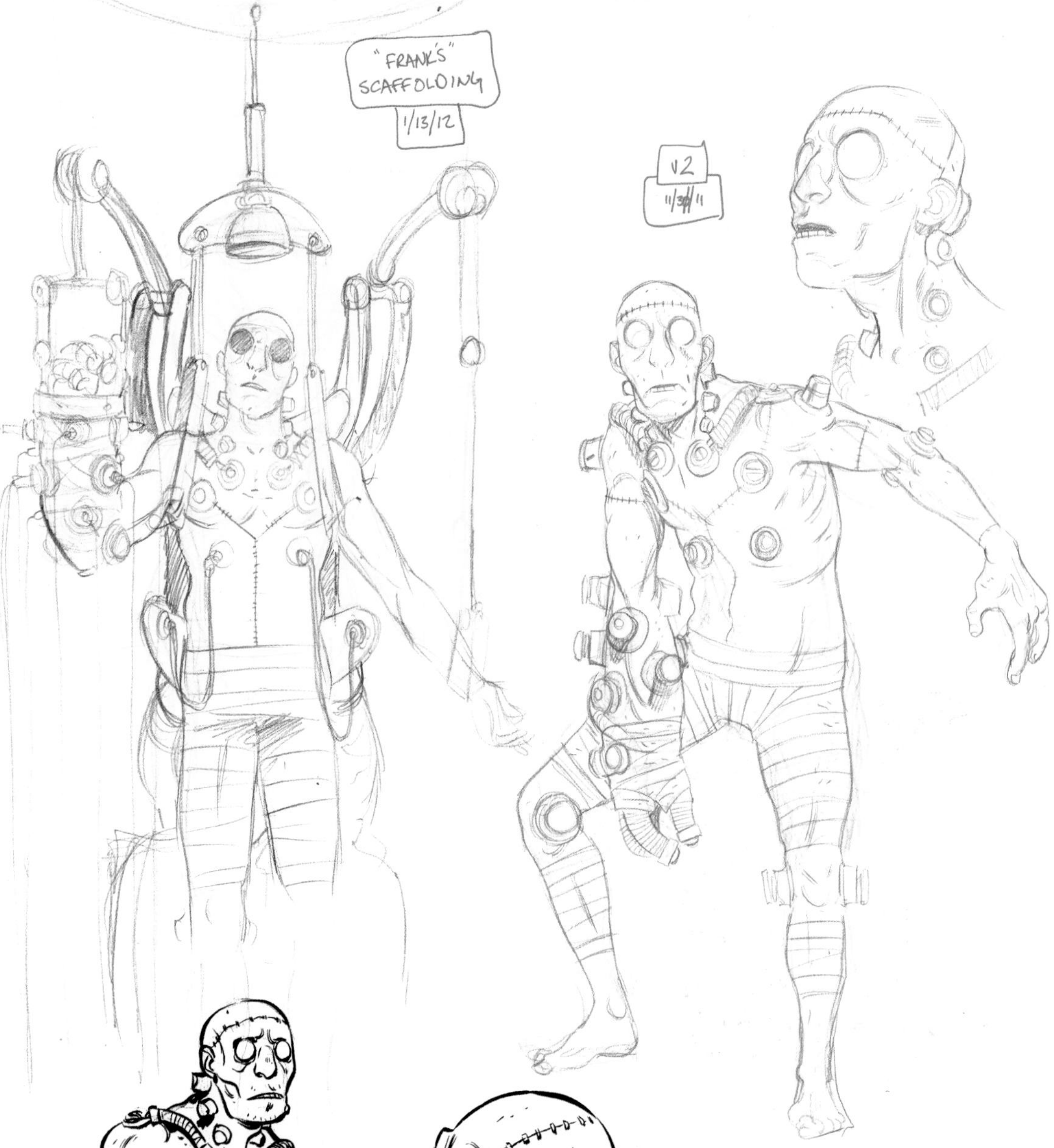
"FRANK'S" SCAFFOLDING
1/13/12
V2
11/30/11

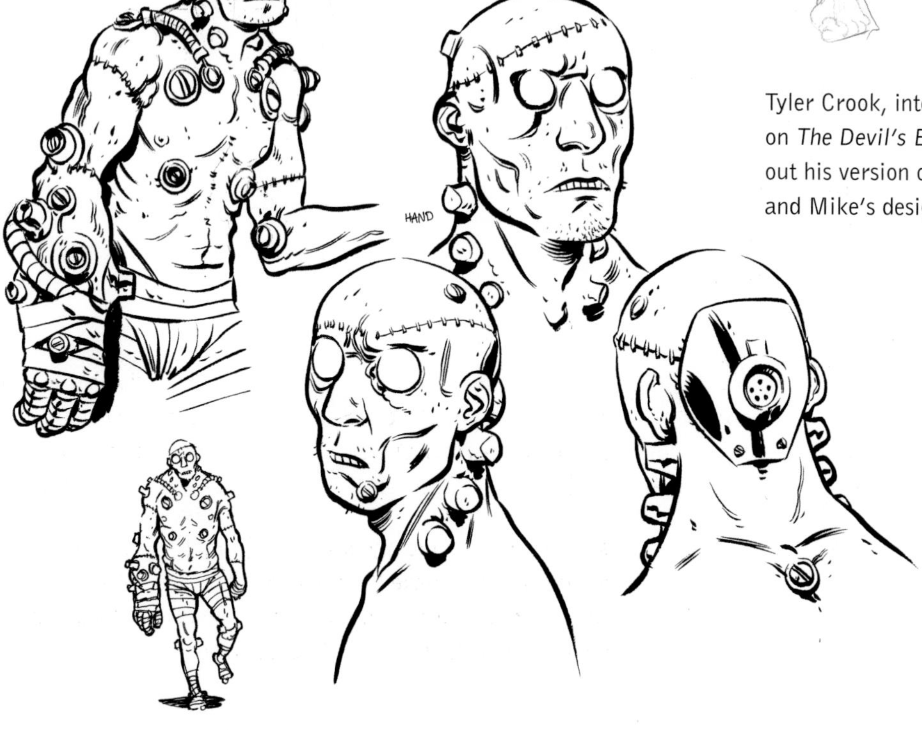
HAND

Tyler Crook, interior artist on *The Devil's Engine*, works out his version of Duncan and Mike's design.

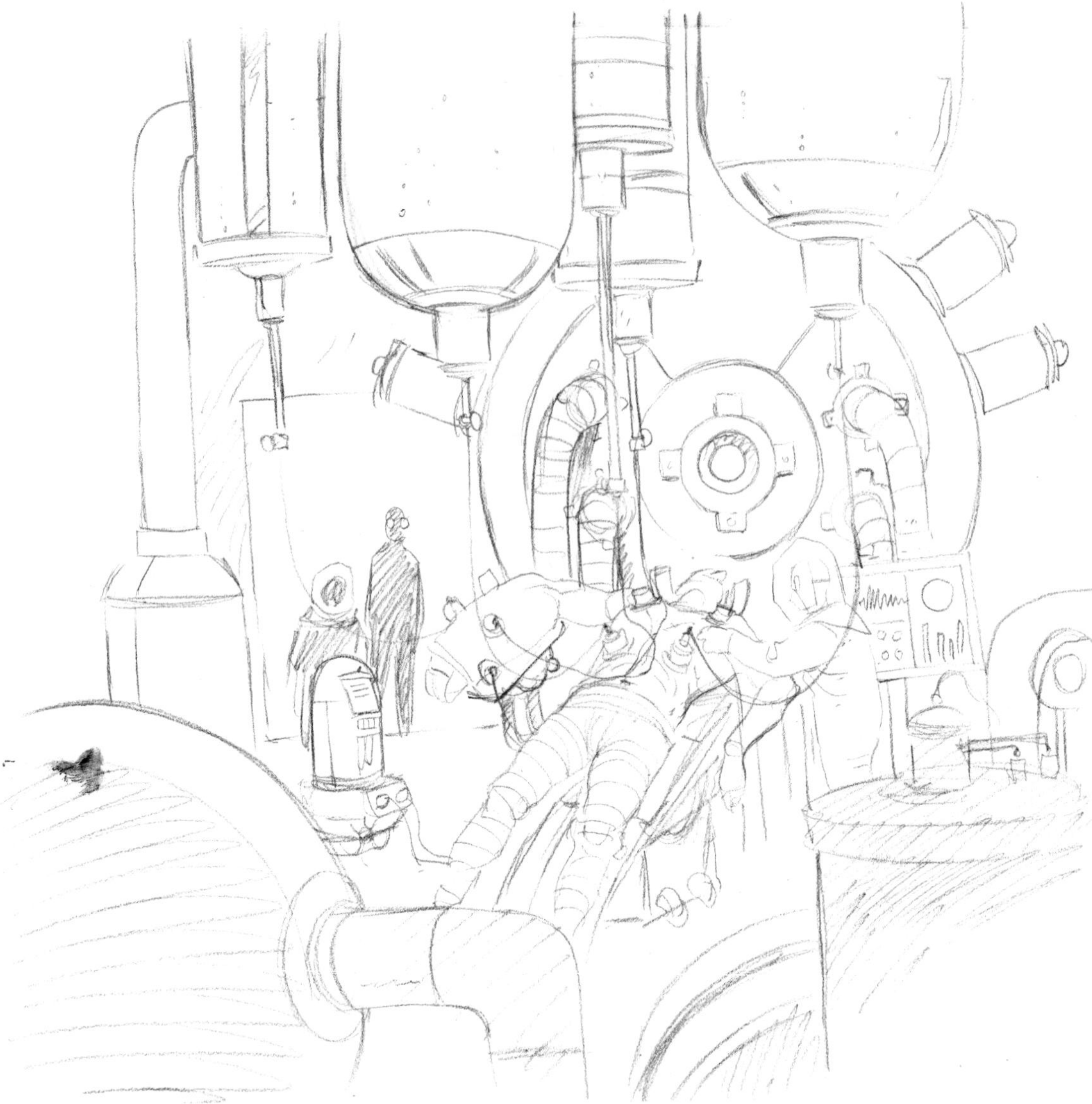

More lab work from Tyler. Arcudi suggested the throne where the Nazis would work on the creature (facing).

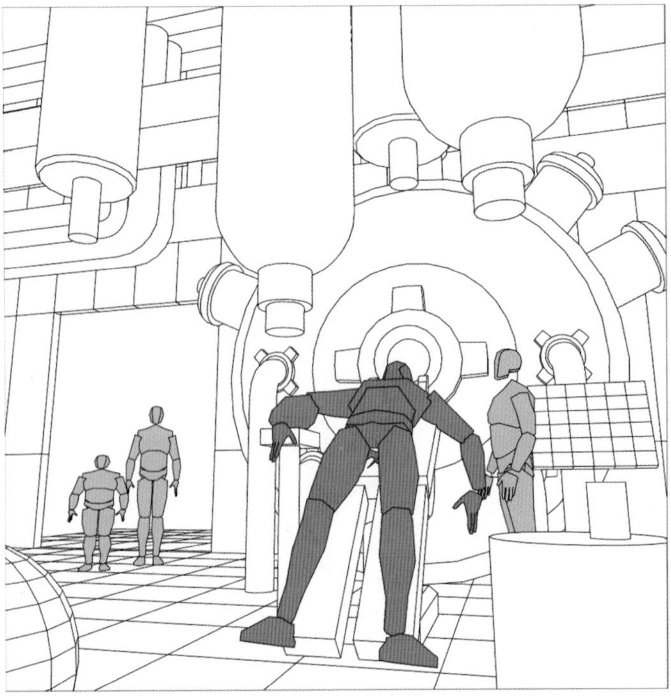

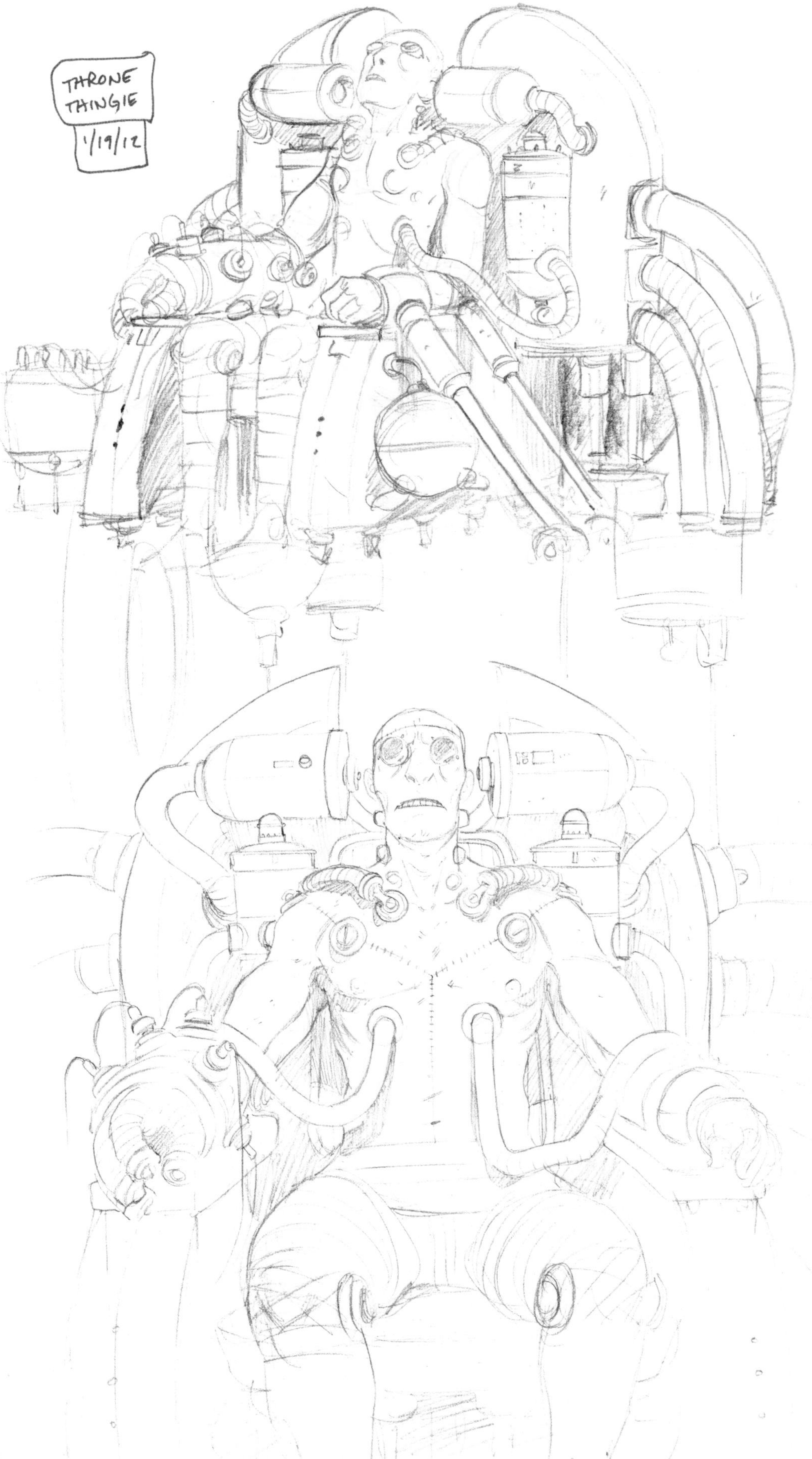
THRONE THINGIE
1/19/12

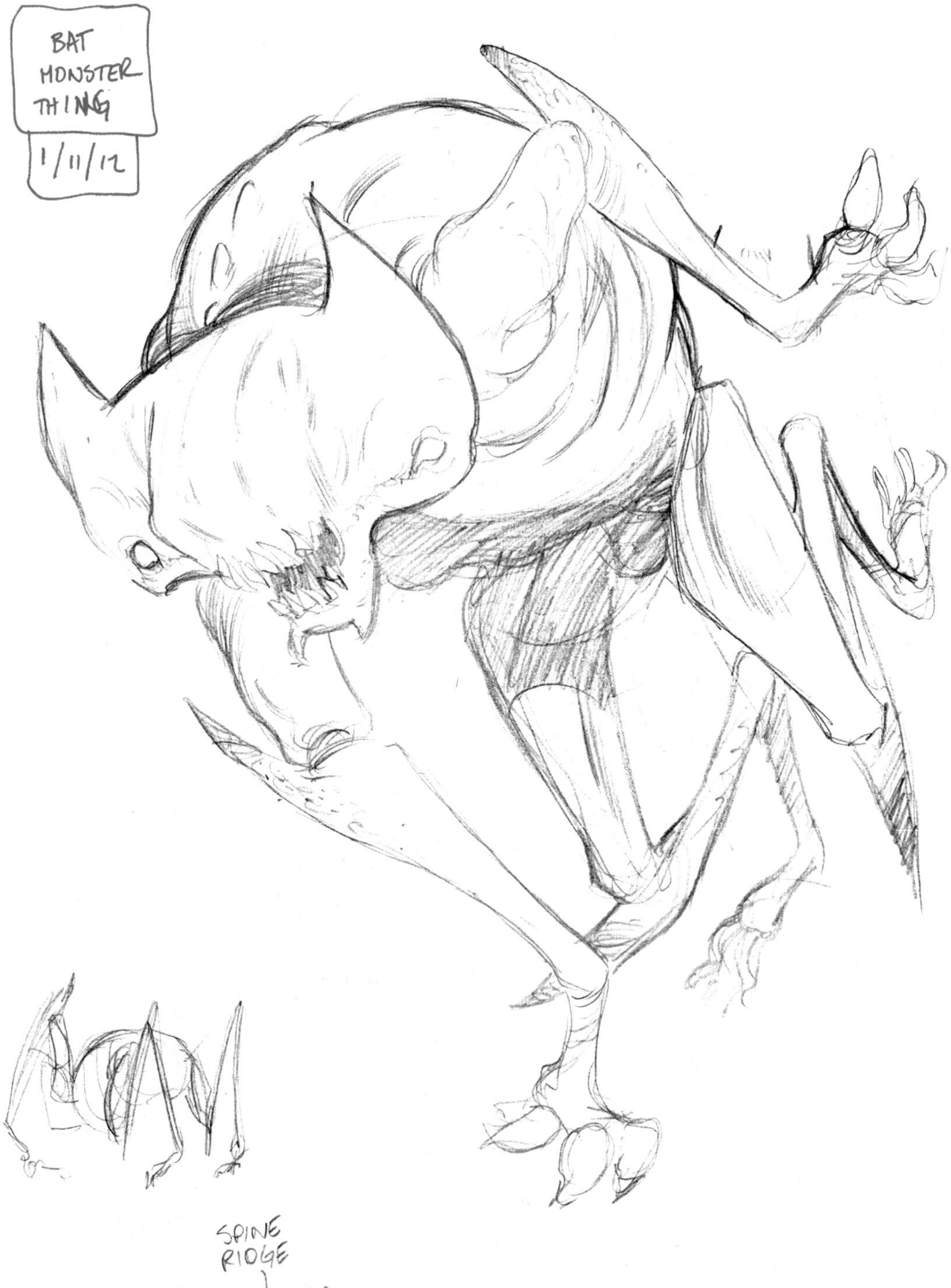
BAT MONSTER THING
1/11/12

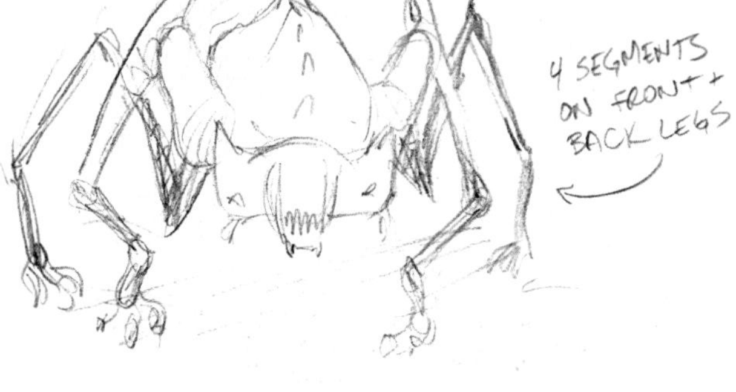
SPINE RIDGE
4 SEGMENTS ON FRONT + BACK LEGS

Guy Davis designed the "bat-headed critters," as John calls them in the script, but new artists adapt the monsters according to their styles.

Facing: Details from the Zinco labs, also adapted from Guy's designs.

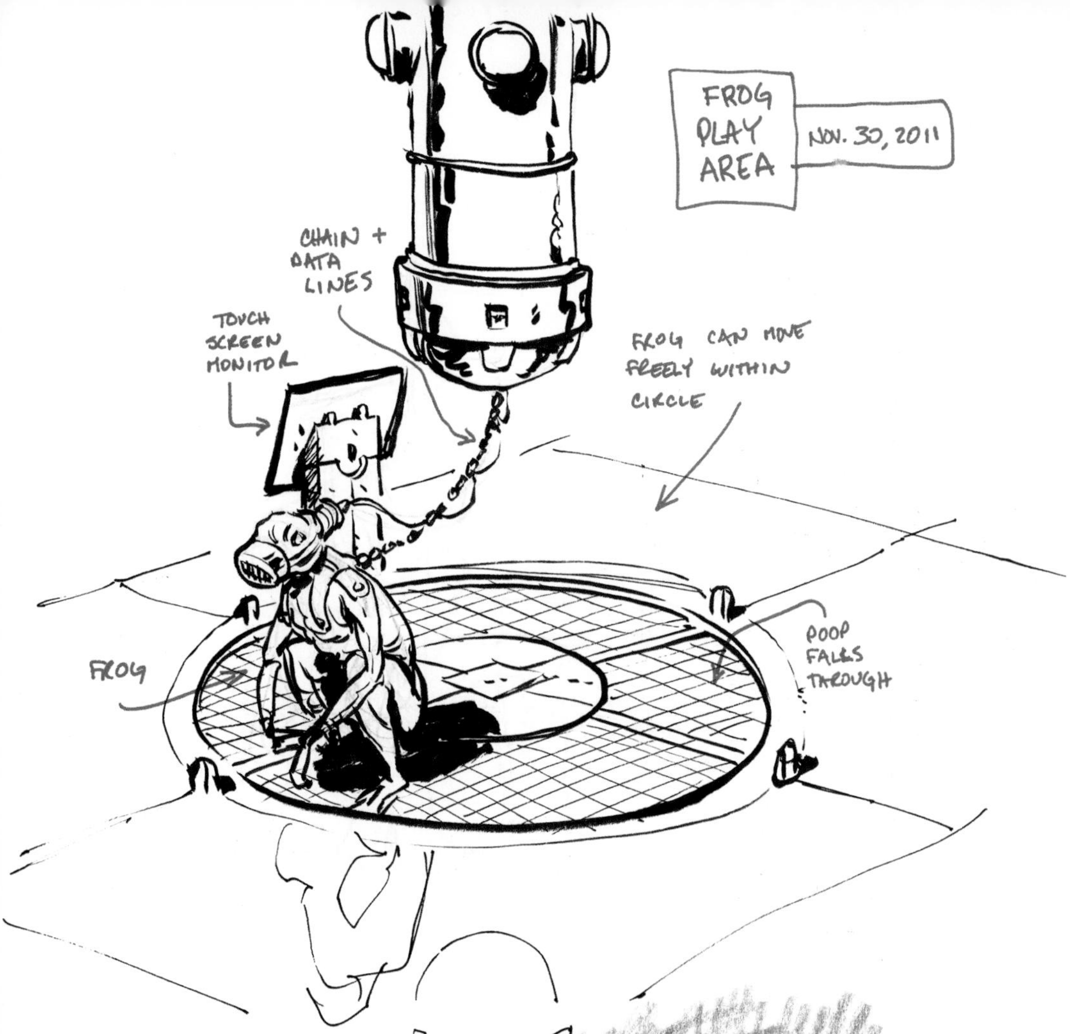
FROG PLAY AREA
NOV. 30, 2011
CHAIN + DATA LINES
TOUCH SCREEN MONITOR
FROG CAN MOVE FREELY WITHIN CIRCLE
FROG
POOP FALLS THROUGH

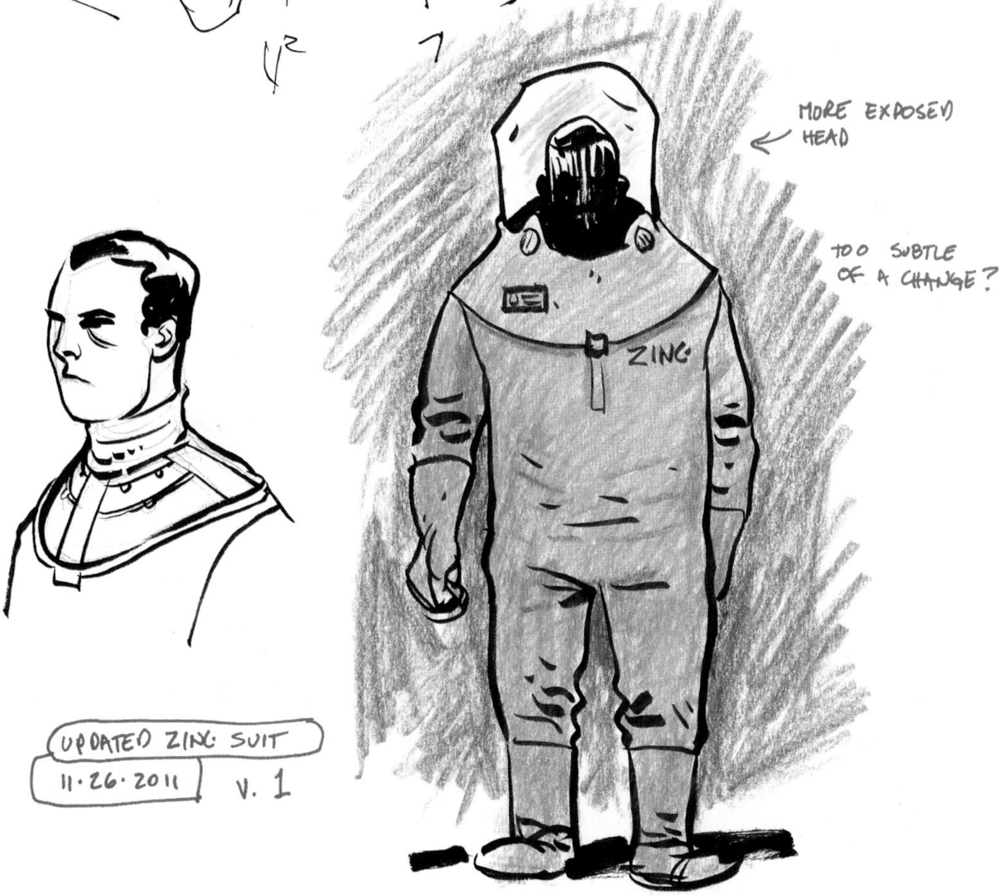
MORE EXPOSED HEAD
TOO SUBTLE OF A CHANGE?
ZINC
UPDATED ZINC SUIT
11·26·2011
V. 1

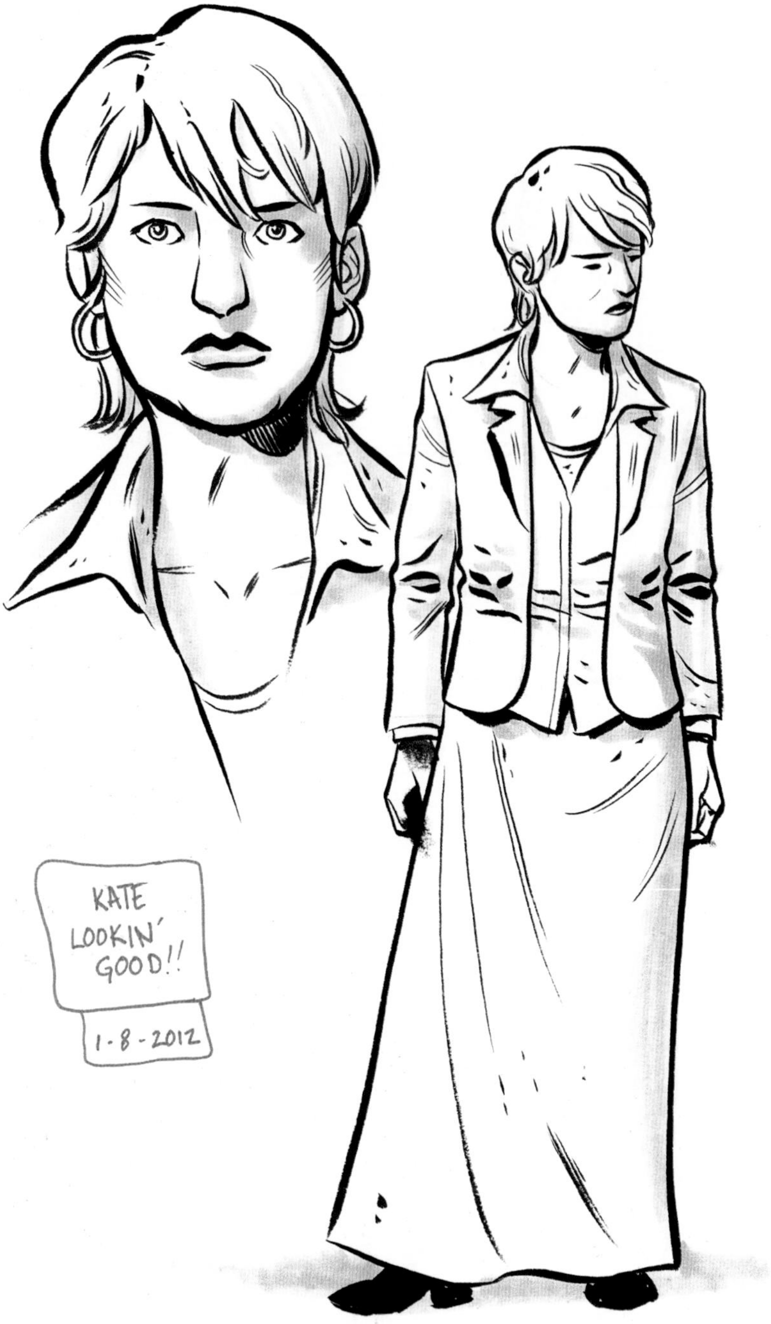
KATE
LOOKIN'
GOOD!!
1-8-2012

Artists provide model sheets to keep the characters consistent from story to story. This is a model sheet for Kate by Tyler, which has gone to Cameron Stewart and James Harren, among others.

Facing: A nasty model sheet for Carla Giarocco. The schedule sometimes requires issues to be drawn out of order. In *The Long Death*, James Harren draws Carla suffering terrible injuries. Before that scene was even written, he provided a schematic of her injuries and how she'd look afterward, so that Tyler, who was already working on *The Return of the Master*, could make sure Carla's wounds matched up.

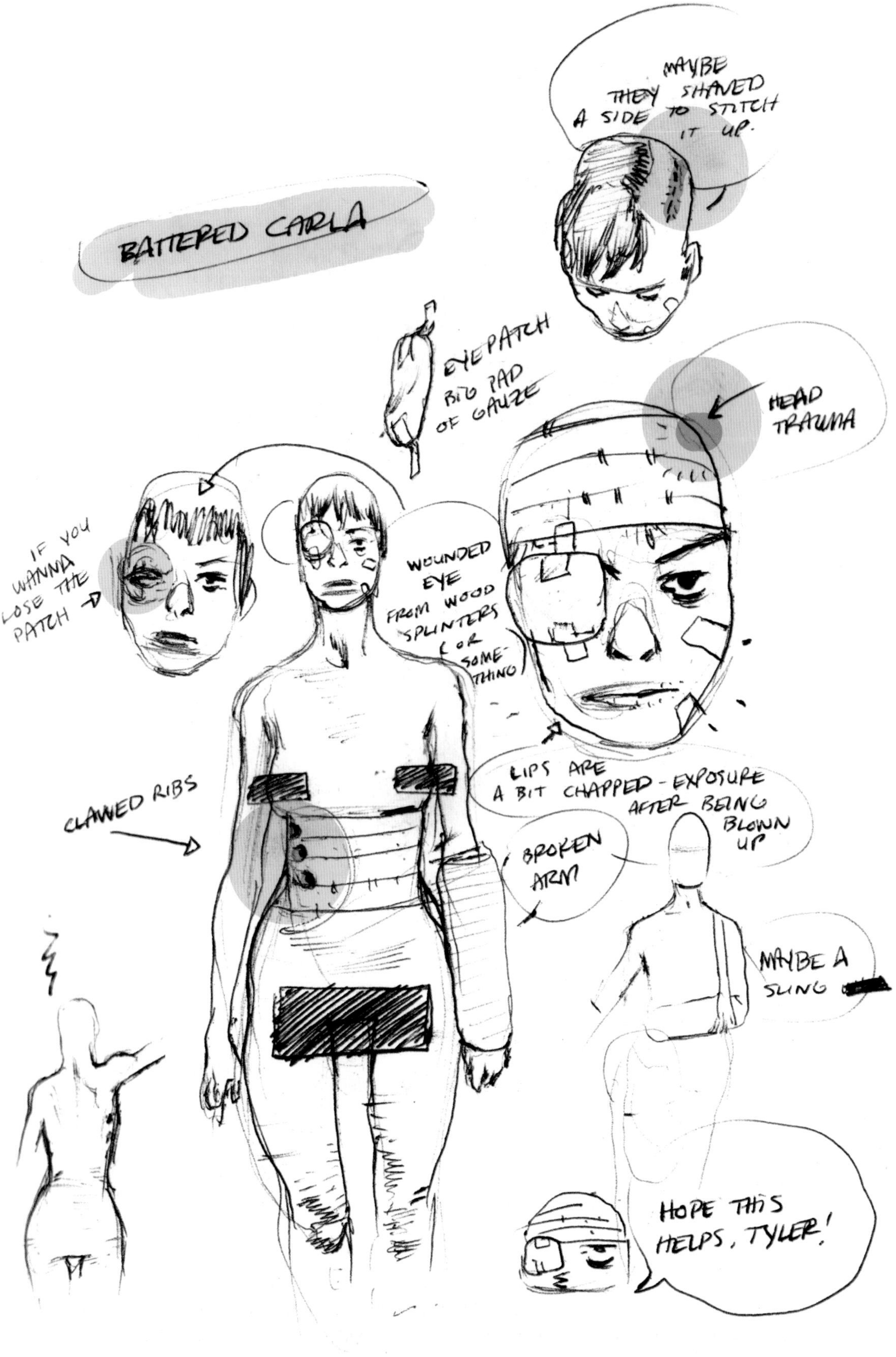
BATTERED CARLA
MAYBE THEY SHAVED A SIDE TO STITCH IT UP.
EYEPATCH BIG PAD OF GAUZE
HEAD TRAUMA
IF YOU WANNA LOSE THE PATCH
WOUNDED EYE FROM WOOD SPLINTERS (OR SOMETHING
LIPS ARE A BIT CHAPPED - EXPOSURE AFTER BEING BLOWN UP
CLAWED RIBS
BROKEN ARM
MAYBE A SLING
HOPE THIS HELPS, TYLER!

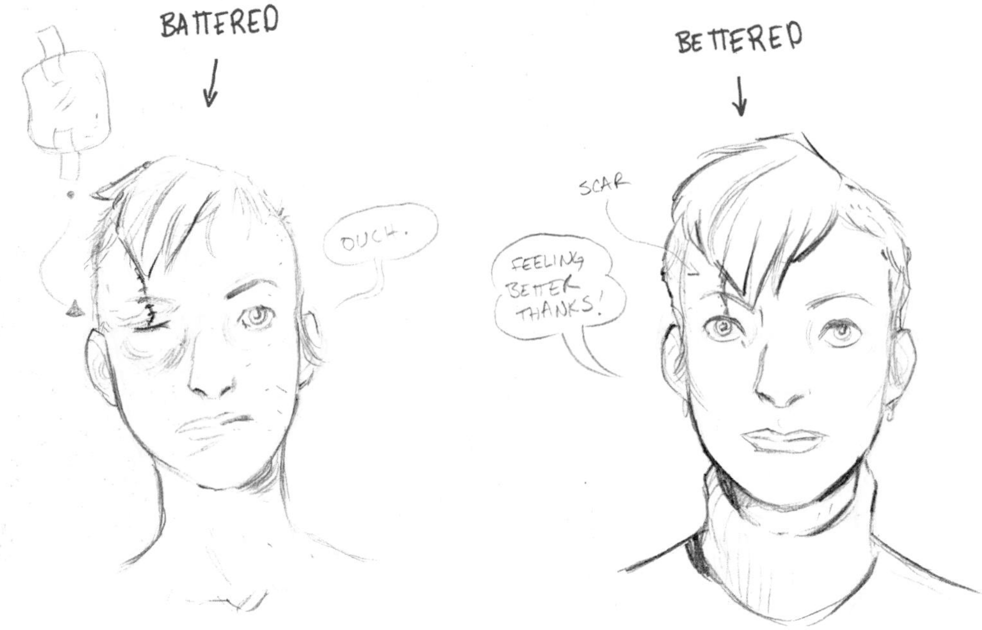

BATTERED
OUCH.
BETTERED
SCAR
FEELING BETTER THANKS!

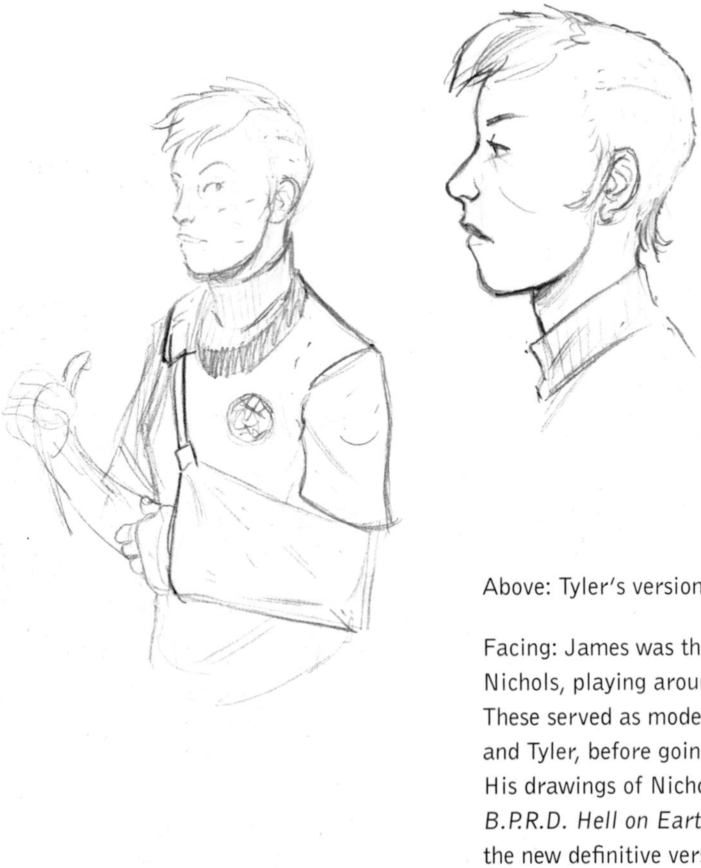

Above: Tyler's version of Carla.

Facing: James was the first to draw Agent Nichols, playing around with different looks. These served as model sheets for Max Fiumara and Tyler, before going to Laurence Campbell. His drawings of Nichols in the upcoming *B.P.R.D. Hell on Earth: Wasteland* have become the new definitive version of the character.

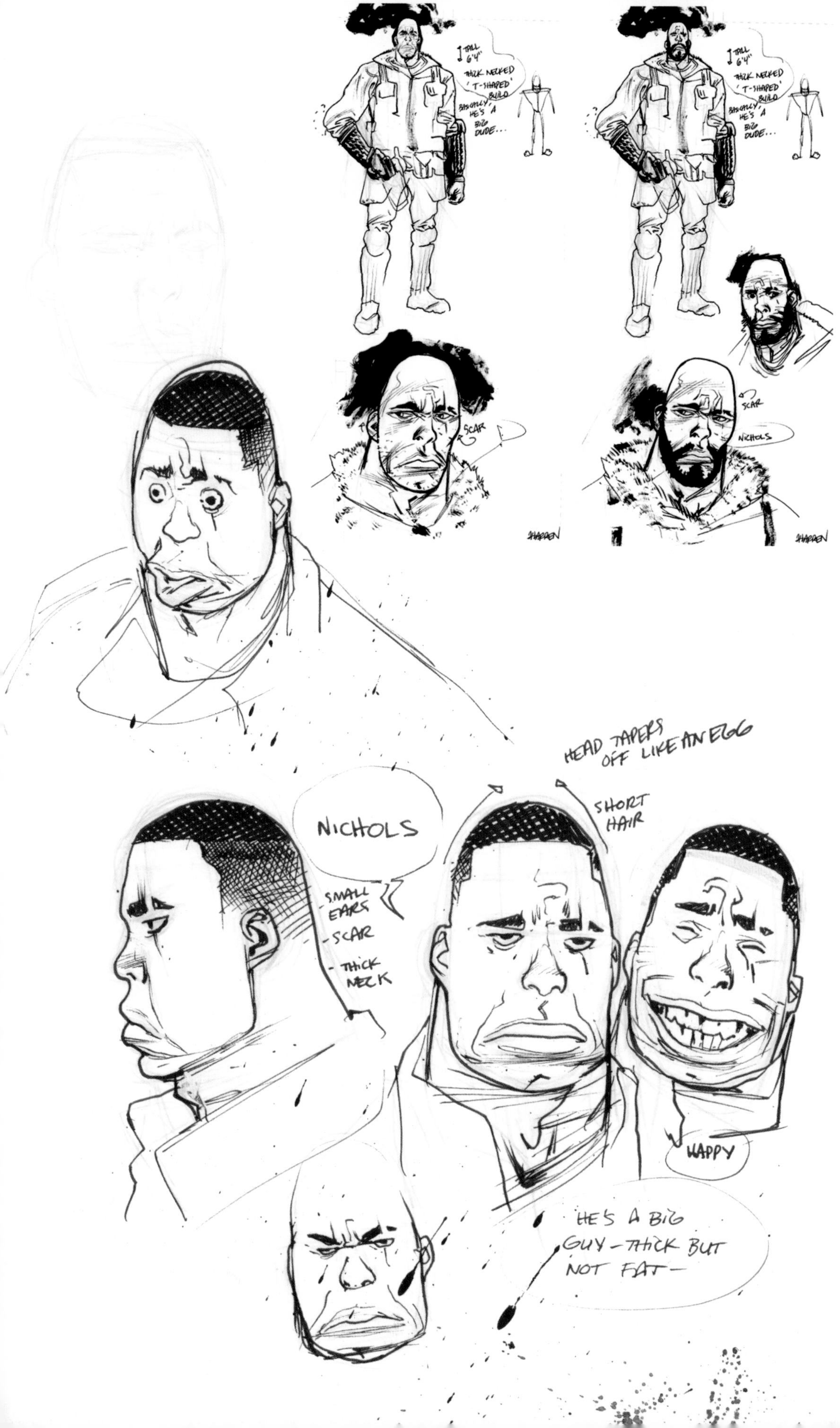

TALL 6'4"
THICK NECKED 'T-SHAPED' BUILD
BASICALLY, HE'S A BIG DUDE...
TALL 6'4"
THICK NECKED 'T-SHAPED' BUILD
BASICALLY, HE'S A BIG DUDE...
SCAR
SCAR
NICHOLS
HEAD TAPERS OFF LIKE AN EGG
SHORT HAIR
NICHOLS
SMALL EARS
SCAR
THICK NECK
HAPPY
HE'S A BIG GUY - THICK BUT NOT FAT -

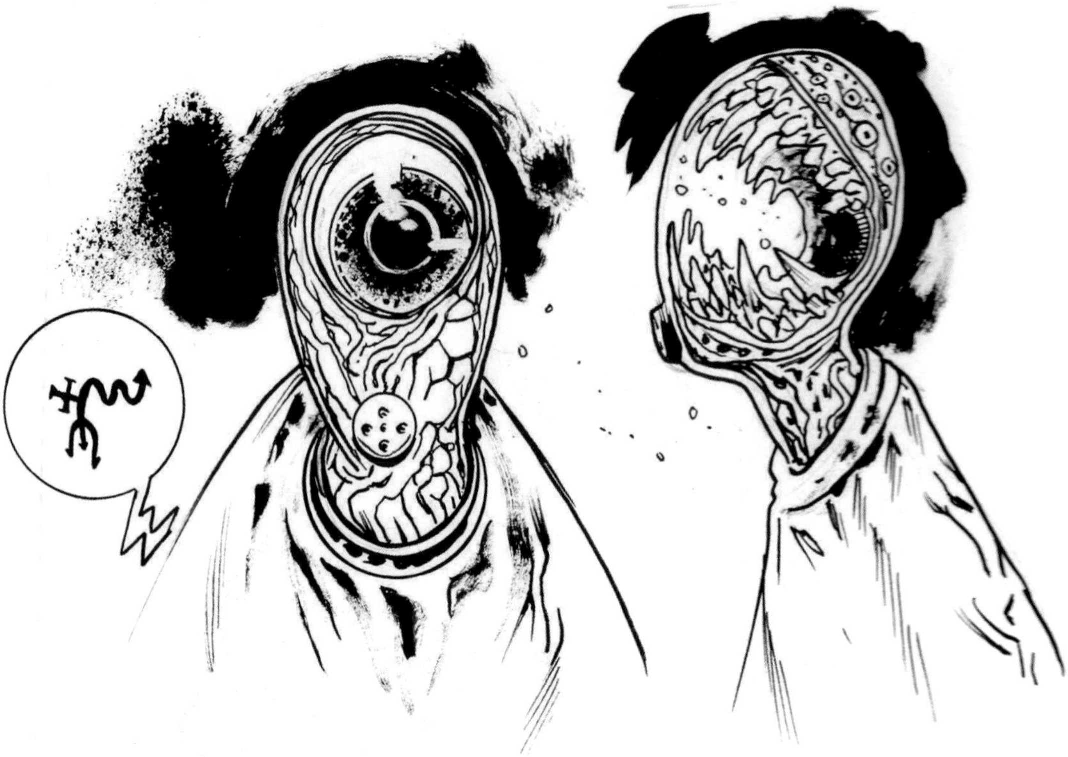

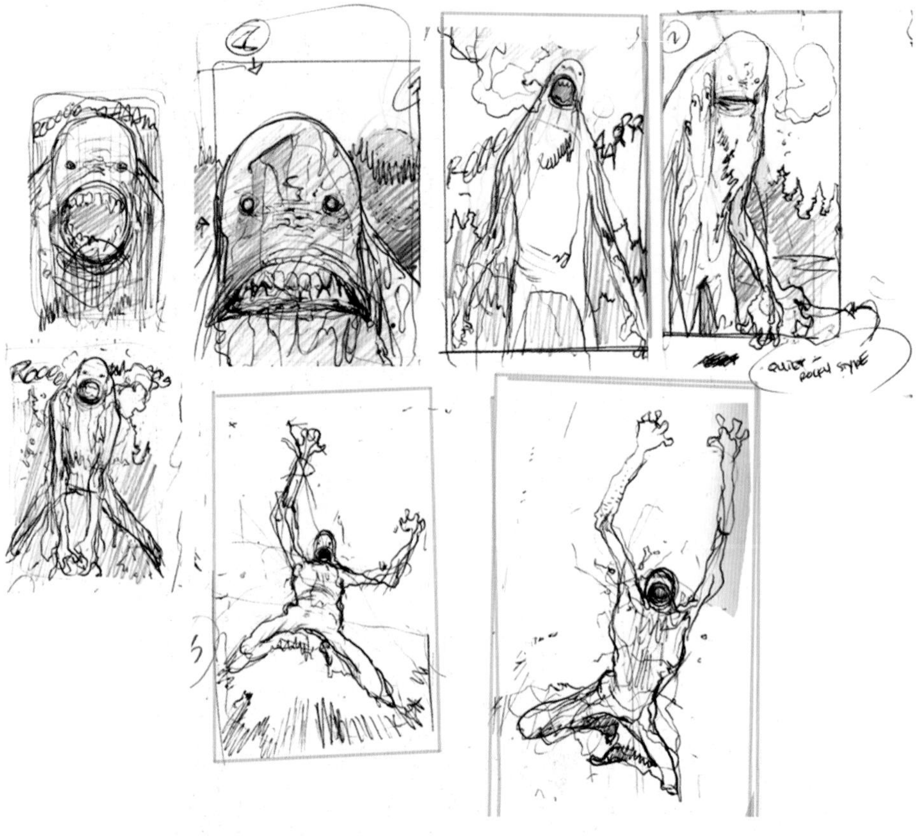
QUIET –
ROCKY STYLE

Facing, top: John got the idea for the scene early on in *The Long Death* #1 when he saw these drawings of Johann.

Facing, bottom: James's ideas for the splash-page reveal of the wendigo and, below, a sketch of the monster.

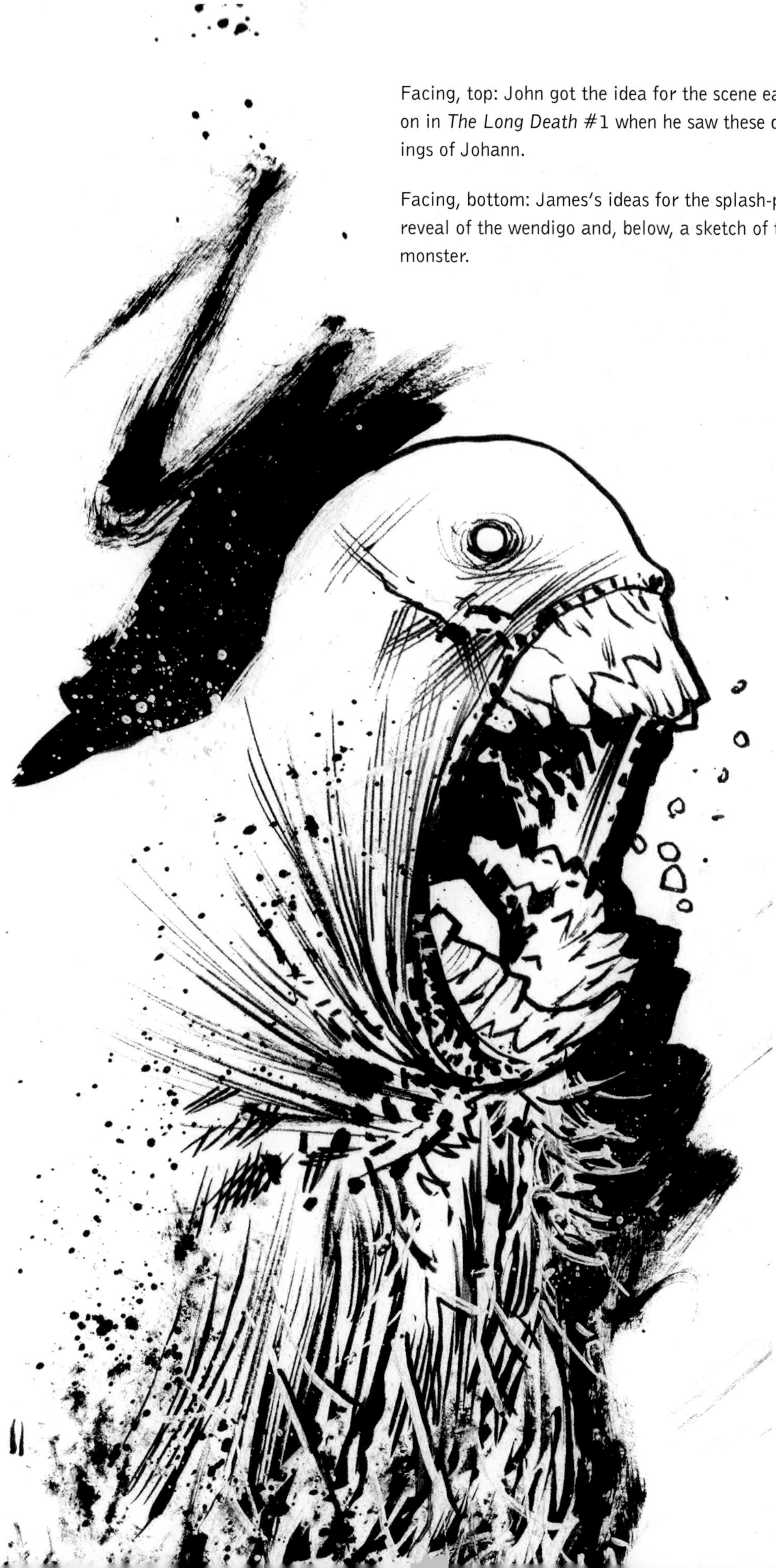

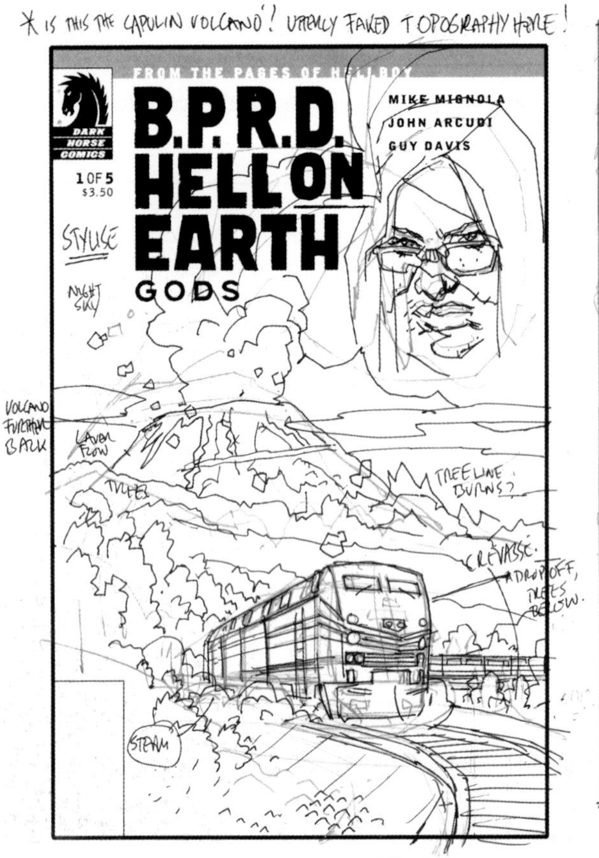
* IS THIS THE CAPULIN VOLCANO? UTTERLY FAKED TOPOGRAPHY HERE!
FROM THE PAGES OF HELLBOY
DARK HORSE COMICS
B.P.R.D.
HELL ON EARTH
GODS
MIKE MIGNOLA
JOHN ARCUDI
GUY DAVIS
1 OF 5
$3.50
STYLISE
NIGHT SKY
VOLCANO FURTHER BACK
LAVA FLOW
TREES
TREELINE BURNS?
CREVASSE. A DROPOFF, TREES BELOW.
STEAM

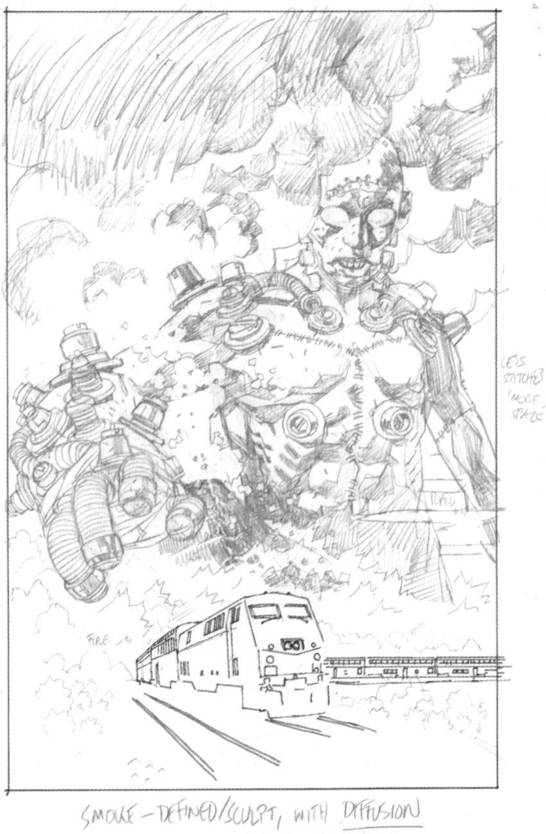
SMOKE – DEFINED/SCULPT, WITH DIFFUSION

Duncan's cover sketches, including his early version of the monster. It was suggested that he remove the creature's hand from the cover, because it overshadowed the volcano, but the hand was just too well drawn to get rid of it.

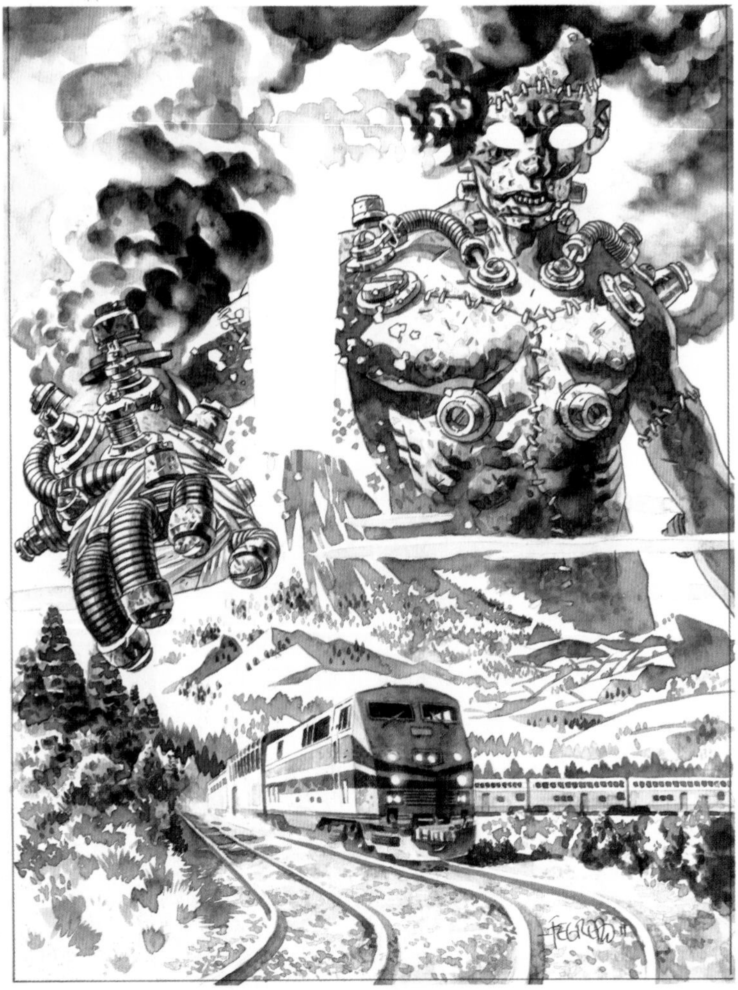

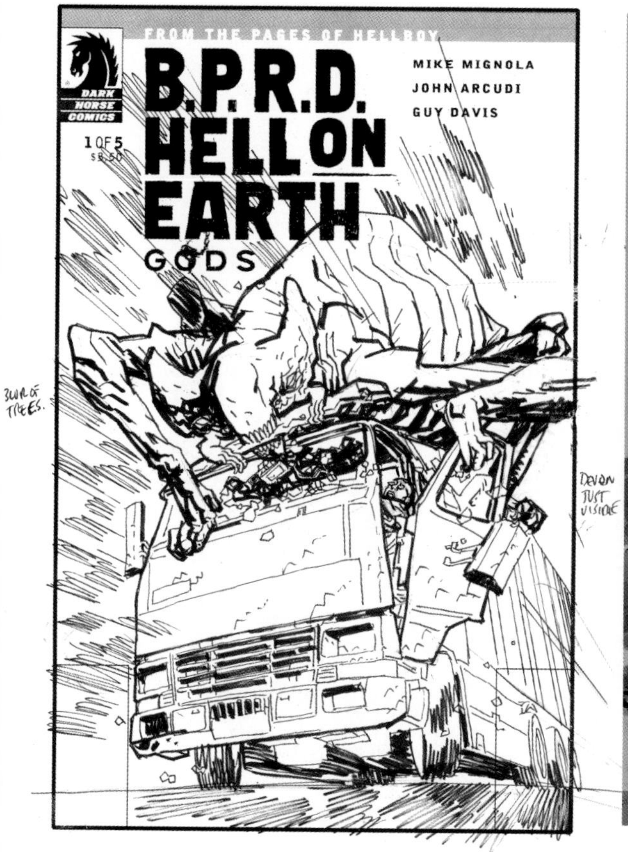
FROM THE PAGES OF HELLBOY
DARK HORSE COMICS
B.P.R.D.
HELL ON EARTH
GODS
1 OF 5
$3.50
MIKE MIGNOLA
JOHN ARCUDI
GUY DAVIS
BURN OF TREES.
DEVON JUST VISIBLE

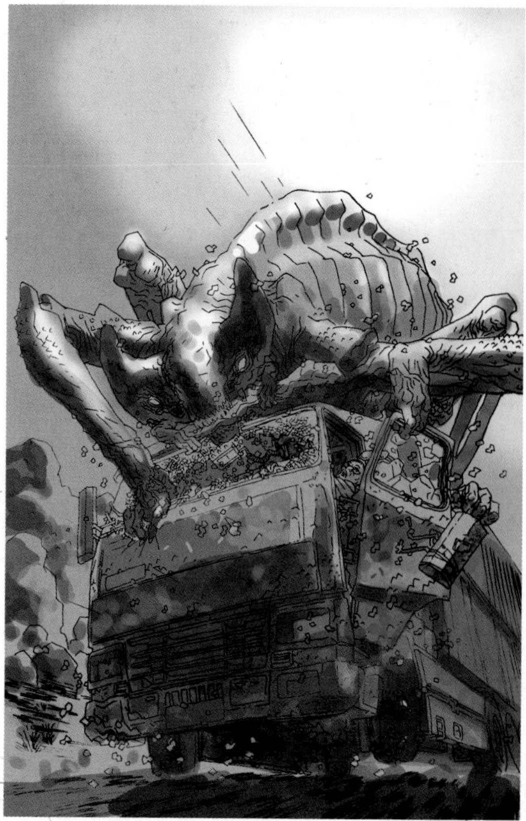

For the second *Devil's Engine* cover, Duncan nailed the concept right away. Note that Duncan was still using an old cover template, from the last series Guy drew.

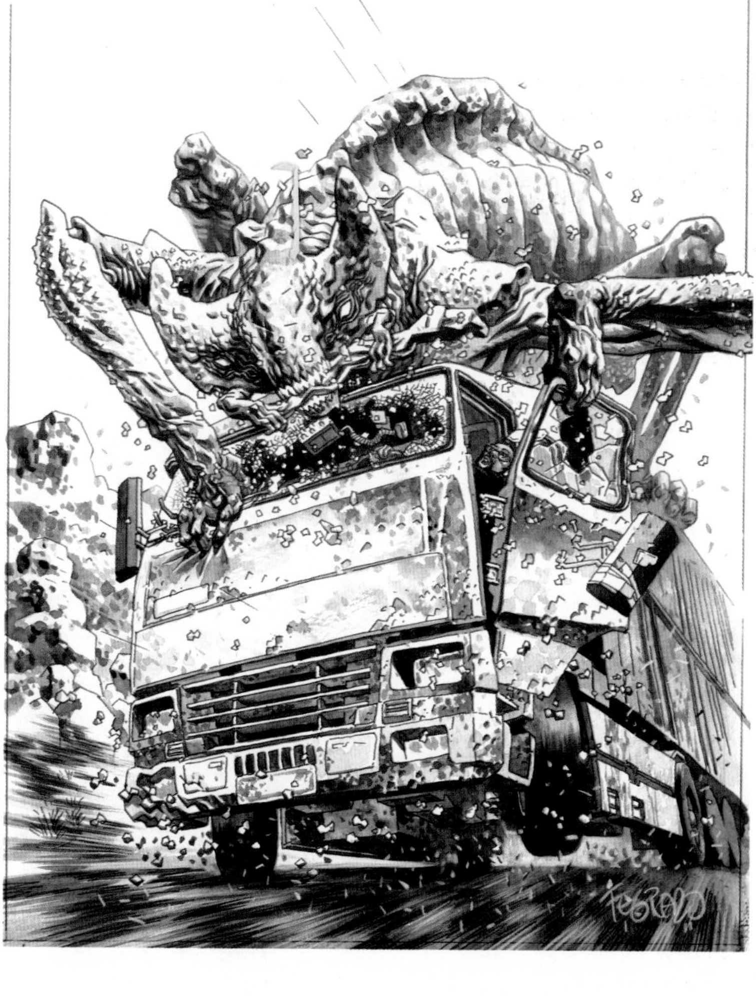

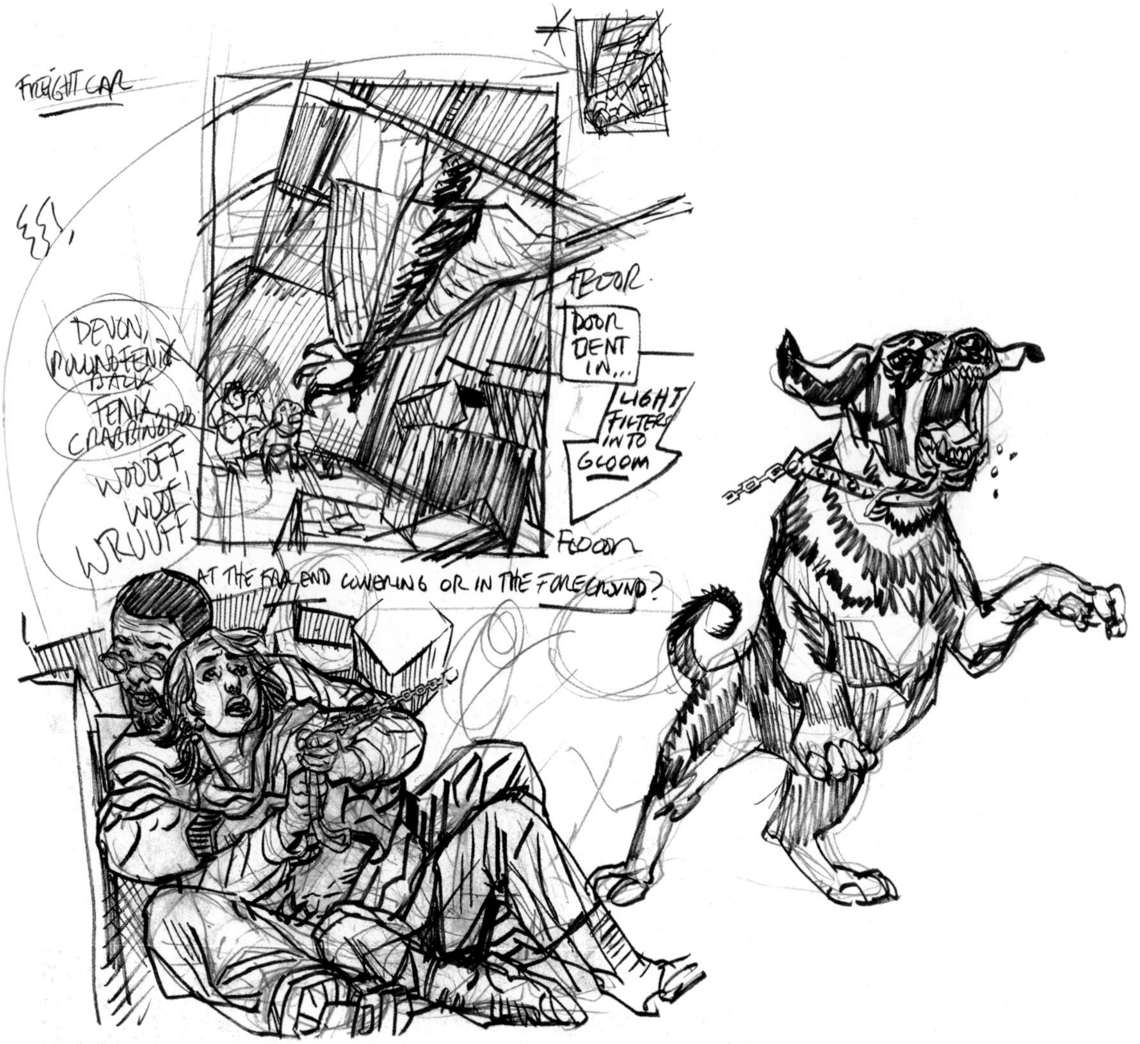
FREIGHT CAR
FLOOR
DOOR DENT IN...
LIGHT FILTERS INTO GLOOM
FLOOR
WOOOFF
WOOF
WRUUFF!
AT THE FAR END COWERING OR IN THE FOREGROUND?

For the final *Devil's Engine* cover, Duncan began with studies of Devon, Fenix, and her dog. They hardly changed through the process. The straight arm of the creature lacked tension, which Duncan resolved by making sharp bends at the shoulder, elbow, and wrist.

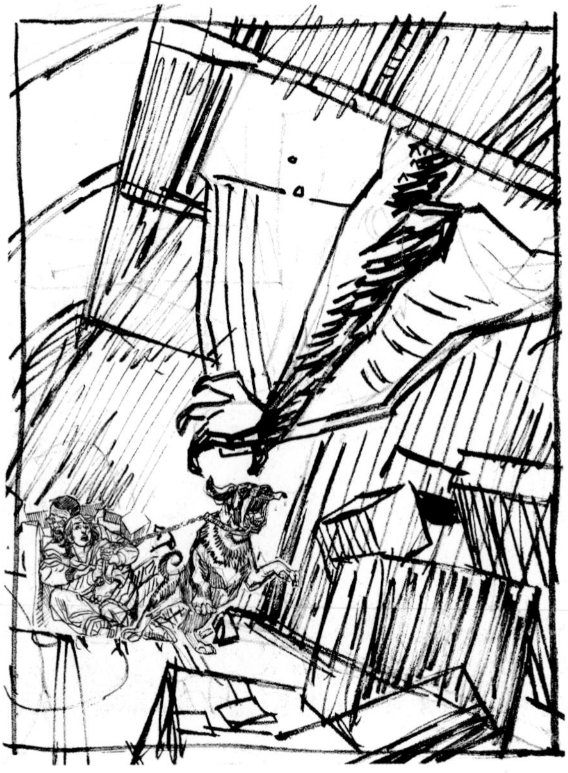

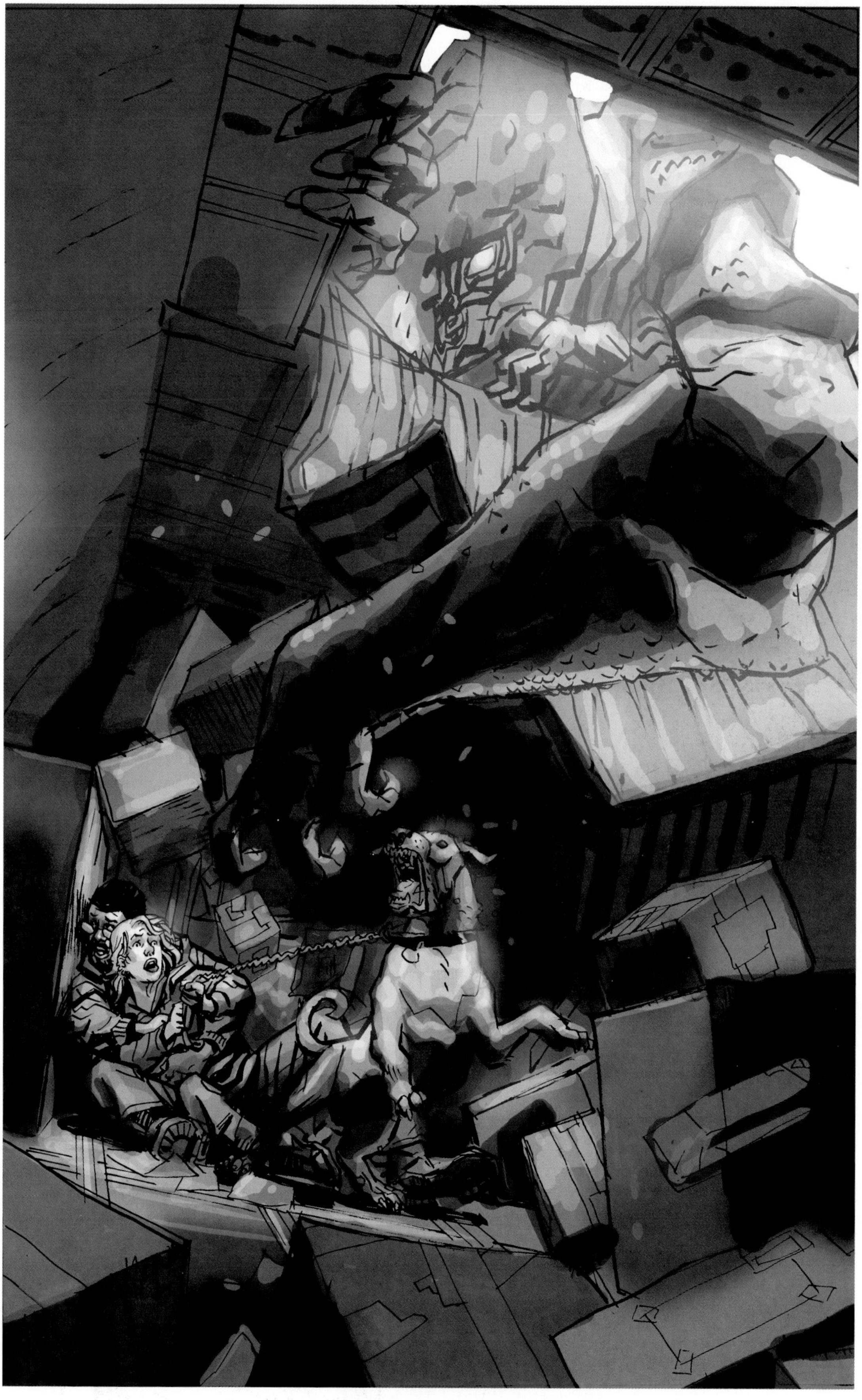

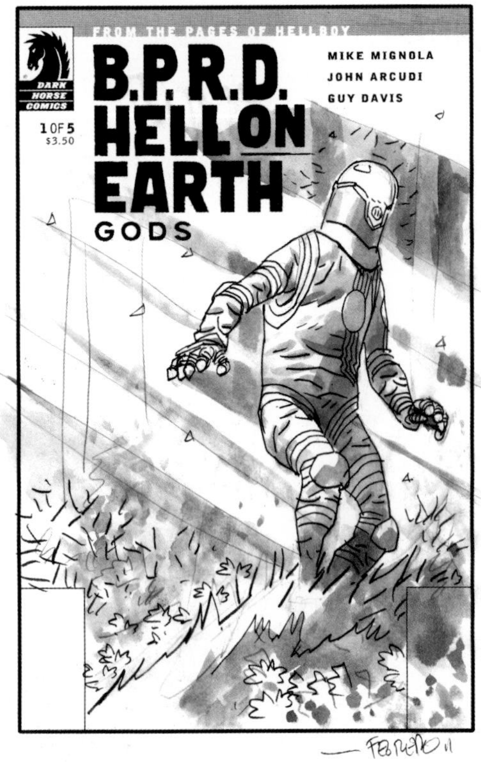
FROM THE PAGES OF HELLBOY
DARK HORSE COMICS
B.P.R.D.
HELL ON EARTH
GODS
MIKE MIGNOLA
JOHN ARCUDI
GUY DAVIS
1 OF 5
$3.50

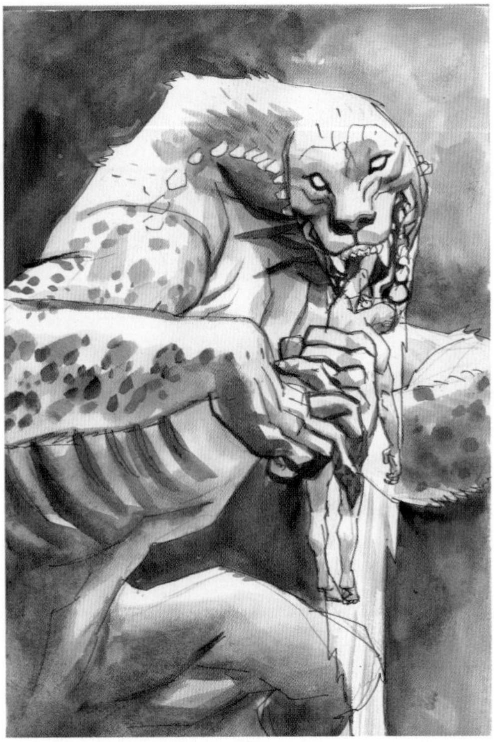

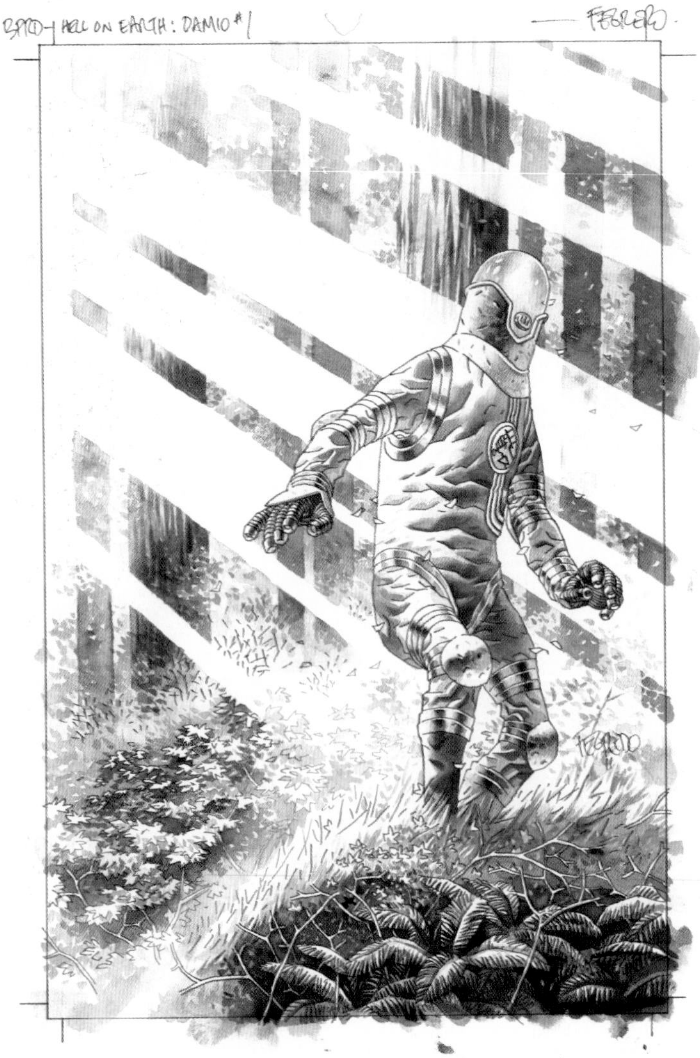

This page, left side: Covers are drawn long before the interiors of a comic, so even though Johann's new suit first appeared drawn by Tyler Crook in *Russia*, this cover for *The Long Death* made Duncan the first artist to actually draw the new suit after Mike and Guy's initial designs. Duncan's drawing became the model sheet for the suit for a while.

Above and facing: This wasn't the first time we'd referenced Goya, or specifically his painting *Saturn Devouring His Children*, in Mike's books.

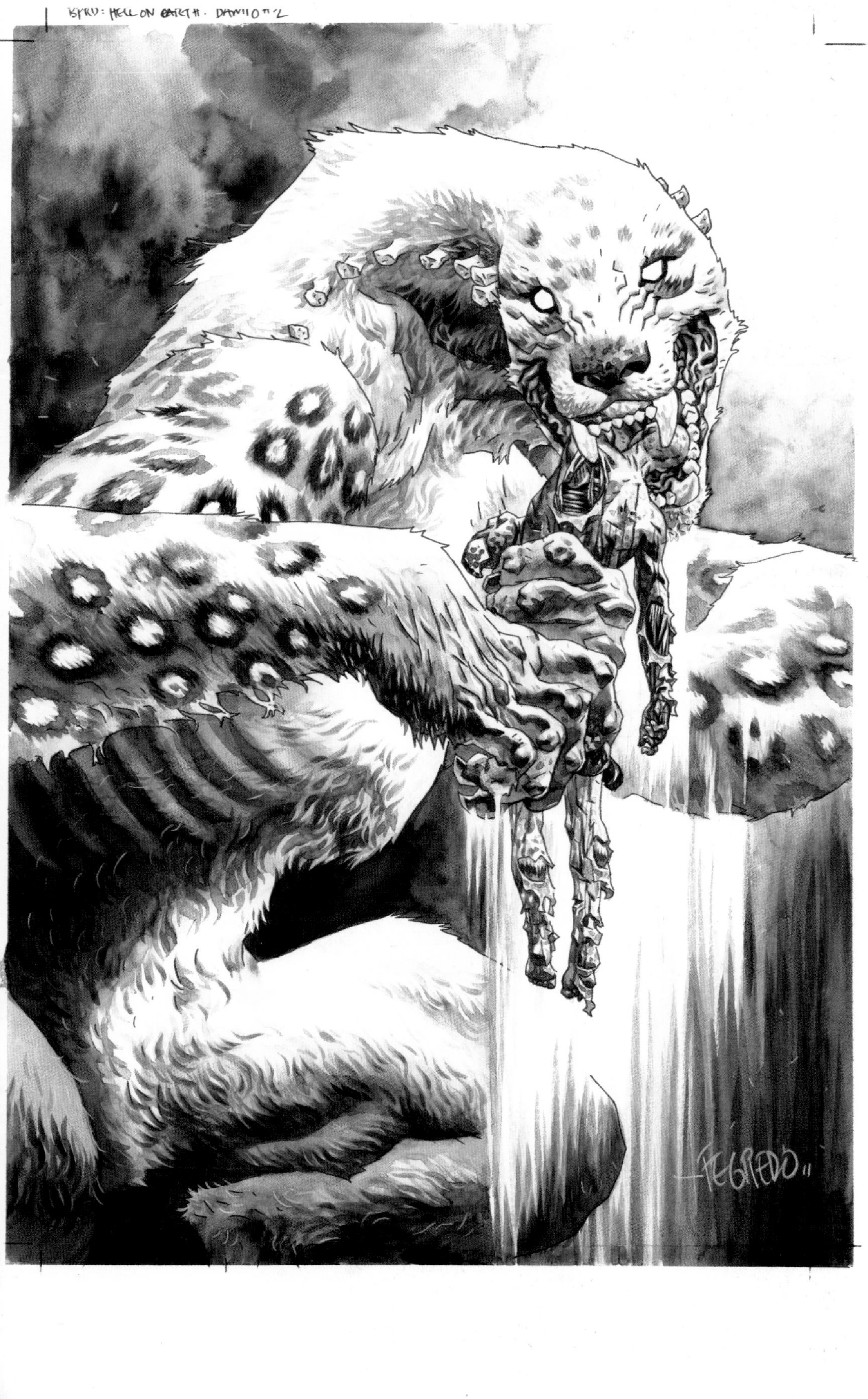
BPRD: HELL ON EARTH. DAMNED #2
FEGREDO 11

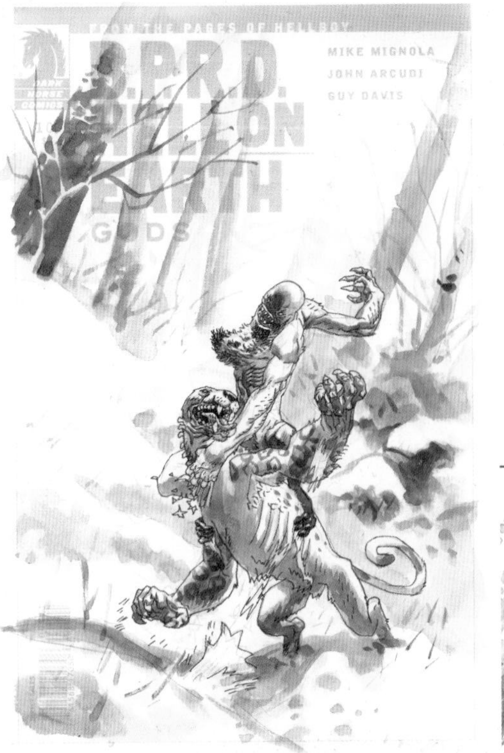
FROM THE PAGES OF HELLBOY
B.P.R.D.
MIKE MIGNOLA
JOHN ARCUDI
GUY DAVIS

We loved this action cover, and had no idea how much more savage the fight would look inside the book once James Harren was let loose on it.

Throughout 2012, Mike did a series of covers called *Year of Monsters*, one variant cover per month, spread across his various titles, featuring his characters going up against his favorite classic monsters. The following images were on the first issue of *The Long Death* and the third issue of *The Devil's Engine*, respectively.

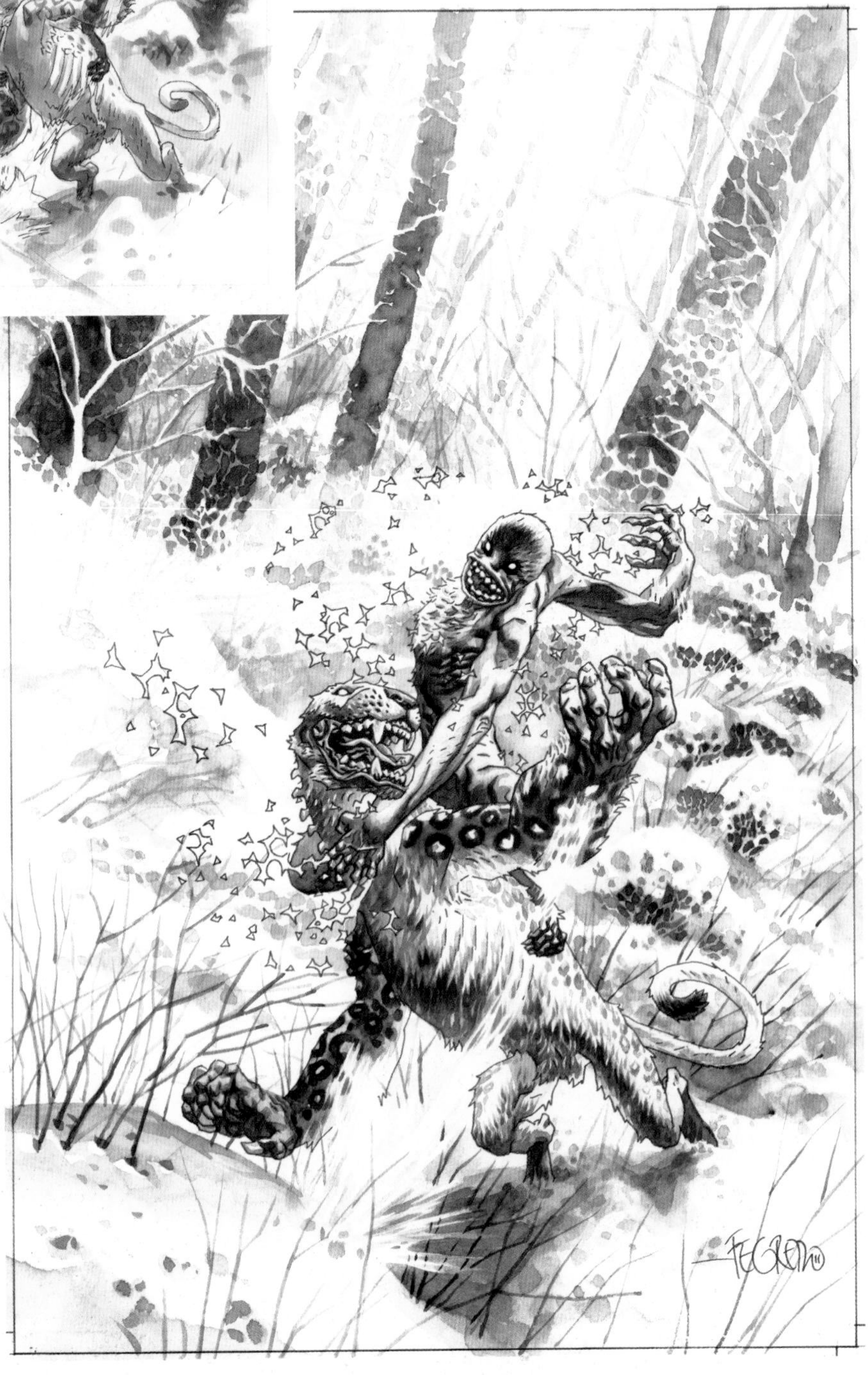

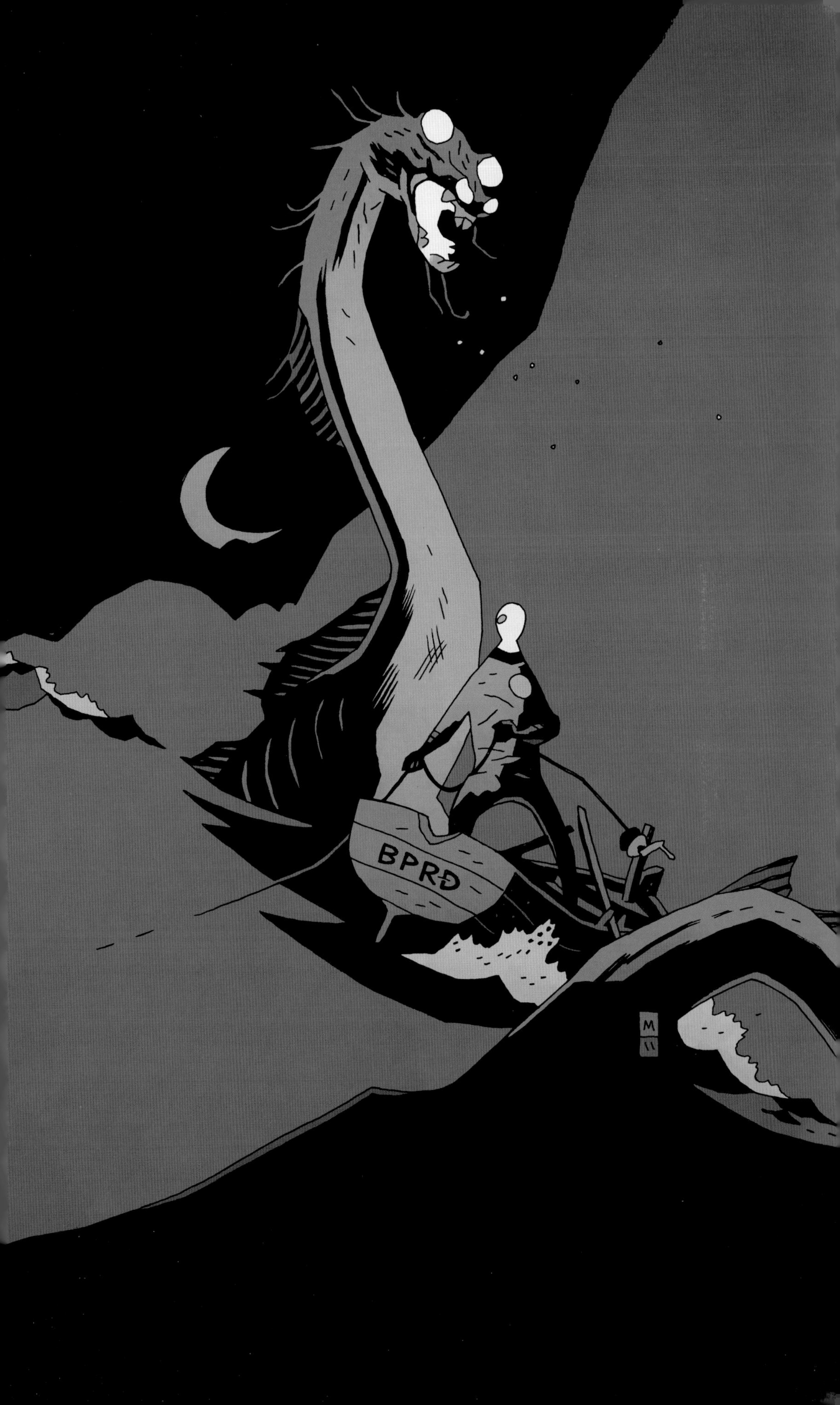
BPRD

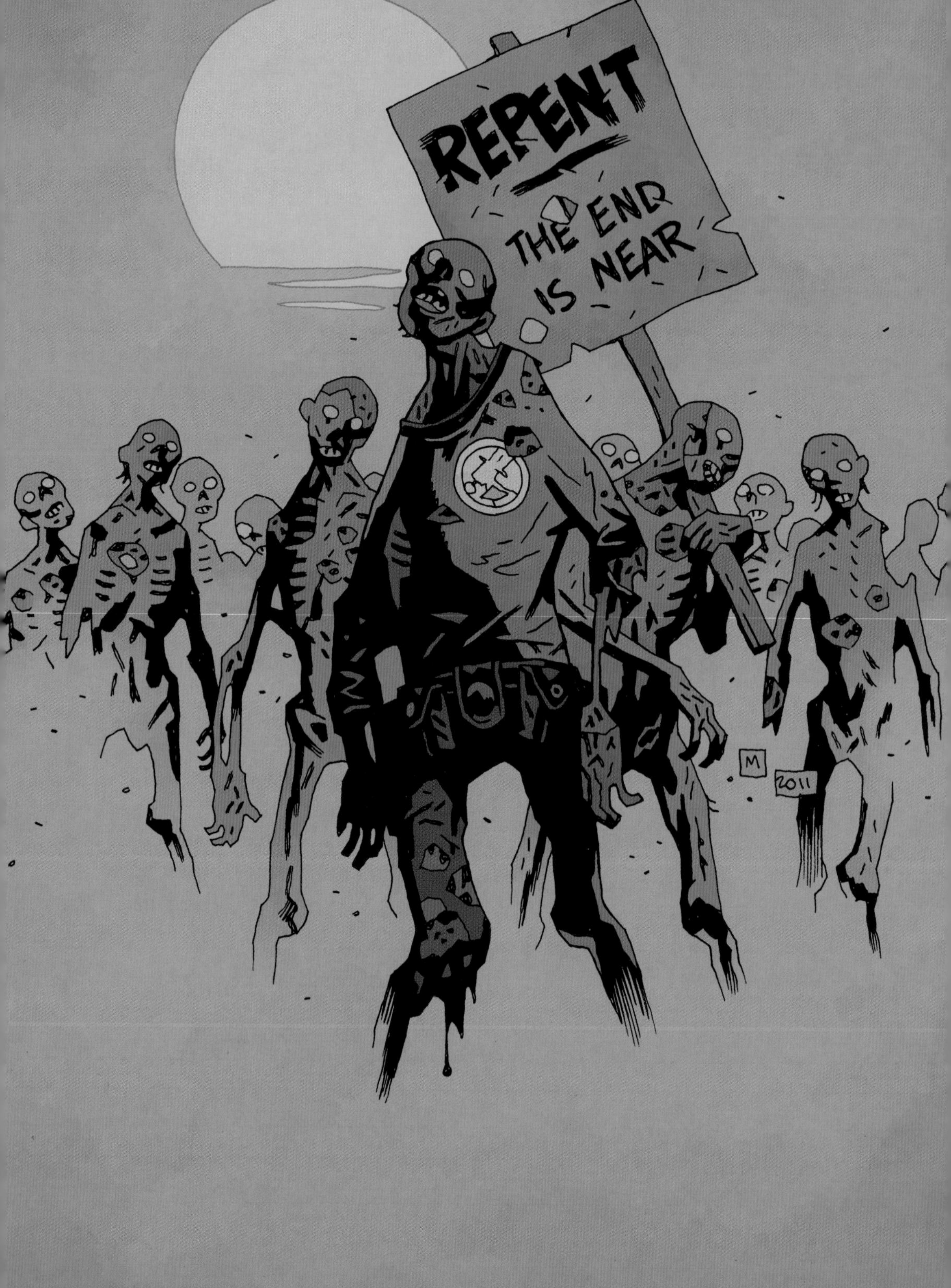
REPENT
THE END IS NEAR
M
2011

Also by MIKE MIGNOLA

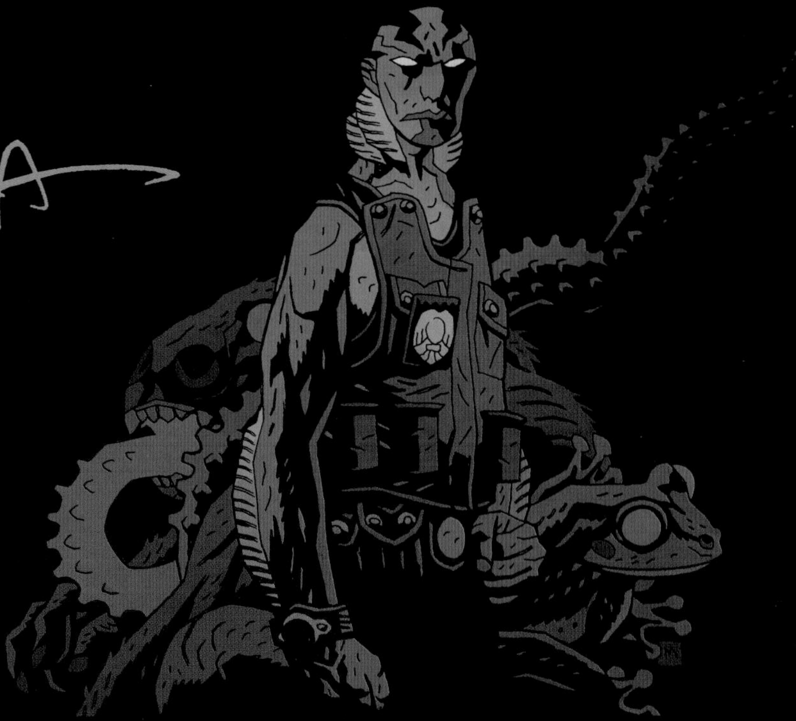

B.P.R.D.: PLAGUE OF FROGS
Hardcover Collection Volume 1
By Mike Mignola, Chris Golden, Guy Davis, and others
ISBN 978-1-59582-609-1 | $34.99

B.P.R.D.: PLAGUE OF FROGS
Hardcover Collection Volume 2
By Mignola, John Arcudi, Davis, and others
ISBN 978-1-59582-672-5 | $34.99

B.P.R.D.: PLAGUE OF FROGS
Hardcover Collection Volume 3
By Mignola, Arcudi, and Davis
ISBN 978-1-59582-860-6 | $34.99

B.P.R.D.: PLAGUE OF FROGS
Hardcover Collection Volume 4
By Mignola, Arcudi, and Davis
ISBN 978-1-59582-974-0 | $34.99

B.P.R.D.: THE WARNING
By Mignola, Arcudi, and Davis
ISBN 978-1-59582-304-5 | $17.99

B.P.R.D.: THE BLACK GODDESS
By Mignola, Arcudi, and Davis
ISBN 978-1-59582-411-0 | $17.99

B.P.R.D.: KING OF FEAR
By Mignola, Arcudi, and Davis
ISBN 978-1-59582-564-3 | $17.99

B.P.R.D.: 1946
By Mignola, Joshua Dysart, and Paul Azaceta
ISBN 978-1-59582-191-1 | $17.99

B.P.R.D.: 1947
By Mignola, Dysart, Fábio Moon, and Gabriel Bá
ISBN 978-1-59582-478-3 | $17.99

B.P.R.D.: BEING HUMAN
By Mignola, Arcudi, Davis, and others
ISBN 978-1-59582-756-2 | $17.99

B.P.R.D. HELL ON EARTH VOLUME 1: NEW WORLD
By Mignola, Arcudi, and Davis
ISBN 978-1-59582-707-4 | $19.99

B.P.R.D. HELL ON EARTH VOLUME 2: GODS AND MONSTERS
By Mignola, Arcudi, Davis, and Crook
ISBN 978-1-59582-822-4 | $19.99

B.P.R.D. HELL ON EARTH VOLUME 3: RUSSIA
By Mignola, Arcudi, Crook, and Duncan Fegredo
ISBN 978-1-59582-946-7 | $19.99

B.P.R.D. HELL ON EARTH VOLUME 4: THE DEVIL'S ENGINE AND THE LONG DEATH
By Mignola, Arcudi, Crook, and James Harren
ISBN 978-1-59582-981-8 | $19.99

ABE SAPIEN VOLUME 1: THE DROWNING
By Mignola and Jason Shawn Alexander
ISBN 978-1-59582-185-0 | $17.99

ABE SAPIEN: VOLUME 2: THE DEVIL DOES NOT JEST AND OTHER STORIES
By Mignola, Arcudi, Harren, and others
ISBN 978-1-59582-925-2 | $17.99

LOBSTER JOHNSON VOLUME 1: THE IRON PROMETHEUS
By Mignola and Jason Armstrong
ISBN 978-1-59307-975-8 | $17.99

LOBSTER JOHNSON VOLUME 2: THE BURNING HAND
By Mignola, Arcudi, and Tonci Zonjic
ISBN 978-1-61655-031-8 | $17.99

WITCHFINDER VOLUME 1: IN THE SERVICE OF ANGELS
By Mignola and Ben Stenbeck
ISBN 978-1-59582-483-7 | $17.99

WITCHFINDER VOLUME 2: LOST AND GONE FOREVER
By Mignola, Arcudi, and John Severin
ISBN 978-1-59582-794-4 | $17.99

THE AMAZING SCREW-ON HEAD AND OTHER CURIOUS OBJECTS
Hardcover Collection
By Mignola
ISBN 978-1-59582-501-8 | $17.99

BALTIMORE VOLUME 1: THE PLAGUE SHIPS
By Mignola, Golden, and Stenbeck
ISBN 978-1-59582-677-0 | $24.99

BALTIMORE VOLUME 2: THE CURSE BELLS
By Mignola, Golden, and Stenbeck
ISBN 978-1-59582-674-9 | $24.99

NOVELS

LOBSTER JOHNSON: THE SATAN FACTORY
By Thomas E. Sniegoski
ISBN 978-1-59582-203-1 | $12.95

JOE GOLEM AND THE DROWNING CITY
Deluxe Hardcover
By Mignola and Golden
ISBN 978-1-59582-971-9 | $99.99

HELLBOY by MIKE MIGNOLA

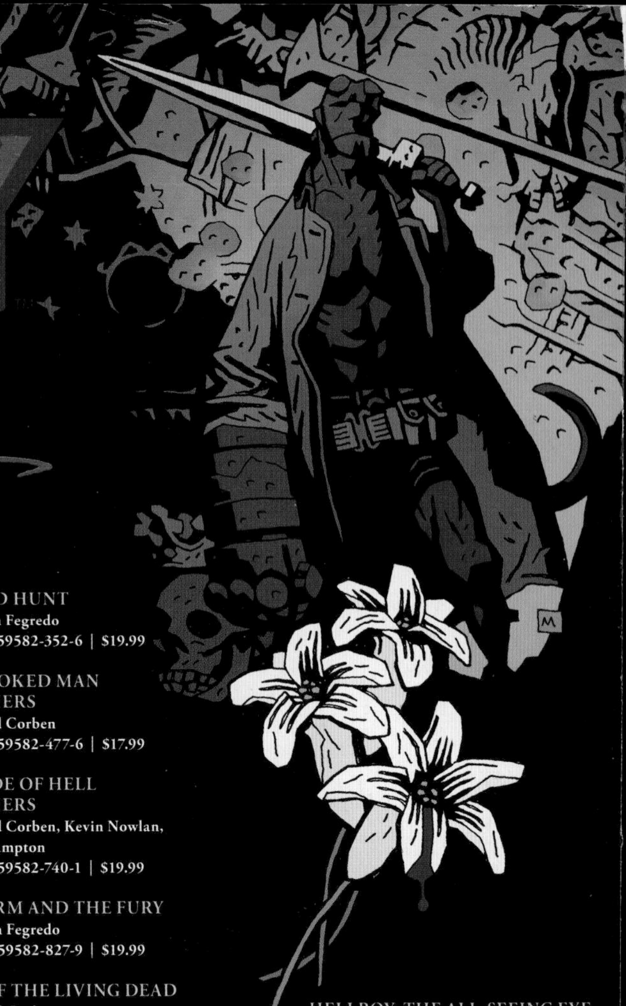

HELLBOY LIBRARY EDITION VOLUME 1:
Seed of Destruction and Wake the Devil
ISBN 978-1-59307-910-9 | $49.99

HELLBOY LIBRARY EDITION VOLUME 2:
The Chained Coffin and The Right Hand of Doom
ISBN 978-1-59307-989-5 | $49.99

HELLBOY LIBRARY EDITION VOLUME 3:
Conqueror Worm and Strange Places
ISBN 978-1-59582-352-6 | $49.99

HELLBOY LIBRARY EDITION VOLUME 4:
The Crooked Man and The Troll Witch
with Richard Corben and others
ISBN 978-1-59582-658-9 | $49.99

HELLBOY LIBRARY EDITION VOLUME 5:
Darkness Calls and the Wild Hunt
with Duncan Fegredo
ISBN 978-1-59582-886-6 | $49.99

SEED OF DESTRUCTION
with John Byrne
ISBN 978-1-59307-094-6 | $17.99

WAKE THE DEVIL
ISBN 978-1-59307-095-3 | $17.99

THE CHAINED COFFIN AND OTHERS
ISBN 978-1-59307-091-5 | $17.99

THE RIGHT HAND OF DOOM
ISBN 978-1-59307-093-9 | $17.99

CONQUEROR WORM
ISBN 978-1-59307-092-2 | $17.99

STRANGE PLACES
ISBN 978-1-59307-475-3 | $17.99

THE TROLL WITCH AND OTHERS
ISBN 978-1-59307-860-7 | $17.99

DARKNESS CALLS
with Duncan Fegredo
ISBN 978-1-59307-896-6 | $19.99

THE WILD HUNT
with Duncan Fegredo
ISBN 978-1-59582-352-6 | $19.99

THE CROOKED MAN AND OTHERS
with Richard Corben
ISBN 978-1-59582-477-6 | $17.99

THE BRIDE OF HELL AND OTHERS
with Richard Corben, Kevin Nowlan, and Scott Hampton
ISBN 978-1-59582-740-1 | $19.99

THE STORM AND THE FURY
with Duncan Fegredo
ISBN 978-1-59582-827-9 | $19.99

HOUSE OF THE LIVING DEAD
with Richard Corben
ISBN 978-1-59582-757-9 | $14.99

THE ART OF HELLBOY
ISBN 978-1-59307-089-2 | $29.99

HELLBOY II: THE ART OF THE MOVIE
ISBN 978-1-59307-964-2 | $24.99

HELLBOY: THE COMPANION
ISBN 978-1-59307-655-9 | $14.99

HELLBOY: WEIRD TALES
VOLUME 1
ISBN 978-1-56971-622-9 | $17.99
VOLUME 2
ISBN 978-1-56971-953-4 | $17.99

HELLBOY: MASKS AND MONSTERS
with James Robinson and Scott Benefiel
ISBN 978-1-59582-567-4 | $17.99

NOVELS

HELLBOY: EMERALD HELL
By Tom Piccirilli
ISBN 978-1-59582-141-6 | $12.99

HELLBOY: THE ALL-SEEING EYE
By Mark Morris
ISBN 978-1-59582-141-6 | $12.99

HELLBOY: THE FIRE WOLVES
By Tim Lebbon
ISBN 978-1-59582-204-8 | $12.99

HELLBOY: THE ICE WOLVES
By Mark Chadbourn
ISBN 978-1-59582-205-5 | $12.99

SHORT STORIES

Illustrated by Mike Mignola

HELLBOY: ODD JOBS
By Poppy Z. Brite, Greg Rucka, and others
ISBN 978-1-56971-440-9 | $14.99

HELLBOY: ODDER JOBS
By Frank Darabont, Guillermo del Toro, and others
ISBN 978-1-59307-226-1 | $14.99

HELLBOY: ODDEST JOBS
By Joe R. Lansdale, China Miéville, and others
ISBN 978-1-59307-944-4 | $14.99

AVAILABLE AT YOUR LOCAL COMICS SHOP OR BOOKSTORE! • To find a comics shop in your area, call 1-888-266-4226.
For more information or to order direct visit DarkHorse.com or call 1-800-862-0052 Mon.–Fri. 9 AM to 5 PM Pacific Time.
Prices and availability subject to change without notice.

DARK HORSE BOOKS
DarkHorse.com